SS-MAJOR HORST KOPKOW

SS-MAJOR HORST KOPKOW

FROM THE GESTAPO TO BRITISH INTELLIGENCE

STEPHEN TYAS

FONTHILL

Fonthill Media Language Policy

Fonthill Media publishes in the international English language market. One language edition is published worldwide. As there are minor differences in spelling and presentation, especially with regard to American English and British English, a policy is necessary to define which form of English to use. The Fonthill Policy is to use the form of English native to the author. Stephen Tyas was born and educated in Yorkshire; therefore British English has been adopted in this publication.

Fonthill Media Limited
Fonthill Media LLC
www.fonthillmedia.com
office@fonthillmedia.com

First published in the United Kingdom and the United States of America 2017

British Library Cataloguing in Publication Data:
A catalogue record for this book is available from the British Library

ISBN 978-1-78155-598-9

Typeset in 9.5pt on 12 pt Palatino
Printed and bound in England

Acknowledgements

I first became interested in Horst Kopkow about twenty-five years ago. At the time, my interest was the holocaust in Eastern Europe and the mass murder of Jewish populations committed there by German SS-*Einsatzgruppen*. As part of my holocaust research, which is still ongoing, I looked at the organisation of the Reich Security Main Office (RSHA) in Berlin, where many of the commanders, officers, and enlisted men that made up the SS-*Einsatzgruppen* came from. I became aware that many officers were not posted to these mobile death squads and, over subsequent years, received no better promotion prospects than those who did go east and become mass murderers. Going east was supposed to increase career prospects not maintain parity. Horst Kopkow and Adolf Eichmann were two senior Gestapo and SD officers who remained in Berlin with their departments and did not personally kill anyone. They became 'desk murderers' instead, sending innocents to concentration camps to be murdered by someone else.

Whereas Adolf Eichmann was a well-documented historical figure, little documentation mentioned Horst Kopkow. Until Gilles Perrault published his book on the Rote Kapelle in 1968, I had seen barely anything about him. Jean Overton Fuller, a scholar working on SOE agents in France, also mentioned Kopkow in her early publications of the 1950s and 1960s.

In 2004, MI5 declassified two Horst Kopkow 'name files', dated 1945–1948. Together with US intelligence agency files on Kopkow, declassified several years before, these added immensely to the material about Kopkow that can be found among different British war crimes investigations. This became the impetus for the research on which this book is based.

I have received help and assistance from a variety of people, not just scholars and historians, who have encouraged my research and writing. Professor Richard Breitman encouraged me, as we both see Kopkow as one of the more significant Nazi war criminals to be recruited by the British secret service, vying with Klaus Barbie who was recruited by American intelligence agencies after the war. Anyone writing about SOE agents will be indebted to the selfless research and digitisation program of Steven Kippax, who runs the SOE Yahoo Group blog. The late M. R. D. Foot, official historian of SOE, also agreed to talk to me about Kopkow, who he saw played the major role in the murder of the captured agents, but had been unable to see all the documents he wanted when writing his official history. I also went up to Northamptonshire to talk about Kopkow with the late Jean Overton Fuller and what her German visitors over the years had told her about him. Jean had a very similar view about Kopkow as that of M. R. D. Foot. Robert Marshall worked on BBC television programs and met Kopkow twice in the 1980s at his Gelsenkirchen and happily shared his impressions and notes from these interviews. Almost twenty years later, in 2004, Sarah Helm went to see Kopkow's widow (he died in 1996) and had surprisingly candid discussions, producing an informative article about it for *The Sunday Times* magazine at the time. Sarah has been especially helpful and encouraged my research. I cannot leave out Duncan Stuart, former SOE Adviser, from a long list of friendly faces who have suggested additional lines of research. Francis Suttill, whose father was murdered on Kopkow's instructions, provided much assistance with the effects of the *Funkspiel* in France.

Fellow scholars in Germany have also encouraged my research: long-standing friends Peter Witte, Florian Altenhöner, Andrej Angrick, Ray Brandon, Rainer Fröbe, and Michael Wildt. Hellmut Götz, whose father worked under Kieffer in Paris, and Hans-Uwe Hartert, archivist of the Dahme Community Council. Mike Tregenza, now living in Poland, has also helped me out with the little Polish material used.

I decided some time ago not to talk to any surviving Gestapo officials or SOE agents who survived the concentration camps. In 2000, the war had ended fifty-five years before, someone aged thirty at that time would now be eighty-five years old—many even older. Looking at my own grandparents, would I want anyone dredging up memories they did not want disturbed? Gestapo officials would still wish to be seen as the good guys and avoid incriminating themselves or showing themselves in a poor light. I did ask Jean Overton Fuller this very question about her former Gestapo visitors. Jean said she was old enough to be their mother and sometimes scolded them when she thought they were embellishing or telling lies. Usually it worked for her, but her visitors came in the 1950s and 1960s.

This book is based on primary archival documentation. It comes from documents used at British war crimes trials, from the interrogation of concentration camp staff, from the interrogation of Gestapo officials by Britain, USA, France, and Germany (East and West). I have also used official documents and reports of the time, including many written by Kopkow and his superiors. It is worth adding that seventy-one years since the end of the Second World War, sixty-five years since Kopkow was last interrogated, there continues to be classified documents by him or about him in the files of MI5 and SIS. Other enemies have come and gone in the intervening years, but files on Nazi criminals are still held back.

The main archives that I visited holding documents about Kopkow and the organisation he worked for are the UK National Archives at Kew, US

National Archives at College Park, and the *Bundesarchiv* Ludwigsburg (the non-active files of the Zentrale Stelle). In Ludwigsburg, archivists Peter Gohle and Nadine Massag have always been very helpful. At the Zentrale Stelle itself, still a prosecuting authority for crimes of the Nazi period, my thanks go to Deputy Director Thomas Will, who took a particular interest in my Kopkow research.

The *Bundesarchiv* at Berlin-Lichterfelde is another tremendous archive for wartime Third Reich material. *Bundesarchiv* Koblenz holds the denazification files of the British Zone, and more recently, it acquired archival material from the BfV (the German equivalent of MI5). Since the reunification of Germany, many files of the former East German Ministry of State Security (the Stasi) have become available at BStU Berlin. I have been particularly well-served in my research there by Archivist Rainer Eiselt, who was always especially helpful and deserving of my thanks.

Researching and then writing means a solitary life tapping away on the keyboard in the office, and naturally I have a long-suffering wife. My wife, Chris, and I have been together for forty-two years and I count my blessings that her fortitude, good nature, and love have enabled me to research and write.

Stephen Tyas, 2016

Contents

1

Germany and London: 1944, 1945–1946

In the morning of Friday 29 May 1945, a low-level Gestapo man surrendered to the British Field Security Post in Lübeck and denounced a group of senior Gestapo men hiding out in Dahme, three weeks after the German surrender to the Allies. A car and a lorry with British military policemen drove 50 km (32 miles) up the coastal road from Lübeck to Dahme, a pretty seaside village on the Baltic coast, and made for the Strandhotel overlooking the beach. Their information was correct, and at 4 p.m., they arrested five Gestapo men, who comprised two officers and three NCOs. The five were driven back to Lübeck and handed in to Marstall Prison for processing.

That same day, a standard form, the Detention Report, was completed by each man—signed and dated.[1] One of the men identified himself as SS-*Sturmbannführer* (Major) *Kriminaldirektor* Horst Kopkow, born 29 November 1910 at Ortelsburg, East Prussia. He was 1.83 metres tall (6 feet), weighed 80 kg (176 lb), and had a false identity document with him; he also had 3,108 Reichsmarks in cash. The career details given on this Detention Report reveal he had been continuously employed and promoted at the 'Secret Police Office Berlin', Dept. IV A2, from 1939 to 1945. His arrest photo shows a young-looking man wearing a shirt and tie under a dark overcoat, with dark hair brushed back. This Detention Report followed him throughout his period in British captivity and shows his progressive changes in place of internment: from Lübeck Marstall Prison to Lübeck Court Prison, Lauerhof jail in Lübeck, Corps Interrogation Camp Prison Neumünster, Internment Camp Neuengamme, and finally to Interrogation Camp Bad Nenndorf. This was not the standard route for automatic arrest prisoners, all members of SS organisations and the Gestapo were subject to automatic arrest. Within two or three days (at most) of his arrest, someone had recognized a valuable prisoner, someone with information, and it did not take long for ex-SS-*Sturmbannführer Kriminaldirektor* Horst Kopkow to realise this himself—that he had something to save himself from an unknown fate, something the Allies would want. Information was the key and he had what they wanted.

In three weeks since arriving at Dahme, with the war already ended, Kopkow had the pressures of working lifted. Three weeks of peace and quiet to mull over a career, Nazi Party loyalty, and decide what to do next. When Kopkow's widow was interviewed by Sarah Helm in 2004, she said that at her first meeting with her husband after the war she professed shock that he had been able to renounce his Nazi beliefs so quickly while still holding hers.[2] Kopkow took a far more pragmatic view than his wife—she did not know what he knew or had done. Kopkow took to heart the words of his last boss, RSHA IV Chief Heinrich Müller, from their last meeting in Berlin on 22 April 1945, shortly before its occupation by Soviet armies. Müller told Kopkow that the western Allies would welcome him because of his knowledge of fighting Soviet agents. Müller was right about this because Kopkow's British captors quickly recognised his knowledge would fill in their own lack of information about Soviet espionage in Germany and former German-occupied territories. In fact, Kopkow's realisation of the means for his salvation took less than eight days to work out from capture, less than eight days when the Nazi of political conviction for fourteen years finally broke with the past, for on the ninth day, his first interrogation report was issued and he never stopped giving information for another three years officially, and at least another fifteen years unofficially.

On the ninth day (7 June 1945), two interrogation reports of Kopkow were issued from Neumünster Interrogation Camp.[3] The first report was sixty pages long, a mammoth document of details 'dictated by Kopkow himself directly into the typewriter' of his former secretary, Berta Rose, who was also imprisoned at this time. Rose was 'consulted' about some of the details to ensure accuracy. Kopkow decided content and layout, British interrogators interrupted when it 'became long-winded' or 'a point required clarification'. Some additional information became appendices. The second report was extracted from the first, giving details of Kopkow the man and his career in the Gestapo.

This report, as dictated by Kopkow and typed by Rose, is a masterpiece of detailed subjects that British Intelligence would find of interest, not only in the detail it revealed, but in his ability to recall such detail and provide context. It is a history of his Gestapo department showing counter-espionage measures in detecting infiltrated Soviet agents, Soviet espionage networks in Nazi-occupied Europe (such as 'Rote Kapelle'), and the huge Gestapo effort to uncover its every agent—how the Gestapo 'turned' enemy agents and how they conducted radio playback games (*Funkspiel*) not only with Moscow, but also with London. It detailed a whole raft of Gestapo investigations into German resistance organisations, such as those involved in the bomb plot against Hitler on 20 July 1944 and his department's final measures in 1945 against the Russians and the western Allies. This long report by Kopkow was the bait British Intelligence swallowed, and with his other reports that followed over the next three years, it was the one that saved Kopkow's life.

Six months earlier, in November 1944, a German SD officer deserted in France, and after some delay, he was brought to London for interrogation. His name was Carl Marcus and at this stage of the war, before Allied troops had set foot on German soil, Marcus proved a valuable source of information on SD intelligence operations and SD personnel. His codename used by MI5, the British security service, was DICTIONARY because he knew and knew of many people.[4] From the interrogation reports so far available in US and UK archives, DICTIONARY (as Carl Marcus) was the concise version; Horst Kopkow was the real thing, the real dictionary of hundreds of names and their place in Gestapo organisations—names in which the British and Americans had a great interest. They needed to ensure that these Gestapo men were under lock and key and not fomenting resistance work in their respective Allied zones of occupation in Germany.

With Kopkow's information, and that from interrogation of other Gestapo personnel in the British and American zones (the two powers shared this type of intelligence material), the bubble of the Gestapo myth (that the Gestapo was everywhere, uncovering every plot in their long black coats and red swastika armbands) was burst and reality took over. The Gestapo was not everywhere, plots came to unsuccessful fruition, many Gestapo men were fat, thin, tall, short, suffered heart attacks, had cancers, were young and old (very old in some cases), wore spectacles, and that they numbered less than 20,000 among a population of 40 million Germans and enlarged by occupation to over 100 million Europeans. They were not on every corner, they waited until someone made a mistake and an investigation into real or perceived crimes against the Nazi state began.

When making this first interrogation report, Kopkow was warned by British interrogators to give truthful information:

> Kopkow realises fully his situation, and knows it is hardly possible for him to hide much or cover up his activities. As a number of his office staff were captured together with him, he is aware that he can easily be cross-checked and he repeatedly said 'If you don't believe me there are plenty of people here you can ask'. His attitude is that his only chance for a milder judgement is to tell as much as possible. He also declared he is fully prepared to make any declaration of loyalty required.
>
> Interrogator made use of this frame of mind. Further it was also realised that it would be hardly possible to catch K. out on contradictions etc. through cross-questioning as he is not only too intelligent for that, but has had a very through criminalistic training; and knows all the tricks of the trade.
>
> Therefore K. was warned from the start, that he would not be treated as any small agent, but if one wanted something from him he would be asked point blank. That had the advantage for him that he always knew where he stood, but on the other hand if he slipped up and tried to con-

ceal something important—and he was bound to be found out sooner or later—then he had damaged his prospects for good and all.[5]

Naturally, at the beginning, Kopkow remained mostly truthful when answering questions, noticeable from his interrogation reports and looked at in hindsight, but the problem facing the interrogators was knowing the right questions to ask. Kopkow and all his men arrested in Dahme regarded themselves purely as criminalists, they had been trained as criminalists, and they themselves were not criminals. When interrogators did get around to asking something approaching the right questions that may have incriminated him, he deflected or, as criminals usually do, blamed someone else. British interrogators faced another problem because they did not fully understand how the different sections of the German security police and security service worked—how they worked in Germany itself and how they worked in co-operation with their offices in the Nazi-occupied territories. Until British and American interrogators of Gestapo and SD men understood the system by which the German security police and security services operated, they would fail to notice how Gestapo and SD men escaped incriminating themselves. The officials working in Berlin blamed the field men and, unremarkably, the field men blamed Berlin.

Kopkow's interrogators were working in the dark to a point—they could only ask questions of which they had knowledge. For the time being, in 1945, Kopkow could answer any question as he saw fit, and for most of that year, the questioning was directed at a who's who in the Gestapo and SD organisations and where they were now. This was safe ground and his interrogations, even when interrogated jointly with other captured Gestapo officers, show Kopkow excelling as a truthful dictionary of these men and their careers.

While Kopkow was under interrogation in Germany, some of his former superior officers had been taken to London for questioning. Ernst Kaltenbrunner had succeeded Reinhard Heydrich, who had been assassinated in Prague by parachute agents in 1942, as head of the RSHA. Kaltenbrunner's interrogations were a tremendous disappointment as he denied everything and refused to answer most questions.[6] Otto Ohlendorf, head of RSHA III (the domestic SD), was in London between mid-June and early October 1945; during this period, Ohlendorf certainly told interrogators about his wartime service in Russia as head of Einsatzgruppe 'D', one of four mobile killing units, and mentioned being responsible for the death of 80,000 people. However, practically all Ohlendorf's statements from this period detailing his killing campaign have still not been declassified by the British authorities, over seventy years later.[7] British intelligence agencies considered they might have better luck with Walter Schellenberg, head of RSHA VI (SD foreign intelligence service), when interrogated in London. Schellenberg turned out to be another real disappointment to them during his sojourn in

Britain between July and October 1945. Reports of Schellenberg's interrogations show 'his demeanour has not produced any evidence of outstanding genius as appears to have been attributed to him. On the contrary, his incoherency and incapability of producing lucid verbal or written statements have rendered him a much more difficult subject to interrogate than other subjects of inferior education and humbler status'. Historians have speculated that British Intelligence had the idea of using him in the British Zone of Occupation in Germany in an intelligence-gathering role, much like the Americans would use the German army intelligence chief in their hands, Major General Reinhard Gehlen. Whereas Gehlen had been an extremely capable German army intelligence officer, Schellenberg proved himself entirely the opposite.

There was a lesson to be learned in London in regard to Schellenberg that would have repercussions for Kopkow in Germany. During Schellenberg's interrogation sessions in London, an unwelcome request dated 1 August 1945 arrived:

> War Crimes Executive are now displaying a regrettable interest in the case; regrettable in the sense that it may result in SCHELLENBERG being taken out of our hands long before we have finished with him or exploited him satisfactorily. The War Crimes Executive are not to be restrained in their enthusiasm by being informed, as the fact is, that no material has come to light which will suggest that SCHELLENBERG is in any sense a proper subject for prosecution. If they cannot get him as prisoner for the dock they appear to be determined to get him as a witness for the prosecution.[8]

The interrogations persisted until 28 October 1945, when Schellenberg returned to Germany and was handed over to American war crimes prosecutors at Frankfurt-Main airport.

The lesson learned was not to tell your colleagues in other branches of the armed services who you were holding. This was a lesson well-learned regarding Kopkow, who was kept in Germany by the Intelligence Division of BAOR (British Army on the Rhine—the military occupation authority in the British Zone of Occupation in Germany) at their Bad Nenndorf Interrogation Centre, near Hannover, and away from any other British agency and the War Crimes Executive. The interrogations of Kopkow at Bad Nenndorf began after his arrival in July 1945, but it was not until 18 October 1946 that BAOR Intelligence Division confirmed to British War Crimes Group/North West Europe that Kopkow was in their hands. On 30 October 1946, BAOR Intelligence Division informed BAOR War Crimes Investigation Unit, part of the Judge Advocate General's office, that 'Kopkow is now at 7 CIC [and] has given a great deal of important information whilst under interrogation, he will not be released without reference to this Headquarters'.[9] Judging by these interrogations, Kopkow provided information that filled gaps in the British (and American) knowledge of the Gestapo and RSHA personnel and its operations. Once this information was exhausted, before the end of 1945, Kopkow was detailing all he knew about Gestapo counter-espionage and counter-sabotage operations that he had controlled from his department at RSHA IV A2, their successes and failures, and the battle against agents from the east and the west. Kopkow gave British Intelligence a great deal of information about communist operations and the 'Rote Kapelle' and its spin-offs in Germany, Holland, Belgium, and France. Tantalisingly for MI5 in London, Kopkow mentioned pre-war contacts between Rote Kapelle in Belgium with secret communist agents in Britain. Such contacts needed to be explored and put to an end if still in operation.

In regard to his departmental responsibilities and liaison with Gestapo operations in France, Belgium, Holland, and other German-occupied territories against British-organised agent operations by Special Operations Executive (SOE), Kopkow was allowed to get away with murder. His BAOR Intelligence Division interrogators and British war crimes interrogators were looking into the murders of captured SIS and SOE agents in German concentration camps during 1944 and 1945, and Kopkow denied any involvement. He claimed it was not his responsibility, blamed others, and stated that two of his own subordinates reported directly to Kopkow's own superior, Heinrich Müller, the chief of RSHA IV, and he was not involved. This from a man who always claimed the limelight for himself from his department's successes, such as the successful uncovering and prosecution of a Soviet espionage group operating in Berlin, 'Rote Kapelle', for which Kopkow received almost three years' salary as a bonus from *Reichsmarschall* Hermann Göring's slush-fund.[10]

Horst Kopkow was always at the front of the successes of his department's counter-espionage and counter-sabotage operations. Kopkow did not shirk responsibility in power, only when out of power, blaming others for his department's misdeeds and denying responsibility for the fate of the captured agents who came under his direct official remit. Yet Kopkow was responsible for all that happened, directing Gestapo field offices to do the bidding of RSHA Berlin, which could be seen from pertinent documentation already held by British war crimes investigators and disregarded by British Intelligence operators at the time. Did they not realise this man was responsible for the murder of their wartime colleagues? Evidence became available from a number of different British war crimes investigations to show Kopkow was involved. Gestapo officers from Paris, who had been brought to the London District Cage in 1946 for extensive questioning about their role in the Gestapo work against SOE agents in France, regularly mentioned Kopkow—not only in connection with the radio games (the *Funkspiel* operations), but also in connection with all the agents being deported from France to German concentration camps.

From declassified files of MI5 and War Crimes Group/NorthWest Europe in Britain and OSS/CIA in the USA, it is clear that Kopkow was never seriously questioned about SOE agents. That Kopkow got away from explaining his responsibility lies in the chaos and ruination of post-war Germany. Documentary evidence was available to indict a large number of major figures from the Nazi German state, but less about the lower figures in power. A great deal of official documents and files had been destroyed during Allied air raids and much else destroyed by burning on instructions from RSHA in spring 1945. Many Gestapo and SD officers disappeared, were missing, or were killed in action at the end of the war. Kopkow's own deputy, Thomas Ampletzer, died during the defence of Berlin against Russian forces in April–May 1945, so he became a scapegoat used by Kopkow.[11]

Horst Kopkow did play the most significant role in the murder of at least 200 captured Allied intelligence agents, who were murdered without trial in German concentration camps and prisons. It can be seen from documentation available at the time of his interrogations that in June 1944, there began a systematic campaign of murder carried out against these agents. The orders went in turn from one concentration camp to another. These agents (men and women) were shot singly or taken in groups to the execution site and shot, hanged, or given lethal injections. Between June and December 1944, at least 125 agents had been murdered in seven different concentration camps. The administration departments of these camps did not decide the fate of the agents, they acted on orders from RSHA Berlin and the relevant department who had sent them. In these cases, it was RSHA IV A2, whose chief was Horst Kopkow, and he had had the agents transferred from their place and country of capture to concentration camps and prisons in Greater Germany. The term 'desk murderer' has been used to describe Gestapo officers like Horst Kopkow, like Adolf Eichmann; these were officers who did not themselves personally murder anyone, but sent out the orders for others to commit murder. Adolf Eichmann escaped prosecution in Germany by escaping to South America from whence Israel kidnapped and prosecuted him in 1960. Adolf Eichmann had a trial in Israel and was condemned to death and executed. Horst Kopkow escaped prosecution in Germany and was recruited and protected by Britain's Secret Intelligence Service, dying of natural causes at the ripe old age of eighty-five years surrounded by his family.

Adolf Eichmann was responsible for the murder of several million innocent Jews, and Horst Kopkow was responsible for the murder of several hundred enemy agents. Only one paid the price, the other got away with it.

2
Into the Gestapo

Horst Kopkow was born on 29 November 1910 at Ortelsburg, East Prussia (now the Polish town of Szczytno), the sixth child of a businessman and hotel proprietor. The family had already moved to the regional capital of East Prussia, Allenstein (now Olsztyn, Poland), before the First World War broke out. Kopkow was still a small child at the time when an invading Tsarist Russian army attacked and almost destroyed Allenstein on 30 August 1914, during its retreat after defeat at the hands of a resurgent German army, known as the Battle of Tannenberg. This was a battle that reignited German patriotism throughout this most eastern of German provinces, sharing a bloody borderland with Lithuania and Poland. The German army also called up his two older brothers; they later died with thousands of others on French battlefields. The deaths of his brothers and Russian armies in East Prussia were to have a lasting effect on Kopkow, turning into a contempt of Bolshevism and communism—a contempt still evident to his later post-war British interrogators, who remarked: '[It] runs like a red thread through the whole statement that is K's [Kopkow's] antipathy towards the U.S.S.R. He is not only through his East Prussian upbringing biased towards them, but also through his career he was … engaged on work against Communism'.[1]

As a schoolboy and student, Horst Kopkow did not shine. After attending grammar school (*Gymnasium*) in Allenstein, at seventeen years old he had failed his exams taking third best results (*Obersekunda*), two steps below matriculation, which would have allowed a university place. Kopkow must have been a lazy student or someone who did not apply himself as he had to take one year's teaching twice. Proud parents were probably very disappointed by his exam results. He left school in April 1928 with little to show prospective employers. Allenstein, with 35,000 inhabitants, was a small country town of agricultural machinery manufacture and matchstick production.[2] Luckily, Kopkow found apprentice work in a pharmacy (drug store). In Germany at the time, it was common practice for many industries and crafts to offer apprenticeships. Most involved two and three years' employment, with training on the job followed by practical examinations; this occurred whether you wanted to be a stone mason, carpenter, or pharmacist, and it became an important yardstick for someone who had flunked his education at the best school in Allenstein—Kopkow had to show he could buckle down to a working environment. He was probably a late developer, which his subsequent career would show.

After his successful pharmacist examination in 1931, Kopkow was retained by the pharmacy where he had trained. As everywhere with unemployment ever present as a political vote catcher, the Nazi Party and Communist Party were vying for votes. Evidently swayed by the Nazi cause, Kopkow first joined the 'Brown Shirts' (*Sturmabteilung*—SA) on 7 May 1931, and the Nazi Party on 1 August 1931 (No. 607,161).[3] Several months before his twenty-first birthday, Horst Kopkow had already decided the Nazi Party as more likely to save Germany from the disastrous economic downturn, from mass unemployment, high inflation, and the lasting effects of losing the First World War. He took to the Nazi cause with relish, leading from the front when communists attacked Nazi rallies. Of this period, Dietrich Orlow stated:

> There can be no doubt that the political street warfare was becoming increasingly bitter in 1931 and that the SA quite literally paid with its blood so that the martyr image of the party as a whole could be maintained.[4]

For someone of slender build, Kopkow certainly did not shrink from such fights. Undoubtedly, the role Kopkow created for himself in the Nazi Party of Allenstein brought attention from his political superiors who asked whether he might accept a political post with the Party. Kopkow turned their requests down on several occasions because his salary from the pharmacy was a good deal more than what the Party offered. The Nazi Party in East Prussia came under *Gauleiter* Erich Koch. *Gauleiters* were political appointments personally made by Adolf Hitler. Koch was very active in *Gau Ostpreussen* and saw the Nazi parliamentary vote increase from 236,507 in September 1930 (22.5 per cent of the electorate) to a whopping 536,278 in the July 1933 elections (47.1 per cent of the electorate), and similar voting patterns across Germany cemented the Nazi Government in power following the January 1933 seizure of power on a tide of popular votes.[5]

In August 1932, Kopkow resigned from the SA 'brown shirts' and joined the SS 'black shirts' on 26 August 1932, member No. 46,034. When considering the numbers accepted into the SS across Germany as a whole, his SS number meant early acceptance into the elite 'black shirt' ranks. His wife would later remark about these days, where she herself worked in the local Nazi Party women's group in Allenstein: 'We were proud to have believed it all before even Hitler became popular. We were young, it was exciting for us'.[6] Young and exciting, the promises of a new political party rather than the older communists who appealed almost solely to the working class. The Nazi Party spread its message across the entire class structure. Kopkow's wife saw his joining the SS as a wise move: 'The SS were the men in black. He was proud to be a man in black and they were pleased to have him. He always wanted to be the best and he was more intelligent than those around him'. Proud, better, and intelligent was just what the SS unit in Allenstein wanted. This unit, 61. SS-*Standarte*, established itself in Allenstein on 19 June 1933, and Kopkow played an active part working not only in their administrative side in his spare time, but also as one of the SS detachment (*Sturm*) commanders. Now the SS began asking Kopkow whether he might make a career with them—offers that continued into 1934. Finally, Kopkow acceded, accepting a post as clerk, with a salary set below that of the pharmacy, in the newly created Prussian *Geheime Staatspolizei* (Gestapo) office established in Allenstein. This was a civil service job, and regardless of the association with the SS, it was a job for life with a pension at the end of it. The possibilities that opened for Kopkow from joining the Gestapo went beyond anything he expected and he grasped those opportunities with both hands. This was a truly new beginning.

There is no doubt that Kopkow started at the bottom as a clerk, a *Kriminalangestellter*, in the Gestapo organisation. This employment began on 1 February 1934, and his rise in SS rank to SS-*Obertruppführer* (sergeant) followed on 4 February. More importantly, on 20 April 1934, his commission followed as SS-*Untersturmführer* (lieutenant); this day was always an auspicious day in the SS for it was Hitler's birthday, and each year, it was the day on which many SS promotions took place. To ensure Kopkow was a fit and proper person to be an officer, he was sent for officer-training at the SS-*Führer-Sportschule* (SS-Officer Sportschool) at Leisnig, south of Leipzig, some 400 miles away from Allenstein. It was probably the first time Kopkow had ever been out of East Prussia. The course began on 27 May 1934 and ended six weeks later on 7 July 1934. A week before the end was the period of the 'Night of the Long Knives', when Hitler ordered *Reichsführer*-SS Heinrich Himmler, Chief of the SS, to put an end to the rise of the SA 'brown shirts' believed to be plotting against Hitler. Across Germany, between 30 June and 2 July 1934, about 100 senior SA men were executed simply by order of Hitler to end their 'homosexuality, debauchery, drunkenness and high living'; the SS also took the opportunity at this time to simply execute some of the political opposition. These events do not appear to have had much impact on Kopkow, though the execution without trial measures would play a part in Kopkow's later career.

Kopkow returned to the Gestapo office in Allenstein in July 1934 ready to begin his new career as both a SS and Gestapo officer. He worked in the department dealing with counter-espionage, carrying out clerical duties to accustom him with office practices. The next stepping stone happened in September 1934 with Kopkow's acceptance as a candidate for training as a *Kriminalkommissar* (KK—many German police ranks have no equivalent among American or British police forces, but this rank is probably best described as a first level 'detective'). His on-the-job training continued with Gestapo Allenstein through 1935, during which time he was further promoted by the SS on 16 June 1935 to SS-*Obersturmführer*, showing that Kopkow was now fully engaged and politically committed to the Nazi cause and its policies.

East Prussia shared a long encircling land border with Poland, connected to Germany itself only via the Danzig corridor and controlled by the Poles. After the Nazi seizure of power, the army began constructing a defensive fortification line along some of the border areas. The Polish intelligence service subsequently took a great interest in these fortifications. In 1935, Kopkow was made assistant to a case worker at Gestapo Allenstein, whose job entailed vetting individual construction workers. With so many workers required and so few Gestapo officials assigned to vetting them, detailed enquiries into the workers' previous employment and residential backgrounds were limited. Finally, the vetting was restricted to excluding communist workers. In 1936, new problems arose due to the return from the Soviet Union of many thousands of German technicians who had travelled there in the 1920s and 1930s on labour contracts. These returnees caused alarm as they were believed in some cases to have been suborned by Soviet intelligence agencies. Gestapo Allenstein received instructions from national Gestapo headquarters (Gestapa) in Berlin that all such returnees crossing the Polish border into their area needed to be interrogated. The subsequent interrogation sessions of fellow Germans by Kopkow gave him practical experience in extracting useful information about the Soviet Union, especially economic factors and Soviet military armament industries. According to Kopkow, these interrogations also 'provided the first authentic inside information on the methods of the NKWD (OGPU). Moreover, a complete picture regarding conditions in the Russian Concentration Camps was obtained'.[7] Some of the returnees admitted Soviet intelligence agencies had only sanctioned their return if they would act on their behalf once back in Germany. Up to a half of the returnees declared they had been forced to sign a declaration to this effect before being allowed to leave Russia. According to Kopkow, the Gestapo had to consult with the Ministry of Justice about these declarations. Both administrations agreed that declarations signed under duress could not be legally acted upon in German law, and the 'only steps taken was to send them for three months to a Transit Camp in Tegel near Berlin, from where they were released to return home'. A very small number of returnees who had been suborned did in fact begin working for Soviet intelligence on return to Germany, but they were quickly arrested once their activities became known. These reports were shared with the army military intelligence service (Abwehr) and Gestapa Berlin. Five years later, when the German armed forces invaded the Soviet Union, Kopkow was the only one to remember the importance of these reports.

Kopkow began courting one of the leading young women in the local Nazi women's movement (*Bund des deutschen Mädchen*), Gerda Lindenau, and they married on 13 February 1936 in Allenstein. His first examination for the career as a criminalist (*Fachprüfung I für Kriminalbeamte*) took place in Berlin over several weeks during September–October 1936; on 16 October 1936, he successfully completed the course. Over the next twelve months, Kopkow's Gestapo work continued and included two mandatory eight-week training courses with the army and six months (March–August 1937) on detached service at the regional headquarters of the criminal police (*Kriminalpolizei*—Kripo) at Königsberg. During this period, Kopkow was again promoted by the SS, 20 April 1937, to Captain (SS-*Hauptsturmführer*). After three years of training as an officer and as prospective criminalist, the next stage in Kopkow's career began in October 1937. All this training now had to be put to the test over a nine-month training course for appointment as *Kriminalkommissar* (KK). This took place at the Security Police and SD Officer Training School (*Führerschule der Sicherheitspolizei und des SD)* located at Schloss Strasse 1, Berlin-Charlottenburg. It began on 4 October 1937 and ended on 2 July 1938. This was the sixth such *Kriminalkommissar* training course of the Nazi period, and comprised about sixty participants, mostly members of the Kripo, with twenty-six Gestapo men and five from the SD. All those attending were *Kriminalkommissar* candidates, few were members of the SS, but Kopkow was senior ranking SS officer as SS-*Hauptsturmführer*; those who were not members of the SS all joined at the end of the course on 2 July 1938 and were commissioned as SS-*Untersturmführer*. These regular courses in Berlin tended to create lasting friendships and similar promotion dates. In Kopkow's case, none of these things happened. In his post-war interrogations, Kopkow named only two officers from this course. Kopkow and Felix Rühl were the only two course participants promoted SS-*Sturmbannführer* (Major) by the end of the war, though Kopkow had advanced further in civil service rankings to *Kriminaldirektor*. Interestingly, Kopkow and Rühl were the only two who had joined the SS before the Nazi regime came to power.[8]

The *Kriminalkommissar* training courses involved both theoretical and practical work led by a number of senior instructors from the Gestapo and Kripo. The participants were accommodated in the *Führerschule* unless they already resided in Berlin; those from outside Berlin who brought their wives to the capital city had to find private lodgings. Classes were divided into groups of about thirty participants and were held every morning until lunchtime (1 p.m.); the afternoons were for individual study, weapons training, and sports. The lectures given over the nine-month period were designed to provide both an extensive knowledge of the German criminal code and justice system, alongside Nazi ideological instruction. One theme explored the development of police work in ancient Greece and Egypt, the French police in Napoleonic times under Fouché, the secret police of the Russian Tsar (the Okhrana), then they were brought up to date with major developments of the German political police under the Weimar Republic, and finally how its purview widened under National Socialism. Under the new Nazi regime that these *Kriminalkommissars* now supported, new political and 'philosophical' enemies were to be investigated: communism, Marxism, Jews, freemasons, churches, Gypsies. To counter these enemies, new laws were available and lectures given on this legislation, criminology, police tactics from the criminal and political police viewpoint, treason, and counter-espionage. Naturally, a Nazi ideological slant across these subjects ensured the candidates realised enemies of the state were political and philosophical. Throughout the course, written and oral examinations took place, and practical exercises involving modern management skills, such as role-playing, were conducted (one example being a murder investigation examined in detail). Other practical exercises involved different instructions to resolve criminal investigations, such as a police warning, initiation of judicial proceedings before the courts, fines, short-term arrest and detention up to twenty-one days without trial, and transfers to a concentration camp. Some courses ended with the *Kommissar* candidates being taken to Sachsenhausen concentration camp, just north of Berlin, to see for themselves what a 'KZ' looked like.[9]

At the end of the course, a final written examination took place, and afterwards, on 2 July 1938, anyone not in the SS was enrolled and given SS-officer commissions as befitted new *Kriminalkommissars* on probation. These new workhorses for the Gestapo and Kripo system—warriors for the ideological war against enemies of the state, the political enemies such as communists and philosophical enemies such as political churches, and Jews whose fate would soon worsen and worsen disastrously within a few years—all returned to their home stations to fulfil their probationary duties and await a fresh posting from Sipo headquarters in Berlin. Kopkow received his posting before the end of August 1938, for in September, he began his new career at national Gestapo headquarters in Berlin, a sure sign that he had impressed people at the *Kommissar* course. As this posting was for an unspecified period, Kopkow moved his wife and daughter from Allenstein to Berlin. He would never return to Allenstein, his future lay in Berlin.

Before and after Kopkow was being trained and examined for a career as a criminalist in Allenstein, the *Geheime Staatspolizei*, or Gestapo (Secret State Police), underwent many changes both of practice and leadership. It began as the Political Department (Department I A) of many criminal police headquarters across Germany, with the remit of investigating and using the rule of law against overtly left-wing and right-wing political organisations; basically, the Communist Party of Germany (KPD) and the Nazi Party (NSDAP). After the Nazi Party formed a government in January 1933, one of Hitler's top men, Herman Göring, became Prime Minister of Prussia and was based in Berlin. The Nazi Party had recognized the significance of having Department I A brought under political control. In Berlin, Göring quickly brought this department out of criminal police headquarters and established it by decree of 26 April 1933 as the *Preussische Geheime Staatspolizeiamt* (Gestapa) under Rudolf Diels.[10] In Munich, *Reichsführer*-SS Heinrich Himmler was appointed Chief of the Munich Police, and on 1 April, he and his top aide, Reinhard Heydrich, took control of the *Bayerisches Politische Polizei* (Bavarian Political Police). The power struggle for control of the political police across Germany by Göring in Berlin and Himmler and Heydrich in Munich would always favour the Himmler–Heydrich partnership. Göring was a tremendous national figure and politician, but Himmler had feet on the ground—his SS organisation had members across Germany. Like dominoes, Himmler proceeded to gain appointment as police chief of all the individual German regional states and acquired control of all their individual police forces. By spring 1934, the only exceptions were Prussia and the tiny Schaumburg–Lippe area. Negotiations took place between Göring and Himmler, and eventually Hitler made the final decision and appointed Himmler as Inspector of the Gestapo with Heydrich as his Director of Operations. Göring remained as Chief of the Gestapo, but his man Rudolf Diels was ousted. Political manoeuvring continued until 1936, with Himmler and Heydrich postulating for a separation of the entire German police forces from the control of the Interior Ministry under Wilhelm Frick. Following an agreement with Hitler, on 17 June 1936, Himmler was named Chief of the German Police within the Ministry of the Interior; the same agreement allowed Himmler to bring together his SS role and his police role, thereby ensuring a more political aspect.[11] However, Himmler remained wholly responsible to Hitler and could and did disregard Frick and the Interior Ministry in his decision making. Werner Best, who would soon be organising and moving the Gestapo as a political police to a new level, remarked: 'Under the leadership of the *Reichsführer*-SS, the German police has become the point at which the movement and the state intersect'.[12]

The Himmler–Heydrich partnership took this agreement from Hitler in their stride and immediately began standardising the individual police agencies of the German states into national entities, centralised in Berlin. Himmler began the formation of Main Offices for the uniformed police services as *Hauptamt Ordnungspolizei* (HA Orpo). The Orpo included the *Schutzpolizei* (Schupo), who carried out the job of uniformed policemen in the towns and cities; the *Gendarmerie*, who did the same job in rural areas; the village police (*Gemeindepolizei*); an emergency technical service (*Technische Nothilfe*); and the fire service (*Feuerschutzpolizei*). In control of HA Orpo, Himmler appointed SS-*Obergruppenführer* and General of Police Kurt Daluege.

Bringing all the political police departments into a central organisation took a little longer, and Göring had to issue another decree to resolve outstanding local problems. In these early days, Himmer and Heydrich created a new Security Police Main Office (*Hauptamt Sicherheitspolizei*) that combined the Gestapo and the criminal police (*Kriminalpolizei*—Kripo). Yet another agency needed to be centralised in Berlin, the Security Service or SD (*Sicherheitsdienst*) that the Himmler–Heydrich partnership created in Munich in 1931. The SD was the intelligence arm of the Nazi Party and had two main tasks at this time; on the one hand, it spied on their political opponents, and on the other hand, they spied upon ranking NSDAP officials to ensure loyalty and discipline. The SD Main Office (*Hauptamt Sicherheitsdienst*) was established on 25 January 1935 in Berlin. Other SS Main Offices would be established in the months and years ahead and cement Himmler's future within the Nazi Government. Heydrich had greater ambitions than controlling the Security Police and Security Service and would later, in pursuit of a new opportunity, fatally suffer from an assassin's bomb.

When SS-*Hauptsturmführer Kriminalkommissar* Horst Kopkow arrived back in Berlin in September 1938 for his posting to the Gestapa, he had ambitions of his own. Kopkow had no base or allies in Berlin who might favour him; therefore, his posting must have been due on merit from aptitude and attitude at his *Kommissar* exams. Although he had been senior ranking SS officer on the course, all the participants held police ranks on a par. In Gestapa Berlin, Kopkow began his new career in Department II A3 and gave its functions as: 'Supervision of Russian Commissions in the Reich; listing of all travellers to and from Soviet Union; Russian underground work [i.e. espionage] in the Reich; supervision of Russian institutions, such as Embassy staff, Consular and trade representatives; supervision of Germans in the Soviet Union. Croatian patriotic movement in Germany'.

In his later post-war interrogations, Kopkow was very descriptive of his posting to Dept. II A3. The causes for concern over German returnees from Soviet Russia he had experienced earlier in Allenstein were just as prevalent in Berlin. While Kopkow could recall a returning German engineer from 1939 who 'attempted to influence soldiers of Stuttgart Garrison with communistic ideas and by theft of weapons from the Wehrmacht to support the Am-Apparat (Anti-Military organisation)' and a returning German communist returnee who 'attempted diversionary tactics on Police and Wehrmacht members and to recruit them into the district special organisation of the Communist Party', he did not say what then happened to these two men. Whereas the fate of others, two communist women for example, who returned from Soviet Russia at this time is much more descriptive.

Josefine Pautz and her husband left Düsseldorf for the Soviet Union in 1931: 'In January 1938 my husband and I returned to Germany after seven years living in Ukraine. Because we were suspected as enemies of the state after living abroad, we were taken into protective custody [by the Gestapo]'. Without any judicial proceedings against them, her husband was sent to Sachsenhausen concentration camp, near Berlin, and detained until liberated by Russian troops in April 1945. Josefine Pautz remained in Düsseldorf police prison before being sent to a women's prison in Berlin. In spring 1939, she was transferred to the new concentration camp for women at Ravensbrück, also north of Berlin, and also liberated by Russian troops in April 1945.[13] More well-known and active members of the German Communist Party, such as Margarete Buber-Neumann and her husband, Heinz Neumann, had fled to Moscow in 1933 soon after the Nazis came to power. They rightly feared arrest and incarceration. In fact, their arrest and incarceration happened in Moscow. During one of the Soviet purges of 1937, Heinz Neumann was arrested and executed; Margarete was arrested in 1938 and sentenced to five years' 'reformatory labour' in the Karaganda Gulag (Kazakhstan), where she worked in the agricultural sector. In summer 1940, Buber-Neumann and about twenty other German communists, mostly men, serving sentences in the Gulag, were returned to Moscow then sent back to Germany by train. On the railway bridge spanning the River Bug at Brest-Litovsk, Russian NKVD guards handed the group over to SS officers who took them to Lublin Prison. Buber-Neumann recalls the prison already held seventeen women and 130 men, all communists, who had also recently been deported from the Soviet Union. After occasional Gestapo interrogations over the following three weeks about her life history and conditions in the Soviet Union, Buber-Neumann and about forty of the men were taken by train and police vehicles to Berlin and imprisonment at the 'Alex'—Berlin police headquarters on Alexanderplatz. Further interrogations were designed to establish she had been sent back as an agent to spy on Germany. These interrogations were in the 'Alex', but on 'several occasions [she] was taken to Headquarters of the Gestapo in the Prinz Albrechtstrasse'; this is where Kopkow worked. In July 1940, a Gestapo order for her 'preventative arrest' and continuing detention was issued together with her transfer to Ravensbrück concentration camp for women.[14] The Pautz couple and Buber-Neumann were typical of the fate awaiting German communists returning to Germany at this time, whether or not they were demoralised or disenchanted with communism.

Summer 1939 saw high-level diplomacy between these two political enemies—Nazism and communism, Berlin and Moscow. German Foreign Minister Joachim von Ribbentrop travelled to Moscow, and on 24 August 1939, he signed a non-aggression pact (the 'Molotov-Ribbentrop Pact'), valid for ten years. In a secret protocol, both agreed to share Eastern Europe by parcelling out German and Soviet spheres of interest. The following day in Berlin, Hitler met with the British Ambassador and stated this non-aggression pact would avoid the problem of the First World War and its two-front military war, Hitler proposing that Britain accept Germany's demands about Poland. Having dilly-dallied politically over Czechoslovakia earlier in the year, when German troops marched in and occupied the country, Britain acted quickly and signed a mutual assistance agreement with Poland on 26 August 1939. This caused a delay to German military plans to attack Poland on 26 August, but within days, German armies invaded western Poland and shortly afterwards Soviet armies invaded eastern Poland as far as their previously agreed new boundaries for the division of Poland, which was soon wholly occupied by German and Russian armies.

Ribbentrop returned to Moscow in September 1939 at the request of Molotov and Stalin. His plane left Berlin on 27 September with a delegation that included Horst Kopkow, who was representing the Gestapo. There was a brief landing at Königsberg to pick up Albert Forster, *Gauleiter* of Danzig, before flying directly to Moscow. Kopkow's participation, in recognition of his expertise about Germans returning from the Soviet Union to Germany, must have received not only the agreement of Heinrich Müller (national

Gestapo chief in Berlin) but also SS-*General* Reinhard Heydrich as Chief of the Security Police and SD. Due to such an important top-level government decision-making involvement, *Reichsführer*-SS Heinrich Himmler would have been kept informed. Kopkow represented Gestapo interests in concluding the German-Soviet agreement of 28 September 1939. The main purpose of this agreement amended the secret protocol signed by Ribbentrop and Molotov on 23 August 1939 that allowed the Soviet Union to take action in Lithuania; it also agreed the resettlement of German minorities in Bessarabia and those in Soviet-occupied Poland, back to Germany. To be included in this diplomatic delegation, rather than a more senior SS officer, indicates an important high-level belief in Kopkow's abilities for this mission, one requiring tact, diplomacy, negotiation skills, and developing relationships with the Soviet side. Although Kopkow only briefly mentioned his mission to Moscow during his post-war interrogations, seemingly his British interrogators failed to question him further about this.[15]

These German minorities (ethnic Germans, *Volksdeutsche*) included in the 28 September 1939 agreement represented a hefty addition to the German population available for work or service in the military: 124,000 in Soviet-occupied areas of Poland and 212,000 in Bessarabia. The former were immediately available for resettlement, the latter not until June 1940, when the Soviet army occupied Bessarabia under yet another Hitler initiative with the Romanians who then held the region. Unlike his earlier experiences with Germans returning from Soviet areas with suspicious motives having been suborned by the Soviet secret police, Kopkow now recognised that the ethnic Germans in Soviet-occupied Poland, and later those from Bessarabia, did not receive 'any training prior to leaving Russia; lack of time, and also the fact that many of these people would have been unsatisfactory in any case as agents, precluded any training being given. The Russian intention was ... merely to use the opportunity to send into Germany a large fraction of people from which a network of agents might be selected as and when the need arose, and which in any case would be out of sympathy with the ideals of the Nazi State'. Whatever the Russian intentions may have been, the June 1941 attack on the Soviet Union put a stop to them. Some of these ethnic Germans were drafted into the Germany army and the SS-*Einsatzgruppen* (task forces) who had the job of exterminating Soviet Jews. Their Russian language skill was used against a state that had recently persecuted them for simply having German antecedents.

Back in Berlin after the mission to Moscow, Kopkow transferred to another Gestapo department, Dept. II A1, whose responsibilities included countering the special communist organisation of the Third International (the Comintern) and Counter-Sabotage. Already in the air was a new Gestapo reorganisation to face the problems brought about by the onset of war. Dept. II A1 had spent the years since 1933 under *Kriminalrat* Kurt Geissler, a close friend of Gestapo-Chief Heinrich Müller, working against German Communists and

Marxists, their organisations in Germany, and those communists and Marxists returning from the Soviet Union to Germany. He had much in common with Kopkow's similar work in Dept. II A3. Kopkow's transfer to this department could be seen as forward thinking by Heinrich Müller and his Personnel Department. Karl Giering was Geissler's long-serving deputy and he was increasingly absent through ill health. Geissler needed career progression, so placing Kopkow in Dept. II A1 can be seen as exceedingly thoughtful. On 27 September 1939, a new organisation was created, amalgamating the Gestapo, Kripo, three SD sections, and their administration and personnel sections into a new entity—Reich Security Main Office (RSHA, *Reichssicherheitshauptamt*), located in Berlin, Prinz Albrechtstrasse 8:[16]

Office I	Administration and Law (Chief: SS-*Brigadeführer* Dr Werner Best)
Office II	Personnel (Chief: SS-*Standartenführer* Dr Alfred Six
Office III	SD (*Sicherheitsdienst*) Inland (Chief: SS-*Standartenführer* Otto Ohlendorf)
Office IV	Gestapo (Chief: SS-*Oberführer Reichskriminaldirektor* Heinrich Müller)
Office V	Kripo (Chief: SS-*Oberführer Reichskriminaldirektor* Artur Nebe)
Office VI	SD-Foreign (Chief: SS-*Brigadeführer* Dr Heinz Jost)
Office VII	SD Research and Archive (Chief: SS-*Sturmbannführer* Dr Paul Dittel)

SS-*Obergruppenführer* Reinhard Heydrich was appointed chief of the new RSHA, reporting to Himmler who reported to Hitler. Consequently, the security police and security service now had a direct channel of communication to the highest level of government. This was a precursor to the ambitions of Heydrich, who now had direct communications with Hitler in the increasingly regular absence of Himmler from Berlin. Himmler and Heydrich created a whole web of senior SS and police generals in positions of authority across the military districts of Germany (the *Wehrkreis*), known as 'Himmler's long arm', whose job was to amalgamate the SS and police forces in their districts under one umbrella. These were the Higher SS and Police Leaders (HSSPF—*Höhere SS-und Polizeiführer*), a position established by Himmler in November 1937. In a few short years, following the invasion of the Soviet Union, three HSSPFs would be transferred from Germany to similar positions in the occupied Soviet territories and begin implementing another key part of Nazi racial policy, the 'Final Solution of the Jewish Question'.

In Berlin, this new Gestapo organisation did not merely adopt new department titles, there was a fresh cross-movement of functions between departments. A complete restructuring in the face of lessening political opposition for the simple reason that some no longer posed a threat to the Nazi regime. Kopkow himself reported that communism and Marxism 'had been of first rank importance' in the early years, 1933–1935, but by 1939, both had diminished or disappeared 'as an independent problem and became more or less a sideline'. Even Kopkow's earlier involvement with 'immigrants gradually fell into the background and eventually disappeared altogether'. In their place, within the new department of RSHA IV A2, came an emphasis on counter-sabotage, industrial security, investigating fraudulent passports, and documents, surveillance of remaining communists and those Germans continuing to return from Russia.

The outbreak of war on 3 September 1939, followed by the establishment of the RSHA on 27 September 1939, encouraged further the implementation of Berlin's authority in the occupied territories of Poland. RSHA IV A2 began to receive reports of sabotage from the newly established Gestapo offices in Poland. These reports of Polish resistance activities with names of resistants involved were checked against the vast card indices of the Gestapa Berlin (now RSHA), including those created in the years of the Political Police departments. Few individuals were new to sabotage, and RSHA indices were capable of showing this. Post-war captured German records contained correspondence between Gestapo Radom to RSHA IV A2 about sabotage acts by Polish resistance groups. Kopkow sent regular teleprinter messages to Radom, providing information on individuals from the RSHA indices.[17] From such correspondence, the extension of RSHA departmental influences can be seen, revealing how RSHA responsibilities continued to spread into the occupied areas, giving the head of RSHA IV, Heinrich Müller, almost unparalleled power to issue orders either directly himself or through his various departmental chiefs.

According to Kopkow, sabotage in Germany before the creation of RSHA in September 1939 was minimal, claiming he could not recall a single sabotage act on the land; however, sabotage of German merchant ships in foreign ports kept increasing. Kopkow falsely claimed sabotage on the land was absent, but failed to explain these two important examples. On 27 February 1940, about 150 skilled workmen and mechanics were reported under arrest in Berlin for sabotage at the Borsig weapons factory; they were sent to a concentration camp.[18] In the winter of 1940–1941, a fire broke out at Berlin Anhalter railway station, destroying half the station before the fire could be contained.[19] The reported cause was a time-bomb in a suitcase in the left luggage office. Such reports as these are typical of those involving RSHA IV A2.

Another important turning point for Kopkow's career happened in November 1939. After Hitler gave a speech in Munich at the Bürgerbräukeller on 9 November, an explosion took place. A bomb had been planted in one of the pillars supporting the building. Himmler immediately sent his sabotage experts from RSHA IV A2, Geissler and Giering, down to Munich as part of a 'Special Commission' to investigate. Borders were closed and stop-and-search procedures began. A man named Georg Elser was apprehended on the Swiss border and taken to Munich for interrogation by members of the 'Special

Commission'. Elser was quickly identified as the bomber and the Gestapo net widened to search for his accomplices. He was transferred to the prison in the cellars of RSHA Berlin, Prinz Albrechtstrasse 8, where Gestapo Chief Heinrich Müller and *Reichsführer*-SS Himmler questioned him. Despite physical abuse, Elser could not tell them anything more than he acted by himself. Elser spent the next five years at Sachsenhausen concentration camp; in 1945, he was transferred south to Dachau, where he was shot by SS men on 9 April 1945 acting on Hitler's express orders.[20]

While Geissler and Giering were in Munich, November–December 1939, Kopkow remained in Berlin as Acting Department Chief RSHA IV A2. When the two returned, Giering was a sick man; he had already been on sick leave between autumn 1938 and summer 1939 with swellings in his face and chest, and 1940 proved no better for him. He was hospitalised again on 2 January 1940, followed by confinement to his home until 28 February. Between 9 April and 7 May 1940, he took a 'Kur' at one of Germany's sanatoriums. Further hospitalisation followed between 20 August and 11 September 1940.[21] In this period of uncertainty, Kopkow acted as Deputy Departmental Chief under Geissler. At this juncture, Geissler himself was absent, having been posted to Holland in May 1940 to investigate ship sabotage by communist groups in the Dutch ports following the German invasion and occupation of Holland. Geissler returned to RSHA IV A2 in July 1940, and before the end of the month, he was given a new posting as Gestapo representative in Bucharest (Romania), advising their state security department on the Comintern (Communist International) espionage abilities (*Berater des rümanischen Staatssicherheitsdeinstes Siguranta in Kominternfragen in Bukarest*). When this appointment came to an end in April 1941, Geissler was posted in a similar position to Greece (*in Athen als Berater des griechischen Polizeichefs abermals in kommunistischen Fragen*) and only returned to RSHA Berlin in January 1942, but not to RSHA IV A2—Kopkow had been promoted to Department Chief.[22]

3

Departmental Chief, RSHA IV A2, Berlin

RSHA IV A2 could not effectively operate without a departmental chief in the absence of Geissler and his deputy Giering: Geissler was out of the picture and abroad and Giering was sick. As a result of personnel discussions with RSHA IV Chief Müller about Giering's future availability for work due to his prolonged ill-health absences, necessity therefore brought about the appointment of SS-*Hauptsturmführer Kriminalkommissar* Horst Kopkow as Department Chief, RSHA IV A2, sometime in July 1940. At the time of his promotion, Kopkow was twenty-nine years old, the youngest in the organisation. According to a RSHA organisation plan of 1 February 1940, setting out departmental responsibilities, RSHA IV A2 combatted sabotage, counter-sabotage measures, and investigated fraudulent documents (*Sabotagebekämpfung, Sabotageabwehr, Fälschungswesen*).[1]

Between 1940 and 1941, under Kopkow's direction, RSHA IV A2 investigated numerous cases of ship sabotage. The historian E. H. Cookridge reported between '1937 and the outbreak of war [September 1939] nine hundred German ships were destroyed or damaged in German or foreign ports and at sea, despite strict security measures and special guards provided by the Gestapo and the SS'.[2] This number of incidents concerning merchant ships is unsustainable for any merchant navy. The Gestapo may well have reduced the threat from communism on the land in Germany, but abroad was a different matter. The German merchant fleet faced considerable threats from communist sabotage measures in Holland in May 1940 (the reason Geissler went to investigate) and in Sweden, such that, in July 1941, Kopkow visited Sweden. With his junior colleague, Erich Mittmann, he travelled to Stockholm and stayed a week, consulting with the Swedish authorities about the sabotage organisation of the well-known communist saboteur, Ernst Wollweber. The agreement reached between Kopkow and the Swedish authorities did reduce the acts of sabotage but not completely.[3]

In a new RSHA organisation plan of 1 March 1941, Kopkow for the first time is listed as Department Chief of RSHA IV A2, and a new responsibility was added to his departmental portfolio: Gestapo provision of industrial security measures (*Politischenpolizeilichen Abwehrbeauftragter*). In the past, these measures had been the responsibility of the military intelligence service, the Abwehr. The Gestapo had become involved due to large numbers of foreign labourers from the western-occupied territories (e.g. Belgium, France, and Holland) now contracted by many German factories to replace German workers drafted into the military. RSHA IV A2 issued guidelines for vetting these new foreign workers and sabotage protection measures against factory production. The individuals in charge of protection measures, the *Abwehrbeauftragter*, were appointed by the Abwehr and agreed by the Gestapo. RSHA IV A2 involvement in these procedures lasted until June 1944, when RSHA absorbed the Abwehr and handed this work over to RSHA IV A3, who were then wholly responsible for industrial security.[4]

Kopkow had his last period of military service between 9 August and 8 December 1941, when he turned out for training with the anti-aircraft defences surrounding Berlin. This allowed Kopkow to attend to his office duties, especially since the war with Russia began on 22 June 1941. In the early months of 1941, during the official preparatory stages for Operation Barbarossa (the attack on the Soviet Union), RSHA IV A2, in common with other RSHA departments, began compiling lists of persons who should be arrested. This included Soviet apparatchiks of the State, Communist Party, and local authorities; it also included numerous German communists then living in various regions of the Soviet Union. Each name listed included the interested Gestapo section. These listings, a 'black book' (though it had a red cover), were provided to all the SS security police units (SS-*Einsatzgruppen*), who combed the rear areas behind the advancing military lines during the invasion.[5] Existing records do not show whether any of those listed in this 'black book' were ever arrested. These SS-*Einsatzgruppen* (four units were deployed) were each divided into four or five sub-units (known as Einsatzkommandos and Sonderkommandos), which carried out liberation and pacification measures along the German Army's lines of communication, the vast Ukrainian prairie hinterlands (the Steppe), and Byelorussian forests. Pacification at the beginning meant shooting resisting populations, male Jews of draft age and Soviet apparatchiks. In the first six months of the campaign, the SS-*Einsatzgruppen* sent radio reports back to Berlin on a daily basis; RSHA IV A1 then compiled a daily situation report summarising the events taking place, where the *Kommandos* had been, and where they were headed. Within a short time, the reports included figures from executions. In August 1941, when the Final Solution of the Jewish Question was implemented across German-occupied territories of the Soviet Union, the execution figures of the four SS-*Einsatzgruppen* increased—half a million Jews had died by SS firing squads before the end of 1941. The distribution lists for these daily situation reports issued by RSHA IV A1 also increased. RSHA IV A2 under Kopkow began receiving a personal copy on 17 July 1941, copy 25 of 34.[6] Through these situation reports, RSHA officers such as Kopkow were fully informed about what was taking place behind the front lines—industrial and callous slaughter of Jews for no reason other than being Jewish. Kopkow could count himself lucky as many of his colleagues who trained with him at the *Kriminalkommissar* course back in 1937–1938 were not only serving in the SS-*Einsatzgruppen* and their *Kommandos*, but actively participating in the firing squads. Kopkow did not mention any of this in his post-war interrogations, however, he had no problems describing his fellow RSHA IV B4 department chief, Adolf Eichmann, as responsible for Jewish affairs and who reported directly to Himmler about these matters.

November 1941 was a month of changes. On 1 November 1941, Kopkow's civil service standard promotion to *Kriminalrat* came through. Three years' unblemished service as *Kriminalkommissar* usually meant a step up the promotion ladder. Due to Himmler's plans to assimilate civil service rankings with those in the SS, Kopkow had now reached the equivalent threshold of SS-*Hauptsturmführer* and *Kriminalrat*. Although Kopkow had attained the rank of SS-*Hauptsturmführer* four years previously, on 20 April 1937, it would be several more years before his next set of promotions and in-line with other ambitious Gestapo officers. A further change of direction for Kopkow and RSHA IV A2 happened on 25 November 1941, when an Abwehr report for the period 11 June to 1 November 1941 made uneasy reading:

> Russian agents equipped with W/T [wireless transmitters] were dropped in groups by parachute over Finland, the former Baltic States, over Poland, Slovakia, Hungary, Rumania and Bulgaria. The agents were nationals of the country concerned, and were given short courses of training. Their mission was both espionage and sabotage, e.g. in Slovakia they were to carry out sabotage against the munitions works at Dubniza and Povanska-Bystrica, in Rumania in the oil districts and the ports. Abwehr arrested about 40 agents and 10 W/T sets.[7]

This same report mentions one agent still transmitting from Warsaw, and three W/T sets captured by the Abwehr when they 'crushed a sub-network of Anglo-Polish' intelligence service, arresting fifty people. A former Polish Army captain acting as a courier between Warsaw and Budapest, when arrested in Kraków, was found to possess $5,000. Another former Polish Army captain, Kuncewicz, was also arrested. Unfortunately for Kuncewicz, RSHA IV A2 wanted him in Berlin for interrogation; he would later be shot at Sachsenhausen camp without trial.[8]

More uneasy reading occurred before the official Abwehr report of 8 July 1942. This report confirmed that between October 1941 and May 1942, the British intelligence service (in this case, SOE Czech Section) had dropped seven groups of parachute agents of Czech nationality into the Czech Protectorate that consisted of Bohemia and Moravia.[9] The Abwehr reports were based 'on statements made by arrested parachute agents in the hands of Stapo Prague' in this period, and these had been circulated to RSHA Berlin. Such important documents would have come via Heydrich to RSHA IV Chief Müller, then to

RSHA IV A2 and Kopkow. These early Gestapo reports from Prague in October 1941 could not have come at a worse time for Heydrich. On 27 September 1941, Hitler appointed Reinhard Heydrich as Acting Reichsprotector of Bohemia and Moravia, the very region where British-trained Czech parachute agents had been dropped. His political actions in Bohemia and Moravia, from his headquarters in Prague, would turn fatal within months.

Before the 1939 German occupation of Czechoslovakia, Prague had been a hotbed of espionage activity and the first stop for German communists seeking refuge from Nazi persecution before heading east to the Soviet Union or west to France and Great Britain. After the German occupation, the newly established Gestapo offices began their work of political and racial persecution. Many Czechs fled to Great Britain, communists and non-communists alike, and a government in exile had been set up in 1940 in London; similar governments in exile in London were established by Poland, France, Belgium, Holland, Denmark, and Norway. Each of them established its own intelligence service and each began liaising with British intelligence agencies.

Following the fall of Western Europe to German occupation in summer 1940, the entire coastal seaboard from the Arctic circle south to Biarritz-Hendaye on the Franco-Spanish border was in German hands, leaving Britain alone to carry the fight back to Nazi imperialism. British Royal Navy warships began a naval blockade of this entire seaboard, stopping merchant shipping headed for German-controlled ports. Prime Minister Winston Churchill wished to carry the fight to the Nazi enemy on the ground, to 'set Europe ablaze' in his words, and, in 1940, he ordered a new organisation be established from Britain's existing intelligence agencies and armed forces, which became Special Operations Executive (SOE).[10] SOE was divided into country sections that determined targets and infiltration and exfiltration of trained agents. The largest was SOE French Section, by virtue of its large population. All the country sections shared training methods and training schools. The arduous training involved tramping across Scottish Highlands and parachute jumps usually from a tethered barrage balloon several hundred feet in the air. Agents would be employed as instructors to train others once deployed in enemy territory, and they were themselves first trained in weapons likely to be supplied by Britain or captured from enemy forces. Saboteurs were trained in various explosives, homemade and industrial, and how and where to place them for maximum effect (e.g. locomotives needed to be blown up in such a manner that whatever waggons or carriages they were pulling came off the tracks causing damage to the track bed). This type of damage to equipment and tracks caused long delays. The agents most in danger of capture were W/T operators, radio operators, who transmitted coded messages in Morse code back to base.[11] Once the Germans realised agents in occupied Europe were on the ground and transmitting illegally, German police units were made available with mobile direction finding vehicles. By triangulation, two vehicles could pinpoint an area or a building where transmissions came from.

Before deployment, radio operators were advised to limit their transmissions from a particular location and change transmission frequencies regularly—in theory, a practical solution to avoid capture, but, in practice, widely abused, and capture became inevitable.

It was against this background that SOE Czech Section trained and equipped two Czech Army NCOs in Britain to assassinate SS-*Obergruppenführer* Reinhard Heydrich, Acting Reichsprotector of Bohemia and Moravia. The Czech government in exile received regular reports of Heydrich's carrot-and-stick approach to the Czech civilian population. The Gestapo carried out waves of persecution to crush resistance, they organised ghettoisation and deportation of Czech Jews and rewarded workers for increasing armaments production at Škoda and other factories. A mission known as Operation Anthropoid was created to assassinate Heydrich. Its two-man team, Josef Gabčík and Jan Kubiš, were dropped by parachute at Nehvizdy, north of Prague, during the night of 28–29 December 1941. Their RAF aircraft had also dropped two other agent groups during the same night, Operations Silver 'A' and Silver 'B', at other locations in the Protectorate *en route*.[12] The three separate groups all converged on Prague, where the men from Anthropoid and Silver 'A' missions began planning the assassination of Heydrich. After keeping Heydrich under surveillance for months, a plan was devised to attack his personal Mercedes staff car, driven only by a SS chauffeur bodyguard, Josef Klein. With no other escort, Heydrich obviously felt himself safe. The assault took place on 27 May 1942 as Heydrich's staff car slowed for a tight bend in the road in northern Prague. Kubiš threw a bomb that exploded by the vehicle's rear wheel, throwing shrapnel everywhere, back at Kubiš himself, but more fatally into Heydrich. Gabčík's machine gun jammed and was useless. The two assassins fled, chased by Heydrich and his driver until Heydrich faltered. However, the damage had been done, Heydrich was taken to Bulkova Clinic, Prague, and treated for several days by Czech and German doctors.

Within minutes of the attack on Heydrich, the Czech police informed Gestapo Prague. When Gestapo *Kommissar* Heinz Pannwitz found Heydrich being treated by Czech medical staff, he immediately requested the clinic be surrounded by SS troops. Senior German security police officers arrived, including HSSPF Protectorate SS-*Obergruppenführer* Karl Hermann Frank. After establishing what had happened, Frank telephoned Himmler in Berlin.[13] After their discussion, Himmler advised Frank to inform the Führer while he took the necessary measures in Berlin. Himmler briefed RSHA IV Chief Heinrich Müller and RSHA V Chief Artur Nebe on what had happened in Prague and they decided to establish a Special Commission to immediately fly to Prague that afternoon and begin investigating the assassination attempt. Müller and Nebe sent Kopkow and KK Dr Bernd Wehner, a Kripo expert. Kopkow outranked Wehner, so he must have been in charge of this Special Commission.

The Gestapo officials in Prague, including Heinz Pannwitz—who became a friend of Kopkow and later worked under his direction in Paris—set about their work of mass arrests and reprisals. Kopkow and Wehner began investigating the actual assassination attempt and methods employed among the 'chaos of catastrophic proportion' around them. Kopkow at least did not stay long in Prague, the scene of the attack on Heydrich and the bomb fragments, plus the jammed machine gun, were easily understood. Having arrived in Prague in the afternoon of the attack (27 May), Kopkow was back in Berlin by 31 May, for he gave a lecture in Berlin on the following morning of 1 June 1942 in the conference room of the RSHA building on Prinz Albrechtstrasse. The was the first day of a two-day meeting of regional Gestapo officials under the chairmanship of RSHA IV Chief Müller; these Gestapo officials discussed the latest measures for their protection of senior figures of the SS and Nazi Party. Kopkow's topic, entitled 'Looking at the teaching aid collection', may well have included the problems caused by senior officials ignoring a security escort and the successful attack on Heydrich.[14] Back in Prague under Pannwitz, the hunt for the two assassins became increasingly frantic. Himmler spent the afternoon of 31 May in Prague visiting Heydrich and later with Heydrich's wife, before a meeting with his SS Generals in charge and an update on what was happening. A lack of suitable antibiotics allowed Heydrich's wounds to become infected, and on 4 June 1942, at 4.30 a.m., he died. Himmler flew back to Prague that afternoon before flying off to Hitler's headquarters in East Prussia to report on events. Heydrich's body was taken back to Berlin on 7 June for a state funeral.

The Special Commission of Kopkow and Wehner had quickly reported on the scene of the attack and weapons used. Through informants, Gestapo Prague eventually identified the two men involved, Josef Gabčík and Jan Kubiš, as well as who was helping them. The network of SOE Czech Section agents in Prague began to be hunted down. Hitler insisted on reprisal measures. The easiest reprisal to organise was the deportation of Czech Jews, and the first train carrying 1,000 Jews from Prague to death camps in Poland left on 9 June 1942; two more trains with another 2,000 Czech Jews soon followed. A false lead led to a search of Lidice, a village just north west of Prague. Hitler was kept informed of the progress of the Gestapo investigation and once Lidice was identified, he gave his orders. All men of the village would be shot (199), and all the women sent to concentration camps (195), children who were suitable for Germanisation would be handed over to SS families to bring up (8), those unsuitable disappeared into concentration camps. Hitler also ordered the entire village be razed to the ground. The action was carried out between 9 and 10 June 1942. It was over a week later when Gestapo Prague had the final piece of information in their hunt for the assassins. In the early morning of 18 June 1942, truckloads of *Waffen*-SS troopers converged on Karl Boromejsky Church near central Prague. They stormed the church, but fell back when met with gunfire. Gunfire, explosives, and water cannon, followed by another storming, finally overcame any resistance. Four dead men, identified as SOE Czech Section agents, including Gabčík and Kubiš, were pulled from the rubble. More agents of SOE agents were soon arrested or killed while resisting arrest. The final total of civilians killed ran into thousands, as did those arrested and incarcerated.[15]

Horst Kopkow could claim these killings and arrests were not his responsibility, but that would not be wholly true. In the Czech Protectorate, Heydrich learned of problems due to the infiltration of foreign intelligence agents and spies, Russian and British, with the job of creating a resistance movement, sabotage, and espionage. In his position as Chief of RSHA, Heydrich ordered counter measures. On 15 May 1942, twelve days before the assassination attempt, Heydrich issued orders on the letterhead of Kopkow's department RSHA IV A2; these orders determined that this department was now responsible for counter-measures against 'Parachute Agents, Terrorists and Saboteurs' not only in the Protectorate, but in adjoining Slovakia, administered by a puppet-government under German control.[16] Within only twelve days of these new responsibilities, Kopkow could rightly claim the killings and arrests regarding parachute agents and terrorists were not his decision when so many senior SS and police commanders in Prague were happy to show their resolve to their superiors.

What can rightly be said of Kopkow is that the assassination of Reinhard Heydrich made his future career in the Gestapo and post-war career with Britain's Secret Intelligence Service. Just two days after Heydrich's death, another order was issued on RSHA IV A2 letterhead, this time signed by RSHA IV Chief Müller. From 6 June 1942, RSHA IV A2 had its remit increased, and it now became responsible for 'Parachute Agents, Terrorists and Saboteurs [whether] English, Soviet Russian or any other agency'.[17] Across Germany and the entire length of Nazi-occupied Europe, Kopkow and RSHA IV A2 were in charge of anything to do with foreign intelligence agents found operating wherever the Gestapo had locations. This is not to say that this area of counter espionage and counter-intelligence was unique to the Gestapo, because it was not. German Army military intelligence, the Abwehr, already operated in these functions across German-occupied territories in the east and the west. One geographical area they could not operate within was Greater Germany itself—this was the province of the Gestapo. With the military occupation of the west, the SS security police followed. Himmler reached agreement with the Army High Command for the establishment of senior SS and police commanders, the HSSPF, in the western-occupied territories (France, Holland, Denmark, and Norway). Under each HSSPF was a Regional Commander of the Security Police and Security Service (BdS—*Befehlshaber der Sicherheitspolizei und des SD*), who organised and co-ordinated the work of pacification and liberation with a network of District Commanders of the Security Police and Security Service (KdS—*Kommandeur der Sicherheitspolizei und des SD*). The KdS established their own sub-offices (*Aussenstelle*) based in towns and villages.

Organisationally, the BdS office followed the departmental structure of RSHA and the KdS offices did the same. This made it much simpler when corresponding with RSHA Berlin or back to the field office, ensuring paperwork was directed to the correct department and did not go astray.

Until 6 June 1942, when the responsibilities of RSHA IV A2 increased to include all enemy parachute agents, later Gestapo activities in France can be seen to have taken a new impetus from this time. The Abwehr in France had been a strong opponent of SOE French Section and 'escape and evasion' lines through France from 1940 for shot-down aircrew trying to escape through France into Spain. Whereas the military regulations governing Abwehr operations demanded captured intelligence agents be brought before military courts, the Gestapo felt no such scruples. In Berlin, RSHA IV A2 began receiving reports from all over the occupied territories about parachute agents being dropped, some being captured and interrogated. In Britain, from various SOE country sections, agents were infiltrated in ever greater numbers from 1942, and although Kopkow's orders specially mentioned 'parachute agents' (*Fallschirmagenten*), Gestapo offices and RSHA IV A2 did not differentiate between those arriving by sea or landed by aircraft.

Kopkow welcomed the extension of his departmental powers to fight foreign intelligence agents as a relief from the caseload of sabotage. The main problem with sabotage actions was identifying and arresting the perpetrators. Modern views of Gestapo men being everywhere and their widespread surveillance are completely false. Many sabotage actions in 1942 were never resolved. In Prague, earlier in January 1942, RSHA IV A2 were concerned in the contamination of woollen stocks with poison, who stole official rubber stamps from the German Consulate in Burgas (Bulgaria), and sabotage on the German railways became a persistent problem. Between April and May 1942, regular correspondence with RSHA IV A2 from BdS Krakau and its KdS offices in Warsaw and Radom concerned Polish resistance organisations and sabotage operations.[18] All these activities were the cause of much correspondence with RSHA IV A2 in 1942, but its Sabotage Section soon took on a minor role as the problem of parachute agents and Russian espionage almost overwhelmed the department in July 1942. Although open to offer advice to officers and offices outside RSHA, Kopkow regarded the other RSHA IV department with a kind of aloofness. According to SS-*Sturmbannführer* Harro Thomsen of the Polish desk, RSHA IV B2, Kopkow kept information about sabotage and *Funkspiel* operations 'almost entirely to himself; they included a great proportion of resistance movement activities and were of great interest to Gruppe (Group) B'.[19] Kopkow appears more than prepared to share his knowledge with senior officers, but not with his contemporaries just down the corridor.

After the invasion and occupation of Holland, Belgium, and France in summer 1940 by the German Army, the Abwehr set up its offices to counter any resistance. During 1941, it came to their notice that three illegal radio transmitters were located somewhere in Brussels. The transmissions were beamed towards Moscow. A radio direction finding unit was brought from Berlin and a transmitter location identified in the Etterbeek suburbs of Brussels. Around 2 a.m. on 13 December 1941, Abwehr officers accompanied by German policemen stormed into the house at 101 Rue des Atrébates and caught a radio operator, Anton Danilov, still transmitting. Two women in the house, Rita Arnould and Sofia Posnanska, were also arrested. The following day, Mikhail Makarov arrived at the house and he too was arrested.[20] Makarov, using the alias Carlos Alamo, had a Uruguayan passport and also acted as a radio operator, transmitting from Ostend. By standard methods of detecting illegal radio transmissions, Abwehr Brussels began unravelling a vast Soviet espionage ring with connections into Holland and France. The next identification and location of illegal transmissions happened on 30 July 1942, when the Soviet-trained German communist Johann Wenzel was caught transmitting by the Abwehr at his Brussels home, 12 Rue de Namur.[21] Investigations into this Soviet espionage ring now codenamed 'Rote Kapelle' (Red Orchestra) by Abwehr Brussels were soon shared with the Gestapo following instruction from Abwehr headquarters in Berlin to allow RSHA IV A2 access to Wenzel, who was then transferred to the RSHA prison in the cellars of the Prinz Albrechtstrasse. Timing was of the essence, so Wenzel was subjected to a brutal interrogation from the beginning. It takes a brave man to withstand torture and physical abuse, and unfortunately for Soviet Intelligence, having been beaten into submission, Wenzel gave Gestapo interrogators all the information they needed to identify their entire underground Soviet espionage organisation across German-occupied Europe. Coding materials for encrypting his radio messages to Moscow, discovered at his Brussels home after his arrest, were soon being used to decrypt the messages he had already sent. The content of these radio messages was astonishing and gave the Soviets top secret German military information that could help them to defeat German armies marching through Russia. The piece of information that caught RSHA Berlin by surprise was the radio message from Moscow, which included three Berlin addresses of Soviet agents working in the capital of the Reich. The conditions had been created for Horst Kopkow to step into the limelight and unravel Rote Kapelle operating in Germany and Western Europe, which was done with surprising speed.

4

RSHA IV A2: Superiors, Office Staff, Peers

When Horst Kopkow took control of RSHA IV A2 in the summer of 1940, his staff numbers were quite small—as far as can be established, less than twenty men and women. During the heydays of the mid-1930s under Geissler, staff numbers were about thirty. Once Heydrich and Werner Best reorganised Gestapa Berlin into RSHA, which began operating in September 1939, a reassignment of officials took place. Heydrich was keen to bring in younger officers from the increasing series of *Kriminalkommissar* training courses. These courses were dominated by men in their twenties and thirties. Geissler's men from the Communism Section were older, many born in the last century, and had been policemen for twenty to thirty years before a posting into the earlier Political Police departments of the criminal police. Before Kopkow took over, at least twelve of the older officials had been sent to other departments; even Geissler's bosses (Reinhold Heller and Paul Opitz) were moved on. The new RSHA organisation of September 1939, especially the new national Gestapo as RSHA IV under Heinrich Müller, wanted a rejuvenated staff with a backbone of not-so-old Gestapo experts and RSHA IV A2 was such an example.

Horst Kopkow was appointed department chief of RSHA IV A2 in 1940 almost by default, but tinged with ambition, it might be expected that the old hands of the department would have been embittered in being passed over. Karl Giering, who had been Geissler's deputy for several years, probably realised his ill health would be the death of him. Despite throat cancer and increasing vocal hoarseness, he survived until November 1945; recognising his abilities, Giering was posted to BdS France, where, in 1942, he began dismantling the Rote Kapelle espionage ring in France and Belgium. Two other Gestapo experts who had worked for Geissler were also retained: Wilhelm Berg and Walter Habecker (born 1891 and 1893 respectively).

Berg was another East Prussian like Kopkow and they both spoke with similar accents. Kopkow trusted him with a detached service posting to BdS Paris in August 1942 to help Giering in tracking down Rote Kapelle agents in France: 'It was rumoured that he used to supply his superiors in Berlin with looted French property'. Once the *Funkspiel* radio games with Moscow began, using Rote Kapelle captured radio sets and ciphers, Berg regularly liaised with Kopkow about the content of the false messages transmitted from France. Berg remained in Paris until August 1944, when the final evacuation of German forces from the city took place. After crossing the Franco-German border, Berg's vehicle came under Allied aircraft attack near Saarbrücken and he suffered a severe shoulder injury. During his post-war denazification trial in the British Zone, Berg reported that his shoulder injury kept him from reporting back for duty until the German surrender in May 1945. This was not the case, however; Kopkow mentioned that in March 1945, Berg had already returned to duty and was deputy of the section leader responsible for anti-sabotage measures whose staff and documentation had been evacuated from Berlin to Hof in northern Bavaria. In March–April 1945, Berg appeared at the nearby Gestapo office in Halle, where he took on the role of case officer for a captured Russian agent, a German officer, Captain Krämer, captured by the Russians and trained by them as an agent. Krämer had been caught following his parachute drop, and although Berg interrogated him, nothing much else happened. With the Allied armies advancing into central Germany and no one stopping them, military defeat was imminent and even Gestapo men realised it was time to disappear. Krämer was captured by the American Army at Erfurt on 12 April 1945 after Berg had released him. Berg himself was later captured by the British Army and interned as an 'automatic arrest' Gestapo man.[1]

Walter Habecker's career had followed the old German criminal police rules on advancement through the ranks. Unlike Kopkow, who went on a *Kriminalkommissar* course, Habecker advanced from *Kriminalsekretär* (October 1934) to *Kriminalobersekretär* (February 1936), then the dead-end career path to *Kriminalinspektor* (April 1941). For men who came up through the ranks of the Weimar Republic police service, this was their career path. The police recruited under the Nazi regime followed a much more training-based advancement scheme, like Kopkow. In April 1944, the Nazi police service recognised that long-serving *Kriminalinspektors*, like Habecker, were being forgotten and unrewarded, so the post of *Kriminalinspektor* was abolished and those in that position were automatically promoted to *Kriminalkommissar*. When asked after the war why this was, he replied 'he lacked education and training'. Walter Habecker was cut from a different cloth than most; as an interrogator, he saw getting information from another person as quickly as possible and by whatever means was a necessary requirement of the job, and he acquired a reputation as someone who freely used his fists and boots to get results. In January 1945, he was sent to Mauthausen concentration camp in Austria; this was where eighteen members of a British and American military mission that were captured in Slovakia before Christmas 1944 were brought. Habecker tortured several of the mission members to obtain information before they were executed.[2]

Neither Berg nor Habecker, nor any of the lower ranked long-serving Gestapo men, raised objections to a junior officer like Kopkow appointed as their department chief in 1940. All the men accepted him and worked diligently for the department—a slightly different meaning than worked diligently for Kopkow. Any initial reservations were swept away as the department's standing within RSHA IV increased, and so did their individual responsibilities. At the end of the war, one or two lesser Gestapo men jealously opined that Kopkow had advanced further than most of his contemporaries and must, therefore, be really favoured. Although these Gestapo men disliked Kopkow, the British believed 'they all considered him a good and efficient superior. On the whole he seems to have bothered more about his staff than other members of the *Führungsstabe* (the Sipo leadership) who only thought of themselves'.[3] In fact, Kopkow's promotions in the SS and the police after 1939 were much in keeping with his contemporaries. In the SS, his promotion to SS-*Hauptsturmführer* occurred on 20 April 1937; his next and final promotion, to SS-*Sturmbannführer*, was six years later, on 9 November 1943. With the police rankings, following civil service guidelines for the police services, Kopkow was appointed *Kriminalkommissar* on 1 February 1939; *Kriminalrat* on 1 November 1941; and *Kriminaldirektor* on 1 November 1944. Kopkow was a reliable department chief who performed extraordinarily well and encouraged excellent teamwork when his department was faced with interrogating individuals after mass arrests: firstly in 1942, with the tracing of Rote Kapelle agents across Germany, and again in 1944, after the 20 July bomb plot against Hitler. In both these cases, several hundred men and women were arrested and interrogated, many until almost the end of the war. At times when the work overwhelmed them, Kopkow called upon other RSHA IV departments to help with interrogations. In 1943, Müller's gave his personnel appraisal of Kopkow, who he regarded as one of his most successful officers:

> Fresh, politically awakened, exemplary diligent and persevering, ready to use at any time experts from outside his department, has excellent writing and presentation skills, lively and energetic. Characterized by his political and ideological reliability. Absolutely reliable in every way, exemplary both as superior and comrade.

In August 1944, RSHA Chief SS-*Obergruppenführer* Dr Ernst Kaltenbrunner approved the citation for the award of German Cross in Silver (*Deutsches Kreuz in Silber*) to Kopkow; approval came from Himmler and the award ceremony took place on 24 November 1944. The citation reads:

> The successful control of the parachute agents, the recording of the radio games and their extraordinarily skilful continuation is due to his quite extraordinary achievements and is to be thanked foremost for his exemplary consistent activities.[4]

What makes the wording of the citation even more revealing is the similar wording of the November 1944 citations for the award of German Cross in Silver to SS-*Oberführer* Friedrich Panzinger, the Group Leader of the six RSHA IV A departments, and deputy of RSHA IV Chief Heinrich Müller.

Panzinger's citation read:

> His merit as Group Leader (Fight against opponents in the Reich), who directed 6 departments which included 18 Desk Officers (*Referenten*) is in itself sufficient justification for an application for the award of the German Cross in Silver (e.g. see the application for this award of his Chief of Department IV A2 [Kopkow]).[5]

The citation for Müller also stresses the award to Kopkow and the reasons for this were included:

> Müller has prevented serious Sabotage and Espionage successes of the enemies of the Reich through lightning-fast action in numerous cases. He has especially distinguished himself by skilful changes of tactics and methods in combating opponents. He has achieved significant successes in the observation of enemy reconnaissance activities. With the *Funkspiel* operation against the enemy, he created better intelligence and material results in largely misleading our opponents. Severe cases of sabotage to the detriment of the Reich have been avoided or prevented through timely arrests of communist groups in the armaments industry and other military-economic centres.[6]

From these three citations for the same medal, it can be surmised that Kopkow's department had taken these measures against sabotage, counter-espionage, and *Funkspiel* radio games, which had played such an extremely important part in their success. The three men could rightly claim they had performed successfully against the enemy and were therefore rewarded in recognition of their achievements. Himmler countersigned each request of RSHA Chief Dr Kaltenbrunner for the awards. What is perhaps even more revealing is how Kopkow managed throughout the war years to maintain a professional relationship with both men. Müller and Panzinger were both Bavarians who had come to Berlin in 1934 with a distinct suspicion of north Germans and especially Berliners in the Gestapo. When Kopkow joined Gestapa Berlin, then RSHA, by the nature of the organisation, he would have had regular contact with Müller, who preferred to be kept informed. Müller was a workaholic who started early and remained late, demanding his department chiefs respond in a speedy manner to problems and requests. As a result, many also started early and stayed late. Kopkow was quickly identified by Müller as particularly efficient and proved his abilities in 1942 when rolling up the Berlin end of the Rote Kapelle espionage ring. The first arrest was made by

Kopkow and Panzinger on 30 August 1942, when they arrived at Göring's Air Ministry building, just across the road from Gestapo headquarters on Prinz Albrechtstrasse, and took into custody Luftwaffe *Oberleutnant* Harro Schulze-Boysen. The majority of Schulze-Boysen's network of agents was soon arrested and filled the prison cells of the Prinz Albrechtstrasse. Gestapo interrogators got to work and soon more arrived—over sixty arrests were made in Berlin alone. A judicial case against Schulze-Boysen and twelve others was prepared by RSHA IV A2 and presented to Prosecutor Roeder of the *Volksgerichtshof*—the People's Court—in Berlin. The trial took place between 14 and 19 December 1942. All were convicted, with nine death sentences, three prison terms, and one sentence that awaited medical reports. Roeder appealed against the prison sentences, but this did not stop the death sentences being carried out. Three days later, on 22 December 1942, Schulze-Boysen and the others given death sentences were executed at Plötzensee Prison, Berlin.[7] The trial and executions were a postscript to Kopkow's final report on his investigations into Rote Kapelle; it was dated 20 November 1942.[8]

Although Panzinger acted as Deputy RSHA Chief IV under Müller, he did have two prolonged breaks from Berlin. Between August 1940 and September 1941, Panzinger was Police Liaison Officer to the Bulgarian Government and stationed in Sofia. His appointment as BdS in Riga followed in September 1943, and he remained until May 1944.[9] During these two breaks, Kopkow became ever closer in personal contact with Müller, showing determination and perseverance in doing his job against opponents of the Nazi regime.

How did Kopkow's contemporaries, his fellow RSHA IV departmental chiefs and other senior Gestapo and SD officers, see him? In June 1944, SS-*Stubaf* Dr Georg Kiessel came to RSHA Berlin from a posting in Serbia. RSHA Chief Dr Kaltenbrunner assigned him to looking at the offices of RSHA IV A departments, and Kiessel spent most of his time in RSHA IV A2 with Kopkow, looking through their files. He described Kopkow:

> [He is] a good character, is convinced Nazi and SS-man, in a reliable sense. Very sharp insight especially against all deviations in the Party and its organizations. Believes strongly in Hitler and is a great critic of Himmler. Strong opponent of Bolshevism, and a strong anglophile.[10]

Many years after the war, in the 1980s, BBC television produced a *Timewatch* programme about SOE in France. They interviewed several former SS officers who had met Kopkow during the war. Former SS-*Sturmbannführer* Josef Schreieder had worked in Gestapo Holland with the *Funkspiel* back to England, using SOE Dutch Section radio ciphers. When asked his opinion of Kopkow, Schreieder said:

> He was a young, good-looking man, very conceited, with polished manners and great charm, with whom I was very cautious because I felt that

> under the veneer there was concealed a great capability for meanness. He was tall, well-groomed and lean and blond—a typical SS-officer. He was obviously very clever and very self-confident....[11]

A more junior SS-*Untersturmführer*, Dr Josef Götz of BdS Paris—who worked on *Funkspiel* using SOE French Section radio ciphers back to England—had met Kopkow in Paris in 1944. He described Kopkow: 'Selfish. He was a man of the Party. He certainly was [an] equally very intelligent man, who was interested in the way of functioning such a thing [the *Funkspiel*]. I think he lived for these things'.[12] Kopkow certainly was a proverbial late-developer, finding a natural ability as a counter-intelligence officer of the Gestapo. He had acquired the polished veneer as both Schreieder and Dr Götz described, but both found something lacking. In 1944, when the most optimistic SS officer would have second thoughts of the abilities of the German Army to fight on two fronts, squeezed by the Soviet and Anglo-American armies, still Kopkow believed in Hitler.

Robert Marshall worked with the BBC *Timewatch* programme, and on 30 June 1983, he interviewed Kopkow at his home in Gelsenkirchen. Even then, Kopkow had a remarkable memory for details of almost forty years previously. At one point in the interview, Kopkow remarked 'I love treason. I hate traitors', to which Marshall noted: 'In a certain sense that was Kopkow's leitmotif as a counter espionage expert'.[13] It certainly was Kopkow's leitmotif. Unlike professional counter-espionage and counter-intelligence officers of today, Kopkow employed his training as a criminal police officer to uncover enemy agents using the vast Gestapo name and subject registry files to help him. He certainly found his leitmotif in RSHA IV A2, and very few enemy intelligence agents escaped the net.

5

Soviet Intelligence Operations Against Germany

The death of Reinhard Heydrich on 4 June 1942 was the turning point in Kopkow's career. Until then, he had been in a RSHA backwater, dealing with sabotage and forgery of official identification documents. His department was hardly glamorous, but it had its peaks—he visited Sweden in 1941. The attack on the Soviet Union in June 1941 soon had Kopkow kept informed of anti-German sabotage acts reported by the SS-*Einsatzgruppen* in the rear areas behind the advancing front line, but these were informatory and involved few responses on his part. The first change in the direction for Kopkow's department came on 15 May 1942, when Heydrich signed an order on RSHA IV A2 letterhead extending the department's responsibilities to include 'parachute agents, terrorists and saboteurs' in the Czech Protectorate and Slovakia. Kopkow can hardly have begun taking on board these new measures when the attack on Heydrich took place in the Prague suburbs on 27 May 1942. He died from his wounds on 4 June 1942. Two days later, on 6 June 1942, RSHA IV Chief Müller issued new orders using RSHA IV A2 letterhead, extending its departmental responsibilities to include 'parachute agents, terrorists and saboteurs [whether] from England, the Soviet Union or another country'. Between Heydrich's fatal wounds and his death, *Reichsführer*-SS Heinrich Himmler paid several visits to Hitler at Führer Headquarters at Rastenburg and had telephone conversations with RSHA IV Chief Müller in Berlin to discuss reprisals and new orders.

By coincidence, on the day of the attempt on Heydrich's life (27 May 1942), Himmler was already at Führer Headquarters in Rastenburg, meeting with Hitler and discussing a long list of subjects. Dutch problems were first on the list and included the dropping of Allied parachute agents into Holland (from SOE Dutch Section). Last on the list was the assassination of Heydrich, and at the end of the discussions, Himmler left for Berlin and Prague.[1] Himmler returned to Rastenburg on 5 June 1942, the day after Heydrich's death. Hitler and Himmler had lunch together, and later that afternoon, Himmler returned to his own nearby headquarters at Friedrichsruh. At 7.45 p.m., Himmler telephoned RSHA IV Chief Müller and, with Heydrich's death much on his mind, ordered 'the most rigorous pursuit of all agents'.[2] That same evening, one of Himmler's staff informed him that a 'parachute agent had deserted'; this probably referred to a group of three Soviet-trained German communists who had been dropped by a Soviet aeroplane near Insterburg, East Prussia, during the night of 18–19 May 1942. Their parachutes were seen coming down and, once on the ground, a fire-fight took place with local policemen. One agent was shot dead and the two other agents surrendered. It did not take long for the local police and Gestapo office to realise who they had arrested and they quickly transferred them to RSHA Berlin for interrogation by Kopkow's men.[3] The man shot dead had been the radio operator, but, fortunately, his ciphers and radio set were captured and the two surviving agents participated in a *Funkspiel* with Moscow. After Himmler's telephone conversation with Müller, expressing the views of Hitler and himself, Müller conferred with Kopkow; the next day (6 June 1942), he issued the order increasing Kopkow's remit to include all parachute agents who now dropped into Germany and German-occupied territories. These orders took Kopkow from the backwaters of sabotage to the limelight of enemy parachute agents—and Kopkow made a great success of it.

The Abwehr during all this time continued to track down enemy agents in the occupied territories. Earlier in 1941, the German agency responsible for tracing illegal radio transmissions (the *Funkabwehr*) expressed surprise at the number of such transmissions that began that year and were directed at Moscow. The numbers had increased as a result of the German attack on the Soviet Union that began on 22 June 1941; wireless transmissions on behalf of the spy-rings in Berlin from the Russian Embassy ceased when the Embassy closed and staff were allowed to return to the Soviet Union—German diplomatic staff in Moscow travelled in the opposite direction. Using radio detection equipment, the *Funkabwehr* established that several groups now in German-occupied territory were transmitting coded messages. One traced to the Berlin area suddenly stopped. A radio transmitter, left behind with one of the Berlin spy rings, was damaged by the operator and therefore it could not be used and was not repaired until October 1941, with fatal consequences. Where one stopped, others increased their radio traffic, and three transmitters were traced to Belgium. Radio detection equipment transferred to Brussels found them operating from the city suburbs. One in particular regularly transmitted up to five hours a night, which made it easier to trace. Rather than track down each address and raid each at the same time, orders from Abwehr headquarters in Berlin to Abwehr Brussels requested an urgent raid on the most prolific. In the early hours of 12–13 December 1941, Abwehr officers, together with a party of German policemen, raided a house at 101 Rue des Atrébates, Brussels-Etterbeek.[4] Inside the house, they found two women and a man who had been transmitting when the raid happened; he attempted to flee the house but was quickly caught. All three were taken to nearby St Gilles military prison. On 13 December 1941, another man called at the house and was arrested when a search of his clothes revealed coded messages. He also was taken to St Gilles military prison. For the moment, all of them stayed silent.

The man who attempted flight from the house was the radio operator Anton Danilov, who had a number of aliases and is most likely believed to have been David Kamy. Despite intensive questioning, he said nothing. The second man who had called at the house the day after the raid identified himself as Carlos Alamo, and he held a Uruguayan passport. In fact, he was a Soviet national, born in Leningrad (1905) as Mikhail Makarov. He had arrived in Belgium from the Soviet Union via Sweden, Denmark, and France. Makarov originally established himself in Ostend and had a radio set that he used to transmit information to the Soviet Embassy in London. After the German occupation of Belgium, during which Ostend was bombed, he moved to Brussels from where he transmitted to Moscow, usually from the Rue des Atrébates address.

Of the two women arrested, one, with papers identifying her as Anna Verlinder, had attempted to shove coded messages into the fire when the raid started. These were rescued by a German policeman with his wits about him. The identity papers of Anna Verlinder were soon dispensed with when her real name of Sofia Posnanska came to light. Posnanska had been trained in Moscow as a coding expert and was brought to Brussels via Paris in 1940. Posnenska refused to divulge any information despite repeated torture sessions and she later committed suicide in St Gilles prison in September 1942. The other woman, the widow Rita Arnould, was completely different. Arnould was a German Jewish woman and communist who had fled from Düsseldorf long before the war. After the death of her husband in 1940, she took up with an old boyfriend, Isidor Springer, and through him, brought into the Soviet spy ring in Brussels. During the raid in the Rue des Atrébates, the Abwehr had not only arrested three people, finding documents, radio sets, and ciphers, they also discovered a secret room devoted to forgery of documents. They found a number of photographs with blank passports, official rubber stamps, and forms. Arnould identified two of the photographs as the 'Big Chief' (Leopold Trepper) and the 'Little Chief' (Victor Gurevich, alias Vincente Sierra, known as KENT). A Polish Jew trained in Moscow, Trepper organised the Russian espionage network based in Brussels and Paris using various aliases, primarily that of Jean Gilbert. Gurevich was a Soviet national, born Leningrad in 1911, and he carried a Uruguayan passport in the name of Vincente Sierra. He had served with the International Brigade in the Spanish Civil War as a Soviet intelligence officer; he began living in Brussels in 1939 and attended university there, studying commerce.

Gurevich undertook a number of missions on behalf of Moscow Centre and is reported to have first visited Berlin in April 1939. Moscow wanted a channel of information from Berlin to Brussels from whence military information would be transmitted in coded radio messages to Moscow. Couriers from Berlin brought secret German military information to Brussels where Gurevich began transmitting it to Moscow, along with the separate intelligence material brought by the 'Big Chief'. It is also suggested that in spring 1940, Gurevich delivered money to the Soviet spy network in Switzerland that was operated by Alexander Rado (the Rote Drei network). Quite how the money, and presumably a substantial amount, was delivered to Gurevich originally is not reported. At the request of Moscow, Gurevich went back to Berlin in October 1941 to resolve their transmitting problems; a coded radio message from Moscow gave him three Berlin street addresses and a coded phrase to identify himself. After the raid on the Rue des Atrébates house, Gurevich fled Brussels for Paris and was reassigned by the 'Big Chief'.[5]

In January 1942, Captain Harry Piepe of Abwehr Brussels reported to Abwehr headquarters in Berlin on what and who they had found in Brussels when uncovering this Soviet spy network. In Brussels, the Abwehr office had decided to dub the affair 'Rote Kapelle' based on its Soviet origins. After Captain Piepe's report in Berlin, it was decided to acquaint RSHA IV with their findings. The Abwehr may have wished to keep the Rote Kapelle investigation within their organisation, but their hands were tied. *Reichsführer*-SS Heinrich Himmler had been appointed Chief of the German Police within the Reich Ministry of the Interior on 17 June 1936. His deputy for the Gestapo and SD, Reinhard Heydrich, had delegated Werner Best to conduct negotiations with the Abwehr over lines of responsibility for increasingly important questions of counter-espionage and counter-intelligence. The negotiations produced 'ten commandments', which were issued on 21 December 1936 and entitled 'Principles governing co-operation between the Geheime Staatspolizei and the Abwehr offices of the Wehrmacht'.[6] Counter-espionage was regarded as the province of the Abwehr, and counter-intelligence that of the Gestapo. Accompanied by earthquakes and trumpets, Moses came down from Mount Sinai bringing stone tablets bearing the Ten Commandments, and their messages would last centuries; the ten commandments of the Abwehr-Gestapo agreement would be honoured more in the breach than in observance. Yet one thing was very clear at this time in 1936: any counter-espionage and counter-intelligence activities within the borders of Greater Germany would be the province of the Gestapo. Once the German military machine began waging a world war in 1939, the Gestapo extended their activities into German-occupied territories, with some early tentativeness in the west, but with relentless vigour in the east.

Due to the importance of the arrests in Brussels and the ramifications that could be plainly seen, the impact of Piepe's visit to Abwehr Berlin meant informing the Gestapo. Admiral Wilhelm Canaris, Chief of the Abwehr, possibly spoke with his opposite number at RSHA, Reinhard Heydrich. They had friendly familial relationships and went riding together in the Tiergarten. Heydrich brought RSHA IV Chief Müller into the meeting when the information was presented to them. They readily agreed that any sensitive German military information being transmitted to the Soviets needed to be urgently investigated. RSHA IV Chief Müller called in Kopkow, whose department, RSHA IV A2, was responsible for counter-sabotage among other things. In recognising the need for a proven investigator and interrogator, the very man had recently returned to duty after his most recent bout of ill-health. Kopkow charged SS-*Hauptsturmführer Kriminalkommissar* Karl Giering with conducting the Gestapo enquiries. According to Gilles Perrault, Giering had ALAMO (Makarov) transferred from his Brussels prison to Berlin, where he sang the 'The Internationale' during his interrogations as an act of defiance before his captors. When ALAMO mentioned he had served in the air force in Spain during the civil war, Giering thought of another way to get him to talk. Living with Giering at his Berlin home was his son, who had recently lost a leg serving as a Luftwaffe pilot. Although his son and Makarov were soon talking avidly about aircraft and their respective times in the air, it all came to naught in regard to Rote Kapelle. Despite every trick of an interrogator, ALAMO said nothing and, after two weeks, duly returned to his prison cell in Brussels. Both Kamy and ALAMO were transferred to the SS-Camp at Breendonk, a former medieval fortress between Brussels and Antwerp, where medieval torture continued but neither man gave anything to the German torturers. To cover Makarov's disappearance, Trepper informed Moscow that he had transferred him to Paris due to the Gestapo hunt for them. This announcement enabled the German use of Makarov's radio set for *Funkspiel Buche-Bob* with Moscow in November 1942 from Paris. In mid-July 1944, when the Germans were beginning to retreat from Paris, they discontinued this *Funkspiel*. Belgian police reports mention a trial of Makarov before the *Kriegsgerichtshof* (the army's military court) that resulted with a death sentence and execution in 1942 at Plötzensee prison in Berlin. Sophie Poznanska committed suicide in St Gilles prison, Brussels, on 29 September 1942. The radio operator David Kamy also appeared before a German military court in Belgium, where he was sentenced to death and executed at Breendock SS-camp on 30 April 1943. Rita Arnould, who told her interrogators the history of Brussels cell of the Soviet spy-ring, was also brought to Berlin and languished many months in Berlin-Moabit prison. In April 1943, she appeared before *Kriegsgerichtshof* Berlin and was sentenced to death and executed at Plötzensee prison on 20 August 1943.[7]

These three Soviet spies appeared before military courts and all were sentenced to death and executed without any publicity. The Abwehr used the judicial process for agents it captured. Due to the highest importance in Berlin for the Schulze-Boysen/Harnack to be tried before military courts, RSHA IV A2 completed its evidence and handed it over to Luftwaffe prosecutor Dr Manfred Roeder for military justice. Once the Gestapo became involved in tracking down Soviet spies across German-occupied territories in 1942, those caught next would not be afforded the luxury of a trial. The concentration camp would be the first and last step before execution without trial.

Heydrich's death and the flurry of RSHA orders extending the role of Kopkow and RSHA IV A2 meant an immediate transfer of men to Brussels. In mid-June 1942, Giering was posted to Brussels together with *Kriminalsekretär* Willi Berg and *Kriminaloberassistent* Richard Voss to work the Rote Kapelle investigation with Abwehr Brussels.[8] Three radio sets had been transmitting to Moscow from Brussels in 1941, and following the raid on the Rue des Atrébates and capture of one set, the other two had stopped transmitting. What had happened? The answers came from Rita Arnould and the information she gave led to the identity and location of others; from this information, the Rote Kapelle house of cards came crashing down. Using Arnould's information, Giering followed the underground communist spy network into Holland and France.

Before Giering and his two assistants had left Berlin for Brussels, there was astonishment in RSHA Berlin with the news that Soviet-trained German communists had been dropped by parachute in East Prussia and in central Poland from aeroplanes of the Soviet air force. During the night of 17–18 May 1942, two teams were dropped at different points near Allenstein, where Kopkow had grown up; during the night of 18–19 May 1942, one team had been dropped at Insterburg and, passing over Poland on its return journey, dropped another team.[9] Four separate teams involving nine agents meant a determined effort by Soviet intelligence agencies to establish networks. Unfortunately for the Soviets, those three teams dropped in East Prussia (six men and a woman) did not establish themselves. The three men dropped on 18–19 May 1942 near Insterburg were spotted by German policemen and, on landing, a fire-fight took place; this resulted in the death of one agent, Wilhelm Freund, and the capture of the two others, Walter Gersmann and Wilhelm Trapp. The two earlier parties were luckier than this threesome as they managed to get away from the drop zone and reach Austria and Germany. Then their luck ran out, primarily because of a complete misunderstanding by Soviet intelligence of the communist parties remaining in Austria and Germany and their ability to hide these agents. RSHA Berlin was quickly off the mark following their interrogation of the two agents captured near Insterburg, who gave details of their four comrades who had dropped into the East Prussia the previous night. On 22 May 1942, RSHA IV A2 sent a special *communiqué* to every Gestapo office across Germany, giving the names and personal descriptions of each agent.[10] The first parachute agent to be arrested was Willi Börner. He had managed to travel from East Prussia, across the Czech Protectorate to Vienna. An informer gave him away to the local Gestapo office, where SS-*Obersturmführer Kriminalkommissar* Johann Sanitzer was the newly appointed Chief of Department IV A2 with Vienna regional Gestapo office (*Stapoleitstelle Wien*). Börner was arrested on 8 July 1942, and a week later, he was escorted by Sanitzer to Berlin and RSHA IV A2 for interrogation. In an interrogation in his post-war CIA name file, Sanitzer said he and Börner met with Kopkow at the Prinz Albrechtstrasse, and as 'the arrest of enemy w/t agent was a new occurrence … they tried to make use of the man for some sort of counter-intelligence work. They finally decided to persuade the agent to begin a series of false radio-messages with his Russian chief'.[11] First of all, they needed his radio set, so Sanitzer and Börner went back to the drop zone in East Prussia where Börner had safely buried it. The two men then returned with their prize to Gestapo headquarters in Vienna, where they began playing Moscow. Sanitzer claims this was the first example of *Funkspiel* operations carried out by the Gestapo. To distinguish the various *Funkspiel* operations, each set was given a name: Borner became *'Quartiermacher I'*.[12] In a show of success for this *Funkspiel*, the Soviets dropped an agent in response to Börner's request for another radio operator to help him with the volume of messages to be transmitted. Emil Kammler had been drafted into the Germany Army and deserted on the Eastern Front in 1942. Once he arrived in Vienna, his task had been the acquisition of military intelligence, cut short when Sanitzer arrested him and used his radio for military disinformation. Kammler transmitted his coded radio messages from Mauthausen concentration camp where he was kept until April 1945; *Gauleiter* Eisgruber requested his execution and Kammler was shot just days before the camp was liberated.[13] In 1943, Börner's radio playback moved from Vienna to Munich, where in May 1943, it was finally broken off. Börner's usefulness to the scheme had probably come to end before then. According to Sanitzer, Börner was 'liquidated' in 1945, no doubt Sanitzer wished to avoid incriminating himself by stating that as 'Willi Hahn' Börner was actually shot much earlier on 7 December 1942 at Dachau.[14] Börner's fellow agent Erwin Panndorf was executed at Sachsenhausen camp on 10 December 1942.[15] Neither man had a trial, they were simply murdered on orders of *Reichsführer*-SS Himmler. An occurrence that would multiply over the next two and a half years when RSHA IV A2 began clearing the decks of captured Allied agents of whatever hue.

In June 1942, Abwehr Brussels was still using radio detection equipment to find illegal transmissions, when one transmitter started with signals directed at Moscow. It took some days to pinpoint the location. During the night of 29–30 June 1942, Captain Harry Piepe, with a party of policemen and some Luftwaffe men from a local barracks, sealed off a street in Brussels-Loeken. The tenement building at 12 Rue de Namur was built on the bridge spanning railway tracks leading to Brussels-Sablon station. When the raid on the house began, they surprised a man found to be transmitting who fled over the rooftops firing his pistol at the Germans, breaking into another house in his endeavour to escape. However, the German cordon was tight and the man eventually found and arrested, putting up a fight before beaten down and taken to Abwehr headquarters. Piepe recalled having the man in his office, handcuffed:

> He was a short, thick-set, hard-featured man, about forty years of age, terribly working class. He did not make much impression on me. His

> first question was whether I was Abwehr or Gestapo, and he was visibly relieved when I reassured him that I was not a Gestapo man. He spoke in French, but badly, and with a heavy accent.... Eventually he calmed down and we started taking in German. He told me that his name was Johann Wenzel and that he had been born in Danzig in 1902.[16]

Wenzel also told Piepe that he would not betray his colleagues and friends before being sent off to the cells in St Gilles prison. What Wenzel would not tell the Abwehr, he would soon be telling the Gestapo after being beaten to a pulp.

Piepe told Karl Giering, newly installed at Gestapo Brussels headquarters, of the arrest of Johann Wenzel and what personal details he had given. Giering sent a message to RSHA IV A2 in Berlin asking for any details they had on him, and the answer came back quickly. The Gestapo card index and registry files contained a large amount of information showing Wenzel's early communist career and recruitment by Soviet intelligence agencies in 1934. In 1935, he began attending GRU training school in Moscow, proving a capable student of espionage and radio transmissions. More recently, in spring 1941, when RSHA began compiling their 'black book' for the military invasion of the Soviet Union, Wenzel's name appears as wanted by RSHA IV A2. However, Wenzel did not act in a vacuum, he controlled an espionage network with agents in Belgium and Holland, acquiring German military information from airfields, navy yards, and army bases. Giering had Wenzel taken from St Gilles prison to Breendonk SS-Camp, where their intensive interrogation methods eventually broke him. At the time, they thought they had extracted every piece of information from him.

While Giering made enquiries of RSHA Berlin about Wenzel, Piepe was on his way to Abwehr headquarters in Berlin carrying vital information. During the search of the Rue de Namur house, Wenzel had left behind a series of coded messages and two messages in German waiting to be enciphered. The contents of these two messages were of such startling detail about top secret German military plans for the Eastern Front that it caused Piepe to personally drive to Berlin. Once Piepe reported the content of the two messages, he was rushed into the presence of Admiral Canaris himself. Canaris and Piepe then drove to the War Ministry and met with Field Marshal Wilhelm Keitel, Chief of the Wehrmacht High Command. In the hands of the Soviets, had these two messages been transmitted, the entire German military thrust into the Caucasus (Case 'Blue') would have been seriously jeopardised, especially as this operation had begun on 28 June 1942, the day before the raid in Brussels. This meant there was a traitor at the highest level of the German armed forces with access to secret military planning, someone who was passing top secret and sensitive military information to Soviet spies, and someone who needed to be caught quickly. The question of who was resolved even quicker than expected.

The history of codebreaking at Bletchley Park in Britain of Enigma radio messages is well-known. What is less well-known is codebreaking by the German *Funkabwehr* under the command of Dr Wilhelm Vauck. A mathematician in civilian life, Dr Vauck controlled a small team of other mathematicians who worked on decrypting the coded messages found not only in the two houses raided in Brussels, but other messages taken down from the ether as Rote Kapelle radio operators transmitted their information to Moscow. The Gestapo interrogation of Johann Wenzel gave them the first clue and Rita Arnould the second that solved the decryption. Very soon, Dr Vauck's team were producing deciphered back-traffic messages sent from Brussels to Moscow dating from October 1941. On 14 July 1942, the decisive message was deciphered, a single message that brought the house of Rote Kapelle crashing down. From 18 October 1941, the deciphered message read:

> KENT from Director personally. Proceed immediately Berlin three addresses indicated and determine cause failures radio links. If stoppages recur undertake transmissions personally. Efforts of three Berlin groups and transmission information vitally important. Addresses: 19 Altenburger Allee, Neu-Westend, third floor right—Coro; 26a Fredericiastrasse, Charlottenburg, second floor left—Wolf; 18 Kaiserallee, Friedenau, fourth floor left—Bauer. Remind Bauer of a book which he gave to Erdberg as a present not long before the war, and of his play Till Eulenspiegel. Password: Director. Report progress by October 20. New (repeat new) plan in force for three stations.[17]

Moscow Centre had committed a cardinal sin, the simplest security breach, with the most devastating results. When this message was handed over to RSHA IV A2, they easily identified the persons living at these addresses, and from 16 July 1942, they put them under surveillance. With guile and perseverance, 'Hitler's guardians of the regime [Gestapo undercover officials] found themselves watching and listening to one of strangest espionage organisations in German history'. The Berlin branch of Rote Kapelle was being uncovered following a Soviet security breach. Unknown to Kopkow, there was also a traitor in the *Funkabwehr*, and a German security breach was trying to warn the Berlin leaders. Corporal Horst Heilmann worked on decoding in Vauck's *Funkabwehr* department and saw a copy of the 18 October 1941 message from Moscow to Brussels with the Berlin addresses. Heilmann did not need to be told who CORO was or who lived at 19 Altenburger Allee in Neu-Westend, Heilmann was already supplying CORO with information from the *Funkabwehr*. Heilmann, having been unsuccessful at telephoning CORO, left messages for him to return his calls. CORO eventually telephoned Heilmann back at his office one evening. In his absence, Vauck answered the telephone and said he could take a message. When Vauck asked the caller for his name and met with 'Schulze-Boysen', the game was up. The revelation that Schulze-Boysen, already identified as CORO and under Gestapo surveillance, knew Heilmann pre-empted the next move by Kopkow. The following morning (30 August 1942), Kopkow and his boss Fritz Panzinger drove over the road to the *Haus der Flieger* (Air Ministry) and arrested Luftwaffe Lieutenant Harro Schulze-Boysen. They drove him back to Prinz Albrechtstrasse. It might have been expected that the Gestapo would then charge about to other Berlin addresses and begin a wave of arrests, but no, the Gestapo seems to have played a watch and wait game with the others identified from the Moscow radio message: WOLF was Dr Arvid Harnack, a senior civil servant in the Ministry of Economics, and BAUER was Dr Adam Kuckhoff, a writer.

Moscow radio traffic to their agents in Brussels, decrypted by Dr Vauck's team, did not only unmask CORO, WOLF, and BAUER, another decrypted message unmasked their agent BREITENBACH in Berlin. On 22 August 1942, before Schulze-Boysen's arrest, RSHA Personnel Chief SS-*Gruppenführer* Bruno Streckenbach made an urgent telephone call from Berlin to *Reichsführer*-SS Himmler at his Hegewald field headquarters in Ukraine. At 11.40 a.m., Himmler made a note in his desk diary as a result of Streckenbach's call: 'Communist cell in the Gestapo. Soviet intelligence organisations'.[18] In Berlin, events moved quickly, and having identified BREITENBACH as *Kriminalinspektor* Willi Lehmann of RSHA IV E1, the fifty-eight-year-old agent was arrested. He had worked on counter-intelligence matters and, according to one account, supplied the Soviets with Gestapo secrets in return for money to fund his gambling habits. What actually happened to Lehmann after his arrest is still obscure and Kopkow is the only source, though his version probably contains a mix of truth and lies:

> [Lehmann] … was shot on written instructions from Himmler, who had forbidden any court proceedings since he did not wish it to become known, even to the courts, that an official of the Gestapa had been working for the Russian IS [intelligence service] for years. The whole matter was hushed up and a statement issued that Lehmann had been murdered by partisans on a journey to Bialystok; a fictious grave was photographed and shown to Lehmann's wife, who was promised a pension.[19]

The report of Lehmann's death appeared as an obituary in the weekly RSHA newsletter, dated 29 January 1943.[20] Lehmann had laid down his life 'For the Führer and the Reich' during December 1942. In fact, Lehmann had been interrogated by Kopkow after his arrest. There was no trial and Lehmann was taken to Sachsenhausen concentration camp, just north of Berlin, where he was shot and his body immediately cremated. Kopkow stated that he was present to witness the two events.

When the Gestapo began arresting Rote Kapelle agents in Berlin, they were mostly staggered: Harnack and his wife, Mildred, were arrested on

3 September; Horst Heilmann, the traitor in the *Funkabwehr*, on 5 September; Kuckhoff on 7 September; and Libertas Schulze-Boysen, Harro's wife, was not arrested until 15 September. The delay in arresting all the Soviet spies following the hurried arrest of Harro Schulze-Boysen may have been due to two major reasons: firstly, the prison cells in the RSHA building on Prinz Albrecht Strasse needed to be emptied and the prisoners transferred elsewhere; and, secondly, it could have been foreseen that RSHA IV A2 only had a small staff of interrogators and therefore had to call on other interrogators from RSHA IV A1 (the communism desk) and RSHA IV E6 (counter intelligence). RSHA IV Chief Müller, a determined anti-communist for twenty years, together with Kopkow, a determined anti-communist for ten years, created a special commission (*Sonderkommission*) staffed mainly by RSHA IV A2 and specially detached interrogators and stenographers from other departments; their task was to root out every possible Rote Kapelle agent and provider of information regardless of where it took them. *Sonderkommission* Rote Kapelle created in September 1942 continued into 1944, when it was overtaken by other events. In Brussels, a detached unit called *Sonderkommando Rote Kapelle* with Karl Giering in charge exhausted every lead in Belgium and Holland, and in 1942, it moved to Paris to continue its work. In Paris, Giering fell ill again as his cancer took over and went on sick leave, never to return to duty. RSHA IV Chief Müller called SS-*Obersturmführer Kriminalkommissar* Heinz Pannwitz to Berlin and, with Kopkow's agreement, appointed him to replace Giering in Paris. After briefing Pannwitz with what was known and what was now expected, Pannwitz travelled to the French capital and took command of *Sonderkommando Rote Kapelle* at the end of July 1943, a command he held through to the end of the war.[21]

At RSHA Berlin, the cells were filling up with men and women directly implicated in the Rote Kapelle network. Kopkow himself initially interrogated Harro Schulze-Boysen, who attempted to save his comrades, telling Kopkow that he had lodged secret documents in Sweden to be released into the public domain in the event of them being executed. Kopkow responded in typical interrogator fashion, promising that he would recommend prison sentences or release from arrest. Schulze-Boysen was taken in by these empty promises, revealing the documents in Sweden did not exist; Kopkow replied that he did not have the seniority to promise what he did and that Schulze-Boysen and his comrades would therefore face the full force of Nazi laws.[22] On 2 October 1942, between 5.30 p.m. and 6 p.m., *Reichsführer*-SS Himmler observed one of Schulze-Boysen's interrogation sessions at Prinz-Albrecht-Strasse.[23] A week later, at Führer HQ in Ukraine, Hegewald, Himmler had a telephone call with RSHA IV Chief Müller about Schulze-Boysen, and a similar telephone call on 21 October. This interest by Himmler indicates the high-level interest in the ever-increasing scope of the Gestapo investigation and where it was taking them.[24] Between September and November 1942, it is reported that 119 men and women had been arrested and interrogated. Some had been released without charge before the trials began.[25]

The first trial of Rote Kapelle members before the central military court (*Reichskriegsgericht*) in Berlin took place on a single day, 14 December 1942. The Foreign Office officials Rudolf von Scheliha and the communist organiser Ilse Stöbe were both convicted of high treason and sentenced to death. The trial did not take long. *Reichsführer*-SS Himmler, at his Friedrichsruh headquarters near the Führer's Wolfsschanze headquarters in East Prussia, received a telephone call from RSHA IV Chief Müller at 11.40 a.m. on 14 December to inform him of the Rote Kapelle case. At this time of day, with the first trial taken place, it can only have been to advise him of the death sentences. Himmler no doubt left little time in advising Hitler himself of the trial outcome.[26]

The second trial began the following day (15 December 1942), and twelve defendants faced charges of high treason before *Reichskriegsgericht* Berlin. A senior judge, Dr Kraell, sat on the bench with two generals, an admiral, and a senior military prosecutor. Presenting the case against the defendants was senior military prosecutor *Oberstkriegsgerichtsrat* Dr Manfred Roeder, who had visited Kopkow at RSHA IV many times to examine the evidence. The trial lasted five days, and with so much evidence against the defendants, the sentences passed on 19 December 1942 still contained a surprise—death sentences for all twelve were expected:

Harro Schulze-Boysen	Sentenced to death
Libertas Schulze-Boysen	Sentenced to death
Arvid Harnack	Sentenced to death
Mildred Harnack	Six years' imprisonment
Herbert Gollnow	Sentenced to death
Horst Heilmann	Sentenced to death
Kurt Schumacher	Sentenced to death
Elisabeth Schumacher	Sentenced to death
Hans Coppi	Sentenced to death
Kurt Schulze	Sentenced to death
Erika von Brockdorff	Ten years' imprisonment
Johannes Graudenz	Sentenced to death[27]

Hitler refused to confirm the prison sentences on the two women and ordered a new trial for them. This took place on 13–16 January 1943 and death sentences were then given.

A third trial before Christmas 1942 also took place. On a single day (18 December 1942), the telecommunications engineer Dr Hans Heinrich Kummerow faced charges of high treason. Although not directly involved with Schulze-Boysen's network, Kummerow had occasionally used their radio operator to contact Moscow. Through a Gestapo *Funkspiel* operation with Moscow, yet again they dealt a fatal blow to their contact. Moscow directed a parachute agent under Gestapo control to make contact with Kummerow, who was arrested attending a late afternoon meeting on 17 September 1942 at Berlin's Potsdamer Platz station. When the Gestapo searched his home, they discovered that Kummerow had already supplied Soviet intelligence with detailed plans for a German surface-to-air missile and now prepared to offer them details of a remotely controlled bomb. When Kopkow's officer, who made the arrest (SS-*Obersturmführer Kriminalkommissar* Johannes Strübing), contacted OKW, they were taken aback that such a top secret project should be in the hands of Kummerow. Strübing was officially warned not to breathe a word about the bomb to anyone. Kummerow was convicted of high treason and sentenced to death. His execution was delayed until 4 February 1944, when he was beheaded in Halle prison. Kummerow's wife, Ingeborg, had also been arrested by the Gestapo in September 1942. She faced a different court in December 1942, when she was sentenced to death for aiding a traitor (her husband); she was executed in August 1943 at Plötzensee prison.[28]

After Hitler's confirmation of the death sentences for von Scheliha and Stöbe, Schulze-Boysen and his comrades (with the exception of Gollnow), the judicial authorities hastened to carry out the sentences. The executions took place on 22 December 1942. Plötzensee prison in Berlin normally used the guillotine and so the three women (Ilse Stöbe, Libertas Schulze-Boysen, and Elisabeth Schumacher) were beheaded, whereas all the men were hanged. This was not the end as seventy-eight men and women would have their trials in 1943. Three were acquitted and thirty-two were given prison sentences, but thirty-three were given death sentences: Mildred Harnack, after her retrial, was executed at Plötzensee prison on 16 February 1943; thirteen more were executed at Plötzensee on 13 May 1943, followed by sixteen on 5 August 1943. Four others were executed individually, with Herbert Gollnow executed by firing squad on 12 February 1943.[29]

The RSHA interrogators and stenographers were given monetary bonuses from *Reichsmarschall* Hermann Göring's slush fund. Göring felt aggrieved that so many military secrets had been disclosed to the Soviets by Luftwaffe officers. He was kept informed of the investigation by *Reichsführer*-SS Himmler and RSHA IV Chief Müller who met with him on 25 September 1942. Müller later met with Göring on 2 and 29 October 1942, on the latter occasion accompanied by Dr Roeder, who would prosecute at the Schulze-Boysen trial. Göring provided RSHA IV Chief Müller with 100,000 RM (*Reichsmarks*) in December 1942 for distribution 'for special achievements in the investigations ... to especially deserving officials'. Two stenographers, Anni Griese and Gertrud Breiter, each received 500 RM, were awarded the *Kriegsverdienstkreuz* II, and a personally signed congratulatory letter from the *Reichsführer*-SS in recognition of their service. Sixty-five RSHA officials received sums varying from 500 to 5,000 RM, totalling 67,600 RM, leaving a balance of 32,400 RM. At least 29,500 RM went to Horst Kopkow, an amount equivalent to almost three years' salary.[30] When the Berlin city authorities confiscated Schulze-Boysen's home and belongings, Kopkow was allowed to take away some of the furniture and kitchen equipment for the princely sum of 20 RM.[31]

The Rote Kapelle investigations in Berlin involved the small departmental staff of RSHA IV A2 between August and early December 1942. During November, Kopkow compiled the final report on the investigation detailing every person involved. This was issued on 20 November 1942 under the title 'Bolshevist High Treason and Treason Organizations in the Reich and Western Europe ("Rote Kapelle")'. It recorded that 119 persons had been arrested in Berlin, ten radio transmitter/receivers seized, and sufficient components that could increase this number to fourteen. The Gestapo investigators also recovered 37,000 RM and 3,450 US dollars. In Holland and Belgium, a further seventeen communist agents had been arrested together with four radio transmitter/receivers. With all these arrests came numerous false documents, travel warrants, photographs, and duplicating equipment for printing political flyers and posters. This long eighty-nine-page document ends by confirming the arrest of five parachute agents who had arrived in Germany to begin activities with Rote Kapelle in Berlin: 'By sending these special operators to mobilise the [Rote Kapelle in Berlin] clearly proves what importance the Comintern and General Staff of the Red Army have given to the traitors and their treasonable groups'.[32]

With the Nazi judicial process completed against those activists in Soviet espionage against Germany and arrested mainly in Berlin, the same could not be said for the parachute agents. In Moscow, both the NKVD and GRU intelligence agencies agreed recognition of a need to expedite the secret military information from their German sources—there was no point in receiving military information late when it had been overtaken by events on the ground. Many German Communists had fled Germany to escape arrest and incarceration in concentration camps and arrived in Moscow during the 1930s. Some had later served on the republican side during the Spanish Civil War, either actively fighting or involved in intelligence work. Soon after the German attack on the Soviet Union (22 June 1941) and the subsequent German advance that almost reached Moscow in December 1941, fuel logistics caused big problems for Soviet aircraft. With the front almost at Moscow, they did not have aircraft capable of a return flight from their air bases to drop agents in Germany. Soviet intelligence therefore decided on another course of action to support their intelligence-gathering endeavours: they would welcome an approach from British intelligence as an ally. Arrangements moved forward quickly. British negotiators from SOE arrived in Moscow and began discussions with the Soviet intelligence agency. Between 14 and 29 August 1941, an agreement was agreed and signed by both parties on 30 September 1941.[33] Even before the signing, a small Soviet liaison team under Colonel Ivan Chichaev was on its way to London.

This agreement and its accompanying 'preliminary survey of joint subversive policy for the guidance of the British and Soviet liaison sections' agreed many actions, several of which the Soviets signed up to and then ignored. The agreement mentions 'subversive activities' and 'attention should also be paid to enemy war industries', highlighting such targets as shipping, canals, road transport, armament factories, chemical industries, electric power plants, and oilfields. Whereas SOE did pay subversive attention to these industries and the British and American bomber fleets did bombard them from the air, the Soviets did none of these things. The foremost and primary interest of Soviet intelligence was using Britain's Royal Air Force to parachute Soviet agents into Western Europe now beyond the range of Soviet aircraft—agents with communication skills who could use radio transmitters and reinforce their existing espionage networks in Germany, Belgium, Holland, and France, networks known to the Abwehr and Gestapo as Rote Kapelle. The Soviet-trained agents, both men and women, who did arrive in Britain, came by ship from arctic north Russian ports, through the stormy north Atlantic seas, some surviving shipwreck. In Britain, they were known as Pickaxe agents.

No sooner had Colonel Chichaev and his staff arrived in London than the first agents were also on the way to Britain. After an arduous sea journey then rail travel from the very tip of northern Scotland, two men and a woman finally arrived in London on 23 November 1941. Their baggage, including radio transmitters, followed a few days later. The men were intended for Germany and had good identification papers for use in Germany, but the woman had no papers and was intended for France. The men were whisked off for parachuting lessons, but the woman refused to parachute so plans were eventually made to land her by a sea on the French coast. The three agents were known as PICKAXE I (the woman, by name Anna Ouspenskaya) and PICKAXE II (the two men, named Pavel Koubitsky and Pyotr Kousnetzov). The two men were the first to be sent on their mission when the RAF attempted to drop them during the night of 27–28 December 1941. The drop-zone location in the Belgian Ardennes region, north of Elsenborn, was covered in low cloud so the aircraft returned to Britain with them still aboard. On landing, the aircraft crashed killing Koubitsky; Kousnetzov survived the crash, but was hospitalised, living to parachute another day.[34] Anna Ouspenskaya received new documents and clothing from SOE for her mission to France, and during the night of 11–12 January 1942, a Royal Navy gunboat crossed the English Channel under stormy conditions; in the early hours, it landed Anna Ouspenskaya on a deserted French beach in Lannion Bay, Brittany. The first communist agent probably ever infiltrated anywhere by a British intelligence agency. SOE people Ouspenskaya had met in London did not think she stood much of a chance as she was very nervous. That said, using her new identity papers supplied by SOE in the name of Jeannette Dupont, she did make it to Paris and, through her contacts in communist underground circles, made radio contact with Moscow. Whatever her successes once deployed in France, she was arrested in mid-1942 by the French police having tried to set fire to a grain store. Handed over to the Abwehr and interrogated, Anna talked. Ten other agents in France were arrested as a result and her radio transmitter and codes were possibly used by the Abwehr for a *Funkspiel* with London and Moscow. When arrested, Anna was using new identity papers in the name of Szyra Lipszyc, and by this name she was executed in July 1942.[35]

The second Pickaxe party, known as COFFEE, proved wholly unsatisfactory. Three men and a woman arrived with no equipment, no documents, and had received no training in Moscow, and they arrived in Britain without knowing what was required of them. Illness, an inability to accept a parachute drop, and other factors caused them to be sent back to the Soviet Union. The third and fourth parties arrived in Scotland during February 1942. One party, known as BRANDY and then renamed RUM, consisted of two men and a woman (all French), and they were destined for dropping in France. The fourth, known as WHISKEY, consisted of two Austrian communists who wanted dropping in Austria. The RUM party needed little training and had decent documents. During the night of 3–4 March 1942, they were dropped from a RAF plane, together with their supplies and a SOE radio transmitter, in Southern France (a little to the north of Montpellier). After landing, these agents made no secret about their intentions to reach Lyon and deliver the radio transmitter. From there, they were to establish radio communications between Unoccupied France and Moscow. Only then would the senior agent, Raymond Guyot (alias Georges Robigot), proceed on a second task to Paris. In fact, Guyot was believed by MI5 to be married to the woman in the party, Annette Fauberge (alias Francine Fromont), but this was not so. It became known in August 1944 that Francine Fromont had been executed by the Germans for espionage; again, this was a case of false information supplied to MI5. After the war, Fromont worked to further the education of the Communist Youth. Like many female agents, her name was revered after the war with streets and schools named after her.[36]

The WHISKEY party also needed little training for their drop, but their parachute dates were cancelled before departure or, having taken off, returned to Britain due to poor visibility over the drop zone. Finally, their aircraft took off on 20 April 1942. Unfortunately, it was presumed lost when it did not return to base. After the war, RAF investigators established the aircraft had crashed into mountains in southern Bavaria with the loss of aircrew and passengers. The two Austrians, despite several aliases, were identified as Lorenz Mraz and Franz Löschl. Their aim had been espionage in Viennese factories and were to transmit their information to Moscow. Lorenz Mraz, had he lived, might have expected to meet his wife, Hildegard, in Vienna during 1943. As it turned out, her agent training continued in Moscow for an eventual parachute drop by the Soviet air force in June 1943 as a widow.[37]

During the night of 24–25 June 1942, Pickaxe party BURGUNDY was dropped by the RAF into Belgium. In one report, sixty-four-year-old Willi Kruyt (father of Jan Kruyt, dropped into Holland) fractured his leg on landing, while another report has him walking about Brussels a day or two later. Kruyt brought with him a radio transmitter believed for communication between Dutch and Belgian Communist resistance groups. MI5, in their post-war assessment of Rote Kapelle, believed Kruyt may have been dropped 'to reinforce Jeffremov's network' in Brussels. Whatever Kruyt's real mission may have been, he did not last out the month, for a Gestapo informer denounced him and his arrest took place on 30 June 1942 at an address in the Brussels suburb of Berchem-Ste-Agathe—a safe house address given to him in Moscow. Kruyt felt the full force of the Gestapo's third-degree measures at Breendonk SS-camp and would not talk or co-operate with a *Funkspiel* using his radio set. It is reported that in July 1943, Kruyt was transferred to Moabit prison in Berlin and executed. This is suspicious as a man in Gestapo custody, especially a trained Russian agent, would normally have been sent to a concentration camp for execution without trial.[38]

While the British and Russians in London agreed co-operation on receiving and dropping agents into German-occupied western territories continued, Kopkow (in Berlin) had been kept busy in the spring of 1942 with Polish Communist-related sabotage taking place in the General Government of Poland. A flurry of teleprinter messages and reports took place in April and May 1942 between RSHA IV A2 and BdS Krakau, KdS Warsaw, and KdS Radom.[39] The names of many of those arrested and suspected in these sabotage activities appeared in Gestapo indices in Berlin, not only their individual names, but the people they associated with. Gestapo round-ups brought in the guilty and the innocent alike. In Germany, sabotage on the railway system increased so much that RSHA IV A2 sent out a circular to all Gestapo offices on 4 April 1942 with advice for examining travellers' luggage, parcels sent by rail for onward delivery, and the passengers themselves.[40] In the aftermath of the attack on Heydrich, Kopkow went to Prague in the afternoon of 27 May 1942 as part of the Special Commission to establish exactly how the attack took place and the means by which it was carried out—the commission was not involved in pursuit of the perpetrators. The Special Commission quickly ascertained the facts about the weapons and explosives used at the crime scene. Heydrich lay dying in a Prague hospital when Kopkow returned to Berlin, where he had a seminar to prepare for. A two-day seminar under the chairmanship of RSHA IV Chief Müller in the Prinz Albrechtstrasse conference room began on 1 June 1942. Planned weeks before, its subject matter was now rather apt; regional Gestapo representatives responsible for '*Schutzdienst*', the protection of senior SS and Party officials, gathered to hear the latest instructions. On the first morning, Müller mentioned the attack on Heydrich and Kopkow followed with a talk about using the RSHA collection of teaching aids for protecting senior officials. Müller reiterated in conclusion of the seminar that there must not be another example of a senior official going without an armed escort, and any excuses to forego an escort by the official should be discarded for his own safety.[41]

The training of Gestapo officials from across Germany continued throughout the war. Four months after the June 1942 seminar, another was held on 22–24 October 1942 at the SD-School in Bernau, on the north-eastern edge of Berlin. Kopkow gave two lectures on the first day that took the whole morning. His first lecture was entitled 'Sabotage by the "philosophical" enemies' (which meant by communists) and his second was entitled 'Sabotage by enemy intelligence agencies'.[42] By this stage of the war, this meant the growing menace from British trained agents dropped into France, Belgium, Holland, and Norway. Unlike the singleton or two-man teams dropped by the Soviets purely for intelligence gathering, British teams were more organised and supplied, and training native resisters to commit acts of sabotage with explosives. In the western territories occupied by German forces, the sabotage threat grew greater into 1943 and 1944. On the last day of the seminar, Kopkow gave a slide show and spoke about 'the latest enemy sabotage materials with explanations'. Throughout the three-day event, Kopkow was supported by three of his staff officers: Ampletzer, Büchert, and Henze. On this last day, Kopkow probably told his audience that the latest Soviet-trained radio operator to be arrested had been brought from Hamburg to RSHA IV A2 in Berlin for interrogation. This was Erna Eifler, the radio operator of the two-man team dropped into East Prussia during the night of 16–17 May 1942; she had been arrested on 15 October in Hamburg as a result of Gestapo informers among the local communist groups. On 20 October 1942, an escort of Gestapo officers brought Eifler from Hamburg to Berlin by regular train service.[43] The following day, her interrogations began with *Kriminalinspektor* Walter Habecker, one of Kopkow's ablest and most brutal interrogators, who had been interrogating communists for the past seven years—throughout the early days of the Gestapo. Willi Fellendorf, who dropped with Erna Eifler, managed to avoid arrest in Hamburg until 28 October, when his luck ran out. Trying to leave the city for Denmark, informers again caused his downfall. Fellendorf remained in Hamburg where his extensive interrogations took place; being the organiser and intelligence-gatherer, his role was considered less important than the designs RSHA IV A2 had for Eifler's radio codes and the possibility of a *Funkspiel* with Moscow. Fellendorf was soon on his way to Sachsenhausen concentration camp, where he was executed in early 1943.[44] Eifler participated in the *Funkspiel* with Moscow, which ran its course probably until early 1944, when she too became expendable and transferred to Ravensbrück camp. Erna Eifler was shot there on 7 July 1944.[45]

The Gestapo hunt for Eifler and Fellendorf was short of information as to their whereabouts when the Soviets dropped two more German Communists, Robert Barth and Albert Hössler. These two were dropped on 5 August 1942 near Gomel in White Russia in the guise of German soldiers returning to Germany on leave. Barth was a long-serving German Communist who had been drafted into the German Army, although he deserted on 3 February 1942 on the Eastern Front. He had been recruited from a POW cage by Soviet military intelligence and taken to Moscow where he trained as a parachute agent. Hössler, on the other hand, had fought with the International Brigades in Spain and went to the Soviet Union in 1938 for training as an espionage agent. Both men were trained for a parachute drop, and they also trained in coding messages and as radio operators. When they were dropped in August 1942, each had a radio transmitter and codes. With good identity and travel papers, both men separated after the parachute drop and independently arrived in Berlin. Their primary task was to help Rote Kapelle agents in place in Berlin with transmission of their information to Moscow. Hössler was most active, as the post-war CIA history of Rote Kapelle mentions:

> Hoessler was introduced by Kurt Schumacher to Coppi with whom he attempted to establish a W/T link with Moscow, first from the shelter of Erika von Brockdorff's house and then from that of Oda Schottmueller. He was instructed to keep in touch with Robert Barth, with whom he had been parachuted and who may have been intended to render a similar service to Harnack's group.[46]

Although Barth also helped out with transmitting Rote Kapelle material from Berlin, one source claims Barth's real contact point was Gestapo man Willi Lehmann. Neither Barth nor Hössler survived long at liberty in Berlin. According to Walter Habecker, one of Kopkow's interrogators at RSHA IV A2, Barth was arrested on 9 October 1942 attending a Berlin military hospital for medical treatment; Hössler had been arrested the previous week at his marital home in Berlin-Schöneberg. Both men agreed to conduct *Funkspiel* operations using their own radio transmitters and Barth sent his first message to Moscow on 15 October.[47] The more committed communist Hössler must have attempted some form of trickery, which was discovered by the Gestapo, because he was executed at Plötzensee prison on 22 December 1942. Barth, on the other hand, carried on with the *Funkspiel* despite being held in cells in a Berlin prison before he was moved to Ravensbrück concentration camp due to air-raids on Berlin; he was kept captive in a cell in the Bunker. In November 1944, Kopkow and some of his staff were now based at a military camp just outside Drögen village, a short distance from Ravensbrück camp. Barth was brought there and given a chance by Kopkow to save his life; he would be taken to the Dudweiler on the western border of Germany, with a radio transmitter, and when the area was overrun by Allied armies, Barth would radio information on Allied military units back to Kopkow. The reality was that Barth did want to save his life, but, at the same time, he did not want to help Kopkow and the Gestapo.

Barth sat out the war in Dudweiler until March 1945, when he surrendered to the Americans. He made himself known as a Soviet agent who needed to be repatriated. Once the Soviets acknowledged Barth's status, he was handed over to the Soviet repatriation mission in Paris, July 1945, who forwarded him to Moscow. Things did not turn out well in Moscow. Following his trial as a traitor, Barth was executed in November 1945.[48]

Eifler had already been arrested and the hunt for Fellendorf in Hamburg was well underway when the Soviets dropped another Soviet-trained German on 23 October 1942. Dropped in their preferred drop zone areas near Allenstein, Kopkow's East Prussian boyhood home, Heinz Koenen was another radio operator destined for the Rote Kapelle in Berlin, and made his way there. Koenen was expected by the Gestapo, news that came from a controlled radio set. On 26 October 1942, he telephoned the home of Ilse Stöbe, a Soviet agent of long service. She had already been arrested by the Gestapo, and a Gestapo secretary now impersonated her. Arrangements were made for a meeting the following day at Berlin's Wittenbergplatz. The Gestapo were waiting and Koenen was arrested. He was brought to Prinz Albrechtstrasse where a search of his belongings took place. In yet another Soviet security breach, Koenen's belongings included a photocopy of a $7,500 deposit slip at a Swiss bank in the name of Rudolf von Scheliha. His identity followed as the Soviet agent 'Arier' and position as a senior German Foreign Office diplomat. Panzinger and Kopkow once again drove through Berlin to the Foreign Office where they arrested von Scheliha on 29 October 1942. Von Scheliha and Ilse Stöbe, who had earlier acted as his secretary and Soviet contact, both faced the first trial of Rote Kapelle agents in December 1942 and were executed. Koenen's radio set was used for another *Funkspiel* operation with Moscow. He was executed without trial at Sachsenhausen camp in February 1945.[49]

While Eifler and Fellendorf had been pursued by the Gestapo in Hamburg, Karl Giering worked on Johann Wenzel in Brussels. Having broken Wenzel physically into submission, *Sonderkommando* Rote Kapelle in Brussels began using Wenzel for a *Funkspiel* operation back to Moscow known as *Beam Weide*. As with all *Funkspiel* operations, the major problem areas included how much truthful material and how much disinformation to tell Moscow. Political-economic information could be fudged in any direction, but military information always needed to be accurate. As a counter check, if the Soviets could get similar information from other agents already under Gestapo control, then inaccurate information could be provided; however, faced with the unknown factor where information could be challenged, the risk of jeopardising a *Funkspiel* operation could not be discounted. Wenzel began working the controlled Gestapo transmissions from Brussels to Moscow in August 1942. Gradually, his Gestapo guards became lulled into a false sense of security at the house on Rue de l'Aurore, just around the corner from Brussels Gestapo headquarters on Avenue Louise, from where the coded radio messages were transmitted. On 18 November 1942, in a careless moment, his guards failed to lock the outside door; taking advantage of this, Wenzel quickly took the key from the lock and locked the door behind him before fleeing. Wenzel disappeared and did not resurface until the Allies had liberated Belgium almost two years later. There are reports that he managed to make contact with a British SIS agent in either Belgium or Holland after his escape from the Gestapo, and also that he asked that the Soviet Embassy in London were informed that the Gestapo were playing back to Moscow at least two radio sets from Belgium.[50] Faced with unwillingness by the German Army to continue providing military information, the escape of Wenzel, and whether he might have found a way to inform Moscow of the *Funkspiel*, the Gestapo eventually discontinued *Beam Weide* in February–March 1944. Afterwards, the radio frequency continued to be monitored, showing Moscow called regularly at the transmission times for three months afterwards.

After breaking Wenzel into submission and using him in a *Funkspiel* operation with his own radio set to Moscow, Giering turned to tracking down other radio operators who had gone silent. For the Gestapo, it became paramount that the remaining Belgian agents, now believed to be in Holland, did not reveal the arrests to Moscow. That would have killed off the *Funkspiel* operational plans of feeding Moscow with false information. Radio operators trained by Wenzel had gone into hiding following the arrests in Brussels. It seems certain that, under torture, Wenzel possibly revealed some names. Giering's men began surveilling an elderly Jewish forger in Brussels, Abraham Rajchmann, who been helping the Russians since 1935. In July 1942, information came through—via an informant of the Abwehr who was in contact with Rajchman—that forged identity papers were to be handed over to a senior communist agent in Brussels. A trap was set, and on 30 July 1942, the Abwehr arrested a Finnish citizen taking the forged papers. He was brought to Abwehr HQ where Piepe and Giering began an interrogation. Eric Jernstroem was every inch a Finn, confirmed by Finnish diplomats in Brussels, but he spoke no Finnish. Not until faced by Johann Wenzel did the pretence drop. Jernstroem's real name was Konstantin Jefremow; known in the spy-ring as BORDO, he was a Ukrainian and a captain in the GRU (Soviet military intelligence), who travelled via Finland and the USA to Belgium in 1939 becoming the illegal resident in Brussels. Wenzel worked for him as radio operator. Under interrogation, Jefremow revealed a second radio operator, August Sesee, working in Ostend, who was arrested on 28 August 1942. With Wenzel and Sesee (together with their radio transmitters) in German hands, two *Funkspiel* operations could begin with complete confidence: *Beam 'Weide'* and *Beam 'Buche-Pascal*. Before the arrest of Sesee, Jefremow had led the Germans to another of his agents, Maurice Peper. In fact, they arrested two agents at the same time as Peper was meeting with a courier, Hermann Isbutzky. The downfall of the Brussels spy-ring, led to the downfall of a similar spy-ring operating from Amsterdam, where Anton Winterink (TINO) was the illegal resident.[51]

Captain Harry Piepe, Abwehr Brussels, realised that Peper could be useful in identifying the Dutch cell leader. Piepe, the terrified Peper, and other Abwehr officers drove up to Holland and made arrangements for the arrests with the local Abwehr and Gestapo offices. Through his usual contacts, Peper arranged a meeting with Winterink in an Amsterdam café. The arrest followed, as did that of Peper's Dutch contacts. Being both the illegal resident and a radio operator, Winterink's home became the centre for a search for his radio set and ciphers. Piepe took Winterink, his radio, and his ciphers back to Brussels, and it took the Germans two weeks to break him—his radio set became *Funkspiel 'Beam Tanne'*, beginning on 22 September 1942. Loose ends in Holland who had avoided arrest had already informed Moscow of Winterink's arrest and his radio traffic therefore became suspect. *Beam Tanne* decided to go on the offensive, reporting that Winterink had escaped from the Germans and therefore the loose ends in Holland (Daniel Gouwlooze and Johannes Nagel) must be under German control. *Beam Tanne* continued transmitting to Moscow until March–April 1944, when it was discontinued. Winterink was executed in Brussels on 6 July 1944.[52]

Winterink was the GRU Resident in Amsterdam and he had connections to another Dutch communist, Daniel Gouwlooze, who represented Comintern activities in Holland and provided political and economic information to Moscow. Gouwlooze also had loose contacts with similar illegal communist groups in Germany. He kept these at arm's length because there existed the danger of Gestapo penetration. To increase his radio transmissions capacity, in 1942, the Comintern arranged for the GRU to provide him with more radio operators and these would arrive via Britain as Pickaxe agents. During the night of 22–23 June 1942, the RAF dropped Jan Kruyt with radio set in woods in central Holland. Kruyt made contact with Gouwlooze shortly afterwards and the two worked together for the next twelve months. A radio operator, Bruno Kühn, was dropped by the RAF in the same area during the night of 29–30 November 1942, and made his way to Gouwlooze in Amsterdam. With his German Communist background, it was intended for Kühn to provide that radio connection to Moscow for Gouwlooze's communist cell in Germany. This cell under Wilhelm Knöchel operated in the Ruhr area of Düsseldorf-Essen-Wuppertal and usually sent couriers to Holland with their information for Moscow. Gouwlooze kept Kühn in Holland when he believed Knöchel's group had been penetrated, borne out by Knöchel's arrest on 30 January 1943. Gouwlooze put Kühn to work with Kruyt keeping Moscow informed. The Gestapo arrested Kühn during the night of 27–28 July 1943; Kruyt called at Kühn's address the following day and managed to avoid being arrested by a plausible cover story. Afterwards, he went into hiding until the liberation of Holland. There is conflicting information about the fate of Kühn: the first is that he committed suicide before or during interrogation; secondly, there are reports that he was shot with Anton Winterink in Brussels on 6 July 1944. Gouwlooze and several others of his cell avoided arrest, and Gouwlooze died in Holland in September 1963.[53]

At RSHA Berlin, Kopkow was being kept regularly informed of arrests and interrogations of captured Soviet parachute agents and whether *Funkspiel* operations had begun. With this influx of Soviet agents in Germany, Holland, and Belgium, together with Kopkow's new responsibility for parachute agents across Germany and the occupied territories, a departmental restructuring of IV A2 took place. Kopkow retained full departmental charge over all these new sections:

IV A 2a	Sabotage	SS-Captain KK Büchert
IV A 2b	*Funkspiel*, Counter Intelligence	SS-Captain KK Ampletzer
IV A 2c	False papers	SS-Lieutenant KK Stempel
IV A 2d	Ship Sabotage	SS-Sergeant KS Fuhrmann

After the war, Kopkow claimed that IV A2a under Büchert and IV A2b under Ampletzer were fully fledged departments in their own right and reported directly to RSHA IV Chief Müller, and therefore they were nothing to do with him. A claim swallowed by his British interrogators whereby they could conveniently not ask him what happened to all the later captured British agents who had disappeared into German concentration camps and murdered without trial. However, it is a fact that Kopkow retained absolute control over these new sub-sections of RSHA IV A2. Parachute agents were a 'growth industry' and, for an ambitious Gestapo officer like Kopkow, it brought him to the attention of the most senior SS officers and Party hierarchy. It even gained the attention of Hitler himself judging by the number of occasions in 1942 and 1943 when Himmler discussed with Hitler not only the growing problem of parachute agents but also his agreement to *Funkspiel* operations with Moscow. It does look rather strange that, on the one hand, Himmler and Hitler discussed this aspect of Gestapo operations against their enemies, yet Field Marshal Keitel, commander-in-chief of the German armed forces did not bring similar Abwehr operations to the attention of the Führer at their daily military briefings. The Abwehr conducted their *Funkspiel* operations to Moscow seemingly on Admiral Canaris' own cognisance.

The Abwehr Brussels, together with the *Sonderkommando* Giering well before the end of 1942, had full control of the Rote Kapelle organisation in Belgium and Holland. They were now supplying Soviet military intelligence in Moscow with a continuous feed of disinformation via the controlled radio transmitters. Time now for Piepe, Giering, and the *Sonderkommando* to follow the steps of the Big Chief (Trepper/Gilbert) and the Little Chief (Sukolov-Gourevich/Kent) to Paris. For this to happen, Kopkow would have needed to discuss the move with RSHA IV Chief Müller, and he in turn would advise the BdS Paris, SS-*Standartenführer* Helmut Knochen, to provide support when the *Sonderkommando* arrived. There is no clear indication of when *Sonderkommando* Rote Kapelle arrived in Paris, but given the timetable of what happened in the last quarter of 1942, the information available suggests the view of Heinz Höhne that Piepe and Giering with his *Sonderkommando* left Brussels for Paris in early October 1942. Perrault, for example, states late summer rather than early autumn 1942.[54] One thing is clear, Piepe and Giering established their Parisian base in the former French Surete building at 11 Rue de Saussaies. Other sections of the Gestapo Paris were also located here.

Before leaving Brussels for Paris, Piepe and Giering agreed using the elderly Jewish forger Abraham Rajchman was probably their best chance of finding the Big Chief in Paris. So before their own departure from Brussels, Rajchman went ahead and began going through his old contacts, leaving messages for a meeting with him. Trepper's own forced move from Brussels to Paris, coupled with Piepe and Giering's success in arresting all his radio operators in Belgium and Holland, had left him bereft of radio contact with Moscow. Moreover, all of his agents who had fled from Brussels to Paris had been sent by Trepper southwards to Lyon and Marseille. Trepper himself apparently wanted to relocate his base in North Africa and run the espionage organisation on the European mainland from there.[55] How Trepper must have cursed the Allies who landed their armies on the beaches of French Morocco and Algeria on 8 November 1942 (Operation Torch). To make the situation worse, not just for Trepper, but for all Allied intelligence agencies working in France, Hitler ordered German armies to occupy Southern France until then controlled by the Vichy government. Abwehr and Gestapo officials now found they could chase suspects the length and breadth of France. At the request of the Abwehr, on 12 November 1942, French policemen arrested the Little Chief (KENT) together with his mistress, Margarete Barcza, at an address in Marseilles. The following day, a Gestapo squad picked them up and brought them to Paris. On arrival, Piepe and Giering decided to take them both to Brussels where KENT could be interrogated and any remaining contacts arrested, ensuring Rote Kapelle in Belgium and Holland was completely eradicated or under German control. After several days of interrogation in Brussels, KENT agreed to give 'King's Evidence', as Heinz Höhne put it, in Berlin at the forthcoming trial of the Schulze-Boysen/Harnack sector of Rote Kapelle in the Reich capital.

Back in France, Abwehr and Gestapo men from *Sonderkommando Rote Kapelle* were searching offices in Paris and Lyon in their hunt to find the Big Chief. They arrested several members of the spy-ring, but not the man himself. Returning to Paris, Giering and Piepe examined every detail found before a chance remark about a dentist recommended for the Big Chief's toothache led to his arrest. On 24 November 1942, in the afternoon, the Big Chief kept a dental appointment at 13 Rue de Rivoli in Paris where Piepe and Giering arrested him.[56] Taken back to their base in Rue des Saussaies, Trepper produced a torrent of information at interrogation, giving away name after name and information provider after information provider, in addition to military and political information being gathered by Rote Kapelle from German military and civilian administration in Paris and other places. His last two main agents, Leo Grossvogel and Henry Robinson, took more time before they too were arrested: Grossvogel at a Parisian restaurant on 16 December and Robinson at a Paris Metro station on 21 December—both deceived by messages arranging a meeting attended by the Gestapo. A few remaining second-string agents remained at liberty until January 1943, when they were picked up in the last wave of arrests.

Grossvogel had been a financier and friend of Trepper since the 1920s and communist agitator in Belgium from 1929, when he and Trepper organised a trading business in Brussels as a front for their espionage activities, known as 'Roi du Caoutchouc'. From Brussels, they conducted espionage activities in Scandinavia through Grossvogel, while Trepper conducted similar espionage operations against Britain. In 1939, when Makarov (using the alias Carlos Alamo) arrived, Grossvogel established a subsidiary company in Ostend for his cover: the Excellent Raincoat Company. All three were being paid in US dollars by Soviet military intelligence. The German invasion of Holland, Belgium, and France in the summer of 1940 caused serious problems for Trepper's organisation and business venture. Trepper and Grossvogel left Brussels for Paris together with many of their assistants; Makarov had been bombed out of Ostend and moved to Brussels with his radio transmitter, where he remained until arrested by the Abwehr. In Paris, Grossvogel established Simex, a trading company that would attract contracts from the German administration of occupied France for the supply of commercial and industrial products. Their need to remain in contact with the operation left behind in Brussels was also the cause of their eventual downfall.

Henry 'Harry' Robinson shared a common Jewish background with Grossvogel and Trepper—his had been German, theirs Polish. Born in 1897 in Frankfurt/Main of a mixed Russian-Polish marriage, he avoided German military conscription in the First World War by studying in Switzerland. Robinson could speak several languages fluently, learning Russian from his parents and German from birth and acquiring English, French, and Italian in Switzerland. Robinson became a full-time communist organiser from 1923, working with the AM-apparat (anti-military) in western Germany and communist youth movements. Together with his mistress, Klara Schabbel, he visited USSR several times in subsequent years. In 1929, he relocated to France, working for the Soviet Resident General Muraille and proving himself capable; in 1930, he found himself in charge of the BB-apparat. This section obtained reports on French factories and businesses, detailing production and problem areas whether manufacturing or personnel. Robinson also did courier work, travelling to Britain and Switzerland. By 1937, he was in charge of espionage networks in France and Britain. When Trepper made contact in 1940, Robinson was in control of a large and successful espionage network in France. How he took to Trepper taking charge of him we may never know; for his part, Trepper possibly stressed that his position with Red Army intelligence was much more important than Robinson's position in the Comintern, which the war had superseded. Robinson held a grudge against Trepper from this time. In 1942, following the arrest of his radio operators—Wenzel (in Brussels) and Hersh Sokol (in Paris)—Trepper lost his radio links with Moscow. Robinson refused to help him out with his own radio network. When Trepper was arrested by Giering and Piepe, Robinson's own arrest followed soon afterwards, so soon that it is suspected that information provided by Trepper was the reason. Like Trepper, Robinson also decided on survival and assisted *Sonderkommando Rote Kapelle* in Paris, which resulted in the arrest of those working in Robinson's network. Robinson spent six months in Paris assisting the Gestapo squad before a transfer to RSHA IV A2 in Berlin. A further round of interrogations in Berlin were based on his early communist career in Germany and training in Russia before his relocation to France. No amount of information could avoid the inevitable. Robinson and his mistress, Klara Schabbel, both appeared before the People's Court, but were sentenced to death and executed in 1943. Hersh and Miriam Sokol were taken back to Brussels for interrogation; he was shot at Breendonk SS-Camp in January 1943, and his wife, Miriam, who also operated the radio transmitter, was sent to Berlin in April 1943 where she died during Gestapo torture by Kopkow's brutal interrogators.[57]

Giering kept Kopkow at RSHA Berlin completely in the picture as regards his progress in Paris. Robinson was arrested on 21 December in Paris, and Kopkow included this detail when writing his report dated 24 December 1942, entitled 'Rote Kapelle', addressed to *Reichsführer*-SS Himmler at his Field Headquarters in Friedrichsruh, a short distance from Hitler's Wolfsschanze headquarters in East Prussia. Kopkow's report mentions both the arrest of the Big Chief (Trepper, who used the alias 'Jean Gilbert' in France) and Robinson along with sources used by Rote Kapelle in Paris to acquire secret German information.[58] What also makes this report out of the ordinary is that is signed by Kopkow himself—RSHA IV Chief Müller usually signed Kopkow's reports. Kopkow probably spent Christmas Day with his wife in Berlin; whereas workaholic Müller spent Christmas Day at the office, where Himmler telephoned him several times during the day. In Moscow, Soviet military intelligence possibly had a small celebration, little realising that their entire network in Western Europe was feeding them with entirely German-controlled information. One simple signals security breach in their radio messages had brought their entire networks crashing down, with the consequent waste of years in planning, training, enormous sums of foreign currency to fund operations abroad, and, of course, the fate of agents who were caught and those who helped them who were arrested by the Gestapo.

The last six months of 1942 were the making of Horst Kopkow. June 1942 began with the assassination and death of SS-*General* Reinhard Heydrich, an action that meant an increase in Kopkow's departmental responsibilities to include enemy parachute agents from the east and west. Kopkow had hardly got himself established with this new role when the Rote Kapelle spy-ring began to unravel. Kopkow was at the heart of the resulting investigation in Berlin, and his men further afield striking in Belgium, Holland, and France. That Kopkow's men, together with the Abwehr, could completely destroy this Soviet organisation with links to the highest levels of German military planning within six months was nothing short of a tremendous achievement. Several hundred men and women had been arrested, representing the top and middle level agents and organisers, and after trial, many had been or were due to be executed. Among those executed without a trial were the spy in the Gestapo, Willi Lehmann, and Moscow-trained German communist radio operator, Erwin Panndorf, both executed during December 1942 at Sachsenhausen camp; Albert Hössler, the other Moscow-trained German communist radio operator, was apparently executed at Plötzensee prison in Berlin on 22 December 1942, the same day and place where Schulze-Boysen and a dozen other of the Berlin group were executed. Kopkow acquired fame and acknowledgement from his superiors both in RSHA, the Nazi Party, and Hitler himself from the Rote Kapelle investigations. It has been pointed out the financial bonus Kopkow received from *Reichsmarschall* Göring; Himmler endorsed Kopkow with an award of his own, a War Service Cross 1st Class with Swords (*Kriegsverdienstkreuz I mit Schwertern*), and the investiture by Himmler took place in Berlin on 30 January 1943. On this day, RSHA personnel assembled in the conference room of RSHA headquarters in Prinz-Albrecht-Strasse, where Himmler introduced the RSHA senior staff to Heydrich's successor as Chief RSHA, SS-General Dr Ernst Kaltenbrunner. This was an appointment not universally celebrated by the RSHA Office Chiefs who had also vied for the position.

For Kopkow, 1943 began with a new remit increasing his responsibilities. A month earlier, on 3 December 1942, RSHA Chief IV Müller had contacted Himmler about an agreement from the Führer to endorse *Funkspiel* operations with Moscow. According to Himmler's diary, he had discussions with Hitler at the Wolfsschanze on 10 December and the entry 'F.Spiel with Moscow' is ticked off. Only a file copy of an official note, simply dated December 1942, has been found in archives. It came from Himmler and was addressed to Müller, and refers to Müller's approach of 3 December and quoted a RSHA IV A2 reference:

> The Führer has given permission for the *Funkspiel* with Moscow, to pass messages by necessity in cooperation with the Foreign Minister and OKW, co-ordinated information to maintain the *Funkspiel* operations, even when such information would be regarded as a treasonable offence.[59]

With such an order, Kopkow and his department moved forward across Europe with Gestapo offices in Germany and throughout German-occupied territories, establishing themselves as the centre for captured parachute agents and the absolute need to recover their codes and ciphers and control of all information for *Funkspiel* operations. After the war, Gestapo officers who had served in France and Holland stated this procedure of control of information for *Funkspiel* plays whether to Moscow or London came from RSHA Berlin—by RSHA Berlin, they meant Kopkow. What this meant is recognition by RSHA IV A2 that it could not have its officials everywhere, with their small staff numbers. Therefore, responsibilities were devolved to the regional and local offices of the Gestapo, Criminal Police, and the SD. On 19 January 1943, RSHA IV A2 (under Müller's signature) sent out a circular to all these offices with new guidelines covering the initial interrogation of captured parachute agents with an emphasis on agents from the Soviet Union being considered 'dangerous'. To obtain standard responses, a list of forty-eight questions to be asked was appended to the circular.

The forty-eight questions were designed to elicit the maximum amount of information from the agent:

1. Personal details, family, personal description, and photograph to be taken.
2. Training, location of schools, instructors, other participants, trained as saboteur or radio operator, codes, ciphering/deciphering, transmission details.
3. Equipment supplied, identity documents, money, food and ration coupons for Germany, weapons, sabotage or propaganda material.
4. In the field, how did they arrive (aircraft type, flight from, drop zone), where they met on the ground by means of signals, route taken away from the drop zone.
5. Interrogation about contacts and orders.
6. Information about the agent's own tasks: military, political or economic targets?[60]

Months later, on 20 May 1943, RSHA IV A 2 (signed Kaltenbrunner) reissued an earlier circular dated 23 September 1942 (signed Müller) to all Gestapo, Criminal Police, and SD offices. This one, entitled 'British Sabotage and Intelligence Schools' in an appendix, listed forty-five 'special schools' that existed for these purposes in England and Palestine.[61] Under RSHA-Chief's Kaltenbrunner signature, Kopkow called for any corrections or amendments to the list and requested 'results of on-going investigations involving British parachute agents'. The letter ended by reminding the addressees of the secrecy required about all captured agents. The appended list reveals a great deal of information about British SOE training schools and its personnel elicited from captured agents. Judging by the content, this information came from agents of many different nationalities dropped by Britain: Czechs, Poles, Danes, Norwegians, Dutch, Belgian, French, and one Spaniard.

At the beginning of the Rote Kapelle investigations both in Belgium and Berlin, and later in Holland and France, the Abwehr and Gestapo agreed not to publicise any details about the arrests or the trials and executions. It was vital for the development of the *Funkspiel* using the captured agents' radio transmitters that the enemy continue to accept information contained in the now controlled and correctly coded radio messages. A vigilant enemy would quickly realise something was amiss if an agent's arrest was publicised and his radio traffic continued. This agreement resulted in growing successes as Soviet intelligence agencies continued to drop their agents to support their agents now in Gestapo hands. When contact was made, arrests followed and new *Funkspiel* operations began. In recognition that RSHA Berlin could not do everything, many responsibilities devolved to its regional offices. For example, SS-*Obersturmbannführer* Adolf Eichmann was a RSHA IV departmental chief like Kopkow. Eichman's office managed the deportation of Jews from Germany to the death camps, but the responsibility in German cities and towns for getting Jews onto the deportation trains had been devolved to the Jewish Department in the local Gestapo offices. Similar arrangements were made for local Gestapo responsibilities in *Funkspiel* operations. On 5 June 1943, RSHA IV A2d (signed Kaltenbrunner) issued new orders for the treatment of captured agents, their radio equipment, and ciphers as a prerequisite to attempt a *Funkspiel* by the local Gestapo office—250 copies of this order had been sent to every office of the Security Police and Security Service across Germany and the eastern and western occupied territories. It reminded the recipients that the enemy 'since the beginning of the war had sought to place their agents in Reich territory, arriving by parachute to carry out political undermining, sabotage actions and acquire military knowledge'. Under Kaltenbrunner's signature, Kopkow requested:

> I request the [local] specialist desk-officer to familiarise himself with the guidelines and expect a quick and smooth cooperation. In future with the capture of agents and their transmitting and receiving radio sets, it will be necessary to obtain my consent when examining possibilities for establishing and beginning a radio counter play which will be successful only through personal initiative and sense of responsibility, by turning the enemy's modern means of warfare against them.[61]

It is evident from German documentation that many local Gestapo offices took up this new initiative for *Funkspiel* operations, primarily against Moscow. None more so than in Vienna, where Sanitzer proved just as clever and subtle as Kopkow in maintaining *Funkspiel* operations with Moscow and also with the new enemy, the American OSS, who landed agents in Italy and Austria and the British SOE station in Bari, Italy. In the latter stages of the war, Gestapo offices in Danzig and Swinemünde, both on the Baltic coast, were sending disinformation to the advancing Soviet armies.

Throughout 1943, Soviet-trained German agents continued to be dropped by the Soviet air force in East Prussia and in Poland. The Royal Air Force flying out of Britain dropped Soviet-trained agents in Germany and France. From available information, it can be established the Soviets dropped nine agents to work in Germany (only one appears to have survived the war) and seven agents to work in Austria (of which three survived). The RAF dropped ten Pickaxe agents on behalf of the NKVD during 1943: three in Germany (none survived), three in Austria (two survived), and four in France (no information on their survival). These are agents who were recorded, others were possibly dropped and captured and their records lost; a high percentage of Gestapo records were burned in 1945 by design, others destroyed by air-raid damage. Whereas the agents dropped in 1942 and captured had clear aims of working for Rote Kapelle, none of the known agents dropped between 1943 and 1945 had such aims. Does this mean the Soviets had realised their organisation in Western Europe had become blown and now a liability so cast them adrift? Pavel Sudoplatov, 'deputy director of the NKVD Foreign Department' from March 1939 and responsible for 'planting of illegals in Western Europe', states 'the performance of the Red Orchestra was viewed with suspicion in Moscow' despite their 'heroic performance in Germany, France, and Switzerland'. He then condemns their espionage activities 'because they produced no hard documentary evidence, only intercepted oral information' and 'its supply of information during the war was secondary for us'.[62] Sudoplatov does make an interesting point about Gurevich (KENT) following his capture by the Gestapo in Marseille on 12 November 1942. During one of his Gestapo-controlled radio transmissions to Moscow, Gurevich inserted information that he was under control. Moscow directed him 'in code to continue to play the radio game'. According to Sudoplatov, Moscow placed more faith in the information coming from their Swiss spy-ring ('Rote Drei'), but they too simply sent radio messages, there was no documentation to exchange. Communist resistance workers in Berlin-Pankow during spring 1943 were providing 'aid to a Soviet girl parachutist' showing at least one safe house known to Moscow was unknown to the Gestapo.[63]

Is this disinformation about Rote Kapelle from Sudoplatov? If their information was of such dubious quality, why would Soviet Intelligence have trained and equipped five radio operators then despatched them to the capital city of the enemy with the task of ensuring Moscow received German secret military and political plans even faster? Was Sudoplatov ensuring western intelligence agencies had only the wartime version of Rote Kapelle to think about, rather than the remaining Rote Kapelle agents who stayed in the west and continued spying for the Soviets? Kopkow told Sanitzer before the end of the war that the Gestapo stopped their Rote Kapelle investigations far too early as they certainly left many spies in place.[64] One reason why Kopkow was actively recruited by MI6 after the war may well have been his knowledge of where to look for such remaining agents.

With the major Rote Kapelle investigations in Berlin now at an end, Kopkow could use the expertise he so recently acquired from interrogating captured parachute agents dropped by the Russians. On 19 January 1943, RSHA IV A2 (signed by Müller) issued an instruction leaflet on the 'Interrogation of Parachute Agents' and sent to Gestapo offices throughout Germany and the occupied territories. It has forty-eight questions with suggestions to prompt accurate answers and additional information. Interestingly, the last question seeks information as to the agent's primary task: military, political, or economic. As the Soviet-trained agents captured in Germany by various Gestapo offices during 1942 had been interrogated differently, the issue of this instruction leaflet shows how specific information needed to acquire through interrogation of captured agents—especially who they were, where they were captured, what were their aims and tasks, where had they been trained, and who had they known there. Copies of these interrogations were to be sent to RSHA IV A2, Berlin, who would provide any background information needed. The letter accompanying the instruction leaflet ended by stating: 'The immediate capture and reporting to RSHA IV A2 of parachute agents in occupied Russian territories cannot be over-emphasized, the special agents are dangerous'. These instructions were developed further on 10 February 1943, when RSHA IV A2 (and signed by the new RSHA Chief Dr Kaltenbrunner) circulated a set of printed forms to report individual cases of sabotage and return them to RSHA IV A2.[65] The circulation of these new instructions together with a copy of the prepared report forms was wide; all Gestapo offices and every BdS and KdS offices from Reval in Estonia to Bordeax in France and the four *Einsatzgruppen* murder squads in Russia received copies. Although the primary task of RSHA IV A2 had changed in 1942 with the Rote Kapelle investigations, it retained strong links to investigating sabotage. In Russia, where sabotage became a daily occurrence in the rear areas, the Abwehr and Gestapo were working hand in glove to investigate and arrest saboteurs and partisans. No mercy was shown to those arrested. They too disappeared into mass graves along with the indiscriminate killing of Russian Jewish men, women, and children. One of the four SS death squads, *Einsatzgruppe* D, travelled from the Romanian border, across southern Ukraine, then one arm moved into the Crimea and a second moved along the north coast of the Sea of Azov as far as Taganrog (2,100 km/1,350 miles from Berlin). The numbers of partisans and others simply described as 'Communists' executed in the sector behind German lines during *Einsatzgruppe* D operations are staggering. Between June and December 1941, *Einsatzgruppe* D reported 221 partisans, 672 communists, and two agents executed; between January and June 1942, it reported 603 partisans, 1,755 communists, and 1,579 persons described as looters, saboteurs, and asocial executed; in addition, fourteen parachute agents were reported executed and eighty taken prisoner—probably also executed. These numbers are derived from the daily reports of the *Einsatzgruppen* distributed by RSHA to departmental chiefs such as Kopkow. In such a report dated 8 April 1942, *Einsatzgruppe* D report its total killings as 91,678 persons. It would be obtuse to believe that Kopkow knew nothing about the 'Final Solution of the Jewish Question' being practised in just one area. The three other *Einsatzgruppen* to the north were reporting killing much larger numbers of partisans, communists, saboteurs, and others opposed to the Nazi occupation forces—quite apart from the several hundred thousands of Jews reported executed. SS officers, such as Kopkow, at their desks in Berlin, when they learned of such actions, no doubt became heartless and hardened to the murder of innocents. Fortunately for Kopkow, he avoided a posting to the *Einsatzgruppen*, and when the time came for him to step up as a 'desk murderer', it was done without wartime qualms; post-war, he blamed others.

RSHA IV A2 became the focal point for reports on sabotage and parachute agents from all corners of Germany and the occupied territories. Information from Russia was interesting to a point, showing patterns of increase in Soviet espionage and sabotage tactics, but due to the distances involved, there was little for Kopkow to do about it. His time continued to be taken up with happenings in Paris where Giering then Pannwitz and the Abwehr were still interrogating the Big Chief, Leopold Trepper. Even today, Trepper is a conundrum. Was he a double agent, a triple agent? Did Moscow and Trepper have a prepared plan in the event of his capture? Apparently, under no pressure during interrogation, he willingly revealed his own organisation and agents, but why did he reveal the radio communications to Moscow of the French Communist Party? After Robinson's refusal, Trepper had been forced to contact the French communists to transmit his coded messages to Moscow after setting up in Paris, following the arrests in Brussels. However, the French communists were a lot more distrustful of any contacts from Trepper after his arrest in November 1942. Gestapo infiltration of the French Communist Party therefore took much longer and under Pannwitz's command of the *Sonderkommando*. Karl Giering had found increasing quantities of alcohol no longer numbed the pain of his advancing cancer. He finally passed the reins to the newly arrived Pannwitz in the summer of 1943, and retired to a sanatorium in Germany where he finally succumbed soon after the war had ended. Pannwitz had to create his own glory in Paris, and Trepper's escape on 13 September 1943 did not help especially when he had to inform RSHA IV Chief Müller. They expected Moscow to be informed of Trepper's escape, who would break off the *Funkspiel* games from France that had been so successful at least in German eyes. Despite a nationwide manhunt for Trepper, the Gestapo never found him. He turned up in Paris after the liberation and the Russian Mission repatriated him to Moscow and Lubyanka Prison.[66]

Soviet-trained German communists continued to be dropped into Germany by the Soviet air force in the east, and the Royal Air Force in the west. One problem the Soviets could not train out of their agents was homesickness. Many had been absent from Germany for years and could not face returning without making contact or visiting their families. This became the downfall of many. One of the first such agents dropped in 1943, a German prisoner of war, had been turned by his Soviet captors and agreed to be trained as an agent. Having been trained as a radio operator, his target area was Danzig on the Baltic coast and his task to radio ship movements in the harbour. In the uniform of army sergeant (*Feldwebel*) and wearing an Iron Cross First Class, he attempted a visit to his family in western Germany, where he was arrested. Taken back to Danzig, the local Abwehr successfully used the man in a *Funkspiel* operation to send deception material. After several weeks, the Russians sent another agent to provide money. This second agent dropped and arrested in August 1943 turned out to be an Austrian Jew. At this juncture, Abwehr Danzig informed Gestapo Danzig who took over the case.[67]

Two more trained German agents were dropped in Poland, four days apart, during March 1943. The first, Josef Weingart, arrived in Berlin having taken an army leave train from Lublin and travelled via Warsaw. The second, Franz Zielasko, made his way via Warsaw and Berlin to Dortmund to begin organising resistance among traditional Ruhr coal mining communities. Weingart (born 1903) had been trained as a radio operator by the German Navy in the 1920s before embarking on a political career in the German Communist Party, finally leaving for the Soviet Union in 1929 and working as a radio mechanic in Moscow. In 1941, he began attending a Comintern special school for intelligence training to prepare him for his later deployment as a parachute agent; Zielasko was older (born 1896) and was a coal miner in the Ruhr when the First World War broke out, and he was called-up for military service in 1916. A late convert to communism, it was 1927 when Zielasko joined the party and 1932 when he left Germany for the Soviet Union. After a short period as a miner, he began attending military schools, and in 1936, he was sent to Spain where he joined the International Brigade (Edgar-André Battalion); he returned to the Soviet Union in 1939, after having acquired a great deal of intelligence gathering knowledge and how to have men follow you. Zielasko was a seasoned military officer with battle experience when he parachuted into Poland in March 1943.

Josef Weingart had been trained in Moscow by the Central Committee of the German Communist Party to act, once in Germany, as their liaison man (*Beauftragter*). Weingart made contact with an old communist couple, Bruno and Maria Stein, in Berlin, who gave him food and lodging. Once he began visiting the illegal communist organisations in Berlin and assessing anti-Nazi resistance, Gestapo informers passed on news of his whereabouts. Weingart was arrested on 23 April 1943, barely a month after his parachute drop; the Steins and some of their relatives were arrested on 7 May 1943.

Weingart saved himself by throwing in his lot with the Gestapo and became one of their informers; his later fate is unknown.[68] The Steins, who appeared before the People's Court in Berlin charged with treason and undermining the military, were convicted and sentenced to death; Bruno and Marie Stein, with three relatives, were all executed in 1944. Franz Zielasko came from sterner stuff than Weingart. Having arrived at Dortmund in the Ruhr coal mining region, he set about establishing communist resistance among the miners. Between April and July 1943, he managed to establish a resistance group of about forty members. Gestapo informers were the bane of communist groups across Germany, and it was no different in the Ruhr region than Berlin. On 7 August 1943, Zielasko and about forty members of his group were arrested by the Gestapo, having been reported by an informer. Kopkow sent his interrogators to Gladbeck prison in Recklinghausen where Zielasko was being detained and began the interrogation. Despite regular torture sessions, Zielasko held out for a week and died under torture on 18 August 1943.[69] His forty followers that were also arrested faced the People's Court; seventeen were executed and the rest were given long prison sentences. To help Zielasko with radio contact, Moscow dropped a radio operator, Elvira Eisenschneider, in eastern Germany, probably East Prussia, during the summer of 1943. She survived the Gestapo roundups in the Ruhr region only to be found by radio detection measures when using her radio transmitter. She was arrested on 23 February 1944. It is reported that Eisenschneider was shot in a concentration camp on 6 April 1944, and the usual camp for captured women agents was Ravensbrück.[70]

Two more groups of Soviet Pickaxe agents were dropped by the Royal Air Force in February 1943: operations 'Tonic' near Freiburg and 'Sodawater' near Vienna.[71] The Freiburg group consisted of Else Noffke (who used the aliases Elena Nikitina and Kersti Poska) and Georg Tietze (alias Henrik Gorelov, Otto Ulnoti, and Ernst Beutge). Noffke was the radio operator and was interested in Cologne and Berlin; Tietze had more interest in the Mannesmann factories in Stuttgart. To the British, Noffke looked to be leader of the group and 'appeared to exude an ineffable sex appeal', whereas the older Tietze (forty-five years old) is noted as a 'funny quiet old man … [who] produced quite a collection of seemingly funny stories'. The second couple, whose target area was Vienna, were Emilie Boretzky (alias Emilya Novikova and Anna Under) who was the radio operator and Hermann Köhler (alias Pyotr Koltsov and Juri Kruus). The thirty-five-year-old '*Hausfrau*' Boretzky had 'great technical knowledge' of radio mechanics coupled with poor clarity of mind and never able to make her mind up. Whereas, the thirty-eight-year-old Köhler possessed a typical Viennese humour but little communist fervour. After several false starts, the RAF finally managed to drop the two groups on the same night using different aircraft. While the RAF was successful, the four agents were not. One group, captured by the Gestapo as they landed, gave away details of the second group dropped several hundred miles away. During the night of 24–25

February 1943, Georg Tietze and Elsa Noffke were dropped in a wooded area a few miles north of Freiburg in Breisgau in south-west Germany. Once on the ground, the two could not find their extra packages containing Noffke's two British radio sets and their clothing. A local farmer found their packages the next day and handed them into the police, who informed the Gestapo and a manhunt began. Tietze and Noffke had already made their way to their safe house in Freiburg and, through contacts with the 'Rote Drei' network in nearby Switzerland, informed Moscow of the loss of their radio sets. Their difficulties would soon get worse as Moscow informed a Gestapo-controlled agent in Berlin to prepare a radio set for Noffke. Since October 1942, a Gestapo *Funkspiel* from Berlin using Heinz Koenen's radio ciphers had played Moscow and now Moscow informed Koenen the safe house address and contact in Freiburg. However, the address had become known to Gestapo Freiburg from a different direction: Vienna.

The same night as Tietze and Noffke were dropped near Freiburg, another RAF plane dropped the second team at Wimpassing south of Vienna and was also expected by the Gestapo. Hermann Köhler and Emilie Boretzky were expected because of another Gestapo *Funkspiel* from Gestapo Vienna to Moscow using Anton Börner's ciphers. Moscow gave Börner instructions to prepare for the arrival of new agents. Johann Sanitzer had a group of his Gestapo men ready to arrest the parachutists as they landed and seize their radio set and ciphers. After their capture, in typical Gestapo fashion, there were two choices for Köhler and Boretzky: help in the *Funkspiel* and you will live, do not and you will be executed. Boretzly's radio ciphers became Gestapo Vienna's *Funkspiel Burgenland* operation. It was the information given by Köhler and Boretzky under interrogation by Gestapo Vienna about Tietze and Noffke that led to their arrest in Freiburg during April 1943. When Noffke saw the German police at the door of the safe house, she attempted suicide by swallowing rather than chewing her cyanide capsule. Rushed to a local hospital, her stomach was pumped removing the poison capsule and Noffke lived to die another day.[72]

Gestapo Freiburg came under the regional Gestapo office at Karlsruhe where Tietze and a recovered Noffke were soon transferred there for interrogation. Interviewed twice after the war about these two agents, Gestapo officer Walter Herberg from Karlsruhe first stated (in May 1946): 'I worked on the case of Nofke [*sic.*] and Beutge [*sic.*]. Beutge was handed over shortly after his arrest to the RSHA Berlin to *Sturmbannfuehrer* Kopkow. I know that he was later condemned to death and executed in Sachsenhausen'. In a second interrogation from August 1946, Herberg stated:

> [Their] case was finally referred to Berlin and they were taken up to Berlin, [RSHA] Amt IV, K.R. Kopkow should deal with all cases of parachutists.... These two persons had been taken to his office and delivered to him personally. Fetzner and Boschert took them up. Novke had

> some 50,000 marks with her. She said she had been given this money in Moscow, in August 1942…

The next part of Herberg's statement revealed:

> She [Noffke] had been told that her true mission would only begin when the British and American forces had invaded Germany. In the meantime she was simply to establish herself in Germany and await instructions. After the arrival of the Allies she was to form an intelligence mission for the Russians.[73]

In Britain, Noffke's companion, Tietze, had studied the Stuttgart industrial area and it was assumed that this was his intelligence gathering area. Herberg gave a different view of Tietze's task in Germany: '[His] mission was to study the air defence of Berlin, night fighter stations, flak positions, etc., and he was to report back by means of Novke's wireless'. After being taken up to Kopkow's office, Noffke was taken to the concentration camp for women at Ravensbrück, north of Berlin. The last news of Else Noffke came from a British SOE agent, Odette Sansom, known there as Odette Churchill after being arrested in France with Peter Churchill; their initial German captors believed that the pair were married and that Peter was related to Prime Minister Winston Churchill. In fact, they were neither married nor was Peter related to the British Prime Minister. However, going along with the German assumption saved their lives. Following her release from Ravensbrück in April 1945, Odette Sansom informed her British interrogators that she and Else Noffke, then using the alias Helene Poska, had become friends at the camp. On 10 January 1945, Poska told Sansom that she was being released and going to Berlin.[74] Poska was never seen again. What is more likely is that during the night of 10–11 January 1945, Poska was shot in the 'shooting alley' at Ravensbrück camp and her body immediately burned in the nearby crematorium. Other Allied agents would meet a similar fate at this spot over the next few weeks.

The usefulness of the two men, Tietze and Köhler, to the Gestapo became irrelevant once their radio ciphers being used for *Funkspiel* operations with Moscow began and continued satisfactorily. Tietze was executed at Sachsenhausen concentration camp, probably in 1943; Köhler survived at Mauthausen camp until March 1945, when local *Gauleiter* Eisgruber ordered his execution.[75]

More agents were dropped from Soviet planes in April and June 1943, all destined for Austria. Ernst Kernmeyer (using the alias Ernst Dorfegger) dropped in Slovakia with his radio set and made his way to Vienna. Sanitzer arrested him and used his radio ciphers for *Funkspiel Alpenrose* and, as a result, apparently uncovered Soviet agents already in positions in Austria. In April 1945, Sanitzer released Kernmeyer, who turned himself in to the

Russian Army. Two Viennese communists, Josef Angermann and his radio operator, Georg Kennerknecht, arrived back in Vienna in June 1943 wearing Wehrmacht uniforms. Their tasks included sabotage and assassinating senior government officials. They survived until January 1944, when they were arrested by Sanitzer in Vienna. Angermann committed suicide on arrest and Kennerknecht's radio ciphers were used for *Funkspiel Felixdorf*. It did not take long for his usefulness to run its course, then Sanitzer had him executed.[76]

A party of three Austrian Communists, a man and two women, were dropped by the Soviets south of Warsaw on 27 June 1943 with orders to make for Vienna. Before setting off from the drop zone, the two women, Hildegard Mraz and Louise Soucek, buried the radio sets they had brought with them. Arriving in Vienna during July, the women began searching for radio components from which they assembled a new radio transmitter and made contact with Moscow. Their leader, Gregor Kersche, began steps to 'organise the entire underground communist leadership' in readiness for future action when the time came. Time ran out for Kersche on 3 January 1944, when he was arrested by the Gestapo. Under torture, Kersche revealed where the two women were staying and they were arrested the following day. Their radio ciphers were used for *Funkspiel Landwurm*, conducted until 5 April 1945 when Sanitzer released all three of them in Vienna. Soon after, all three reported themselves to the Soviet authorities in Vienna, and they were arrested and sent to Moscow for trial. They were all given prison sentences and Mraz died in a Soviet Gulag.[77]

On 12 May 1943, the RAF dropped another Pickaxe agent (Operation Ararat) on behalf of the NKVD. This was Ignace Fallière (alias Igor Feldmann), who appeared to be about twenty years old and Parisian; he was dropped in wooded areas between Mantes and Vetheuil, north-west of Paris. He was carrying a radio transmitter probably to assist the already arrested Rote Kapelle network. British intelligence officers who arranged the drop did not believe he would last long, and later no trace was ever found of him.[78] The last Pickaxe agents to be dropped in France, Operation Orange, took place on 14–15 September 1943. They had a number of aliases and were described as Basque, Spanish, or French Spanish. Their drop zone was east of Avignon, in the Malemort-au-Comtat/Murs district. British intelligence believed their intention was to support the Rote Kapelle network in France, a network now under Gestapo control. The fate of these three men is unknown.[79] Later that year, during the night of 5–6 November 1943, the RAF dropped another Pickaxe agent (Operation Rigi) in Germany, between Schleiden and Schmidtheim, towards the border with Luxemburg. Otto Bach (alias Ivan M. Botsevich)—described as a 'very tough and obviously discreet' working class German—was apparently required in Holland or Belgium to support two other Pickaxe agents dropped earlier, not knowing that both had already been arrested by the Gestapo. His fate, like Fallière in France, is unknown, but Bach was believed to have been captured and executed.[80]

The last known Soviet-trained German agents dropped in 1943 by the Soviet air force, and perhaps the most famous, were dropped in Poland during the night of 7–8 October 1943. Käthe (Katja) Niederkirchner and Theo Winter were dropped by arrangement into an area controlled by a Polish Communist partisan group. Their radio traffic with Moscow was already being intercepted by Bletchley Park and decrypted. In decrypted messages dated 8 and 31 October, Niederkirchner is called 'Katie', 'Keti', and 'Kitty' (such are the vagaries of decryption), and the partisan group had the job of ensuring her safe journey to Berlin.[81] They also assisted Winter, who travelled separately with his radio set. Niederkirchner travelled alone on the Warsaw–Berlin train, and at Kutno, near Lodz, an examination of her travel and identity documents revealed shortcomings that resulted in her arrest. On 3 November 1943, the Polish Communist group informed Moscow of her arrest. There is still some doubt about where Winter was arrested; there are reports that the arrest took place like Niederkirchner on a train heading for Berlin, or in Berlin itself.

Born in 1909 in Berlin to a politically active working family, the teenage Käthe Niederkirchner became active in the communist youth movement, joining the German Communist Party in 1929. Her communist activities increased to giving speeches and handing out leaflets. Her arrest by the Nazis in March 1933 spurred her to leave Germany after her release. Both her parents had already left for Moscow and Käthe followed them. The execution of her brother by the NKVD in the 1938 purges does not appear to have dimmed her politics, and she gave regular talks on Radio Moscow broadcasts transmitted to Germany. After the German invasion of the Soviet Union in June 1941, the Soviets began training German Communists in underground and espionage work for future deployment. Although Käthe Niederkirchner did not know it at the time, Kopkow's department had already listed her for arrest in the 'black book' (with an incorrect date of birth) issued to the SS-*Einsatzgruppen* for use in Soviet Russia. Her arrest on the Warsaw–Berlin train must have been a severe blow for Soviet intelligence and their lack of accurate knowledge about the situation in Nazi Germany, whether illegal communist groups existed and an assessment of their future capabilities. After her arrest and handover to the Gestapo, they brought Niederkirchner to Warsaw and placed her in a prison. Interrogations began and it is said she refused to budge from the story in her identity documents. After a reported four months of interrogation in Warsaw—possibly in March 1944—Niederkirchner was transferred to Berlin. It is believed that torture took place, but she refused to say anything under such severe duress.

There can be no doubt that both Niederkirchner and Winter, when brought to Berlin for interrogation in 1944, were the responsibility of Kopkow's department. The torture also carried out by Kopkow's interrogators meant it came under his managerial responsibility. Kopkow had Winter sent to Sachsenhausen camp in spring 1944; in autumn 1944, Winter was brought back to Berlin and shot, although it is not known by whom or where. He has a gravestone in the central cemetery of Berlin-Friedrichsfelde. After the conclusion of her interrogations, Niederkirchner arrived at Ravensbrück camp on 31 May 1944 'without details' and was recorded as Prisoner No. 40569. Assigned to Block 3, where other German Communist prisoners were quartered (although celebrated as a parachutist from Moscow), she still had to work like the other prisoners; she worked in the textile unit where German Army uniforms were repaired. A decision about her fate eventually came from RSHA Berlin, and on 18 September 1944, Niederkirchner was transferred to one of the cells in the Bunker prison building. During the night of 27–28 September, Niederkirchner was brought to the 'shooting gallery' together with four or five Polish female prisoners and shot in the back of the head by SS-Sergeant Arthur Conrad. All the bodies were burned in the nearby camp crematorium.[82] In 1951, the East German authorities, with a touch of irony, renamed Prinz-Albrecht-Strasse, where Gestapo headquarters had once stood, as Niederkirchnerstrasse.

The year 1943 saw a shift in emphasis for the Soviet parachute agents. With minor exceptions, they were no longer aimed at supporting Rote Kapelle operations. Did this mean Soviet intelligence agencies had received so many warnings about Gestapo control of the organisation in Western Europe—not just in Germany—that it had now been written off? Did they play the *Funkspiel* radio games in the hope that occasional nuggets of information would be transmitted to Moscow and, at the same time, save the lives of captured agents? In a wartime situation, there could be no salvation for captured agents, especially ones from the 'philosophical war' between opposing dictatorships: Nazism and communism. From this changing emphasis in 1943, it can be concluded that Moscow had written-off the Rote Kapelle network. Agents would now start from scratch, which can be seen in the aims of agents sent to Germany, such as Käthe Niederkirchner and Theo Winter, who would have arrived in Berlin in late October 1943 had they not been arrested. Their tasks were to search out any existing illegal communist organisations and establish whether any form of resistance and presumably sabotage could be undertaken. Unfortunately, Soviet intelligence agencies consistently misunderstood what had happened on the ground in Germany in regard to communism and communists. The Gestapo across Germany had rooted out local communist branches, closed its offices, and riddled what remained with informants—some of whom were communists released from concentration camps who did not want to go back into the camps. Where communists were not arrested, they had been called up to the army like any other citizen. Dozens sent to the Eastern Front deserted. The German military defeats in Africa (El Alamein) and at Stalingrad not only undermined German military capabilities, but caused a reassessment of them. After a speech in Berlin by Joseph Goebbels on 18 February 1943, in which he called for a 'Total War', Nazi Germany had ramped up German public opinion to face serious dangers ahead if Germany and Europe as a whole were to survive, should the war be prolonged and a German victory take longer to achieve. Naturally, the principal enemy behind Goebbels's speech was the Soviet Union and 'Bolshevism'. Two years and two months before Soviet armies entered Berlin, Goebbels could already see the writing on the wall, despite ending his Berlin speech with a call to arms: 'Now, people rise up, and let the storm break loose!' Against this background, increasing the age range for military call-up began, those in their fifties and seventeen-year-olds now found themselves drafted. Factory manpower changed as German workers were drafted into the military and their place taken by concentration camp prisoners as slave labour with no pay and poor food. Communists and non-communists alike were not immune from this process. Therefore, when agents came calling to find a safe house, they found in many cases no one at home to help them.

Naturally, Soviet intelligence agencies took little notice of Goebbels or his speech as they increased the infiltration of agents into Germany and Austria throughout 1944. During the first quarter of 1944, the British RAF dropped the last Soviet Pickaxe agents in Austria, Germany, and France. They completed the Austrian and German missions in a matter of days. The first on 4 January, a singleton agent with a radio set, Siegfried Schmidt, was dropped near the border with Luxemburg between Schmidtheim and Stadtkyll. He was described as a pleasant working class German 'quite unmoved at the prospect of his task' of acquiring information about the military situation in the Rhine-Ruhr region. Unfortunately, Schmidt did not get that far as the local Gestapo office in Trier arrested him soon after his arrival. Like Otto Bach, who had been similarly dropped in the same area just two months previously, he also had been arrested by Gestapo Trier. The Gestapo undertook *Funkspiel* operations with both their radio sets. What eventually happened to Bach and Schmidt is unknown, but they are believed to have been executed.[83]

The next two-man teams, dropped into Austria during the night of 6–7 January 1944 and into Germany the following night, had similar disastrous results. The Austrian group of Albert Huttary and Josef Zettler (radio operator) did not appear to get on well together even when waiting in Britain for a suitable flying date. There is also some confusion about what happened to them after they were dropped near St Pölten, to the west of Vienna. One account has them arrested by the Gestapo on landing, but Johann Sanitzer, the Gestapo officer in Vienna responsible for parachute agents, states he did not arrest them until 31 March 1944 'as a result of trying to find an apartment with AC [electrical] power supply'. According to Sanitzer, their primary task on behalf of the NKVD was to collect military intelligence about the Luftwaffe airfield at Munchendorf-Gross Wien. Their radio ciphers were used for Gestapo *Funkspiel Rote Mauer* (transmitting from Vienna), which continued until April 1945. Huttary was kept in Vienna and Zettler was sent to the fortress prison at Theresienstadt in Bohemia (Czechoslovakia). Both survived the war, with Huttary in Austria and Zettler in East Germany, where he died in 1974.[84]

The last pairing of Eugen Nesper (a radio operator) and Hermann Kramer arrived in London on 13 November 1943 by sea from the Soviet Union. Both had a number of different aliases. According to British intelligence, Nesper 'had no particular personality, but Schmidt [Kramer] had the bearing of a German officer of the Prussian type, with good manners and a sense of security'. They were dropped in southern Germany between Reutlingen and Hechingen during the night of 7–8 January 1944. Their parachute descent came under observation and, on landing, shots were fired at them, resulting in the wounding of Kramer; although wounded, he covered Nesper's escape. Nesper reached Stuttgart, about 25 miles (40 km) from the drop zone, where he had communist friends known before the war. Without his luggage and radio set, Nesper was adrift in the Nazi sea and a huge Gestapo search was started to find him. Nesper made contact at the safe house of the Schlotterbeck brothers whose address he had been given in Moscow. He had known the Schlotterbecks in Stuttgart before the war so he felt safe. The Stuttgart Gestapo, with a long memory based on the registry files and index cards, began combing through people perhaps known to Nesper and it was only a matter of time before his arrest. The Stuttgart Gestapo chief SS-*Obersturmbannführer* (Lt-Col.) Friedrich Mussgay had been in Stuttgart since the Nazi seizure of power in 1933, a known 'communist hunter' who treated Nesper like an old friend come to visit. Mussgay knew Nesper from the 1930s, when he had been one of the Gestapo informers betraying his communist friends. In spite of Nesper's sojourn and agent training in the Soviet Union, after he had deserted from the German Army on the Eastern Front, Mussgay still had a use for him. He wanted to use him as a Gestapo informer again, and to this end, he denied requests from RSHA Berlin, from Kopkow, and from the army who wanted to prosecute him for desertion. There are also reports that Nesper, having been reunited with his radio ciphers after the shootout at the drop zone, began a Gestapo *Funkspiel* with Moscow that did not last long. Therefore, Mussgay put Nesper back on the Stuttgart streets and first wanted all those who helped the Schlotterbeck communist cell. Nesper would report back via Gestapo department IV N, a department used throughout all Gestapo offices to control their network of informers. In Stuttgart, IV N also had its own anonymous office where informers could report. Nesper duped the Schlotterbecks into providing him with information on the Stuttgart armaments industry, but also finding out who supplied the information to them. On 10 June 1944, Nesper disappeared from Stuttgart and made his way to the Swiss border near Schaffhausen where he shot a German border policeman who tried to stop him getting over the border. Mussgay had to eat humble pie with RSHA over Nesper's escape and launched a savage series of arrests of communists in Stuttgart, all those connected to the Schlotterbecks. Ten of those arrested, including Schlotterbeck family members, both men and women, were taken to Dachau camp on 29 December 1944 and all shot the following morning.

Hermann Schlotterbeck, one of the brothers, survived until 18 April 1945 in Riedlingen prison before he too was shot.

A report came to the Foreign Office in London during June 1944:

> It was reported that Swiss Police were holding a man giving the name of Nagel, and other details which identified him as being Schmidt [a mistake for Nesper].... He said that he and his companion had been captured by the Gestapo some time after landing and had been forced to transmit false information to Russia. He requested an interview with some member of the British Legation in Berne, but in view of the danger of his being also a German agent, it was decided to disassociate ourselves entirely from the affair.[85]

Nesper remained in a Swiss police cell until the end of the war, when he was repatriated to Germany. He appeared before a Stuttgart denazification court on 14 July 1948, convicted as a 'main culprit' for his Gestapo informer days, and sentenced to ten years' internment. He next appeared before a civil court in Konstanz where he was charged with the murder of the border policeman in 1944; he was convicted on 19 July 1950 and sentenced to three years' imprisonment.[86]

Of the unfortunately wounded partner of Nesper, Hermann Kramer, it is believed he survived his wounds, only to be executed at Sachsenhausen concentration camp.

The last Pickaxe agents were dropped in France by the RAF and they, at least, avoided the Gestapo. Two agents, Antoine Laurier and Simon Stephan, were dropped on 5 February 1944 in the Lyon region. They are described as French students and were trained to work for the NKVD. It seems they did not make radio contact with Moscow until November 1944, when their radio traffic was intercepted and decrypted at Bletchley Park. They were working for Guyot, the French communist dropped by the RAF in 1943, and their messages were 'extracts from the local press on political and economic conditions in France', which, by this time, had been almost liberated by the Allies. Their last message was sent on 30 June 1945.[87] The last agent to be dropped had the aliases S. V. Rozov and Simon Valerien Rosière—his real identity was never disclosed. He was dropped with his radio set on 5 March 1944 near Vlermont de l'Herault in southern France. He began transmitting to Moscow on 3 June 1944 and he too had his radio traffic intercepted and decrypted at Bletchley Park. The mainly political content of his messages reported on how the French populace viewed the second front (i.e. the Normandy landings of 6 June 1944). Before long, Moscow asked whether he could make contact with Spanish communists and arranging a meeting for him with Guyot in Lyon; this occurred in October 1944. His last transmission on 23 March 1945 was followed by Moscow continuing to make radio contact until they stopped on 9 August 1945.[88]

In July 1944, another event took centre stage for Nazi Germany when quite literally a bomb went off. On 20 July 1944, during the midday military briefing at Führer headquarters in East Prussia, Wolfsschanze, a bomb left under the conference table exploded. It killed two senior military officers and a stenographer, plus a dozen others, including the Führer himself, were wounded to various degrees. It quickly became apparent that Colonel Claus von Stauffenberg, who had left the meeting and departed the area by aircraft for Berlin, was the main culprit; in Berlin, a coup against the Hitler regime began. Stauffenberg had announced Hitler's death to the plotters in the highest positions in Berlin's military circles, who put Operation *Walküre* (Valkyrie) into operation across Germany. Unfortunately a radio broadcast to the German people by Hitler later that night brought the coup to a halt, despite efforts by the main plotters to keep it going. Hitler told the radio audience that 'a very small clique of ambitious, wicked, and stupidly criminal officers forged a plot to eliminate [him] and, along with [him], virtually the entire leadership of the Wehrmacht'.

As soon as news reached RSHA Berlin, there was a delay. Where was *Reichsführer*-SS Himmler to give them directions? Historians have argued that Himmler's absence from Berlin that day must mean he knew of the plot and was waiting to see what would happen before reappearing. In fact, Himmler's absence was due to a more mundane but pressing appointment on 20 July 1944. Gudrun Potthast, Himmler's mistress, had given birth on 3 June 1944 to their second child, a daughter, at the SS clinic in Hohenlychen, north of Berlin. Himmler needed to appear before the Registrar of Births in Lychen to acknowledge in person that he was the child's father.[89] That afternoon, having heard that there had been explosion at Führer headquarters, Himmler immediately made for Berlin. In the meantime, RSHA IV Chief Müller, at the direction of Himmler, sent SS-*Oberführer* Humbert Achamer Pifrader over to Berlin military headquarters, the Bendlerblock, to arrest Stauffenberg. Arriving at 5 p.m., Pifrader found himself arrested by the plotters. Bendlerblock became a hive of activity as the plotters endeavoured to have military commanders near and far accept Hitler was dead and the army now in charge. Before midnight in the Bendlerblock, disloyal senior military commanders decided the attempted putsch was over and tried to cover their own involvement by shooting the main plotters. General Olbricht, Stauffenberg, and his aides, Mertz and Haeften, were shot by firing squad in the courtyard on orders of General Fromm—another plotter trying to save himself. The leading army General Ludwig Beck, who had worked on the plot with Stauffenberg, was shot out of hand on Fromm's orders before the executions in the courtyard.[90]

The following day, RSHA began taking control of the situation and set up a new enquiry team, *Sonderkommission 20.Juli*, under SS-*Obersturmbannführer* Georg Kiessel. It consisted of eleven groups responsible for different elements of those involved in the attempted coup against the regime. SS-*Sturmbannführer*

Kriminalrat Horst Kopkow was head of Group 1—Crime Scene. The crime was classified as 'sabotage' and, as such, came under Kopkow's departmental remit. Kopkow stated:

> As sabotage specialist I was appointed to lead the examination of the attempted attack on the Führer. I had orders to determine the exact facts and in particular clarify the origin of the explosive device. I was sent the same day with a staff of assistants, including officials of the Forensic Institute of the Kripo to Wolfsschanze in East Prussia, and provide detailed report of the incident.[91]

Himmler left by plane on 21 July 1944 for Hitler's headquarters accompanied by SS-*Sturmbannführer* Horst Kopkow, who was acting as 'scene of crime officer'. In June 1945, not even a year after these events, Kopkow could not recall more of his work at Wolfsschanze; in the same document, he was able to name twenty-eight individuals involved in the plot. In his 1961 interview with the West German police, Kopkow recalled that he spent 'many weeks' at Wolfsschanze working on the explosive device before returning to Berlin. Very quickly, RSHA Chief Dr Kaltenbrunner began producing regular reports from Berlin addressed to Nazi Party Secretary Martin Bormann; these showed the progress in establishing exactly what had happened, who did it, Gestapo arrests of those involved, and the hunt for more. On 26 July 1944, Kaltenbrunner provided the first results of Kopkow's findings, mentioning that the bomb itself had 'English chemical-mechanical timer ignition parts'; he also noted that, at the nearby airfield and army unit, they had found an 'English chemical-mechanical timer firing pin for a 30 minute delay attached to a detonator' that had been apparently thrown away. Kopkow, though unnamed in the report, probably established the nature of the bomb and pieces for a second bomb thrown away, also establishing that Stauffenberg must have been the perpetrator.[92] On 3 August 1944, Kaltenbrunner informed Bormann that the English bomb material was captured in the occupied territories, and in October 1943, it was handed over to Stauffenberg by another of the plotters, Colonel Henning von Tresckow, Chief of Staff with an army group in Russia, during a visit to Berlin. This report was the last to mention the sabotage investigations at Wolfsschanze and Kopkow had most likely returned to his usual Berlin duties by this point.[93] Kaltenbrunner continued to inform Bormann and, through him, the Führer, of RSHA actions to track down, question, and hand over the guilty to the People's Court for judicial proceedings.

Why Kopkow decided to forget most of his part in the Gestapo investigation may have been due to two factors: the first being the execution of many of the plotters, and secondly, his department RSHA IV A2 was still alive and investigating other suspects from its base in Potsdam as late as January 1945. A whiff of cordite from firing squads executing people was something Kopkow needed to distance himself from in the post-war world.

Naturally, as Soviet armies recovered the occupied areas of the Soviet Union from German domination and advanced toward Germany itself, there was no longer a need for NKVD agents to be dropped by the British RAF. Soviet aircraft with a much shorter flight from the recovered territories could now drop all their agents themselves. As a result, a significant increase in Soviet agents into Germany and closely adjoining territory began. For example, the Soviets found it difficult to drop agents into the immediate region around Vienna, in eastern Austria, due to high population levels. Therefore, agents were dropped into southern Czechoslovakia where sparsely populated areas were common, areas where agents could easily bury their parachute equipment and then make their way into Austria. These agents continued to be Austrian or German communists trained in Moscow and, increasingly, a number of German Army deserters or prisoners of war who volunteered to return as an agent. Towards the end of 1944 and in 1945, the Germans began capturing Soviet-trained agents dropped behind their retreating lines who had the task of military reconnaissance, establishing troop movements, railway transports of material heading for the front, and the lay of the land. These were not single agents, but groups, some up to six, seven, and eight persons. Not all were captured by the Gestapo, with most able to survive until overrun by Soviet armies intent on encircling Berlin. A last *Funkspiel* occurred in mid-April 1945 by the local Gestapo office in Swinemünde on the Baltic coast, but this was discontinued within days when Soviet armies approached the town. This agent, Rudi Fey, was released. Similar cases had happened in February–March 1945, further south at Halle, when the Gestapo captured two agents, Krämer and Dietrich. During the evening of 20 February 1945, the two had been dropped near Bitterfeld, captured the following day, and handed over to Gestapo Halle. Krämer proved the more willing to save his life and helped in establishing a *Funkspiel* with his Soviet base. By the end of February 1945, he was being interrogated by Kopkow's men, Strübing and Müller, who had been evacuated from Berlin to Hof in northern Bavaria and out of the way of Allied air raids. Afterwards, Krämer was returned to Gestapo Halle to continue the *Funkspiel* with Moscow, which continued until the last transmission on 30 March 1945. On 9 April 1945, the Gestapo released Krämer, who began making his way to his Giessen home, 250 miles away westwards. Three days later, Krämer was captured by advancing US armies at Erfurt. By June 1945, Krämer had been taken to Britain for interrogation.[94]

What Krämer had to say about his career as a Soviet agent came as a surprise to the Allies. Army Captain Krämer surrendered to superior Soviet forces at Stalingrad on 30 January 1943. After several months as a POW, he was selected by a German communist commission for training as an espionage agent in November 1943. This is a typical recruitment story for many Germans trained as agents by Soviet intelligence; conditions in the POW cages were awful, lacking in sanitation and food, just like their counterparts in German camps where Soviet POWs were held. Some of those chosen for agent training did have a communist background and some did not; that some saw an opportunity of getting home cannot be denied. Krämer is another example of Soviet intelligence shortcomings. Interrogated in June 1945, he told the British of three other parties of Soviet-trained Germans also dropped in the Halle area during March and April 1945. All were caught by the police and handed over to Gestapo Halle by Kopkow's men.

6

Allied Intelligence Operations (SOE, SIS-MI6, OSS)

After the war, SS-Major Horst Kopkow was held in several prisons and internment camps for initial questioning. In August 1945, he arrived at Britain's Combined Services Detailed Interrogation Centre/West European Area (CSDIC/WEA), located in Bad Nenndorf, west of Hannover, for more intensive interrogation. When being debriefed and interrogated on behalf of SIS (Britain's Secret Intelligence Service, also known as MI6) and MI5 (Britain's Security Service), Kopkow proved invaluable and voluble when asked who was who in the Gestapo and on how best to combat Soviet infiltration agents. He was less forthright and voluble about Allied intelligence agents from the west, especially those of SIS and SOE, to the point of disavowing all knowledge of them. His refusal, for this is what it was, to mention his responsibilities for SOE agents went against statements by captured Gestapo officers from Holland and France in the same early post-war period. These Gestapo officers not only made statements under oath about Kopkow's responsibilities for SOE agents, but repeated them on the witness stand when undergoing their own war crimes trials, including the British military court in Wuppertal where Kopkow himself appeared as a prosecution witness. These statements must have been known to British intelligence services as well as war crimes investigators. Yet in February 1947, BAOR Intelligence Division at Herford (Germany)—basically the SIS organisation—allowed its fellow officers in the Judge Advocate General's War Crimes Branch to examine their Kopkow interrogations. These were returned a week later, and stated: 'It is regretted that the interrogations carried out at CSDIC did not touch on the subject matters referred to…'[1] This can only mean that, despite all the evidence from other sources, by February 1947, Kopkow had not been questioned about his knowledge of SOE agents and what had happened to them. Did SIS bury its head in the sand on this point, for the evidence available to them indicated that Kopkow had played the major role in the murder of the captured SIS and SOE agents in German concentration camps? Kopkow had already mentioned under interrogation that he knew what had happened to the Soviet-trained German communists dropped into Germany and German-occupied territories; did SIS really not believe Kopkow played a role in the fate of their own former agents and those from SOE caught by the Gestapo? Were they more intent on acquiring Kopkow's knowledge about fighting Soviet agent infiltration operations in readiness for the imminent Cold War, and forgetting a duty of care to agents who had just disappeared in the wreckage of war? Former SOE 'F' Section officer Vera Atkins went to Germany in 1945 and 1946 and made serious efforts to establish what had happened to 'her' lost agents, eventually interviewing Kopkow and producing a remarkably poor statement from him.[2] SIS appear to have done nothing at all about their lost agents. The journalist Sarah Helm established fifty years later that the SIS had not informed the widow of one agent the circumstances behind the death of her husband who had fallen victim to Kopkow

In 1940, the new British Prime Minister Winston Churchill instigated the establishment of a new British intelligence agency, Special Operations Executive (SOE), reportedly saying it should 'set Europe ablaze'. Its sister organisation, SIS, from whom SOE acquired some personnel, was primarily concerned with intelligence gathering, whereas SOE would take on another role—that of sabotage and training others on the ground as saboteurs. Together with the European governments in exile now based in London (e.g. Belgium, Czechoslovakia, Denmark, France, Greece, Holland, Poland, Norway, and Yugoslavia) and remnants of their secret services, SOE set up individual country desks and training schools at various locations across Britain. Suitable candidates were chosen for training in stamina, sabotage, weaponry, and ciphering/deciphering for radio transmissions. Some of the early agents were infiltrated by sea using the Royal Navy; a later stage involved parachuting from aircraft; and from 1941, a new development was landing aircraft on the ground, especially in France and Belgium, where the single-engined Lysander (two seats including the pilot) proved an excellent aircraft for this purpose. As the war progressed, and especially in 1943–1944, SOE graduated to using the twin-engined American Lockheed Hudson aircraft to land larger numbers of agents and bring more back to Britain. The SOE air liaison officer based in Paris, Henri Déricourt, after his parachute infiltration in January 1943, found areas in France where agents could be dropped by parachute and fields where aircraft could land safely at designated spots to reception committees. Supplies and weapons would be dropped by the RAF when requested, and that request would primarily come via a coded radio message from the agent on the ground to SOE headquarters in Britain. As with Soviet intelligence, coded radio messages from agents on the ground in enemy territory were the primary means of communications with their base. The Abwehr and Gestapo had effectively used direction finding when tracking down Rote Kapelle agents in Germany, Belgium, and Holland, so sending similar units and equipment to France became inevitable. Radio direction finding in conjunction with informers would prove a formidable and successful tool among other German counter-intelligence measures in their fight against Allied subversion in the west.

In August 1940, following the end of German hostilities and their occupation of Western Europe, from the Franco-Spanish border to the tip of northern Norway, it was the Abwehr who began conducting counter-intelligence and counter-espionage measures against British-inspired incursions onto the European mainland. It is widely recognised that British intelligence had no 'humint' (spies and agents) on the ground in Germany at this time, and they only had a small number of individuals left behind and overrun by German forces in France and possibly in other countries—although these proved capable of supplying information. SIS had been taken completely by surprise in summer 1940, when the German Blitzkrieg war attacked and occupied Western Europe. SIS officers fled back to London with diplomats and everyone else who feared the Germans. The 'phoney war' was over, the real one just beginning.

In Berlin, these overwhelmingly successful military campaigns were rapturously received and people flocked to the cinemas to see the latest newsreels. With no television service in those days, cinema, newspapers, and radio broadcasts were the providers of news. With military success came political success, and the Führer revelled in a new popular adoration of his personality cult. The Nazi regime riding high on a wave of popular support, Kopkow and his wife no doubt felt the world was at their feet, confirming their early adoption of Nazi politics. In summer 1940, when Kopkow replaced Kurt Geissler as department chief RSHA IV A2, still a backwater involving cases of sabotage and counter-measures, his influence began to spread beyond Germany and Poland into the newly occupied western territories. The Security Police and SD, in agreement between the Army High Command and RSHA (Heydrich), established central offices in the new capital cities, followed by offices in the provincial cities and towns. These followed the organisational model of RSHA, and in each office, a desk officer became responsible for investigating sabotage, just as another desk officer became the Jewish expert. These desk officers may have shared other responsibilities, such as communists and freemasons respectively, but, in essence, they carried out their activities using official guidelines for their jobs provided by RSHA IV A2 (Kopkow) and RSHA IV B4 (Eichmann). Regardless of where these desk officers worked, whether in Oslo, Paris, or Warsaw, the same guidelines applied.

In many ways, the further away from Berlin, the more latitude devolved to the local Gestapo offices in the occupied territories. In Norway, few captured agents were sent to Germany: twenty-four were executed in Norway and fifteen agents killed in action fighting German forces. A number of British commandos were captured in Norway following a number of raids between 1941 and 1943. Some of those captured were executed by Gestapo firing squads in Trondheim and Oslo, and others were sent to Germany. They were later executed at Sachsenhausen concentration camp in 1945, almost certainly on Kopkow's orders. In Denmark, SOE and Danish intelligence were slow to get going until 1943, when the pace quickened. Between 1943 and 1945, fifty-seven Danes trained by SOE were dropped by the RAF and six were killed in action fighting the Germans—one committed suicide rather than face capture. SOE Czech Section, who organised the assassination of Heydrich, had a dozen of their agents commit suicide rather than face capture after his death; six agents parachuted later and were killed fighting German forces and three captured agents were executed. SOE Polish Section dropped its first agent on 15 February 1941, followed by forty-five others in drops during the winter 1941–1942. The biggest problem for Britain at this time was a lack of suitable long-range aircraft capable of flying to Poland and back to Britain. Yugoslavia was under direct German military occupation and Britain parachuted in several military missions to assist the partisans (initially Mihailovic, then Tito). Seven agents were killed fighting the Germans and Italians, and three captured agents were executed. In Greece, a British and an Allied Military Mission were sent; three captured agents were executed in Averoff prison, Athens, yet four members of a SOE raiding party (Force 133), captured in May 1943 after attempting to block the Corinth Canal using explosives, were sent over 1,000 miles north to Sachsenhausen concentration camp where they became Kopkow's responsibility.

Local Gestapo excesses against captured agents were mitigated in those countries where the Abwehr retained control. Such Abwehr control prevailed in countries where the German Army administration dominated—a prime example is Belgium. It was in Belgium that most of the captured SOE agents remained under Abwehr arrest until brought before military courts for trial. Depending on the sentence by these courts, some agents that were given a death sentence were subsequently executed in German prisons or shot at the shooting range of TIR National in Brussels-Schaerbeek. Many captured Belgian agents given terms of imprisonment and held in German prisons and concentration camps survived the war and returned home. This is completely different to what happened in Belgium's neighbours, Holland and France, where practically all the captured agents became the responsibility of the local Gestapo before their transfer to concentration camps in Germany, at which point, responsibility switched to RSHA Berlin and Kopkow. Barely twenty agents survived incarceration in the camps.

In the months following the successful German Blitzkrieg in Holland, Belgium, and France, it was the Abwehr who carried out the first counter-intelligence and counter-espionage measures against local resistance activities. In France, the country became divided into the 'occupied zone' and the 'unoccupied zone'. Based in Paris and under German control, the occupied zone covered the entire northern and western coastlines from Dunkirk via the Brittany peninsula to the entire Bay of Biscay coastline, then south to Biarritz and the Spanish border. The 'unoccupied zone' was governed by Marshal of France Philippe Petain and was based in Vichy, some 200 miles south of

Paris; it covered almost as much land area as the occupied zone and the entire Mediterranean coastline. The Vichy regime governed from July 1940 until November 1942, at which point, German military forces entered the unoccupied zone and took control of the entire country. External events were the cause of full occupation and followed Allied military operations in North Africa. On 23 October 1942, British and Commonwealth armies attacked German and Italian armies (the *Afrika Korps*) on the Libya–Egypt border and began the Battle of El Alamein. It was hard fought and ended on 11 November 1942 with German forces in retreat. Three days earlier (8 November 1942), a joint American and British military assault, Operation Torch, began on Vichy-held territory in Algeria. This was the first deployment of American troops in Europe of the war and it met with great success. Within six months, all German, Italian, and Vichy-French troops had either surrendered or had been evacuated from North Africa to Italy. The defeat of the *Afrika Korps* paved the way for the Allied invasion of Italy and southern France in 1943 and 1944 respectively.

In France, during the first months of German occupation, a demoralised civilian population cowed by German troops did not immediately believe in resistance or sabotage—there were more important things to consider such as their livelihood, work, a salary, and food on the table for their families. Once the occupation settled down, some sections of the civilian population began to encourage resistance and actively sought to commit sabotage and organise a resistance movement. Within twelve months of German occupation, isolated and individual acts of sabotage in France became more organised and widespread as resistance groups formed. In April and May 1941, German Army reports mention 'major attacks on railways, factories', other army locations, and the cutting of telephone cables became quite common. The following is one German's view of the increase in sabotage: 'With the outbreak of the war against Russia, underground activity in France assumed an entirely new aspect. Whereas resistance against the occupation had previously been carried out by the De Gaullists, it was now seriously taken up also by supporters of the Left'. By 'the Left', he meant the French communist underground.[3] German counter measures entailed increased surveillance by all German security organisations of the army (Abwehr, Field Gendarmerie, and Secret Field Police), the Gestapo and SD, and the French police service. Further encouragement to resistance by civilian populations across Europe came from the BBC London, on which those governments in exile sponsored radio programmes directed at their citizens now under German occupation. On a regular basis, the French government in exile under (then) Colonel Charles de Gaulle began making regular radio broadcasts to France, and BBC radio services gave its resistance movements a messaging service that used agreed phrases to warn them of an event about to happen, such as an air drop of agents or supplies or both. Such BBC radio messaging was later used in May and June 1944 to warn the French resistance organisers that the invasion was imminent and they should increase sabotage activities.

One of the first resistance groups was established in Paris by former Polish army officers who had sought refuge in France and were caught out by the German occupation. Shortly after the occupation of Paris, the Poles had a transmitter sending messages from Toulouse in unoccupied France (governed by the Petain regime) to the Polish Embassy in Madrid. Eventually, Madrid was replaced by London, when SIS and the Polish Intelligence Service took over this resistance group. Its original name TUDOR was replaced by INTERALLIE, and it was commanded by former Polish air force officer Captain Roman Garby-Czerniawski. In October 1941, he was brought to Britain for debriefing on conditions in France, meeting with General Wladyslaw Sikorski, who was Prime Minister of the Polish government in exile in London and Commander-in-Chief of the Polish Armed Forces. Sikorski awarded Garby-Czerniawski with the Polish Medal for Gallantry (*Virtuti Militari*) before he returned to France by parachute drop in November. His freedom did not last long. Sergeant Hugo Bleicher of the German army's Secret Field Police (GFP, *Geheime Feldpolizei*), began rounding-up INTERALLIE personnel on 17 November 1941. Poor security resulted in large numbers of them being arrested; the increase in numbers due to Garby-Czerniawski's assistant, Mathilde Carré (codename *La Chatte*, the Cat), cooperating with Bleicher in return for her life and his bed. Within three days, acting on Carré's information, the Abwehr identified and arrested 'the entire network', which proved 'disastrous for SIS'.[4] However, it did not prove disastrous for SIS networks alone; a French Sûreté report of 8 June 1945 notes that Mathilde Carré betrayed three other networks to the Germans: OVERCLOUD, a BCRA organisation; PHILIPPE, another Polish intelligence organisation; and LUCAS, a SOE network.[5] All three networks closed as a result of her betrayal, as well as causing the arrest of numerous activists. The SOE radio operator of LUCAS, Alan George Boyd (in reality, the Frenchman Georges Bloch), had been dropped on 6 October 1941 and sent messages until 12 November, when he was arrested. He was held in Le Mans prison and suffered torture during Gestapo interrogations: 'The Gestapo despaired of eliciting any information from him and he was executed on 11th April 1942'.[6] He was the first SOE victim of the Gestapo in France.

After several months under Abwehr arrest, in February 1942, Carré used her resistance contacts to be picked up off the French coast by a Royal Navy vessel and taken to Britain. British intelligence were not impressed by her story and she subsequently languished for most of the war in a British prison because of her duplicity. After Carré's departure for Britain, the Abwehr used the INTERALLIE radio set operated by Czerniawski from Fresnes prison in Paris for a *Funkspiel* with SIS. This continued until July 1942 when Czerniawski himself, ostensibly as an agent for the Abwehr, travelled to Spain and made contact with the SIS Madrid station. Brought to Britain, he revealed all that the Abwehr wanted of him to his British interrogators. He became a double agent for MI5 as BRUTUS, playing the Abwehr to almost the end of the war.[7]

With INTERALLIE based in Paris, SIS grew a second network, ALLIANCE, based in Vichy, capital of unoccupied French territory. This network had two radio transmitters sending messages to London, which SIS shared with de Gaulle's intelligence service, BCRA (*Bureau Central de Renseignements et d'Action*). Their intelligence gathering very quickly required further channels of radio communications and SIS had three transmitters taken into France. Two were established in Monaco and Marseilles and the third was held in reserve. September 1941 arrived and two additional radio sets were on their way—these were destined for Lyons and Paris. ALLIANCE spread its intelligence gathering across France, and the SIS supported them with additional agents trained in Britain, one of whom, following capture by the Abwehr and turning into a double agent, began informing. Following discovery of his treachery, the SIS recommended his execution, which was accomplished by poison. ALLIANCE served its purpose until 1943, when network security was breached by the Abwehr and arrests began—over 150 of its agents were captured, among them was Commandant Leon Faye, ALLIANCE's head of operations.[8]

A third SIS sponsored network, JADE AMICOL, operated from a nunnery in Paris. Its intelligence gathering came from the French railwaymen, an invaluable source of German troop movements in the months preceding D-Day in June 1944. Philippe Keun (using the alias Gerald Kane), SIS agent and assistant commandant of JADE AMICOL in Paris, was arrested on 29 June 1944 shortly after returning from London briefings. Imprisoned at Fresnes, Keun was deported by the Paris Gestapo to Buchenwald concentration camp along with many other captured SOE agents six weeks later in August 1944.[9] Kopkow's order for their execution came to the camp in September 1944, when a series of agent executions began.

Having described SIS operations in France, SOE espionage and sabotage operations were on a much larger scale across the whole country. In France between 1941 and 1944, the RAF special duty flights landed 140 agents from aircraft on the ground and 900 by parachute from four different espionage and intelligence organisations: SOE French Section, RF Section, SIS, and Polish intelligence.[10] Certainly between the first days of the German occupation of France in 1940 and May 1942, the Abwehr ruled the roost as far as investigating Allied networks and arresting agents, together with escape lines for prisoners of war and shot-down aircrew. On 18 May 1942, the military commander in France, General von Stülpnagel, issued instructions to his *Geheime Feldpolizei* (GFP, Secret Field Police) and Abwehr in France relating to 'Co-operation with the Senior SS and Police Leader in France' (the HSSPF), SS-Major General Karl Oberg.[11] This instruction resulted from the Hitler Decree of 9 March 1942 issued by the Army High Command in Berlin following complaints to Hitler by *Reichsführer*-SS Heinrich Himmler that the army and German Ambassador Otto Abetz had denied the Security Police (Gestapo and criminal police) and SD for almost two years from taking executive measures in the country. To reinforce their new position, RSHA Chief Reinhard Heydrich travelled to Paris, and on 5 May 1942, he met with his HSSPF Oberg and General Heinrich von Stülpnagel, the Army Commander in France. The instructions by von Stülpnagel issued two weeks later settled the matter, giving the Gestapo a free hand.[12] The Heydrich-Oberg meeting had another agenda point. Since August 1940, SS-*Obersturmbannführer* (Lt-Col.) Dr Helmut Knochen had been stationed in Paris where he worked under Oberg as Plenipotentiary of the Chief of the Security Police and SD for Belgium and France within the area of the Chief of the Military Administration in France (*Beauftragten des Chefs der Sicherheitspolizei und des SD für Belgien und Frankreich für den Bereich des Chefs der Militärverwaltung Frankreich)*. On the day of Heydrich's visit (5 May), Knochen was promoted to SS-*Standartenführer* (Colonel) and his office now became BdS France (*Befehlshaber der Sicherheitspolizei und des SD in Frankreich*) stationed in Paris, with responsibility for the regional commanders (KdS, *Kommandeur der Sicherheitspolizei und des SD*) and their offices in the major cities of the occupied zone. The organisation of BdS France closely followed that of RSHA Berlin and the officer in charge of Department IV (the Gestapo) was SS-*Sturmbannführer* Karl Boemelburg; his office was in charge of counter-espionage, Dept. IV E, and the man who would take on SOE was the formidable SS-*Hauptsturmführer* Hans Kieffer.

Boemelburg was a career policeman and fifty-five years of age when he arrived in Paris after spending many years with Gestapo regional headquarters in Berlin and a year establishing the Gestapo regional headquarters in Prague. Although in overall charge of all Gestapo departments in Paris, he retained one section under his charge that dealt with informers. Section IV N acquired information from a wide range of French informers—from street level to senior officials. The more senior were controlled by Boemelburg personally. In 1943, before his departure from Paris for Vichy as the Security Police commander (KdS), one of his informers, known as BOE 48, was Henri Dericourt, who acted as SOE air liaison officer based in Paris from January 1943 until returning to London with his wife in February 1944. MI5 began questioning him about his loyalties, and after the war, Dericourt faced charges of treason before a French military tribunal, where the trial witnesses included former German SS officers of BdS Paris, French civilians, and former SOE Major Nicholas Bodington. The tribunal preferred to accept the words of Bodington to those of their former occupiers and Dericourt was acquitted.[13]

Hans Kieffer had a similar police career as Boemelburg. Born in 1900, Kieffer had a brief military career when conscripted on his eighteenth birthday in 1918, and he was demobilised the following year. He joined the police service in 1920 and carried out street patrols before joining the criminal police as a detective. Following the Nazi seizure of power in 1933, he switched to the political police service. Kieffer had a successful career with the political police in Karlsruhe, an organisation that became the Gestapo, and already in 1939 chief of the counter-espionage department. For the French campaign, the Secret Field Police (*Geheime Feldpolizei*—GFP) of the German Army conscripted Kieffer, and on 27 June 1940, uniformed as a *Feldpolizeidirektor*, they despatched him to Paris; from 10 July 1940, Kieffer found himself reassigned to Knochen's staff as a Gestapo man, replacing his *Feldpolizei* uniform for that of a SS-*Hauptsturmführer* (Captain) and *Kriminalkommissar*. His experience in counter-espionage, pre-war co-operation with the Abwehr in Karlsruhe, and, more importantly, knowing RSHA IV Chief Müller made him the ideal SS-officer for the work now developing in France. Knochen, Kieffer's boss, stated:

> Kieffer was an official trained and experienced in all counter intelligence matters. He was known in Berlin on account of his detailed [pre-war] work. He worked in close liaison with Military Counter Intelligence [Abwehr] and on account of his high conception of duty, he was well spoken of by other military headquarters as well.[14]

Together with the newly arrived Boemelburg as Department Head IV (Gestapo) and Kieffer as Section Head IV 'E' (counter-espionage), they worked from the former French Sûreté offices on Rue des Saussaies in Paris, establishing a political police service. From the first days, Department IV sections undertook intelligence activities and responded to acts against all branches of the German armed forces now stationed in France. Sabotage and attacks on German personnel, including woundings and assassinations, were investigated and, where possible, the culprits arrested. The second major objective was investigating the French communist party and its association with German communist *émigré* circles in France. Captain Hermann Giskes of the Abwehr was stationed in Paris in 1940 before his later transfer to Holland. Giskes later commented: 'At this time the S.D. and Stapo were only responsible for matters concerning communists, German emigrants, freemasons, Jews, and Church affairs but encroachment on Abwehr territory was not long delayed'.[15] As in Germany, the Gestapo, though fewer in number in France, could not be everywhere or have the linguistic skills to interrogate people. They took steps to create their own collaborator police force of thugs and establish a growing army of informers across French society, especially among the French communist party. Between July and August 1941, Boemelburg and Kieffer made a long journey through the occupied and unoccupied zones (Vichy–Dijon–Lyon–St Etienne–Montélimar–Aix en Provence–Marseille–Toulon–St Raphael–Nice–Monte Carlo then across the Italian border at Ventemiglia to San Remo) and along the Riviera coast. They were accompanied by a recent appointment to their Paris staff, SS-Sergeant and detective Friedrich Dohse, who had been posted from Gestapo Kiel. Dohse spoke French well and describes what happened:

> The intention of this journey was partly to pay visits to the French police authorities, and partly to get into touch with the 'V-Männer' [informers], who were working for the German Sicherheitsdienst in the occupied and in the non-occupied parts of France. Bömmelburg [*sic.*] had before the war been an exporter for 8 years at St Etienne and Lyon, so consequently he had many connections.[16]

Dohse did not attend all the meetings with these informers, adding: 'All of them were occupying high positions within the Vichy Government's various administration lines. Bömmelburg spoke French perfectly'. They also met several French police officers known to Boemelburg.

After Heydrich's meetings in Paris with Oberg and von Stülpnagel in early May 1942, he returned to Berlin prior to his posting to Prague where, at the end of May, he was assassinated. Due to Heydrich's assassination, it was June 1942 before Kopkow was able to turn his departmental interests westwards because his official responsibilities now included British parachute agents and those of other nationalities being dropped into France and Holland, and to a much lesser extent Belgium. In Paris, on 10 July 1942, Oberg issued a public declaration. While most French people went about their lives quietly, 'some support the English and Soviet sides who commit assassinations and sabotage acts against the German occupation troops, and as a consequence of these acts endanger the lives of the French population'. It was not simply English agents creating mayhem in France, French communists were also fighting back. The senior SS and Police Commander in France, Oberg, issued a stern public warning to those who helped saboteurs and assassins. Those who helped such people would be shot along with all their family members over eighteen years of age, and all female family members would be sent to forced labour, and any children of seventeen years old and younger were sent to educational establishments. To reinforce the warning over the following two months, the Gestapo had 155 French civilians shot for aiding the enemy.[17]

Throughout 1942, SOE increasingly infiltrated agents from Britain by parachute drops and aircraft landings, who would then establish resistance networks. SOE also infiltrated agents into southern France via Gibraltar using submarines and feluccas (small coastal sailing ships). In their fight against enemy agents and home grown ones, the Gestapo and French police used informers everywhere. As in Germany, where remaining German communist cells had been infiltrated by informers, the system worked just as well in France. Informers on the ground had their purposes, but SOE radio operators transmitting information back to London faced another formidable enemy: radio detection. The Abwehr worked closely with the Luftwaffe and *Ordnungspolizei* radio detection units that would pinpoint areas where enemy agents transmitted.[18] The Abwehr Chief in Paris Oskar Reile noted the research of his colleague, Major Ernst von Bary, into enemy radio transmitters operating across German-occupied Europe by western and eastern intelligence services; at the end 1943 to the beginning 1944, German radio detection units had noted 500 enemy radio transmitters operating from German-occupied territories and their number continued to increase.[19] However, some radio operators operated more than one set at different locations to avoid carrying them around when the danger of baggage searches by German patrols could uncover the radio sets and lead to the operator being arrested. This does not lessen the fact that 500 radio transmitters sending illegal radio messages from German-occupied territories meant well over 400 radio operators. Little wonder German radio detection units were overwhelmed by the work of uncovering illegal transmitters.

Heydrich's visit to Paris in May 1942 allowed Knochen, BdS Paris, to increase his responsibilities for tackling French resistance movements and bring in more staff. SOE French Section began infiltrating trained agents into various regions of France; they were a mix of French nationals and French-speaking English officers. Once the English officers began to be captured, Kieffer recruited his own English speakers for interrogations. Kieffer's department IV E in their Rue des Saussaies headquarters consisted initially of a small staff of professional Gestapo officials, and the expansion of Gestapo activities in France under BdS Knochen required an increase in staffing levels. Rather than post more officials in from Germany, a decision between the army and RSHA meant that on 22 November 1942, some 1,500 men serving with the GFP in France were taken into the *Sicherheitspolizei*.[20] Many did not consider this a good career move as some dropped a rank and therefore salary. Two such GFP men assigned to Kieffer were Dr Josef Götz, a former teacher of modern languages, and Josef Placke, a businessman. Both men spoke French and English and both had worked for GFP Group 733 in Paris. A third German recruited, Ernst Vogt, had been working in Paris since 1926; he was a civilian called up after the German occupation began.[21] All three men would play a leading role with Kieffer in tracking down, arresting, and interrogating SOE agents and their French helpers across France. SOE radio operators were the prime target for the Abwehr and Gestapo. The successful German ability of using these captured radio sets and associated ciphers meant an increased success when playing back these radio sets to a gullible London, who accepted many of these false messages. This hoodwinking of London led to the seizures of supplies, weapons dropped by aircraft, and, more importantly, the arrest of other agents especially in the drop zone. Radio operators captured in this way presented the Gestapo with a completely controlled field of operations and means of disinformation that could further their control of the resistance movement.

No sooner had Kieffer's section become involved in taking the fight to the French resistance that they arrested their first SOE 'F' Section officer. Georges Gilbert Turck, a radio operator, parachuted into the unoccupied zone (at Saint-Désiré) during the night of 5–6 August 1941 with his organiser,

Jacques Vaillant de Guélis, and after escaping the Vichy police headed for Marseilles where they set up a resistance circuit. In October 1941, the Vichy police and gendarmerie began arresting most of the agents operating from Marseilles; Turck states he had a forewarning and simply disappeared, making his way to Paris where his fiancée lived—he went to ground in her apartment. In July 1942, 'a too casual meeting' in the Paris suburb of St German des Prés led to his arrest by the Gestapo. Turck suffered Gestapo torture when interrogated and said nothing; he suffered in French prisons until January 1944, when he was deported to Buchenwald. Turck survived the camp and returned to France after the war.[22] He was lucky in this respect, as were most other SOE agents who fell into the hands of the Gestapo in 1942 and early 1943. Christopher Burney had been organising a resistance cell in Paris for three months before his arrest on 15 August 1942. He then spent over a year in Fresnes prison in Paris until deported to Buchenwald.[23]

These arrests in the unoccupied zone had been incited by a German task force that operated in Vichy territory from September 1942 until the German entry and occupation of the rest of France in November 1942. German direction-finding (D/F'ing) had already plotted large numbers of radio transmissions directed at London and Algiers from the unoccupied zone. According to SS-*Untersturmführer* Arthur Katzemich, a Gestapo counter intelligence officer with nine years' service, a special German task force assembled at Vincennes near Paris for 'Operation Donar on 1 September 1942. It comprised about 250 men: one-third German Army personnel (W/T experts and D/F monitoring squads), one-third Orpo personnel (W/T experts and D/F monitoring squads), and one-third Sipo personnel. Overall charge lay in the hands of SS-*Sturmbannführer* Boemelburg who addressed the assembled men, informing them that their major task would be 'the liquidation of information sources for the Allies'—in other words, illegal radio transmitters and receivers of Allied agents, as can be seen by the large number of radio direction-finding (D/F) squads and W/T personnel capable of operating radio sets. From Katzemich's description, the army and the Orpo (Order Police) did the technical side of the operation, establishing exact transmission points, and the Sipo (Gestapo and Criminal Police) liaised with the Vichy police in arresting suspects. The task force divided into five groups with its headquarters at Charbonnières-les-Bains on the western fringe of Lyon. Katzemich remained here in charge of the Sipo contingent. When questioned after the war, he claimed to remember only three arrests in his area. An SOE agent captured transmitting in Lyon in mid-October 1942 (not a month earlier as claimed by Katzemich) was able to set fire to his coding material just as the Gestapo and Vichy police burst through the door. This agent, Georges Brault, was imprisoned, but he was able to escape shortly afterwards. Also in October, two Frenchmen transmitting information via Switzerland to Moscow were caught, undoubtedly part of the Soviet 'Rote Drei' espionage ring operating out of Lausanne. Polish intelligence working out of their government in exile in London also had their agents working in France among Polish circles. Katzemich mentions the arrest of 'two Poles, one an elderly diplomat' transmitting south of Clermont-Ferrand, probably in October 1942: 'Interrogations were carried out by the French Police at Clermont-Ferrand'.[24]

Allied landings in French North Africa on 8 November 1942 (Operation Torch), resulted in a hurried German reassessment of the Vichy regime and the unoccupied zone. Three days later, German armed forces marched into the zone, and within days, they had complete occupation of France. This also meant the end of 'Operation Donar', and Katzemich was recalled to Paris in December 1942. The new appointment of Boemelburg as KdS Vichy and other SS-officers in similar positions in cities of the former unoccupied zone led to a consolidation of Gestapo control across France; this would increase the difficulties for all Allied agents to operate clandestinely and was the reason why, over the next eighteen months, many would be caught in road blocks and railway checkpoints as Gestapo consolidation and surveillance techniques tightened up.

Reichsführer-SS Himmler was kept informed of events and mayhem being caused by Allied sabotage efforts on a daily basis by his HSSPF in France and Holland. A few original documents from these senior SS and police leaders escaped destruction in the last stages of the war when the Gestapo and SD began the wholesale burning of paper documents. Several 'Blitz' (urgent) teleprinter messages from Karl Oberg, HSSPF France in Paris, to Himmler survive.[25.] On 25 October 1942, he reported that a 'terror group' consisting of a Hungarian, two Romanian men, and two Romanian Jewish women under the command of a Slovakian Jew had been arrested in Paris. Since 5 August 1942, they had carried out a number of armed attacks on German soldiers, with four killed and forty wounded. A second teleprinter message on the same day mentions the arrest of fourteen members of a communist organisation. On 26 October, Oberg reported to Himmler about arrests in Sartrouville (north-west of Paris), where German soldiers had been attacked. These three reports from Oberg were the basis for Himmler's own report to the Führer (dated 26 October 1942)—'Report to the Führer re anti-bandit operations'. One of the last actions by Operation Donar squads took place in Marseille on 14 November 1942, when two French colonels and two French majors of the Deuxième Bureau had a secret meeting with three activists. One of their French informants let the Gestapo know that these French secret service men employed in Vichy were preparing plans for stealing German weapons and retaining secret information. BdS Knochen informed *Reichsführer*-SS Himmler by teleprinter message on 27 November 1942, and it was copied to RSHA IV (Müller) and RSHA VI (Schellenberg). Although such reports were interesting for Kopkow, his interests were better served in a 'Blitz' teleprinter message from Himmer to Party Comrade Martin Bormann at Führer Headquarters (dated 18 December 1942).[26] At the time, Himmler was staying with his family in Gmund (Bavaria, south of Munich) for the Christmas period. Himmler asked Bormann to put his 'Blitz' message before the Führer and sought his approval for various measures to be taken in France in regard to the French army, police, and secret services. These would either be disbanded or absorbed. The advice of Eichmann and Kopkow, via RSHA IV Chief Müller, reflects the importance Himmler and Müller placed on these two main enemies of the Reich. Eichmann wanted his Jewish Section in Paris deporting French and stateless Jews from France to Auschwitz, and Kopkow showed his concerns at the growing threat from Allied intelligence agencies infiltrating France. Himmler wanted approval for 'the creation of a special police unit to combat the political enemies of Europe (communists, freemasons, Jews, saboteurs, intelligence agents and spies). In establishing this police unit, the German police would have the ability to provide help, advice and assistance'. Not only that, Himmler wanted approval from Hitler for the 'removal and emigration of Jews to the East and the arrest of foreigners, English and Americans, and their transfer to internment camps in Germany'. It would also be a continuation of the 'radical fight against communism, all its helpers and their accomplices'. Both Eichmann and Kopkow wanted a Führer decree to encompass their work in France and cover all eventualities. Himmler's proposals, tying together the Jewish 'philosophical enemies' of the Reich with the communists and Allied 'political enemies', revealed how serious he and RSHA top management viewed these two enemy groups and their importance by bringing these proposals to the attention of the Führer for approval.

The new year (1943) brought about an office move. Kieffer's department moved from the old Suréte building on Rue des Saussaies to the more well-known Avenue Foch 84 in Paris. His staff began to expand and he now had two floors of the building with a couple of holding cells. Helmut Knochen, BdS Paris, would later explain that the drive behind the work against Allied intelligence agents, 'this very important type of work', came from SS-Major Kopkow at RSHA IV A2 in Berlin. Furthermore, according to Knochen, Kopkow in Berlin 'had decreed an absolute centralisation for the direction of these radio deception plans and all matters concerned with them. All radio messages originating from London had to be reported at once to Kopkow's Sub-section'. Ordinarily, this was done by Kieffer's desk officers or in more important cases by Knochen himself or his deputy (SS-Lt-Col. Henschke). Once the messages from London arrived with Kopkow in Berlin, he and his desk officers would sift them for any requests about military information. Such information could be obtained following the agreement Himmler obtained from Hitler in December 1942, when Kopkow proved capable of *Funkspiel* operations with Moscow using Rote Kapelle radio sets. Having obtained the necessary information from army, navy, or Luftwaffe High Command, Kopkow sent detailed replies back to Kieffer for transmission to London for their *Funkspiel* with SOE radio sets.[27]

With Knochen ordering Kieffer to increase his operations, Kieffer had his men interrogate the SOE agents captured in Paris during 1942 or brought to Paris from other cities. There were three Paris prisons of choice: the largest and old established one in Fresnes on the southern outskirts of the city; Cherche-Midi, a former French military prison used by the army and Abwehr; and the smaller one under Gestapo control at 3 bis Place des États-Unis, a sturdy brick building converted into holding cells. The Gestapo would use all three and Avenue Foch, depending at what stage of interrogation the captives were undergoing. First they needed captives to interrogate. SOE 'F' Section officers Christopher Burney and Charles Grover-Williams had parachuted blind into an area near Le Mans during the night of 30–31 May 1942. Burney was a former commando and Grover-Williams a former Grand Prix racing driver who had lived most of the 1930s in Paris. Burney had orders to make contact with SOE circuit AUTOGYRO in Caen, but approaching the address, he found it under observation and decided to make his way to Paris where he made contact with Grover-Williams who was setting up SOE circuit CHESTNUT for sabotage work. The two decided it would be best for Burney to return to Britain, taking the long route down through France and over the Pyrenees into Spain. Before he could get away, the Gestapo burst into his hotel room and arrested him in the early hours of 15 August 1942. Burney suffered many brutal Gestapo interrogations and gave away nothing; subsequently, he spent almost eighteen months in solitary confinement in a Fresnes prison cell before deportation on 29 January 1944 to Buchenwald, along with the earlier Gestapo prisoner Georges Gilbert Turck.

Edward Zeff landed from a submarine on the southern French Riviera coast in April 1942. His task from SOE was W/T operator for Virginia Hall in Lyon, who passed him onto the SOE organiser in Lyon, Georges Dubourdin. Zeff spent many hours transmitting to London, sometimes for six hours at a time.[28] In February 1943, London recalled him and he proceeded to the Pyrenees, intent on crossing into Spain; however, the Gestapo arrested him on 18 February 1943 at Amélie-les-Bains, south-west of Perpignan, with the mountains looming ahead. In April, he arrived at Fresnes and suffered brutal interrogations for maintaining his silence. Despite deportation to German prisons and concentration camps, Zeff survived to be liberated at Mauthausen.[29] Other SOE agents fell into Gestapo hands, and on 13 April 1943, the Gestapo office in Toulouse arrested a W/T operator and his organiser, Marcus Bloom and Maurice Pertschuk. When Toulouse informed Kieffer of their capture, it was decided to attempt their first attempt at *Funkspiel* with London using the radio set and ciphers of Bloom. Kieffer sent his new radio expert Dr Josef Götz down to Toulouse. For this first attempt, as Götz readily admitted after the war, he had with him an army radio expert and one of Kopkow's deputies from Berlin, SS-*Obersturmführer Kriminalkommissar* Karl-Heinrich Büchert. They were hampered by Bloom's steadfast refusal to help them. Götz described what happened:

> The decoy transmissions went on for about four weeks but had no practical result. After it was concluded I travelled back to Paris and went on leave from there. When I came back from this there were two decoy transmissions in Paris which I had to take over. One of these two lasted only a short time; the other, much longer.[30]

Both Bloom and Pertschuk were brought to Fresnes prison and in 1944 deported to German camps. Neither survived.

What were the 'two decoy transmissions in Paris' mentioned by Götz that happened during his leave? Götz was in Hamburg on 19 June 1943 for the birth of his son and later told British author Jean Overton Fuller that he received a telegram from Kieffer recalling him; on his return to Paris, 'Kieffer told him they had arrested the chiefs of an important group'.[31] During the night of 15–16 June, two French-speaking Canadians recruited by SOE—the organiser Frank Pickersgill and his radio operator John Macalister—had parachuted into a French reception committee of SOE agents Pierre Culioli and Yvonne Ruddelat. On 21 June, the four were in a car taking the two Canadians to the railway station at Beaugency where they would all board a train for Paris. When passing through Dhuizon village (100 miles south of Paris), they were stopped by a German gendarmerie roadblock checking papers. All four got out of the car at the town hall for the check. The papers of Culioli and Ruddelat passed muster and they returned to the car and waited for Pickersgill and Macalister. Minutes went by and the two Canadians did not return, with sounds of unrest beginning, so Culioli and Ruddelat went off in the car and soon found themselves pursued by German vehicles. Gunshots at another checkpoint brought an end to the chase when Ruddelat received a head wound and Culioli a shot in the leg. The car ended up in a ditch.[32] The two Canadians were taken to Gestapo headquarters in nearby Blois for interrogation. Culioli was left to suffer his leg injury, untreated, for three days until interrogated in Blois. The prize for the Gestapo was Macalister's radio set and ciphers, which were unused. The three men and the radio equipment were soon at Fresnes prison and Götz would begin his first successful *Funkspiel* with London that lasted for nine months until March 1944.

The background to Götz's second successful *Funkspiel* also happened when he was on leave. In Paris, the Gestapo, through Boemelburg personally, had been playing Henri Dericourt, the SOE air movements officer stationed in Paris. There are several versions as to how Dericourt came to know Boemelburg, and once they were in contact, what did Dericourt then tell London, to SIS and SOE? There are numerous versions about the career of Karl Boemelburg, most of them mythologising his past either with the German Embassy pre-September 1939 at what seems to be a Police Attaché post or at the International Criminal Police Commission (Interpol) in Vienna, when he would have known senior French policemen. None of these posts are borne out by his SS-Officer file. While by no means providing a complete set of career postings, the timelines of Boemelburg's SS-Officer file and documents bearing his signature indicate that he did not go to France at any time in the 1930s and had no connection with Interpol.

Born on 28 October 1885 in Wuppertal, Boemelburg attended elementary and secondary schools between 1891 and 1900—he did not attend a grammar school or go to university. Leaving school in the summer before his fifteenth birthday, he would have joined a business apprenticeship scheme. In Boemelburg's case, this was in the confectionary trade and this remained his career path before later joining the Gestapo. When twenty-one years old in 1906, he felt sufficiently capable of standing on his own because he moved to Paris as a self-employed 'technical businessman'. Over the next five years, Boemelburg lived in Paris and became fluent in French and a successful businessman. In 1911, he returned to Germany, and in September 1914, he was called up by the German Army as an infantryman. When the First World War broke out, his infantry regiment spent four years on the Western Front in France. These war years brought him an Iron Cross 2nd Class and the Wound Badge in Black after being lightly wounded in action. He also received a campaign medal and ended the war as a corporal (*Unteroffizier*). Boemelburg was demobilised on 8 December 1918 and, in the new year, lived in Berlin and began working again in the confectionary trade. The economic downturn and unemployment that affected Germany in the 1920s and early 1930s had no effect on his own job. Sweets and biscuits being the very last items people will stop buying when times are tough. These tough times indicate Boemelburg had acquired the necessary skills to maintain his job and standard of living. They also brought about his political thinking, and between the communists and the Nazis (the new political standard battlers for the governance of Germany after the disasters of the Weimar Republic), Boemelburg decided to join the Nazi Party, joining the Party and their SA Brown Shirts on 1 December 1931. He did not last long with the Brown Shirts (barely six weeks) before leaving them for the more glamourous SS Black Shirts. His newly acquired political stance saw him recruiting and organising the Nazi Party in Grunewald, a middle-class area in western Berlin. In January 1933, the Nazi Party came to power and Boemelburg's contribution was evidently recognised when he was invited to join the new political police being organised in Berlin by Hermann Göring—the *Geheime Staatspolizei* (Gestapo). On 25 February 1933, Boemelburg made a career change, beginning on the bottom rung of the Gestapo as a clerk. Yet Boemelburg had the edge over other new recruits—his fluency in French. At this early stage of life for the Gestapo, it was payback time for communists. Gestapo Berlin was organised with many sections dealing with various aspects of political life (i.e. anti-Nazi) being dealt with by various desk officers. Boemelburg's section, designated II 1A1, handled communists and Marxists. As he was fluent in French, his desk actively sought information on German communist *émigré* circles in France and French communists. In 1934, he was translating French articles into German from the French newspaper *L'Humanité* about French workers protesting at working conditions and a variety of documents obtained in France. By this stage, Boemelburg had been promoted to the next rung in career progression as a detective-candidate (*Kriminalassistent-anwärter*). In September 1935, Boemelburg was probably the oldest in a group of about twenty other men to be trained as officer-grade senior detectives, *Kriminalkommissar*, when the eight-month course in law, forensics, arrest, and detention procedures began at SS and Police Officer Training School in Berlin-Charlottenburg. Known under previous governments as the *Polizeiinstitut*, after the arrival of *Reichsführer*-SS Heinrich Himmler and his deputy SS-*Gruppenführer* Reinhard Heydrich, who were now in control of the Gestapo Berlin, it became *Führerschule der Sipo und des SD*. Now it had a political edge using new National Socialist principles against other enemies of the state. The course work included sections on Jews, the churches, and freemasonry. Passing the written test at the end of the course meant a SS commission. On 20 April 1936, Boemelburg was commissioned SS-*Untersturmführer* (second lieutenant) and probationary *Kriminalkommissar*. As usual with new *Kriminalkommissars*, they were soon posted to another station to broaden their experience. In Boemelburg's case, he transferred from the national Gestapo office in Berlin to the regional Gestapo Berlin office, Section II A, and continued to investigate communists and Marxists and their organisations. His career followed normal police civil service advancements, which also meant an equivalent rank in the SS; these dual elements having brought into effect following the appointment of *Reichsführer*-SS Heinrich Himmler as Chief of the German Police in 1936 and his standing as Chief of the SS. His SS promotions to SS-*Obersturmführer* (first lieutenant) and SS-*Hauptsturmführer* (captain) followed his rapid advance from *Kriminalkommissar* to *Kriminalrat* in two years, instead of the usual four years. In using his experience as head of the anti-communist department to make his name at Gestapo Berlin, Boemelburg became first choice in March 1939 as department chief of the same department at the newly established regional Gestapo office in Prague.

The March 1939 military invasion and total occupation of Czechoslovakia followed the international Sudeten crisis of October 1938. The western powers persuaded the Czechoslovak government to accept Hitler's proposals for the German absorption of the Sudetenland, Czech territory where as many as 800,000 ethnic German speakers lived. This region also included many Jews who now found themselves under German control. The occupation in March 1939 led the Germans to create two distinct regional spheres. The central and western regional areas of Czechoslovakia became the German 'Protectorate of Bohemia and Moravia' based in Prague; the eastern region became the German puppet state of Slovakia, based in Bratislava (Pressburg). Prague was where most German communist *émigrés* had sought refuge from Nazi Germany after January 1933; it was also a centre for Soviet intelligence operations. Boemelburg's job as department head II A was to sweep all these communist party officials and agents off the streets and into concentration camps. Taking any necessary measures against Czech communists, and after a successful year in Prague, Boemelburg was rewarded with a posting in summer 1940 to newly German-occupied France.[33]

In May 1940, the long-serving SD officer SS-*Sturmbannführer* Dr Helmut Knochen was appointed head of a Sipo-SD *Einsatzkommando* bound for Paris, following victorious German armies into the French capital. His Paris organisation, known as '*Beauftragten des Chefs der Sicherheitspol. u.d.SD für Frankreich u. Belgien—Dienststelle Paris*' (Plenipotentiary of the Chief of the Security Police and SD for France and Belgium – Paris Office) established its offices in 72–74 Avenue Foch. Boemelburg's posting to Paris probably happened in August 1940 and he was appointed 'Leiter IV' (Office Chief IV), responsible for every department and section of the Gestapo in occupied France, not just Paris. With his deputy, Hans Kieffer, who ran Gestapo counter-intelligence and counter-sabotage sections from the same time, he established their Paris offices in the former French Sûreté building at 11 Rue des Saussaies. In January 1943, they moved to the infamous 82–84 Avenue Foch.

In the early post-occupation period of 1940 Paris, the more organised French communist party became the first offenders against German military rule. With their long experience of combatting communism in Germany and the Protectorate, Boemelburg and Kieffer set about combatting French communism. When he arrived in Paris, Boemelburg was fifty-five years old, avuncular, slim, almost 6 feet tall (1.8 metres), with greying hair; four years later, before the retreat, he was a drunkard with a 'blue bloated face'. Kieffer was younger by fifteen years and shorter by 5–6 inches; his athletic build and broad shoulders that he began with in Paris turned into a slight stoop, worn out expression, and nervous manner. The war years in Paris were unkind to the health of both Boemelburg and Kieffer, with the idea of a posting to a sophisticated carefree Paris having given way to endless office work and pressures to get things done—to do the bidding of RSHA Berlin without complaint.

The intervening years since the end of the Second World War have seen the Dericourt myth explored by many authors. Not least by Jean Overton Fuller who corresponded and talked with him at length over many years until his death in November 1962, when his aircraft crashed in Laos.[34] The question asked of Dericourt but never satisfactorily explained is the nature of his betrayal of so many SOE agents to the Gestapo in Paris which resulted in their deaths? Dericourt never refuted the knowledge that he was paid by the Germans. Did he provide Gestapo Paris with the means of arresting these agents or did he simply allow them to copy written reports of the agents (both coded and *en clair*) being given to him for transmission to SOE London headquarters? As the SOE air liaison officer, Dericourt arranged for British aircraft to land agents at suitable spots in rural France and take others back to Britain together with any written material for SOE headquarters. Dericourt claimed that senior SOE and SIS officers in London were aware of what he was doing 'for the greater good'. Betrayal is betrayal in anyone's language and no SOE and SIS reports currently available in archives confirm Dericourt's claims, not even the extensive interrogations in his MI5 'name file' available at UK National Archives[35]. The obituary of Jean Overton Fuller in the British newspaper *The Guardian* (18 May 2009) states 'her judgment could suffer from a tendency to become emotionally attached to her subjects' as can be shown by her biographies of SOE agent Noor Inayat Khan and Henri Déricourt. Contrary to the image described by Fuller, *The Guardian* obituary more accurately describes Déricourt as 'an unscrupulous conman whose contact with the Germans earned him money and sent British agents to their deaths'. SOE historian M. R. D. Foot, writing in 1966, had a more charitable view when quoting Dericourt's interrogation by the French DST (the internal security service) from 4 November 1946.[36] In this interrogation, Déricourt claims that around May 1943 (he says late spring), he was taken for a drive by two Luftwaffe officers who he had known before the war, and a third man who introduced himself at Dr Götz. During the drive, Dr Götz told Déricourt all that the SD (where Dr Götz worked) knew about his clandestine work, including agents landing by parachute and by aircraft. It was Dr Götz who asked for his collaboration with the SD. Déricourt claims he felt 'more or less a prisoner' and agreed to collaborate. Apparently, he made no mention of the financial rewards. At Déricourt's trial in Paris (1948), Dr Götz told French judges that this drive described by Déricourt did not happen, instead describing how he, Boemelburg, and Déricourt had dinner together in the evenings. After the meal, Boemelburg observed as Déricort gave Dr Götz his new information. Almost forty years later (1985), Dr Götz—when a guest at the home of Jean Overton Fuller in Northamptonshire while Fuller was researching her biography of Déricourt, later published in 1989—again denied Déricourt's version of what had happened in Paris.[37]

When did Déricourt begin his collaboration with the SD (a misnomer for the Gestapo) and betrayal of SOE agents? All the indications lead to some time in May 1943, when Déricourt began allowing Kieffer's section to copy written reports and letters being sent from SOE agents in the field to London using aircraft organised by Déricourt that landed agents. Most of these documents copied came from the Paris-based PROSPER network, led by SOE Major Francis Suttill.

The downfall of the PROSPER network began from another direction—Holland. The Gestapo and Abwehr in Holland worked closely together against SOE operations in the country to such an extent that all SOE and most SIS agents infiltrated into Holland during 1940–1943 had been captured. They were now held in Dutch prisons. All the SOE wireless communications in Holland to SOE Dutch Section in London were part of a vast *Funkspiel* operation, called 'North Pole' by the Germans. As a result, between 1942 and 1943, the Gestapo captured all fifty-five SOE and SIS agents landing in Holland.

Throughout 1942–1944, SOE continued to drop weapons, supplies, money, food, and agents all into the arms of the waiting Gestapo. London, however, wanted agents in Holland to return for debriefing. For obvious reasons, the Germans put this off for some time until coming up with a plan. Why not have two English-speaking Germans travel down the escape route to Paris where they could be openly arrested. Two English-speaking Abwehr men from Holland, Richard Christmann and Karl Boden, masquerading as SOE Dutch agents, travelled via another German-controlled SOE agent in Brussels to Paris. On 20 May 1943, after asking around, they eventually found SOE agent and radio operator Gilbert Norman playing cards with other SOE agents in a Parisian café. It was agreed the two 'Dutchmen' would return to Brussels while Gilbert Norman arranged a Lysander operation back to Britain. They all agreed to meet again in the Paris cafe on 9 June 1943. The evening meeting place was subject to a German patrol and one of the 'Dutchmen' was arrested.[38] The other, Christmann, having established his *bona fides* with Gilbert Norman and the PROSPER circuit, was soon providing the local Gestapo Paris with contact details for the SOE agents.[39] Kieffer claimed 'PROSPER was arrested in his house after the house had been watched for about a fortnight', and Kieffer must have meant Gilbert Norman as Suttill was living in small hotels.[40] With such poor attitudes to personal security in Paris, SOE 'F' Section in London joined in and provided the second piece of information that betrayed the PROSPER circuit to the Gestapo.

The two Canadians (Pickersgill and Macalistair) were searched by Gestapo men from Blois following their arrest on 21 June 1943 at Dhuizon. Among the various objects and messages found on them were 'some new [radio] crystals and detailed instructions for their use for Gilbert Norman'.[41] SOE 'F' Section thus played a role in the downfall of the PROSPER circuit. Two days later, in the small hours of 24 June, the arrests began in Paris. Norman and his courier Andrée Borrel were arrested together at a Paris apartment. Their organiser, Francis Suttill, was arrested the following morning at a small Paris hotel. It is said that none of them talked for several days in the belief that their operatives would realise their sudden disappearance meant they had been arrested, and in turn make them disappear from their usual haunts. With the two Canadians now brought to Paris and imprisoned with Borrel, Norman, and Suttill, the Gestapo men set about interrogating them. The SOE agents had received a couple of day's instruction in holding up to interrogation during their training in Britain. Very few arrested agents were able to withstand for long professional Gestapo officials with interrogation techniques going back years. Kieffer stated after the war that his section had been watching Norman for about two weeks before his arrest. This indicates that Christmann had provided Kieffer with the necessary information about Norman on 9 June or very soon afterwards. The notes for Norman found after searching the two Canadians were simply confirmation. After several days of interrogation, according to Kieffer, the first to break was Norman.

Kieffer showed Suttill and Norman the photographs of their reports they had passed to Dericourt for despatch to London by one of the Lysander aircraft operations:

> At this time I did not attach much importance to this material. It was, however, put to very good use during the interrogation of PROSPER [Suttill]. PROSPER did not want to make any statement, but GILBERT/ NORMAN, who had not the integrity of PROSPER, made a very full statement. Through NORMAN and through the documentary material available we received our first insight into the French Section, and also through DENISE [Borrel].[42]

Josef Götz, having been recalled from his leave in Hamburg by Kieffer, quickly set about two *Funkspiel* operations with SOE London courtesy of material found on the two Canadians; they had their unused radio set and ciphers and also their radio transmission schedule, plus new radio crystals for Gilbert Norman's radio set. With this unused transmission ability, Götz immediately began deceiving SOE 'F' Section in London. The *Funkspiel* using Norman's radio ciphers did not last long as other SOE agents at freedom in Paris reported his arrest to London. Any news about the two Canadians was not reported as no one knew of their arrival and capture. SOE wanted them to set up a new circuit, ARCHDEACON, based in Sedan, east of Paris. The ciphers given to the Canadians were used by Götz as *Funkspiel* ZEUSS back to SOE London to disastrous effect as they parachuted in both agents and supplies over the next twelve months.

As Dr Götz got to work on the *Funkspiel* material, Kieffer and his interrogators got to work on Norman and Suttill. A chain of interrogators worked continuously on the two men, allowing them food and drink, but denying them sleep for two days. Finally, Kieffer showed them photocopies of their written reports sent to London via Dericourt's Lysander aircraft operations. This broke their spirit. Was there a traitor in London? Kieffer did not explain how he came by the reports, allowing them to worry over it. At this point, according to Kieffer, Norman and Suttill began asking what would happen if they talked; would the French people who helped them be arrested or killed? The question of a pact was discussed. What would Kieffer's superiors guarantee in return? Kieffer discussed the situation with SS-*Standartenführer* Knochen, who informed SS-Major Kopkow at RSHA Berlin. Kopkow knew what to do and what to offer, the same scenario had come up in the Rote Kapelle investigations in 1942 when Russian spy Harro Schulze-Boysen claimed he had lodged papers in Sweden and wanted the lives of his fellow Soviet spies spared. Kopkow obliged him with a worthless signed and certified document of intent and Schulze-Boysen confirmed there were no documents in Sweden. He and his fellow conspirators, including his wife, went to the gallows.

Kopkow therefore had no compunction in agreeing to another worthless signed and certified document from his office. It was sent to Paris within a matter of days, agreeing terms, such was the urgency:

> Kieffer asked Suttill and Norman to give him precise details of all of their activities for the French Section in England and in France, to point out all of their helpers in France, to give the location of all of the depots of arms and material, the names and addresses of the people who created these depots or were guarding them. They must also both undertake that they would order their helpers with whom they were confronted, to behave in the same way as themselves. In exchange, Kieffer would undertake, on their giving their word of honour, that they would both, together with their helpers, be treated fairly and not be placed before a tribunal but purely and simply sent to a concentration camp in Germany until the end of the war. Suttill and Norman accepted on condition that the only people to be arrested would be those who had taken an active part in their clandestine activities and not those who were simply aware of their activities, for example, their families. Kieffer agreed. To my knowledge the conditions were adhered to strictly by both sides.[43]

The Gestapo then went about arresting fellow agents of Norman and Suttill and also confiscating what arms and supplies they had received from London and secreted in various locations. Within days, the PROSPER circuit across Paris and adjoining regions suffered large numbers of arrests, seizures of arms, supplies, and radio transmitters. No doubt Kieffer was fully aware of the subterfuge created by Kopkow's letter and played his part in the arrests and seizures, occasionally taking Norman along to help in uncovering arms and supply dumps. Norman and Suttill had been completely deceived by the Gestapo and possibly Suttill voiced dismay as he was soon sent from Paris to Sachsenhausen concentration camp north of Berlin, arriving on 3 September 1943.[44]

The arrest of Norman and loss of his radio transmitter meant there was only one SOE radio operator still at large and working in Paris—Noor Inayat Khan. There had been a double Lysander landing during the night of 16–17 June 1943, arranged by Déricourt, north of Angers, bringing SOE agents Inayat Khan, Diana Rowden, Cecily Lefort, and Charles Skepper.[45] None of them would survive. Inayat Khan (codename MADELEINE) had been sent to Paris as a radio operator to assist the CINEMA/PHONO circuit, a sub-circuit of PROSPER. A week later, she escaped being arrested with Norman and Suttill and was now forced to change address regularly, keeping the radio transmitter with her while finding somewhere safe and retaining contact with the rest of circuit. The arrest of Norman left Inayat Khan to frustrate the Gestapo squads that were arresting dozens of agents and informants across the Paris area between June and August 1943, following the Kopkow 'pact' with Norman and Suttill—all the time trying to maintain radio contact with SOE London. It is believed Inayat Khan was betrayed to the Gestapo when they arrested her on 13 October 1943 in a central Paris apartment.[46]

Robert Dowlen, a radio operator for the CHESTNUT network had been DF'd working one of two radio transmitters he used—not the one in Paris, but a second at a farm near Mery-sur-Oise, north of Paris. He was caught transmitting on 31 July 1943 by a Gestapo squad from Paris that brought him back to Aveue Foch. It is possible that Dowlen was brought face to face with Gilbert Norman, who talked with him about the Gestapo 'pact' he had arranged. This seems more likely as two days later, on 2 August 1943, a Gestapo squad came to Auffargis, just to the west of Paris, and arrested his organiser, Charles Grover-Williams. Brought back to Avenue Foch, Grover-Williams decided to say nothing, regardless of the 'pact', and despite many interrogations, he remained steadfast in his silence. It was probably in early January 1944 when Grover-Williams was sent up to Berlin and incarcerated in the cellars of the RSHA building where Kopkow's men waited for him.[47] It was many weeks later before Grover-Williams was sent up to Sachsenhausen concentration camp to join Francis Suttill.[48] Dowlen was sent to Flossenbürg camp.

Kieffer's men, Götz and Placke, were soon unable to use Norman's ciphers for a *Funkspiel* with SOE London because Inayat Khan had informed them of his arrest. The arrest of Inayat Khan resulted in a huge bonus for Kieffer as, contrary to security instructions—or her failure to understand these instructions before infiltration into France with her transmitter—the Germans found copies of all her back radio-traffic to and from London, complete with security checks. Using Inayat Khan's ciphers and security checks as *Funkspiel* DIANA, Götz was able to hoodwink SOE London into believing she was still at liberty and thus the veracity of their messages. In a post-war interrogation report, Kieffer said Inayat Khan was resolute in not answering questions about her work or SOE organisation and attempted escape twice from her cell in Avenue Foch. These escapes must have happened in October, in the two or three weeks after her arrest, as in November 1943, Kieffer claims he had her sent to Karlsruhe; in reality, Inayat Khan went to Pforzheim Prison and was shackled day and night to preclude further escape.[49] After the war, Götz reported that they initially thought SOE London 'were not really deceived', but they continued with *Funkspiel* DIANA, and by the end of 1943, Götz felt their acceptance.[50] Their *Funkspiel* messages requested supplies and money that were dropped and recovered. The various radio deception games with London continued and increased, so much so that Götz's section had more men assigned. To some extent this may have been due to the loss of one of their English translators, August Scherer.

Not all Gestapo raids went smoothly and not all agents were captured without a fight. In November 1943, another SOE radio transmitter was located by DF'ing at Tours in the Loire valley, some 120 miles south-west of Paris. On 8 November, a Gestapo Paris squad assembled and raided the location, surprising the radio operator in the act of transmitting. A firefight took place and August Scherer, a Gestapo translator, was shot dead by the SOE agent, who also wounded the other English translator Ernest Vogt. The SOE agent André Dubois (codename HERCULE) was shot and badly wounded by returning gunfire.[51] The Gestapo men returned to Paris with Dubois' radio transmitter and ciphers; Dubois himself was treated for his injuries at a Paris hospital before being imprisoned in Fresnes. A new radio game was established using these newly captured ciphers as *Funkspiel* HERAKLES (the German for Hercules). Before the end of November 1943, another two SOE radio operators were captured: John Young (18 November, in Dijon) and Marcel Clech (19 November, in Paris).

In 1942, Kieffer's section had managed to capture four SOE agents, two organisers and two radio operators. These four men were still in Paris prisons at the end of 1943. During 1943, Kieffer increased the pace and targeted SOE agents with greater persistence through denunciations, document checks at railway stations, and DF'ing. These measures led to the capture of forty SOE agents, including thirteen radio operators, most in the last six months. In addition, a British raiding party of five saboteurs (Operation SCULLION II) was dropped by parachute during the night of 17–18 August 1943 to attack a synthetic petrol refinery at Autun, 180 miles (300 km) south-east of Paris in Burgundy. They were able to plant their bombs, but the resultant explosions did little damage. Afterwards, four of the five saboteurs managed to reach Paris, and before the end of August 1943, all four had been arrested and imprisoned at Fresnes.[52]

SOE historian M. R. D. Foot rightly believed 1943 was calamitous for SOE, not just for Kieffer's actions from Paris, but also for the loss of Jean Moulin, beaten half to death by SS-Lieutenant Klaus Barbie in Lyon. Moulin had parachuted into France on 1 January 1942, and had been appointed by de Gaulle as a Delegate on the French National Council based in London. Moulin's job was to unify the various sections of the resistance in France and travelled widely from his base in Lyon. On 21 June 1943, when attending a secret meeting of resistance leaders in a Lyon suburb, the Gestapo surrounded the house and arrested those attending the meeting. Moulin and the others were taken to nearby Montluc prison. Barbie brutally beat and tortured Moulin, who remained silent throughout a series of daily interrogations. In July 1943, Moulin was sent up to Paris where he was put on a deportation train for Germany. Moulin had died (or committed suicide) by the time the train arrived at Metz on 21 July 1943.[53]

Both Kieffer and his boss, Helmut Knochen, were fully aware that Kopkow, in Berlin, and his bosses were very concerned about SOE 'F' Section activities in France. They were not only worried about their actions on the ground, but their likely reactions in the run-up to an Allied invasion. German expectations were that any Allied invasion would be somewhere along the French coastline. The invasion did not take place in 1943 despite many SOE agents expecting it, so 1944 would be the year. Kopkow urged Kieffer to get details of the invasion date as a priority. Although Kieffer claims not to have sanctioned torture as a means of obtaining information, his section did commit acts of torture. Whereas Emil Rühl and Josef Stork admitted to water-boarding Frenchmen, no one wanted to admit beating and torturing SOE agents.[54] Such non-self-incriminating statements do not bear comparison with what happened to some agents in Paris and at the regional Gestapo headquarters—the women sometimes being mistreated as much as the men. Most were beaten and bloodied about the face. Brian Rafferty, an organiser arrested in June 1943 and brought to Dijon prison, was reported 'in a lamentable condition, arm broken, unrecognizable, bruised'.[55] Some were beaten on every occasion when interrogated—Christopher Burney was beaten with an ox-tail whip.[56] Tommy Yeo-Thomas said he was beaten, water-boarded, and given electric-shock treatment at Avenue Foch.[57] Odette Sansom states she had her fingernails pulled out.[58] Maurice Southgate, an organiser, was arrested on 1 May 1944 at Montluçon when calling at a house where his radio operator transmitted without realising the danger signals of a German presence. They had DF'd the location, raided the house, and arrested the radio operator Rene Matthieu; he would later die under interrogation at Avenue Foch.[59] By the end of May, Southgate was at Avenue Foch in Paris where Ernest Vogt, the Gestapo translator of English, told him 'that they were sorry for any bad treatment given to British officers by the Gestapo in the provinces—"the latter didn't know any better"'.[60] In their training in Britain, SOE agents were taught techniques about interrogations should they be caught—it is one thing to be taught in a safe environment, but completely different in a hostile and menacing environment. It takes a strong character to withstand hostile interrogation and not every agent was able to do so. There are reports some broke down within hours of arrest. The organiser in Rouen, Claude Malraux, was arrested on 8 March 1944 and was 'reported to have broken down under torture'. That night, thirty to forty men of his network, including his radio operator, were arrested by the Gestapo and 35 tons of arms recovered.[61] Radio operators were subjected to severe treatment, both Marcus Bloom captured near Toulouse and Yolande Unternahrer (Beekman) in northern France at St Quentin were both beaten bloody in efforts to obtain their ciphers, bluff checks, and true checks (which were used to add truthfulness to the radio messages and the knowledge that the operator was still at liberty).[62] Southgate reported: 'Time after time for different men, London sent back messages saying: "My dear fellow, you only left us a week ago. On your first message you go and forget to put your true check"'.[63] This meant more beatings for the radio operator who had tried to put London in the picture, only to be demoralised by London's failure to recognise what had happened. As London failed to recognise the signs of German control of the radio sets, more agents would be lured to landing grounds controlled by them, enabling the Gestapo to literally nip in the bud anyone sent to create havoc and resistance in France by agents who brought more radio transmitters. With the turn of 1943 into 1944, this is exactly what happened.

The arrest of agents and the helpers in 1944 continued with greater intensity. On 13 January 1944, German DF'ing brought a Gestapo squad to an address in St Quentin where radio operator Yolande Beekman was caught transmitting. The raid also brought the capture of her organiser Gustave Bieler. The radio set and her ciphers were brought to Avenue Foch in Paris. February 1944 could be rightly said to have been a disaster for SOE. It began on 3 February when two agents, Gaillot and Vallee, making for a Lysander pick-up to take them to safety in Britain were arrested at a checkpoint. The failure of London to recognise radio sets under German control resulted in two parties of agents (four agents on 8 February near Poitiers and five agents on 29 February near Chartes) being captured on the landing grounds. Between these two actions, on 15 February at Montbéliard near Dijon, SOE instructor Eric Cauchi fearing Gestapo arrest was shot and killed during a street firefight with them. March 1944 was an even greater disaster for SOE, with the Gestapo squads seemingly everywhere. Two separate groups of agents (six in total) were arrested at their landing grounds during the night of 2–3 March as a result of German control of radio sets. As far afield as Bordeaux, Marseille, and Paris more arrests followed. In the first quarter of 1944, the Gestapo arrested thirty SOE agents. The second quarter of 1944 brought in another twenty-one agents, and not just from SOE; the Gestapo net had caught four French BCRA agents who recently landed near Limoges through another captured radio set, their first OSS agent Rene Matthieu (mentioned above) and SIS agent Gerald Keun in Paris.

By the end of June 1944, with the Allied invasion forces now firmly established in Normandy, it was the regional Gestapo offices who were catching agents. *Waffen*-SS front-line divisions also caught agents. Violette Szabo, for example, was caught on 10 June 1944 at a roadblock manned by SS men of the 2.SS-Division '*Das Reich*' at Salon-la-Tour near Limoges, who were being hampered by resistance obstacles on their way north to Normandy. Using a Sten light machine gun, Szabo held the *Waffen*-SS men at bay covering the escape of her comrades with gunfire.[64] With ammunition exhausted, she surrendered and was handed over to the local Gestapo office in Limoges before her transfer a few days later to Kieffer's men in Paris. Two more SOE agents were less fortunate. On 8 July 1944, SOE radio operator Maurice Larcher was shot and killed transmitting by SS men of the 1.SS-Division '*Leibstandarte Adolf Hitler*' at Pierrefitte-en-Cinglais (Calvados) just outside the western edge of the Normandy bridgehead. His organiser, Jean Renard-Dandicolle, also suffered gunshot wounds and was apparently executed on the spot.[65] Another SOE radio operator, Alcide Beauregard, captured by DF'ing in Lyon on 16 July, was executed a month later in Montluc prison on 20 August 1944.[66]

Two women, SOE radio operators Eileen Nearne and Lilian Rolfe, were caught in the last ten days of July 1944 (Nearne in Paris, Rolfe in Nargis, south of Paris).[67] Both were heavily involved in transmitting information on German troop movements northwards to stem the Allied breakout from their Normandy bridgehead.

It was now time to remove all the captured agents being held in Paris prisons. After the war, Kieffer declared:

> We received instructions from [RSHA] Berlin concerning transports to Germany in the case of the French Section nominal rolls, signed either by *Obergruppenführer* Müller or Kopkow; possibly also, sometimes by K.R. [*Kriminalrat*] Ampletzer or Büchert or Müller. I remember a transport of four officers who were being considered for exchange purposes, amongst them [Peter] Churchill. As far as I can remember, three transports went to Ravitch [*sic.*]; about 42 were involved in matters of the French Section; one transport went to Flossenburg [*sic.*]; two were sent to Ravensbrück; one or two to Karlsruhe; also to Buchenwald. One transport for Ravitch consisted of 24 people and was accompanied by Woelere [*sic.*—Wörle]. Otto went to Ravitch once with a transport of 10/15. One small transport was sent with about six people.[68]

Kieffer was reasonably accurate about the number and destinations of the transports, but was out on the numbers of agents concerned. What Kieffer's statement does confirm is that the Gestapo staff in Paris had no influence on where the agents were sent, and that once beyond the borders of France, responsibility for the agents' welfare now lay in the hands of RSHA Berlin and especially Kopkow.

The various Paris prisons used by Kieffer holding captured SOE agents had not been emptied, and some, like Christopher Burney, endured almost sixteen months of solitary confinement at Fresnes prison under appalling sanitary and nutritional conditions. On 27 January 1944, Burney was included on a deportation train with Maurice Pertschuk, the two Newton brothers, and Gilbert Turck to Buchenwald concentration camp in Germany.[69] The next to go was Peter Churchill on 14 February 1944, via RSHA Berlin to Sachsenhausen concentration camp.[70] There was a lull in transports until April. On 9 April, fifteen British and French agents left Paris for Flossenbürg concentration camp near the Czech border.[71] A few days later, another twenty-four British and French agents were sent on transport and arrived at Rawitsch penitentiary (now in Poland) on 18 April after five days of travel.[72] On 12 May, when eight female SOE agents were sent to Karlsruhe prison, only one would survive (Odette Sansom); according to John Starr, they left from Avenue Foch in a charabanc.[73] The final agents were sent off in August; on 8 August, a train with forty agents departed, with thirty-eight men destined for Buchenwald and two women (Lilian Rolfe and Violette Szabo) destined for Ravensbrück. Only six of the men would return. A final train left Paris on 11 August with 102 women most destined for Ravensbrück, among them were four BCRA agents captured in Limoges during April as a result of a *Funkspiel* with the French intelligence service.[74]

On 7 July 1944, a container drop of weapons organised through a *Funkspiel* with SOE London would turn into a nightmare for Kieffer. The drop zone at Noailles near Paris had Kieffer's men waiting for the containers, but instead of containers, twelve commandos of 1st SAS Regiment parachuted in. Two of them escaped, two were killed, and eight were captured after a firefight that resulted in three of them being wounded. They were brought to Paris, with the wounded sent to 'La Pitie' hospital, and the remaining five were questioned by Kieffer's interrogators. Information about the captured SAS went up to Knochen, Oberg, and the Abwehr. Knochen informed Kopkow at RSHA Berlin:

> A reply came immediately by teleprint from Kopkow's Subsection, that we were to wait for further decisions and orders in this matter. On the express orders of Berlin, Paris could not give any instructions concerning the Commando men. They were in fact in the power of RSHA.[75]

Kieffer's interrogation teams continued to interrogate the SAS men through mid-July 1944 and only stopped on 20 July 1944. The army command in France followed the Operation Valkyrie orders from Berlin announcing the Führer's death and the army had taken over control of the State. Their orders required them to arrest all senior Security Police officers, and as a result, both Oberg and Knochen were taken into custody by the army, leaving their Paris offices in disarray and leaving their subordinates wondering what was happening. It was twenty-four hours before the army released Oberg and Knochen following the collapse of the coup by Stauffenberg. This meant the SAS men were saved for the moment. With Hitler back in control and his revenge taking place, it was against this background that a teleprinted message dated 6 Aug 1944 arrived in Paris and addressed to Knochen. The message from RSHA IV Chief Müller reported that the Führer had ordered the immediate shooting of the SAS men held captive in Paris.

After consulting with Oberg, Knochen spoke with Kieffer and an execution party was organised. During the morning of 7 August 1944, the SAS men had to remove their uniforms and put on civilian clothes, before they were taken out towards Noailles and shot. One SAS man managed to escape into the woods as the firing squad assembled. Kieffer reported back to Knochen on the shooting and the escape who reported it back RSHA IV Chief Müller. A reply came back ordering an investigation into the escape, but events on the ground in France overtook any further explanation.[76]

The last August 1944 trains departing from Paris took prisoners to concentration camps across Germany, and Kieffer and all Gestapo Paris sections were packing files in readiness for their own departure due to the advance of the Allied armies. Kieffer sent off most of his staff, and a few days later, on 17 August, he and his remaining staff left, heading east for Nancy then Strasbourg, finally leaving French territory. On 1 September 1944, they established their base for future operations at Offenburg in Germany, 16 miles (25 km) across the River Rhone from Strasbourg. Kieffer's radio experts Dr Götz and Placke were still continuing their existing *Funkspiel* operations with SOE London.[77]

What did SOE achieve in France and what effect did Kieffer's counter-espionage operations have on their activities? From a baseline of no agents on the ground in September 1940, in the following four years, British intelligence agencies trained and infiltrated into France at least 1,784 agents, both men and women.[78] One agent died of illness, fifteen agents died fighting the Germans, 122 agents were deported to concentration camps (of which thirty-four survived), nine died in captivity, and seventy-nine were executed. These numbers are relatively few in comparison with many thousands of French men and women who helped the resistance in various ways and were deported to German concentration camps as 'NN' or '*Nacht und Nebel*' (Night and Fog) prisoners whose return was 'undesirable'. Thousands died of disease, malnutrition, and forced labour.

One of the main aims of these agents was to train French resistance people in the use of weapons and explosives. To support these aims, the RAF and USAAF, over almost four years, flew 7,498 sorties (air operations) and dropped 10,485.5 tons (106,530 kg) of materiel, including 1.34 tons (1,361 kg) of explosives (mainly plastic explosives). The guns and ammunitions were used to protect sabotage attacks and local uprisings. In 1943 and 1944, numerous acts of industrial sabotage were carried out on French factories producing military equipment and components for the German war machine. Some attacks had little effect, while others had a tremendous effect.[79]

Kieffer's section of the Paris Gestapo, regional KdS offices across France, the Abwehr, and French informers all participated in curtailing the sabotage and arresting agents. They proved unable to stop it as shown by the numerous acts of sabotage. The number of agents arrested disrupted rather than stopped SOE activities. However, the ability of Kieffer's men to seriously hamper communications to SOE London during 1943 and 1944 cannot be overestimated. DF'ing and arrests of radio operators followed by *Funkspiel* operations gave the Gestapo an advantage when they arrested trained agents on their landing grounds.

SOE Activities in Holland, 1940–1945

It is against this background of *Funkspiel* operations that attention is now drawn to SIS and SOE Dutch Section activities in Holland during the war. It does not matter how you look at it, between 1940 and the summer of 1943, SIS and SOE activities were a complete disaster. German penetration of the agent networks and arrest of new agents landing by parachute and the subsequent use of their radio ciphers meant the German security services and Abwehr were in complete control of all British and Dutch intelligence operations in Holland. The Abwehr called it Operation North Pole (*Unternehmen Nordpol*) and the Gestapo, the England Game (*Englandspiel*). The capture of trained men and women, alongside the air supply of arms and munitions, food and money, and loss of aircraft and aircrew, is a terrible indictment of SOE Dutch Section, who failed to recognise radio signals with missing security checks from their operators in the field, which led to the most awful waste of human and material resources.

The original plan following the German occupation of Holland was intelligence gathering. What was happening in Dutch cities and towns, how were the population coping, and could active resistance begin? SIS began its operations first in 1940, and SOE dropped its first agents in 1941 when SOE Dutch Section had some inkling of Dutch resistance movements and their organisers. A 1945 SOE report discussing the situation in Holland during 1941–1943 stated:

> …Most of them [resistance organisations] carried out clandestine resistance to the Occupying Power in some form or other, while some were concerned with the preservation of Dutch institutions and culture against German encroachment and absorption. All were, unfortunately, permeated with political rivalries, survivals of the previous Dutch heterogeneous political system, and this was a source of considerable weakness, since most valuable time was wasted and much energy dissipated on unprofitable squabbling, the main object being often lost sight of.[80]

The two main resistance groupings, the Orde Dienst (OD) and Raad van Verzet (RVV), were spread through Holland. As both were too loosely organised, with little in the way of a central command, the Germans found it easy to penetrate and be kept informed of their activities. A third organisation created in 1942, O.S.VI, and reported to be soundly based, carried out bureaucratic sabotage (destruction of population ledgers, supplying false identity documents and ration coupons, and helping Dutch Jews) and 'elimination of undesirables'. Illegal presses were established, producing such newspapers as *Het Parool*, *Je Maintiendrai*, and *Trouw*, and their publication persisted until the liberation in 1945, despite numerous German attempts to track down the presses. British plans to support resistance and political measures would be thwarted by successful German counter-espionage against the agents sent out from Britain to train resistance workers in sabotage.

The first agents were sent by SIS: Lodo van Hamel was sent by parachute on 27 August 1940 (a surprise since Holland surrendered to Germany on 17 May 1940), followed nine months later during the night 11–12 June 1941, by Hans Zomer and his radio operator Wiek Schrage. Aart Alblas, another radio operator, was sent in by parachute on 5–6 July 1941. Over the sixteen months (from the end of August 1940 until the end of December 1941), fifteen SIS agents were infiltrated into Holland by parachute drop and from the sea by the Royal Navy, although only four returned—one of which, Lotti Röell, survived several years in Ravensbrück concentration camp for women. Two men of the fifteen agents are presumed to have died at sea while attempting to return to Britain in November 1941. Of the remaining nine agents, five were murdered in German concentration camps, two (van Hamel and Zomer) were tried by German Military Tribunal and shot for acts of espionage, and the remaining three are unknown and un-commemorated.[81]

Radio transmissions of coded messages to SIS and SOE London from agents in Holland were intercepted and tracked by German direction-finding units. As a result, most of the early SIS agents were arrested and unsuccessful *Funkspiel* operations took place. SIS very quickly recognised these messages were made either under duress or by another person due to the lack of security checks and they broke off further radio contact. SOE made serious mistakes about missing radio security checks almost from the beginning. The first SOE Dutch Section agents, Huub Lauwers (radio operator) and Thijs Taconis (organiser), were dropped by parachute over central Holland during the night of 6–7 November 1941. After landing, they made for The Hague and set about their tasks: organise resistance and organise sabotage. It did not take long for Lauwers to discover his radio set had a fault, which he had to have fixed, then he discovered an indoor aerial precluded transmission of signals. On 3 January 1942, he finally succeeded in making his first radio contact with London from The Hague.[82] Meanwhile, Taconis set himself up in Arnhem and found organising resistance difficult; many people he approached refused to join them. Making contact with a Dutch resistance group already in existence was a card they played. By such small careful steps to maintain their security, they missed the devil on the doorstep. As everywhere, the Abwehr and Gestapo had an informer network and Holland was no exception. The resistance group they contacted had been penetrated by George Ridderhof, an alcoholic, profiteer, diamond-smuggler, and Abwehr informant.[83] Lauwers kept regular radio contact with London, which sent him a message to find a drop zone where the RAF could drop weapons. His increasing regular radio transmissions with intelligence material was intercepted by German direction-finding. With the weapons drop fixed for the night of 28–29 February 1942, Taconis and the Dutch resistance group that included Ridderhof, who provided a lorry to take away the weapons, were staring into the night sky when an aircraft went over and two containers with parachutes drifted down. One was lost in a local canal and the second was retrieved and taken away. The Abwehr and the local Gestapo could not have British weapons distributed among the Dutch resistance, so Lauwers was the first to be arrested on 6 March 1942 after breaking off his regular radio transmissions as German vehicles had been seen in the near vicinity. He was walking away when stopped by the Abwehr. The Gestapo arrested Taconis in Arnhem on 9 March through another informer. The Abwehr held Lauwers and shared the results with the Gestapo and the Gestapo held Taconis and shared their results with the Abwehr.[84]

The officers in charge of the Abwehr investigations and those in charge of the Gestapo investigations reached a broad agreement about these agents: they would work together, but the Gestapo would keep them in a Dutch prison under their control.

Major Hermann Giskes arrived in Holland during August 1941, having being posted from Abwehr Paris. Giskes had an army background, serving in the First World War as an officer; after the armistice, his army service continued, apart from ten years in civilian life as a businessman (1924–1934), before he returned to the army. In 1938, he joined the Abwehr in Münster, and in 1940, Major Giskes was posted to Abwehr Paris, counter-intelligence section. On arrival in Holland, his new role at Abwehr station in The Hague was Departmental Chief III 'F', in charge of counter-intelligence throughout Holland. He brought in new ideas and got rid of old wood, bringing in new people. One of these, Gerhard Huntemann, would play a major role in deceiving SOE Dutch Section, as already noted, by also deceiving SOE French Section agents in Paris. It took some time for Giskes to get his organisation how he wanted, leaving the Gestapo to carry out the important counter-espionage activities with the German police DF'ing unit and make the early arrests (SIS agents van Hamel, Zomer, ter Laak, Ortt, de Jonge, and others). Giskes was ready when Huub Lauwers and Thijs Taconis were arrested in March 1942 in a joint action between the Abwehr and Gestapo. Lauwers because the first agent they 'turned', and from the moment he began transmitting deception messages to SOE Dutch Section in Britain, Operation North Pole began. It was a success for the Abwehr-Gestapo partnership, and a disaster for SOE Dutch Section as they accepted Lauwers radio transmissions even when he missed his security checks.[85]

There were moments when Operation North Pole might have been discovered by SOE following other agents being dropped blind in March and April 1942. Organiser Leo Andringa and his radio operator Jan Molenaar dropped on 29 March; Molenaar was seriously injured on landing and rather than hold back Andringa, he took his own life with the SOE supplied cyanide tablet. Andringa went on his way and was arrested a month later on 29 April. Organiser Gosse Ras and his radio operator, Hans Jordaan, landed during the night of 29 March—they were arrested on 1 and 3 May 1942 respectively. In April, organiser Barend Kloos and his radio operator, Henk Sebes, dropped on 5 April—they were arrested on 29 April and 8 May respectively. The final drop was by Jan de Haas on 18 April, a radio operator sent in to replace Molenaar. He was swept up on 28 April. By the end of the first week of May 1942, the Abwehr and Gestapo now had five organisers and four radio operators (with their radio ciphers) in custody and they controlled the entire SOE agent network in Holland. It was time for Operation North Pole to begin its mass deception of SOE through *Funkspiel* operations.

SS-Captain *Kriminalrat* Josef Schreieder was a career Gestapo officer. Born in Munich in 1904, he came to Holland in August 1940 with the first Security Police unit. Following the establishment of BdS Holland, with headquarters in The Hague, Schreieder became the head of Department IV 'E' (counter-espionage), the equivalent of Kieffer in Paris; like Kieffer, he was responsible for espionage cases, sabotage, and armed resistance. Giskes said of Schreieder: '...Well-intentioned, but often prevented from carrying out promises by Deppner. Tried to establish good relations with the Abwehr and was not in entire agreement with the SD on many matters...'.[86]

Schreieder himself confirmed the views of Kieffer about RSHA Berlin's express interest in the captured SIS and SOE agents. Unlike Kieffer, who mentions Kopkow by name, Schreieder does not and simply states RSHA Berlin. Since Kopkow was responsible for all Allied agents across German-occupied territories, it is safe to assume that Schreieder did normally communicate with Kopkow about the agents:

> In accordance with directions from the RSHA, whenever agents were caught, the question of a possible *Spiel* had to be examined thoroughly. When the report of a capture was rendered, notice had also to be given as to whether a *Spiel* was to be attempted, or on what grounds a *Spiel* was considered impossible. If a *Spiel* was to be attempted, then a report was to be made on the proposed lines of the *Spiel*, and the contents of the first messages which would be transmitted. The RSHA then approved the *Spiel* and gave it a name.
>
> In order to maintain regular times of transmission, messages of a general nature such as routine signal messages, notification of dropping points, etc. were transmitted without the previous authority of the RSHA. The content of these messages was later reported to the RSHA, and all messages had of course to follow the lines laid down or approved by that office.[87]

Schreieder found, as did Kieffer's section in Paris, Kopkow's section at RSHA Berlin could be tardy in supplying information: '...the obtaining of material was such a complicated and slow process, and the material itself was so poor in quality and quantity, that its use was avoided wherever possible'.[88] By the end of 1943, one of Kieffer's *Funkspiel* experts in Paris, Götz, no longer asked Kopkow's section for information, having now found it could be established from army headquarters in Paris—later appraising Kopkow of the messages sent to SOE French Section. Schreieder found he and Giskes would do the same in Holland.

SS-Captain (later Major) Dr Erich Deppner had also arrived in Holland in August 1940 and was originally in charge of Department I/II, responsible for administration. In autumn 1942, he was placed in charge of Department IV, and he was responsible for all Gestapo matters in Holland. According to Giskes, he was a 'brutal SD-man and Nazi; did all he could to further the SD at the expense of the Abwehr, untrustworthy and secretive'.[89] It is little wonder that, in their post-war memoirs about Operation North Pole, neither Giskes nor Schreieder had much to say about Deppner. Deppner was the equivalent of Boemelburg in Paris, with none of his abilities.

With the capture of all the SOE agents in Holland by early May 1942, this left the remaining SIS agents at large. Three were arrested before the end of May, a fourth agent (active in the field since July 1941) was arrested on 16 July 1942. The fifth and last, dropped on 29 March 1942, remained at large until October 1942. Some of the SIS agents had radio sets and sent their own messages. When agents were captured and *Funkspiel* operations began with their ciphers, SIS London quickly recognised the subterfuge and broke off contact. If SIS were not taken in by these false radio messages, it raises the question as to why their sister organisation, SOE, failed to recognise German-controlled radio messages after their agents began falling like dominos into German hands. SOE Dutch Section began transmitting to captured agents in Holland that new agents were being dropped to designated drop zones as specified in the *Funkspiel* messages. In this period of German control, between the end of May and the end of December 1942, SOE dropped seven more radio operators and twelve organisers. Little wonder that Schreieder could record that, in late September 1942, he had seven captured radio sets sending information back to SOE.[90] Between February and May 1943, before SOE Dutch Section realised something was amiss, another three radio operators and twelve organisers had been dropped into German-controlled drop zones. On 10 February 1943, Schreieder recorded their thirteenth radio set was now in contact with SOE London. Quite apart from the agents, SOE had also dropped an enormous amount of money, arms, and munitions intended for armed resistance.

The HSSPF in Holland, SS-General Hanns Albin Rauter, kept *Reichsführer*-SS Himmler fully informed about the SOE and SIS agents being caught. In his daily report of 28 October 1942, he reported that, the previous night, two agents (numbers 39 and 40) had been captured at the drop zone along with '18 tons' of material, including radio transmitters. On 11 November 1942, Rauter informed Himmler of further developments:

> In the course of E-Spiel [*Englandspiel*] an instruction came yesterday at different times and on different radio sets, that for the time being they should not carry out operations and await further orders and instructions by radio. An English request whether two more long planned agents should be sent at this time was answered in the affirmative.[91]

In turn, also on 11 November 1942 in Munich, *Reichsführer*-SS Himmler informed Hitler in his 'Report to the Führer re Partisan warfare' (*Meldungen an den Führer über Bandenbekämpfung*), repeating the exact words from Rauter's report. On 12 November, Rauter sent a much longer report to Himmler, who again, in his own report to the Führer, repeated the same wording. This time, the report concerned radio messages from SOE London to Holland and the *Funkspiel* messages sent from Holland to London. The last message from London confirmed that a new 'dropping period' would begin on 16 November, a new period when the moon was full, giving good visibility and enabling RAF aircraft dropping agents to identify the pattern of lights on the ground for the reception committee.[92]

The same scenario that happened in France was repeated in Holland. Himmler's representatives, the HSSPF, were providing daily updates on how their *Funkspiel* operations were developing, with Himmler placing the information before Hitler. Whereas the Abwehr carried out *Funkspiel* operations on their own cognisance, Himmler requested authority from Hitler for their similar operations.

By October 1942, all the captured agents held in various places were taken to a special prison at Haaren, converted from a seminary, and controlled by the Gestapo. Agents captured after October 1942 were also taken there directly after capture and interrogated.[93] Things did not always run smoothly because there were hiccoughs for the Abwehr and Gestapo. Agents escaped from Haaren prison, and this meant that the secret of Operation North Pole, well-known among the imprisoned agents, might leak to the British if the escaped agents were able to make contact. The first two to escape from Haaren prison were Pieter Dourlein and Ben Ubbink during the night of 29–30 August 1943.[94] After some deliberation between Giskes and Schreieder, they decided on a simple measure. Using one of the *Funkspiel* radio sets, they informed SOE Dutch Section that these two agents had been captured and turned by the Germans and now they had been persuaded to return to Britain bearing false messages. Dourlein and Ubbink remained in hiding in Holland for ten weeks until the manhunt mounted by the Gestapo died away. In November, they began their escape via Belgium and France towards Switzerland; eleven days later (22 November 1943), they successfully crossed the border and made their way to the British Consulate in Berne. The SIS station chief, Count Frederick Vanden Heuvel, sent a coded radio message to SIS London with the sensational news of German penetration measures in Holland:

> Lieutenant Johan Bernhard Ubbink, cover-name Edema and codeletters CEN, parachuted into Holland during the night of 1 December 1942, and Sergeant Pieter Dourlein, cover-name Diepenbroek, code letters ACO, dropped during the night of 10 March 1943, have both arrived here. Both report that they were met by a reception committee who knew their cover-names yet turned out to consist of Dutch Nazis and German SD, who immediately arrested them. During their interrogation it became clear that the Germans were completely aware of the whole organisation

> with its codes and passwords. For a long time the Germans have been transmitting to England pretending to be agents. They guess that at least 130 men have been arrested in this way so that the whole organisation is in German hands. During the night of 30 August 1943 they escaped from prison. They suspect Major Bingham of treachery without daring to accuse him outright and press for the utmost caution with this message. On 25 November I can send them to Spain using our normal route, but arrangements have to be made to ensure that they spend as little time as possible in Spain, in view of the importance, in my opinion, of their information. Do you agree with this or do MI6 want to give them a new assignment? Please let me know immediately if they really are who they say they are. Description of first mentioned. Height 1.82 m, face long and thin, hair blond, blue grey eyes, quite a large nose and somewhat crooked scar on left knee. Of the second, height 1.78 m, face thin and somewhat triangular shaped heavy chin, prominent jaw, dark blond hair, eyes green grey, heavy eyebrows, nose long and thin, damaged middle finger left hand, on right arm tattooed anchor.[95]

Galling as it was for SOE to receive such devastating news from SIS, SIS quickly sent radio messages to its own agents in Holland: 'Sister service totally infiltrated by Germans. We therefore urge you to break off all contact with their agents and keep clear of them. Please warn OD [Orde Dienst] and other organisations'.[96]

Such damaging news, though unknown in Holland at the time, did not stop three more agents, Art van der Giessen, Jan van Rietschoten, and Klaas Wegener, escaping from Haaren prison during the night of 22–23 November 1943—the day when Dourlein and Ubbink reached safety in Switzerland. The three men managed to avoid German pursuit and go into hiding. Wegener went off on his own and found a safe house, and week later, he attempted to contact a SIS contact; however, this contact avoided any communication at all, having taken to heart SIS London's very clear radio message about agents from their 'sister service'. In early 1944, Wegener decided to go down an escape line towards Spain. It was winter, and he was captured after crossing the border into Belgium and returned to Haaren prison.[97] Meanwhile, SOE Dutch Section had given agreement for Ubbink and Dourlein to be sent to Britain.

On 5 May 1944, van der Giessen and van Rietschoten came out of hiding and took a train from Rotterdam south to Zeeland, the less populated island estuaries towards the Belgian frontier. They had acquired intelligence material and were intent in having it taken to London. They were recognised after attempting to obtain false papers, and were followed onto the train and arrested. How they would proceed from Zeeland is unknown. What is known is that van der Giessen and van Rietschoten were shot in June 1944 at the German camp established at Vught (Herzogenbosch), central Holland.[98]

Horst Kopkow. (*US NARA, Berlin Document Center, SS-Officer file*)

Kopkow with his wife and son in his SS staff car. (*Courtesy of Sarah Helm*)

RSHA Berlin (Prinz Albrechtstraase). (*Max Williams archive*)

SS-*Obergruppenführer* Heinrich Müller at Hegewald. (*Max Williams archive*)

SS-Captain Theodor Ampletzer. (*US NARA, Berlin Document Center, SS-Officer file*)

Kriminalkommissar Walter Habecker. (*US NARA, Berlin Document Center, RuS file*) 007 Heinz Barth, a Soviet-trained German communist parachute agent used in the first radio games (*Funkspiel*) between Berlin and Moscow. (*The National Archives, Kew*)

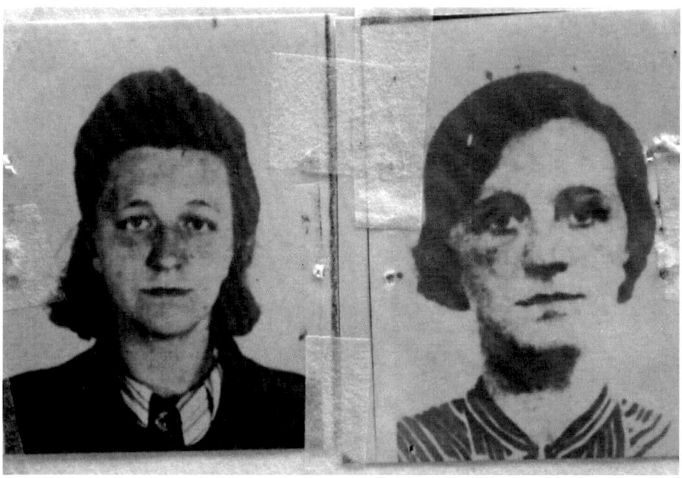

Erna Eifler, along with Barth, was a Soviet-trained German communist parachute agent. (*The National Archives, Kew*)

SS-General Karl Oberg. (*Max Williams archives*)

Above left: SS-Colonel Herbert Knochen. (*The National Archives, Kew*)

Above right: SS-Major Hans Kieffer. (*The National Archives, Kew*)

Below left: SS-*Leutnant* Dr. Josef Götz. (*Fotosammlung Familie Götz*)

Below right: SS-General Hanns Albin Rauter. (*Max Williams archive*)

SS-Major General Wilhelm Harster on the left. (*Max Williams archive*)

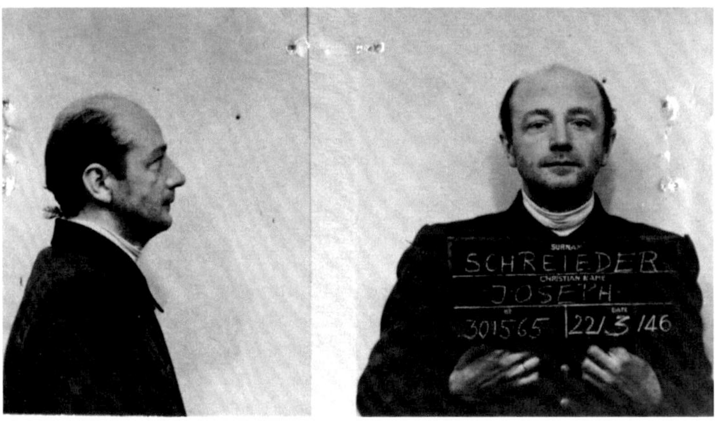

SS-Major Josef Schreieder. (*The National Archives, Kew*)

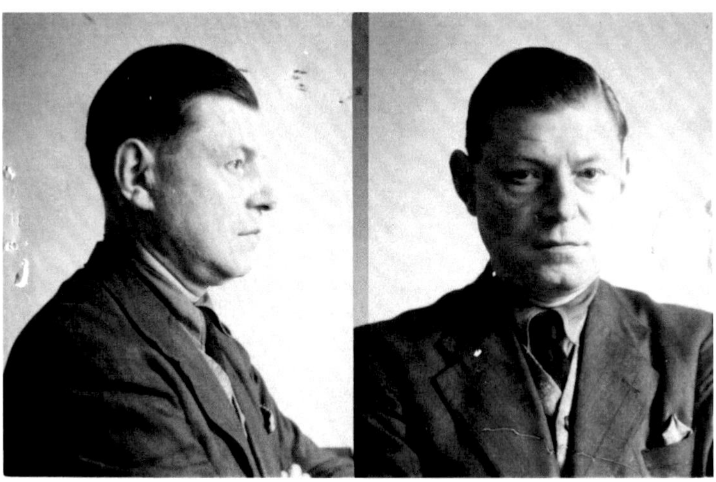

SS-*Leutnant* Ernst May. (*The National Archives, Kew*)

KL Gross Rosen camp entrance. (*Author's Collection*)

KL Gross Rosen, commemorative plaque for the agents. (*Author's Collection*)

KL Natzweiler camp entrance. (*Author's Collection*)

KL Natzweiler, Crematorium building where the first four female agents were murdered.

KL Dachau camp entrance. (*Author's Collection*)

KL Dachau. Solitary grove where 4 female agents were shot. (*Author's Collection*)

KL Mauthausen (Austria), camp entrance. (*Author's Collection*)

KL Mauthausen, crematorium, where the agents were taken after being shot. (*Author's Collection*)

Above left: Eliane Plewman. (*The National Archives, Kew*)

Above right: Yvonne Unternahrer (Beekman). (*The National Archives, Kew*)

Below left: Madeleine Damerment. (*The National Archives, Kew*)

Below right: Denise Bloch. (*The National Archives, Kew*)

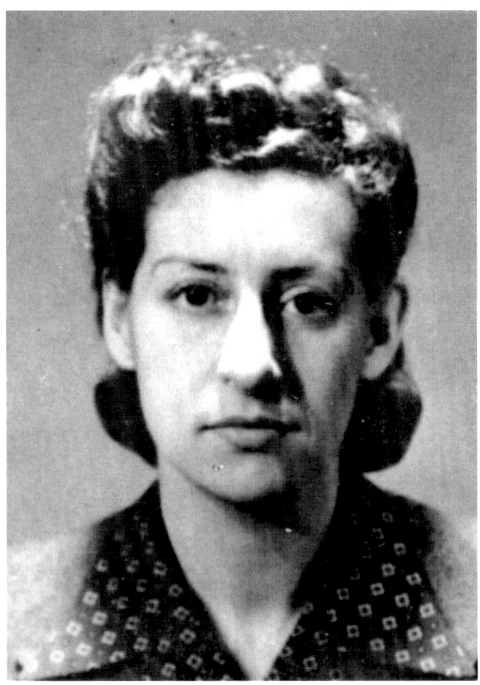

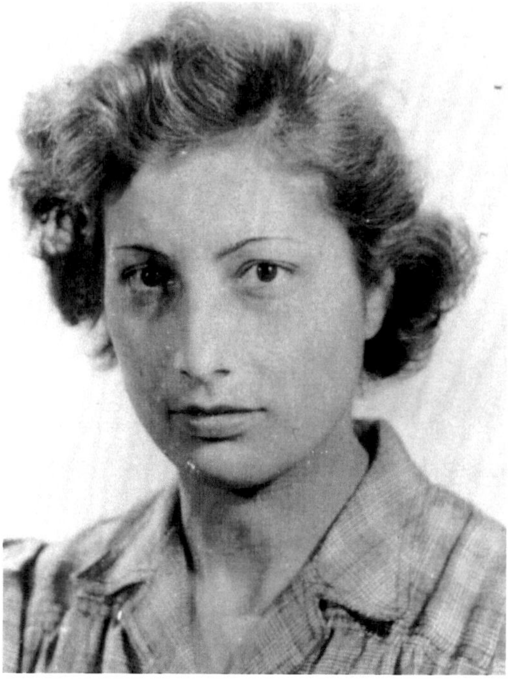

Above left: Noor Inayat Khan. (*The National Archives, Kew*)

Above right: Andrée Borrel. (*The National Archives, Kew*)

KL Buchenwld, camp entrance. (*Author's Collection*)

KL Buchenwald crematorium, the agents were murdered in the cellar rooms below the crematorium. (*Author's Collection*)

KL Sachsenhausen, camp entrance. (*Author's Collection*)

Left: KL Sachsenhausen, where agents were shot. (*Author's Collection*)

Below: FKL Ravensbrück, camp entrance on the left of the administration block. (*Author's Collection*)

FKL Ravensbrück crematorium, agents were shot on top the steps on the left. (*Author's Collection*)

KL Flossenbürg camp entrance. (*Author's Collection*)

KL Flossenbürg Cell Block showing foundations of the individual cells where the agents were held in solitary confinement for a year. (*Author's Collection*)

Home of SS-General Heinrich Müller, Cornelius-Strasse, Berlin, where Kopkow received his last instructions, April 1945. (*Author's Collection*)

After the second escape, the remaining agents held at Haaren were transferred on 27 November 1943 to a real prison at Assen. There were no more escapes. In April 1944, the order came from RSHA Berlin to send the remaining agents held at Assen to Germany. Fifty-one captured agents of SIS and SOE arrived at Rawitsch penitentiary on 15 April 1944.[99] Schreieder later said 'that the Sipo in Holland wished to keep these agents in Holland, but the matter was taken out of their hands by Amt IV RSHA'.[100] Why would Schreieder wish to keep these agents in Holland when Operational North Pole had finished? There is no real reason why RSHA (and Kopkow) wanted the agents left behind in Holland, their usefulness had ended and their lives were forfeit. None of the Dutch agents survived the year.

The last SOE agents dropped directly to a German-controlled drop zone occurred on 21 May 1943. By this time, SOE Dutch Section had realised something was wrong in Holland. Dourlein and Ubbink had not yet escaped from Haaren prison, so something in the radio messages must have raised doubts. Or SIS informed SOE about Germans taking over the radio ciphers of their captured agents and had immediately broken off contact, which caused SOE to look at the back traffic of their agents. Whatever they found, no further SOE Dutch Section agents were dropped that year. SIS, having paused to rethink their strategies for Holland, dropped two radio operators in September 1943 and one more on 5 November 1943. None of these three survived capture. In 1944, SIS continued with its policy of dropping agents and SOE recommenced its operations, but on a much smaller scale. Both organisations placed greater emphasis on maintaining personal security, but captures did take place. Some agents did manage to survive capture, the following did not:

Year	SIS Organisers	SIS W/T	SOE Organisers	SOE W/T
1943	-	3	-	-
1944	2	9	5	3
1945	1	-	1	-

The SOE figures for 1944 include one organiser and one W/T operator from MI9, dropped to organise 'escape and evasion' lines for shot down Allied aircrew seeking to escape German captivity. The Abwehr and Gestapo captured twenty-four agents that had been dropped in 1943–1945, most of whom lost their lives. According to Schreieder, his section attempted more *Funkspiel* operations with newly captured radio ciphers, none with their earlier success rate.[101] One with SIS ciphers (the ciphers of Henk Letteboer, arrested 3 February 1944—he managed to survive the war) went on for two months, but 'without success'. Two more attempts in 1945 were also unsuccessful. Radio security had improved, but radio operators on the ground in Holland continued to be captured by DF'ing. In a sense, they helped the Germans to find them by transmitting for too long, transmitting too long on the same frequency, or simply transmitting from the same place. All these scenarios greatly assisted German DF'ing, which was extremely effective.

In 1945, Allied armies were advancing eastwards into Germany, Belgium, and Holland after liberating France. In the early evening of 6 March 1945, HSSPF Rauter was travelling in his personal staff car with two bodyguards on the road between Arnhem and Apeldoorn in eastern Holland. About midway at Woeste Hoeve, the car was shot up by resistance workers, killing his bodyguards and leaving Rauter severely wounded. When the news reached Himmler, he ordered reprisal actions. These happened on 8 March 1945, when at least 263 prisoners from camps and prisons in Holland where shot at three different locations. Captured agents were included in the victims. Among those shot on this day were three at Waalsdorpervlakte near The Hague (two SOE men and one SIS man) and three more at Woeste Hoeve (one MI9 man and two SIS men).[102]

In France, the geographic size of the country meant that Abwehr and Gestapo capture of Allied intelligence agents while hampering some resistance activities did not bring it to a halt, simply slowing it down momentarily in some areas. In Holland, a much different set of events took place: the Abwehr and Gestapo had complete control of all the agents who had arrived and who would arrive between 1941 and summer 1943. There were no agents at large in Holland attempting to foment resistance. Not until 'blind' parachute drops of agents in 1944–1945 did SIS, SOE, and two newcomers (OSS and the Jedburgh teams) begin encouraging and supplying arms for resistance among local underground groups working against German rule. The reprisal in 1945 after the attack on Rauter was not the first, many other reprisals had happened in 1944 after attacks by the resistance on German personnel and railway sabotage.

The attempt on Rauter's life and the resultant murders of 8 March 1945 were not the last executions. In April 1945, when the German surrender must have been known to most, the Gestapo continued to exert its power and murdered four more captured agents (two SIS men, one from MI9, and one from SOE).

What happened with SOE Dutch Section and its failure for almost two years to recognise that all its radio traffic came from German-controlled sets was a complete and utter disaster. The failure can, of course, be claimed to have been a battle between SOE (British) amateurs and Abwehr and Gestapo professionals. There is a truth in this, but from the British side, there were recriminations for not having the foresight to record the 'fist' of the radio operators, each having a slightly different technique to one another. Such recordings could later be played back with the 'fist' operating in the field of operations to ascertain any change. Be that as it may, SIS broke off all contact when their agents, following capture, did not give their captors their radio security check. On the other hand, SOE appears to have time after time failed to recognise the absence or incorrect security check and ignored periodic warnings that some agents in Holland had been captured.[103] As a result of these failures, fifty-one agents deported from Holland to Rawitsch penitentiary would be murdered in German concentration camps on orders from SS-Major Horst Kopkow.

7

Building on Success: Agent Arrests, Radio Games (*Funkspiel*) with London and Moscow

RSHA IV A2 in Berlin became the national office for counter-intelligence measures conducted against enemy radio operators. It carried out this work itself and co-ordinated and controlled similar measures undertaken by Gestapo offices across Germany and German-occupied territories. The nature of Nazi Germany and its population control meant that, in wartime, citizens could not travel outside its borders without Government approval permits. Enemy secret agents could hardly revert to invisible writing on letters, the telephone, or coded telegrams via post offices as these methods were subject to examination and censorship. Such methods were simply too slow, cumbersome, or impractical for modern secret warfare. The fastest and most employed means of sending information by an enemy agent in Germany was enciphered radio messages from a radio transmitter sent in Morse code over the airwaves. The airwaves were open to anyone who tuned in to various wavelengths and messages could be intercepted, but not stopped. Two German agencies, one from the Army and another from the uniformed police service, tuned into wavelengths likely to be used for clandestine and therefore illegal radio transmissions. Morse code is the same the world over, a series of dots and dashes that represent individual letters and numbers. Although interception of the wavelengths could not be avoided, a message in Morse code could not be understood if enciphered and the interceptor did not have the method of deciphering. If the code could not be understood, then steps needed to be taken to find the sender of the radio transmission. In its simplest form, tracing an illicit radio transmission was done by direction finding, commonly known as DF'ing. Needless to say, the Germans had a highly efficient direction finding department within the signals intelligence division of the army high command, known as OKW/Chi. Its radio stations in Germany were capable of triangulating illegal radio transmissions and giving a city or town where transmissions originated. Its mobile radio direction finding vans then travelled the streets of that city or town to pinpoint the house, which was raided and the radio set and ciphers seized. The Order Police (*Ordnungspolizei*), the uniformed police of Germany under the control of Himmler, also had mobile radio direction vans and these were gradually used throughout Western Europe by Gestapo officers at the BdS and KdS offices. The Abwehr also used them when the army DF'ing vehicles were not available. This seizure of coding materials and ciphers became rich products for German counter-intelligence agencies—the Abwehr and the Gestapo—to replace the illegal radio operator transmitting intelligence material to its base and use their own radio operators to transmit disinformation to mislead and misinform the enemy. These operations were known as radio playbacks and radio games, or by the Germans as *Funkspiel*, and became immensely important counter-intelligence activities as the war developed. The radio operators sending clandestine messages to Moscow or London, for example, were exceptionally brave and also foolhardy. They transmitted for far too long and from the same place, which made German direction finding much easier. As the war progressed, SOE and SIS began providing each radio operators sent into Europe with several radio sets. These could be stored at different locations, which made it more difficult for the Germans to locate and had the added advantage for the agents by not having to lug the suitcase-sized transmitter in public places, such as railway stations, where German patrols had regular checkpoints or stop-and-search initiatives. Despite these simple measures to avoid German detection, their direction finding still located Allied radio operators in Holland and Germany who were arrested and shot as late as April 1945.

Coupled with establishing that enemy agents were using radio transmissions to send enciphered radio messages, the army's intercept unit (*Funküberwachungsstelle*) first heard a Rote Kapelle message on 26 August 1941 at 3.58 a.m., hearing 'KLK de PTX'. The intercept station had been established after the Polish campaign in 1939 on the Baltic coast at Cranz, 21 miles (34 km) north of Königsberg (today, Cranz is Zelenogradsk in the Kaliningrad enclave, governed by the Russian Federation). The alert operator took down thirty-two different messages in five different ciphers using these call-signs and sent them by teleprinter to the Army Central Signals Office (*OKW-Amtes Wehrmachtnachrichtenverbindungen*—WNV) in Berlin, and passed to section Fu III. This section, like Britain's Bletchley Park establishment and the US National Security Agency, investigated coded radio messages and deciphered them. Initially, Fu III were unable to decipher the messages sent from Cranz and turned to Abwehr headquarters in Berlin to help in tracking down the source of the radio signal. When the PTX signals were traced to Belgium, active direction finding began.[1]

In the early part of the war, certainly since September 1939, the Abwehr carried out the search for clandestine and illegal radio transmissions. Following the German invasion of the Soviet Union in June 1941, the Abwehr were quickly DF'ing and arresting Soviet agents, whether stay-behind or recently parachuted into the vast hinterland behind advancing German lines. In July 1941, the

Abwehr reported seventy-eight radio transmitters working to the Comintern Moscow; a year later, 325 illegal radio transmitters were reported, mostly from German Army rear areas in Russia and growing in numbers throughout German-occupied Western Europe.[2] In all *Funkspiel* operations, whether by the Allies or the Germans, these operations developed along two distinct lines. The first line was obtaining information and knowledge of what your enemy wanted to know, and how he intended to react to such information; secondly, the provision of disinformation and misinformation to mislead the enemy. Abwehr officer Oskar Reile, who operated on the Eastern Front, reported that by 1942 the Abwehr had about thirty radio sets being worked back to the NKVD, one of the other intelligence agencies charged with defending the Soviet homeland. By necessity, Soviet agents dropped behind the front lines required information on military units and their dispositions to ascertain weak spots on the frontline where a successful counterattack could be made.[3] NKVD officer Pavel Sudoplatov has a slightly different view of the *Funkspiel* operations. His section had forty 'minor' *Funkspiel* operations, with the Abwehr and Gestapo providing disinformation. Furthermore, the later Colonel Rudolf Abel (working for Soviet intelligence under cover when caught in 1957 by the FBI in New York, USA) was at this time in charge of a NKVD section engaged in these radio games with the Abwehr and Gestapo.[4]

SS-Captain Horst Kopkow played no part in these *Funkspiel* operations by the Abwehr in the German-occupied territories of the Soviet Union. However, he was kept informed of the Gestapo role in this territory from reports of the murder squads, the SS-*Einsatzgruppen*. As well as their extermination actions in killing almost half a million Soviet Jews before the end of 1941, the SS-*Einsatzgruppen* also had counter-intelligence and counter-sabotage functions. Their daily reports sent by radio back to RSHA Berlin were compiled and edited by RSHA IV A1 and issued to a growing number of individual RSHA offices, police, and army authorities. Kopkow's department, RSHA IV A2, first appears on the distribution list of Daily Report No. 25 (*Ereignismeldungen UdSSR Nr. 25*) dated 17 July 1941; Eichmann's department, RSHA IV B4, did not begin receiving their personal copy until a week later with Daily Report No. 32 dated 24 July 1941.[5,6] Both Kopkow and Eichmann played no part in their respective spheres of work in Russia, and these reports were sent for information purposes only. Neither officer could afterwards deny that such information about mass shootings and mass killings was unknown to them during the war, just as neither could deny what went on in concentration camps and extermination camps—especially as both officers sent innocent people to such camps to be murdered. Kopkow well understood the antipathy of the senior ranks of the RSHA and the Nazi Party towards communists and Jews when writing the first report on the Rote Kapelle investigation in November 1942, entitled 'Bolshevik Treasonable Organisations in the Reich and Western Europe ("Rote Kapelle")' ('*Bolschewistische Hoch- und Landesverratsorganisation im Reich und in Westeuropa ("Rote Kapelle")*').[7] Some of those arrested were pointed out as Jews and in an organigram of the Rote Kapelle in Paris, three of them had a Star of David by their names. In his later reports, Kopkow regularly mentioned those arrested who were Jews.

On 15 May 1942, SS-General Reinhard Heydrich extended the departmental responsibilities of RSHA IV A2, Kopkow's department, to include 'parachute agents, terrorists and saboteurs' in the Czech Protectorate (where Heydrich was Acting Protector) and Slovakia. Additionally, in May 1942, there was a reorganisation at Stapoleitstelle Vienna and their IV A2 section, whose new officer in charge was SS-*Obersturmführer Kriminalkommissar* Johann Sanitzer. In Vienna, this section had slightly different responsibilities to the national centre at RSHA under Kopkow. Sanitzer's IV A2 section investigated sabotage, illegal weapons and ammunition, forged identity papers, industrial counter-intelligence among armament factories in the Vienna region, and parachute agents and their radio operators. During the night of 16–17 May 1942, an aircraft of the Soviet air force circled over East Prussia before dropping four Soviet-trained German communists—three men and a woman. Two of them were radio operators, Erna Eifler and Willi Börner, and they would be the first to be used by the Gestapo in radio games with Moscow.

After landing safely, they buried the two radio sets in the drop zone, although they retained the ciphers and schedules of transmissions. In two groups, they set off for nearby Allenstein, from where they took the train for Berlin. Once there, Eifler and her organiser, Wilhelm Fellendorf, began looking for the agents that they were to contact in the Rote Kapelle network. Following their arrival in Berlin, Börner and his organiser, Erwin Panndorf, set off for Thuringia, where Panndorf had family who would take them in. These two were supposed to begin their intelligence work here, acquiring 'military and political intelligence and to furnish weather reports'.[8] Panndorf was mistaken about family loyalty because his sister reported his approach to the Gestapo. Their attempts to contact communist resistance had not get them very far, so, with the Gestapo on their heels, they decided to separate. Panndorf would go to Berlin and try making contact with communist resistance workers there, while Börner went to Vienna to do the same.

With a successful agent drop by the Soviet air force behind them, they made another drop two days later during the night of 18–19 May 1942. Three Soviet-trained German communists were dropped in a different region of East Prussia, near Insterburg. This is where Soviet plans unravelled for these three agents, the four before them and the ones to come. On this cool May night, the three parachutists were observed descending. A local gendarmerie unit, together with a number of soldiers, rushed towards where they would land and opened fire on them, killing Wilhelm Freund who happened to be the radio operator, and capturing the other two, Walter Gersmann and Wilhelm Trapp. It did not take long for the arrest to be reported to RSHA Berlin, with the report landing on Kopkow's desk via that of RSHA IV Chief Müller. The two survivors, with all their equipment and documentation, were quickly escorted to Berlin for interrogation and examination. Gersmann was unable to withstand Gestapo methods and provided information that identified the four who dropped earlier and more who would arrive in the future, people who they had trained together in Moscow. As a result of Gersmann's information, on 30 May 1942, RSHA IV A2 sent a teleprinter message to Gestapo offices across Germany announcing the arrival of 'three ex-KPD functionaries by parachute from Soviet aircraft near Insterburg'. In Nuremberg, the Police President SS Lt-Gen. Benno Martin also distributed the message to all Gestapo offices across his district giving a description of Börner and Panndorf, and calling for 'the most intensive search measures'.[9]

In Vienna, the new IV A2 expert at Gestapo headquarters, Johann Sanitzer, probably had all the Gestapo informers instructed to report if Börner came to Vienna. He did not have long to wait for on 8 July 1942, Sanitzer arrested Börner in Vienna. Under interrogation and an examination of his belongings, Sanitzer found his cipher and schedule of transmission, and Börner stated he and Erna Eifler had hidden their radio sets in the drop zone near Allenstein. According to Sanitzer and without seeking permission from RSHA IV A2 in Berlin, he took Börner back to Allenstein and found the two radio sets then returned to Vienna. This return trip was not a few hours there and back. Vienna to Warsaw then north to Allenstein before returning to Vienna, is about 1,300 miles (2,000 km). On their return to Vienna, Sanitzer informed Kopkow in Berlin, who gave orders to bring the prisoner Börner and the radio sets and ciphers to Berlin. In consultation with Kopkow, who undoubtedly realised he had the first in a brand-new series of Russian agents, Sanitzer agreed to begin a *Funkspiel* with Moscow using Börner's codes.[10] This new phase in the careers of Kopkow and Sanitzer was delayed for a few days. Taking into account Börner's arrest in Vienna on 8 July 1942, several days of interrogation, and the overnight trip to Allenstein to retrieve the hidden radio sets, the visit to Kopkow at RSHA Berlin probably took place around 18 July 1942. Sanitzer claims Börner, after their return to Vienna, would not begin the *Funkspiel* until the Gestapo had arrested his drop partner Erwin Panndorf. Börner then provided the means by which this happened. He told Sanitzer that he had been given by NKVD Moscow a recurring meeting with an agent in the woods at Meerane on the 5th, 15th, or 25th of each month. Sanitzer and Börner must have been with Kopkow at RSHA Berlin after 15 July because, as noted above, Käthe Tucholla was the woman arrested by the Gestapo at Meerane on 25 July, which then led to the arrests in Berlin on 27 July 1942 of her husband and Erwin Panndorf.[11]

Panndorf arrived back in Berlin on 5 June 1942. He made contact with the communists Käthe and Felix Tucholla who lived in Berlin-Rummelsburg and were involved in anti-Nazi activities. Käthe Tucholla was known to the Gestapo and when on a visit to Meerane, about 20 miles south of Leipzig, contacting communist circles on 25 July 1942, she was arrested, betrayed by Börner. Mrs Tucholla did not withstand Gestapo interrogation. On 27 July

1942, back in Berlin, the Gestapo raided her home and many other houses, arresting numerous communists including Käthe's husband, but more importantly the prize of Erwin Panndorf.

By this time, the last week of July 1942, Kopkow was now busy investigating the Rote Kapelle in Berlin after the arrest of Soviet radio operators and the capture of their ciphers in Brussels. On 1 August 1942, the first *Funkspiel* transmission of the Kopkow era was sent by Börner from Vienna, a *Funkspiel* operation named Quarter Master One (*Quartiermacher Eins*).[12] This first coded radio message was accepted by Moscow. Afterwards, regular transmissions took place two to three times per week, and they were 'rather lengthy, sometimes four or five hours'. These are long hours and it is surprising that Moscow did not realise something was wrong. Possibly they were interested in the intelligence being fed to them with military information from Abwehr Vienna and political intelligence provided by Sanitzer and approved by Kopkow before transmission. According to Sanitzer, the military drew the line at including weather reports as this could be construed as treason. To avoid any real judicial charges, Sanitzer reported the transmissions to the German Army DF'ing station at Hitzing near Linz (85 miles (140 km) west of Vienna), which monitored and examined radio traffic sent outside German territory and the German Police DF'ing unit in Vienna.

Börner managed to hang onto his life in Vienna with Sanitzer urging Moscow to send in additional agents due to the increasing work. They would eventually send an agent to Vienna in October 1942. Back at RSHA Berlin, Kopkow's department had broken one of three agents, Walter Gersmann, who had been dropped into East Prussia and met on the ground by gunfire, killing one of the agents, during the night of 18–19 May 1942. The two survivors, Gersmann and Wilhelm Trapp, were brought to RSHA Berlin and put in the cells in the cellar for interrogation by Kopkow's men. Gersmann was 'turned', and on 14 July 1942, he was officially mentioned as a Gestapo informer (*V-Mann*) for RSHA IV A and sent to Hamburg to help find the still missing parachute agents from the earlier drop, Erna Eifler and Wilhelm Fellendorf, reported to have gone to ground in Hamburg.[13] The 'turning' of Gersmann appears to have been a double cross on his part. Instead of trying to find the two agents in Hamburg, he was trying to establish a route for himself out of the country—into Denmark and then Sweden. This is reported in Kopkow's Final Report on the Rote Kapelle investigations (dated March 1943), by which time Gersmann had been shot at Sachsenhausen concentration camp. His drop partner, Wilhelm Trapp, appears to have given information and was afterwards sent to Sachsenhausen as a prisoner and liberated at the end of the war.

The Gestapo search for Erna Eifler and Wilhelm Fellendorf intensified in Hamburg. They were eventually found in October 1942. The five months between July and early November 1942 were especially successful for Kopkow because his department arrested and rolled up the entire planned Soviet networks to be operated by Soviet-trained German communists, which had been dropped by parachute in various locations by the Soviet air force and arrested in Germany and Austria:

Willi Börner, dropped 16–17 May 1942, East Prussia—arrested 8 July 1942, Vienna
Erwin Panndorf, dropped with Börner—arrested 27 July 1942, Berlin
Erna Eifler, dropped 16–17 May 1942, East Prussia—arrested 15 October 1942, Hamburg
Wilhelm Fellendorf, dropped with Erna Eifler—arrested 28 October 1942, Hamburg
Walter Gersmann, dropped 18–19 May 1942, East Prussia—arrested on landing
Wilhelm Trapp, dropped and arrested with Gersmann
Wilhelm Freund, dropped with Gersmann and Trapp, killed at the drop zone
Albert Hössler, dropped 5 August 1942, Gomel, Russia—arrested September 1942, Berlin
Robert Barth, dropped with Hössler—arrested 9 October 1942, Berlin
Heinz Koenen, dropped 23 October 1942, East Prussia—arrested 29 October 1942, Berlin
Emil Kammler, dropped November 1942, Slovakia—arrested November 1942, Vienna

Most of the arrests were connected to Moscow's desire to reinforce the Rote Kapelle network operating in Germany. Those recruited to carry out this work were German communists (both men and women), who had emigrated to the Soviet Union in the early 1930s. They had all written to their families from the Soviet Union before June 1941 (the German invasion of the Soviet Union), mail that had been intercepted and recorded by the Gestapo. This made it much easier for the Gestapo when their names became known and the search for them began. Like all police forces, they started with the families in the search for the culprits and the very extensive Gestapo card index system provided much information on likely addresses. Kopkow believed these agents were well trained, possibly 'the best agents' the Russians had at their disposal, but they 'failed largely because of their ignorance as to actual conditions in Germany' and because they had been instructed by Moscow that 'they would easily be able to get in touch with communist groups in the Reich who would help them in their work'. Such ideas were totally the opposite of reality in wartime Germany because, as Kopkow pointed out, 'conditions in Germany had altered considerably since 1935, and the contacting of communist groups had become almost impossible'.[14]

The next problem when agents made radio contact with Moscow from Germany was more technical. Some of the radio sets provided to the agents were damaged or faulty and needed repair. Where in Germany would the radio operators obtain spares to repair the sets? Making contact with businesses who might help could well lead to a call to the Gestapo. Their fall-back position by necessity meant former comrades in the German Communist Party and making contact with them would come to the notice of Gestapo informers. Obviously the Gestapo could not allow intelligence agents parachuted into German territory to remain at large and every effort was made to arrest agents whenever knowledge of them came to their attention. Of the eleven Soviet agents arrested in 1942, seven were radio operators, and it was in this way that Kopkow began serious *Funkspiel* operations with Moscow (Soviet intelligence agencies GRU and NKVD)—two from Vienna, Börner (*Funkspiel* Quarter Master I) and Kammler (*Funkspiel* 'Crown (*Krone*)), and five from Berlin. To ensure continuity and control of their *Funkspiel* system of operations within RSHA IV A2, Kopkow set about reorganising his department into two (and later four) different sub-sections: RSHA IV A2a, Sabotage, RSHA IV A2b, *Funkspiel*, and Counter-Espionage. Undoubtedly, all Kopkow's officers wanted to be at forefront of this new sub-section running *Funkspiel* operations. Most were young and ambitious, full of Nazi zeal, and control went to SS-*Obersturmführer Kriminalkommissar* Thomas Ampletzer, who became directly responsible to Kopkow. When discussing their careers afterwards with the CIA following their respective returns from Soviet captivity (Pannwitz was released in January 1956), both Pannwitz and Sanitzer exaggerated their own position with *Funkspiel* operations under their control. Such exaggerated control was designed to suggest to the CIA their own importance in the operations and possibly jockeying for recruitment as counter-intelligence officers.[15] Naturally, both Pannwitz and Sanitzer were supervised by Kopkow, who played the crucial senior role between what information should be passed to Moscow after primary agreement from top level of the Security Police and the Armed Forces about its content.

The information being passed in *Funkspiel* operations was not only secret, but passing it to the enemy was a treasonable offence. Himmler kept Hitler informed about these radio games with Moscow and Himmler decided it must be put on an official footing, if only to give his SS officers like Kopkow, Pannwitz and Sanitzer legal protection should such activities become known outside the small circle of RSHA IV A2. Himmler made regular 'Reports to the Führer' on different subjects. Report No. 55 (dated 11 November 1942), entitled 'Report to the Führer re partisan combat' (*Meldungen an den Führer über Bandenbekämpfung*), described the radio games with England from Holland. England had asked whether they could send two more agents and a positive answer was given.[16] On 3 December 1942, RSHA Chief IV Müller informed Himmler that possibilities had arisen for making *Funkspiel* contact with Moscow using radio ciphers of the Rote Kapelle. In his meeting notes for discussion with Hitler on 10 December 1942, Himmler noted '*F.Spiel mit Moskau*' (*Funkspiel* with Moscow) and this entry is marked with a tick.[17]

Himmler prepared a report for Müller with Hitler's affirmation and the only copy extant is dated '12.1942':

> The Führer has given the necessary approval for the *Funkspiel* with Moscow, co-ordinated messages from the Reich Foreign Minister and Army General Staff (OKW) will be used to maintain the *Funkspiel* operations, even when they meet the requirements of high treason.[18]

With the Führer's permission, Kopkow could now vigorously pursue *Funkspiel* operations against all enemy intelligence services from the east and west. Contrary to the exaggerated views of Pannwitz and Sanitzer, it would be Kopkow who would hold the whip, and it would be Kopkow who gained recognition again after his success in rolling up the Rote Kapelle network in Germany. After the appointment of Ampletzer to take control of the RSHA IV A2b (*Funkabwehr*, Radio Counter Intelligence), Kopkow was able to increase his departmental staff in Berlin to ensure exploitation of the *Funkspiel* to maximum effect. Kopkow's men quickly discovered that the Soviet agents were not just from one intelligence agency in Moscow. They came from the GRU (Red Army Military Intelligence), the NKVD (Soviet Ministry of the Interior), and the Comintern (Communist International), and all competed for military, political, and economic intelligence. In 1944, with Soviet armies in Poland and Romania, agents arrived to acquire military dispositions immediately behind the German front lines and find weak spots capable of being exploited. Within a year, Kopkow had twenty-three SS officers and officials working solely on *Funkspiel* operations. With the number of these operations increasing, it became impossible for RSHA IV A2 to do all the practical work so it was farmed out or retained by the Gestapo office where enemy radio operators were captured.

SS-*Obersturmführer Kriminalkommissar* (later SS-*Hauptsturmführer Kriminalrat*) Thomas Ampletzer, a thirty-two-year-old from Bavaria when he took charge of the *Funkabwehr* section, had had a similar early SS career as Kopkow. Ampletzer's *Kriminalkommissar* training course had followed that of Kopkow, and afterwards, he was posted to the Gestapo office in Dessau where he had worked on the communism and Marxism desk. Two years later came his posting to RSHA IV A2 in Berlin, where he would remain until the end of the war as Kopkow's deputy. The directives of Heydrich, then RSHA IV Chief Müller, in May and June 1942 that extended the departmental responsibilities of RSHA IV A2 for enemy parachute agents and their radio operators, created new challenges for both ambitious SS officers. Kopkow proved a most capable departmental manager and Ampletzer began knowing nothing about ciphers and secret agents and established himself as a capable controller of the captured enemy agents and the completely new *Funkspiel* operations of the Gestapo, especially those with Moscow. The learning curve for Kopkow and Ampletzer began with the intensive interrogations of Albert Hössler in

September 1942, then Erna Eifler and Walter Gersmann in October 1942.[19] They learned to ask questions about fellow trainees, agent training schools, and their personnel; similar questioning of SOE agents and subsequent reports became part of the subtle demoralisation techniques of Gestapo interrogators to trick agents into giving new information. In return for this knowledge, the information requirements of Moscow were economic, political, and military. From the very beginning of the *Funkspiel* operations with Moscow, Kopkow and his officers believed any information sent should be regarded as verifiable by other sources open to Soviet agencies. Economic material, such as food rationing in Germany, the black market, transport, and results of the Allied bombing of German cities, could easily be provided by the Gestapo. When it came to military information, their point of contact in the Abwehr became increasingly difficult and uncooperative. As a result, the *Funkspiel* from Berlin regarding military information became evasive, unlike in Paris and Vienna, where Pannwitz and Sanitzer respectively enjoyed better relations with the local Abwehr.

The first *Funkspiel* operation of RSHA IV A2 from Berlin used the ciphers of Albert Hössler, who they had arrested in September 1942. Hössler had been despatched by Moscow to help Schulze-Boysen and transmit information from the Rote Kapelle network. Hössler arrived too late as the network had been penetrated and most of them arrested by Gestapo. According to Kopkow, Hössler arrived with two radio transmitters, and after his arrest, he 'was the first WT play-back with Moscow and was the basis of the many play-backs which developed later'.[20] Despite brutal interrogations, Hössler did not fully agree to Kopkow's plan to play-back to NKVD Moscow because 'he tried again and again to spoil the play-back, and, as things went on, it came out that on a large number of points he had not told the truth'. Himmler took exception to these attempts to warn Moscow and ordered Hössler's execution. This really was a problem of Kopkow's own making. He would learn that you do not allow the captured agent to transmit *Funkspiel* messages on your behalf as the agent can slip innocuous errors into them and so alert his headquarters. Despite this, Hössler's ciphers were used to request Moscow for another agent to help them with the information from the German Foreign Office sources. A suitable and trained German communist, Heinz Koenen, was dropped in the Soviet's favoured area of Allenstein in East Prussia during the night of 23–24 October 1942.

Heinz Koenen's father, Wilhelm Koenen, was a communist member of the German parliament, the Reichstag, who fled to France in June 1933 and eventually came to Britain where he spent most of the war years. Heinz had migrated to Russia at the same time after his engineering studies were stopped by the Nazis. He was thirty-two years old when he returned to Germany as a trained radio operator with the job of reinforcing the transmission capacity between the Rote Kapelle in Berlin and Moscow. To accomplish his primary task, Koenen arrived back in Berlin with the address of Ilse Stöbe. The success of their first *Funkspiel* operation meant Kopkow knew in advance that an agent would be coming and where the first point of contact would be made. The address given was now a front for Gertrud Breiter, a Gestapo stenographer, standing in for Stöbe who occupied a cell in Gestapo headquarters on Prinz Albrechtstrasse. Koenen spoke with Breiter and arranged another meeting for the following day (29 October 1942), where Kopkow's men pounced on him. A search of his belongings produced another treasure trove for Kopkow that identified a new Soviet source in the German Foreign Office, diplomat Rudolf von Scheliha. Koenen came from Moscow with a transmitter and ciphers, and to encourage von Scheliha to again provide intelligence material, there was a photo-static copy of a bank draft from 1938 showing a Soviet payment into the Swiss bank account of von Scheliha, leading to his arrest by the Gestapo.[21] In December 1942, Ilse Stöbe and Rudolf von Scheliha were the first of the Rote Kapelle network of agents to be tried by the People's Court (*Volksgerichtshof*) in Berlin. The two were convicted of high treason on 14 December and executed at Plötzensee Prison, Berlin, on 22 December 1942. That same day, Albert Hössler was murdered in the cellar of Gestapo headquarters on Prinz Albrechtstrasse.[22] Hössler's codes were used in a *Funkspiel* to trap another victim. In November 1942, a message came from Moscow with a Berlin telephone number that Kopkow's men quickly traced, and to their astonishment, identified a Gestapo officer, *Kriminalinspektor* Willi Lehmann. A political police functionary from 1933, Lehmann had been recruited by Soviet intelligence in 1934 and now worked in RSHA IV E1 combatting Soviet espionage in German armament factories, an ideal source for letting the Soviets know what he was supposed to be protecting from them. Interrogation of Lehmann revealed he had been recruited in late 1934 and is said to have passed on 22 June 1941 for the German attack on the Soviet Union. Lehmann's arrest became the responsibility of Kopkow's department, and when they ended, he was taken to KL Sachsenhausen. In an interesting choice of words, Kopkow later said he 'was present at the cremation'. Lehmann was shot on 13 December 1942 and immediately cremated. According to Kopkow: 'The whole matter was hushed up and a statement issued that Lehmann had been murdered by partisans on a journey to Bialystok; a fictitious grave was photographed and shown to Lehmann's wife, who was promised a pension'.[23]

The second *Funkspiel* by Kopkow from Berlin used the ciphers of Heinz Koenen, who had been 'turned'" and agreed to work his radio transmitter. This took place in Berlin-Spandau. As ever, Kopkow knew the bitter truth about Koenen and told his own British captors what they wanted to hear: Koenen 'was largely instrumental in exposing the ramifications of the Russian IS [Intelligence Service]. He was assured that he would be allowed to go completely free at the end of the war' after imprisonment in 'special quarters in Sachsenhausen concentration camp'. Despite these comments by Kopkow, Koenen was executed at Sachsenhausen camp in February 1945 on Kopkow's orders.

The case of Robert Barth, the radio operator dropped with Albert Hössler and arrested in Berlin on 9 October 1942, is one that Kopkow preferred not to mention. Barth survived Gestapo interrogation and incarceration in several concentration camps, surrendering to American forces in Dudweiler, near Saarbrücken, on 20 March 1945. Kopkow had sent the 'turned' Barth to Saarbrücken in November 1944 with a radio transmitter to await Allied occupation then report by radio what was happening and US troop movements. At the first opportunity, Barth surrendered and was interrogated by US forces. In Paris during July 1945, Barth, as an acknowledged Soviet agent, was handed over to the Soviet Repatriation Mission who took him back to Moscow. After a trial before a Soviet Military Court, where he admitted his 'traitorous activities', Barth was executed in November 1945.[24]

Barth admitted when interrogated by the Americans in April 1945 that he had been arrested by the Gestapo and forced into the *Funkspiel* operations against Moscow. Following his arrest in Berlin in October 1942, Ampletzer had taken control of him. Ampletzer went through every aspect of his training, ciphers (enciphering and deciphering), his security checks, and 'a detailed analysis of his style in framing messages'. Barth could hardly mislead Ampletzer as the five messages he had managed to transmit to Moscow before his arrest were also found on him. In this way, Ampletzer's section could encipher messages without having to ask Barth. When the *Funkspiel* with his ciphers began at the end of October 1942, Barth did the transmissions himself. This *Funkspiel* operation last until March 1944, when Ampletzer closed it down. Barth, however, was positive from the beginning that Moscow knew he was transmitting under duress.[25] From March to October 1944, Barth languished in a prison cell at Ravensbrück concentration camp for women, though several men were held in the cells, and he noticed several men and women who had trained with him in Moscow. In October 1944, Kopkow recruited Barth for a Gestapo operation in the west as shall be seen later.

By the end of December 1942, Kopkow had instigated and now controlled a number of *Funkspiel* operations directed at Moscow from Berlin, Austria, and Belgium:

From Berlin:

1) From June 1942, the ciphers of Gersmann/Trapp;
2) From 9 October 1942, the ciphers of Albert Hössler (known as *Funkspiel* 'R.K. Berlin') closed down on 25 February 1943;
3) From October 1942, the ciphers of Robert Barth (*Funkspiel* 'Amateur'), closed down in March 1944;
4) From November 1942, the ciphers of Erna Eifler (*Funkspiel* "Biene') operated beyond November 1943;
5) From December 1942, the ciphers of Heinz Koenen (*Funkspiel* 'Quartiermacher Zwei'), still in operation in November 1943.

From Austria:

6) From end July 1942, the ciphers of Willi Börner (*Funkspiel* 'Quartiermacher Eins'), closed in June 1943;
7) From late 1942, the ciphers of Ernst Kammler (*Fumkspiel* 'Alte Krone'), closed in June 1943.

From Belgium:

8) From 2 August 1942, the ciphers of Johann Wenzel (*Funkspiel* 'Weide'), closed on 3 September 1943;
9) From 22 September 1942, the ciphers of Anton Winterink (*Funkspiel* 'Tanne'), closed on Moscow's advice, March/April 1944;
10) From 17 October 1942, the ciphers of GRU Captain Konstantin Jefremov (*Funkspiel* 'Buche-Pascal', first in Brussels, then from Paris), closed in July 1944;
11) From 24 October 1942, the ciphers of Hermann (Bob) Izbutski (*Funkspiel* 'Buche-Bob'), closed down in July 1944.

During 1942, the two British intelligence agencies operating clandestinely, SIS (Secret Intelligence Service, also known as MI6) and SOE (Special Operations Executive), fared no better than the Russians. In Belgium, the ciphers of at least six SOE agents were being used in an Abwehr *Funkspiel* back to SOE Belgian Section in London.[26] In Holland, the situation was worse. The Abwehr and the Gestapo counter-intelligence officers of BdS Holland were working together in 1942 and controlled the entire SOE Dutch Section network. Of eleven SOE radio operators captured in 1942, most had been caught on landing by parachute following the very first *Funkspiel* operation. Their ciphers were then successively used to bring more SOE agents and air drops of food, money, weapons, and explosives. *Funkspiel* operations by the Abwehr and Gestapo in Western Europe especially were used to lure not only agents, but supplies, unlike in Germany, where the Soviet air force were unable to conduct air operations to supply their agents.

With at least eleven *Funkspiel* operations being used against Moscow and at least seventeen against London, this amounted to large quantities of diverse accurate and inaccurate information being fed to Germany's enemies. Little wonder that Kopkow wanted a guarantee that he and his officers would not be charged with treason by supplying secret information wanted by their enemy.

From the beginning of the Gestapo *Funkspiel* operations, Kopkow directed his Gestapo co-ordinators in Austria, Holland, and France that all messages received from Moscow or London would be relayed by teleprinter to him at RSHA Berlin. They would provide the answers to the questions raised. The Abwehr was a military intelligence service and a foreign secret service had capable officers on the ground in Austria, Holland, Belgium, and France who could act independently, though keeping Abwehr headquarters in Berlin informed of their actions without the qualms of possible treason charges applying to them. After all, the Abwehr chief Admiral Wilhelm Canaris reported directly to the Chief of the German General Staff who advised Hitler personally on military matters.

What information did the Allies want and what did the Abwehr and Gestapo provide? With so many captured agents with diverse operational activities, answering the questions posed caused considerable manpower requirements. When Kopkow established a new section in 1942 to control the *Funkspiel* under Ampletzer (RSHA IV A2b), it soon received new staff to manage the workload and create a card index system to control the information. Different agents under Gestapo control could be asked for the same information as a verification measure. Johann Wenzel had been arrested by the Abwehr in Brussels on 30 June 1942 through DF'ing, and at first, he refused to answer questions of his interrogators.[27] Captain Harry Piepe of Abwehr Brussels had led the raid on the house where Wenzel transmitted and seized the documents Wenzel used. These included ciphered radio messages already sent to Moscow and other messages in plain language awaiting ciphering. These latter messages were astonishing by Abwehr standards. Piepe claimed: 'There were precise details of German aircraft and tank production, of our losses and our reserves'. Another was the key document that unmasked the Rote Kapelle network in Berlin: 'In one of the telegrams there was mention of a Berlin address which was of special importance and must on no account be discovered by the Germans'.[28] However, it was; the Berlin address quoted of agent 'Schubo' was revealed as that of Luftwaffe Lieutenant Harro Schulze-Boysen. In agreement with the Brussels Abwehr Chief Colonel Hans-Karl von Servaes, Piepe drove to Berlin and reported the Wenzel document seizures to Admiral Canaris.

Only after he had been beaten to a bloodied and unrecognisable shambling figure by Gestapo interrogators did he agree to work for them. Wenzel provided the cipher that unlocked his back radio traffic, which allowed the Gestapo to grasp the breadth of secret military and economic information Moscow had demanded. An examination of the eventually deciphered past messages revealed top secret information from the highest levels of the Reich military machine in Berlin. Kopkow later discovered the courier link from Berlin to Brussels for this material. Although Wenzel's ciphers were soon in use in *Funkspiel* operations by the Gestapo, they did not know that Moscow had already been informed on 15 July 1942 by Jefremov (BORDO) of Wenzel's arrest. According to Wenzel's 1945 statement, he began his *Funkspiel* with Moscow on 2 August 1942, advising Moscow that he had needed to change his address and had lost contact with BORDO. It did not take long for the Abwehr and Gestapo to trace BORDO and he was arrested at the end of July in Brussels.

A further example of what information Moscow wanted, what was transmitted, and the difficulties involved is reported by Rudolf Rathke. SS-*Sturmscharführer* (warrant officer) and *Kriminalsekretär* Rudolf Rathke had served in the Gestapo Brussels office since 1940, and in 1942–1944, he worked on the Rote Kapelle investigation and its later *Funkspiel* operations:

> All information transmitted to Moscow on these *Funkspiel* had to be passed by Abteilung IV A2b of the RSHA in Berlin. Economic information concerning the food situation, black market activities, production and transport conditions, was furnished by the Gestapo, and was, as a rule true, since the Gestapo assumed that Moscow was in a position to verify the information. Other information concerning partisan activities, sabotage, misconduct of Germans in occupied territory, reaction of the population to German occupation, results of Allied bombings, were also truthfully relayed. However, the transmitting of military information furnished by the Abwehr became more and more difficult because of the uncooperative attitude of the military authorities. Particularly Maj. Möhring of the Military Intelligence Service sabotaged the work of the RSHA units and refused to give any military information to be passed on to Russia. Questions of a military nature had to be left unanswered or were answered in an evasive, unsatisfactory manner which led to the discontinuance of most of the Belgian transmitting beams.[29]

Numerous examples of the material sent before the arrests of the Soviet network can be found in archives. At the former Stasi archives in Berlin, eleven pages of such messages can be found in date order from November 1940 until June 1941, provided by Soviet intelligence in 1966 to the East German state security office.[30] These messages from Harro Schulze-Boysen (cover name 'Starschina') and Arvid Harnack (cover name 'Korse') were taken by courier to Brussels for transmission to Moscow, and the subject matter is startling. One, dated 2 April 1941 from Harnack, stated that the Luftwaffe high command had already prepared plans for the invasion of the Soviet Union; on 11 April 1941, Schulze-Boysen explained that 'Hitler [was] the initiator of plans for the invasion of the Soviet Union'. Two months later, on 11 June 1941, Schulze-Boysen warned that the military was now fully armed, German fighter aircraft had been deployed to Hungarian airfields, and Göring would move to his new Staff Headquarters on 18 June to await the German attack on the Soviet Union. It would be another year before Schulze-Boysen and Harnack were arrested. Couriers continued taking their material to Brussels after the German invasion of the Soviet Union, and attempts to create their own transmission centre in Berlin remained beset with technical difficulties. One of the main reasons why Soviet intelligence decided to parachute agents into East Prussia in spring and summer 1942 was making contact with the Rote Kapelle network in Berlin and expedite transmission of their information.

There are few other *Funkspiel* messages that survived the war and are available in archives. Another set of Funkspiel message can be found in the Stasi archives and involves the provision of information by the Abwehr for *Funkspiel* EIFFEL in 1943.[31] Leopold Trepper began establishing the Rote Kapelle network in Belgium during 1937–1938 as part of long-range plans by the NKVD. They would be prepared in the event of war. At this early stage, Trepper began pushing Soviet espionage into France, Britain, and Scandinavia. When war did break out in summer 1940, 'the big Chief', as Trepper was known, decided to move to Paris under a new identity, while most of his organisation remained in Brussels. Under German occupation, Paris opened new intelligence gathering doors and Trepper set up the Simex company to exploit them, primarily through the new offices of Organisation Todt on the Champs- Elysées. In his memoirs, Trepper states Organisation Todt 'supervised all works of construction and fortification for the Wehrmacht' in the occupied zone and Simex 'could furnish the materials they needed on the black market'.[32] His radio operator Sukolov-Gurevich (KENT) had fled Brussels after the Abwehr raid that netted Makarov in December 1941, and he made for Marseilles in the unoccupied zone of France. According to Trepper, KENT was demoralised by all that happened and seemingly no longer transmitted, but he had his ciphers with him. He was not alone in Marseilles, he brought along his mistress, Margarete Barcza. Although Trepper had his information sent up by courier to Wenzel for transmission, some also went to Winterink in Amsterdam, but this all came to stop following their arrest in summer 1942. He was forced to make use of a Jewish communist pair, Hersh and Myra Sokol, who transmitted to the Soviet Embassy in London. Their radio set was DF'd in the Paris suburb at Maisons-Laffitte and raided in June 1942. Both were arrested and tortured, but they refused to say anything that would help the Germans. Their ciphers were not used in a *Funkspiel*. Trepper then fell back on the transmitters of the French Communist Party. With the Brussels network completely in the Gestapo bag, the *Sonderkommando* under Giering left for Paris to chase Trepper. It took several months, with Giering following every lead, and it was not until November 1942 that they found success. The German Army marched into the unoccupied zone of France on 8 November 1942 and brought the entire country into one German-occupied zone. The Gestapo and SD squads following behind established their own offices in the newly occupied towns. On 12 November 1942, KENT and his mistress were arrested in Marseilles. Trepper states KENT talked to the Gestapo willingly as long as he was not separated from Barcza.[33] Trepper himself, despite his own carefulness, was arrested in Paris by Giering two weeks later (24 November), when visiting his dentist. The other members of his Paris network soon followed.

Although Giering's abilities and those of his *Sonderkommando* (all long-serving criminal police officers now with the Gestapo) had been dogged in their pursuit of the Soviet networks in Brussels, Amsterdam, and Paris, it would be Kopkow who took the rewards. Kopkow's long reports on

Rote Kapelle in November and December 1942 were copied by Himmler to Martin Bormann, head of the Nazi Party Chancellery and Hitler's secretary, as well as to Göring. RSHA IV A2 personnel took the financial rewards from Göring's slush funds with the lion's share going to Kopkow. Back in Paris, Giering's health was fading as cancer took its toll, alleviated by heavy drinking. It would be summer 1943 before he had to admit defeat, returning to Germany for his cancer treatment. Giering managed to survive the war and died in Halle on 9 November 1945.

The year 1943 began on a bright note for RSHA IV A2 and its growing *Funkspiel* operations across German-occupied territories in Western Europe. In France, KENT agreed to begin transmitting from Marseilles to Moscow (as *Funkspiel* MARS) sending disinformation. In spring 1943, KENT and his mistress were moved to Paris so that *Funkspiel* MARS and *Funkspiel* EIFFEL (Trepper's cipher) could be worked in tandem. The *Funkspiel* messages available between Moscow and Paris reveal Moscow's interest in German troop movements and their armaments, in addition to French politics. The *Sonderkommando* continued its work with the DF'ing units, detecting French communist radio sets transmitting to Moscow from Paris (at Le Raincy), Bordeaux, and Lyon. When the *Sonderkommando* made a raid on a house at Choisy le Roi (south-eastern suburbs of Paris), they found evidence 'of contact with Comintern, Switzerland and England'.[34] The French communists were made of sterner stuff than the Soviet communists arrested in Brussels in resisting torture, as no *Funkspiel* operations were made on these sets.

In Germany, RSHA IV A2 found it less time consuming for the individual Gestapo offices to carry out *Funkspiel* operations when agents were captured in their areas. From Kopkow's home town, Gestapo Allenstein conducted a *Funkspiel* with a captured German communist youth leader who had been dropped in the area. Another *Funkspiel* began in Danzig. On this occasion, a German Army sergeant captured in Russia had been turned and dropped into East Prussia with a radio set. This man decided he wanted to get back to his family in western Germany where he was arrested. Having been brought to the attention of the Abwehr, the sergeant was brought to Abwehr offices in Danzig where the counter-intelligence officer began a *Funkspiel* with the man's ciphers. The messages sent back to Moscow induced them to drop another agent to help in the work. In August 1943, a Soviet-trained Austrian Jew was dropped at an agreed point and arrested on landing. At this point, the Abwehr turned the operation over to Stapostelle Danzig (SS-*Sturmbannführer Kriminalrat* Jakob Lölgen) for further development. Kopkow later mentioned this as *Funkspiel* KIEBITZ.[35]

The first two Pickaxe agents landed on German soil in 1943. Else Noffke (alias Yelena Nikitina and Kersti Poska) and Georg Tietze (alias Henrik Gorelov and Otto Ulnoti) were German communists trained by Soviet intelligence as radio operators with individual ciphers. The two had been among a party of four NKVD agents travelling by ship from Archangel to Britain.

En route, their ship had been torpedoed and sunk by a German submarine, and having been saved by another ship, they eventually arrived in Britain on 28 September 1942 with only the clothes they were wearing—most of their equipment and everything else having gone down with the ship. Noffke did manage to save 30,000 Reichsmarks given to her in Moscow. SOE re-equipped them with documents, a radio set, and suitable clothing. They were dropped from a RAF aircraft flying from Britain during the night of 24–25 February 1943 into Endingen-Kaiserstuhl, north of Freiburg im Breisgau, in south-western Germany, with fields backing up to a hilly forested area. Noffke ended up in the forest with her parachute caught in the branches and it took some time before she could struggle free. There are conflicting reports about the circumstances leading to their arrest by the Gestapo during early April 1943 at a house on Albrechtstrasse, Freiburg im Breisgau. Kopkow recalled a *Funkspiel* being carried out in East Prussia that mentioned the safe house in Freiburg where a family called Müller lived, 'and a Russian female agent whom they were sheltering'. The house was kept under surveillance for three weeks by the Gestapo until an agent appeared. In April, they called at the house and there was a scuffle with Tietze who had a pistol, but he was overpowered and arrested without a shot being fired; Noffke swallowed her poison tablet, so they rushed her to a local hospital and had her stomach pumped, saving her life.[36, 37] On recovery, Noffke and her arrested partner, Georg Tietze, were taken to Gestapo Karlsruhe for interrogation. Tietze was taken up to RSHA Berlin and handed over to Kopkow, who sent him to his death at Sachsenhausen camp. Meanwhile, for a short time, Noffke was held in Karlsruhe prison for interrogation about her tasks before her transfer to RSHA Berlin. Kopkow and his immediate superior, SS-*Standartenführer* (colonel) Friedrich Panzinger, interviewed Noffke in Berlin. Panzinger remembered her as a very attractive woman of about twenty-three years, who migrated to Russia with her parents in the early 1930s. According to Panzinger, Noffke had already made radio contact with Moscow before her arrest and been told to wait for further instructions from them. For reasons not explained by Panzinger, he and Kopkow agreed to have her *Funkspiel* operated from Köln.[38] 'The W/T station and code were seized intact and since then has been played back with false information', and on 9 August 1943, SOE informed the NKVD liaison officer in London (Colonel Chichaev) of Noffke's arrest 'that the wireless set is now being used by the Germans to deceive the originators of the enterprise'—an indication that SIS via Bletchley Park had her radio communications under scrutiny.[39] Gestapo arrests of the Müllers, who rented the house in Freiburg im Breisgau, closed down a long-standing courier route for Soviet agents into Switzerland.[40] There can be little doubt that the *Funkspiel* with Noffke's ciphers did not last more than a few months. On 23 December 1943, Noffke arrived at Ravensbrück concentration camp for women and was registered as a prisoner.[41] On 10 or 11 January 1945, she was executed with a shot in the back of the head and then cremated.

Sanitzer's 1942 successes in Vienna continued into 1943: four more *Funkspiel* operations with Moscow were undertaken, including those of two more Pickaxe agents dropped in Austria by the RAF flying from Britain. Emilie Boretzky (cover names Emilya Novikova and Anna Under), a radio operator, had dropped with Hermann Köhler (cover names Pyotr Koltsov and Juri Kruus) near Eisenstadt and the Neusiedler See, south of Vienna, during the night of 24–25 February 1943. The two had been among the other NKVD agents (Noffke and Teitze) travelling by ship from Archangel to Britain and lost everything when the ship was sunk. SOE re-equipped them.

Having landed safely from the parachute drop, Boretzky and Köhler made their way to Vienna. According to Sanitzer, like other Soviet agents, they had difficulty finding an apartment with AC power supply—a rarity in Vienna. This possibly gave them away as Boretzky was charged on 31 March 1943 with treasonable activities by the Gestapo. The photograph of her at this time, available on the website of DÖW Vienna, shows Boretzky in what appears to be her parachute combinations and safety helmet. Sanitzer began *Funkspiel* BURGENLAND with Boretzky's ciphers and transmitting frequencies. When Sanitzer informed Kopkow in Berlin of their capture, he immediately sent Ampletzer off to Vienna to help interrogate this new type of agent and assist in the *Funkspiel*. Under interrogation, Boretzky and Köhler mentioned other communists they had trained with in the Soviet Union, what was planned for them, and where would they operate. The pair also mentioned two other agents who had come with them via the sunken ship to Britain. *Funkspiel* BURGENLAND transmitted from March 1943 to March 1945, with Sanitzer continuing to use Boretzky. At this point, Köhler was sent to Mauthausen concentration camp, 106 miles (170 km) west of Vienna near Linz—he did not survive. Boretzky was sent Ravensbrück concentration camp for women, north of Berlin, and she was recalled to Vienna in January 1945 by Sanitzer. She turned herself into the Russians in Vienna during April 1945, and after a trial for treason, she was sent to a Soviet gulag. Boretzky survived this experience.[42]

Sanitzer found parachute agents on the increase in 1943, dropping in Poland and nearby Slovakia then making their way to Vienna. Through a message sent in Börner's ciphers over *Funkspiel Quartiermacher I*, Moscow dropped another agent with a radio set and cipher. Ernst Kammler dropped into East Prussia during November 1942 and made way to his mistress, Viola Sandroos, who lived in Reichenberg, bringing with him his radio transmitter. After a week, in December 1942, Kammler left for a rendezvous in Vienna with Börner. Sanitzer arrested him and his ciphers were used in 1943 for *Funkspiel* KRONE. Viola Sandroos was 'enticed to come to Vienna and was arrested'. After a time, Sanitzer had Sandroos sent to Prague, where she participated in another *Funkspiel*. Unfortunately for Kammler, his *Funkspiel* KRONE only lasted until June 1943 when Moscow broke it off. With no further use for him, Sanitzer sent him to Mauthausen camp where he was shot in April 1945.[43]

In April 1943, the next Soviet-trained Austrian communist, Ernst Dorfegger, fell afoul of a police checkpoint at a Vienna railway station and arrested. Sanitzer stated that the twenty-one-year-old Dorfegger was 'easily persuaded' to begin *Funkspiel* ALPENROSE with his ciphers. This *Funkspiel* resulted in the unmasking of a Soviet agent serving as a senior staff officer with the Nazi Governor of Posen District and another agent.[44] *Funkspiel* ALPENROSE operated until April 1945 and Dorfegger turned himself into the Russians.[45]

The last two Soviet-trained Austrian communists parachuted into Austria in 1943 arrived at Whitsuntide. Josef Angermann and Georg Kennerknecht arrived in German Army uniforms, working for the NKVD with a mission to commit sabotage and assassinate senior Nazi officials in Austria. Their instructions from Moscow included assembling a new network from communists who had fought in the Spanish Civil War and young communist circles in Austria. Angermann initially stayed with his father while looking for an apartment, which probably led to their denunciation and arrest. Sanitzer discovered a treasure trove when searching for them: 'A sum of about 6000 RM [Reichsmarks] was found in Angermann's father's place. A certain amount of German explosives (regular TNT), explosives caps and safety fuse was found in Felixdorf in a cache; also a German machine pistol' plus a radio transmitter with cipher.[46] When Sanitzer began *Funkspiel* FELIXDORF with Kennerknecht's cipher, they sent details of alleged sabotage activities. Moscow responded by saying assassinate *Gauleiter* of Vienna, Baldur von Schirach. RSHA Berlin were informed and RSHA Chief Kaltenbrunner responded that no action should take place. Eventually, Moscow responded to the *Funkspiel* messages, according to Sanitzer, and 'insisted that no radio traffic was to be had with them until Schirach was killed so the play was finished there and then'.[47] In January 1944, Josef Angermann committed suicide by grabbing the bayonet of one of his SS guards and cutting his throat. Sanitzer covered this up by having a newspaper report his death when assembling an explosive device for terrorism. Kennerknecht reported this to Moscow, word for word, who then said he should go into hiding. According to Sanitzer, Kennerknecht escaped Gestapo custody around this time and made for Switzerland. He was apprehended after an exchange of gunfire in which one of Sanitzer's men received a bullet wound. Kopkow responded from RSHA Berlin ordering the shooting of Kennerknecht.[48]

Sanitzer had success in Austria and Ampletzer in Germany; in Holland, German control of SOE Dutch Section activities was complete. Operation North Pole, the *Englandspiel* by the Gestapo, was a complete success on the German side and a complete disaster for SOE. Every new team of SOE agents dropped into Holland in 1942 and 1943 were arrested on landing by the Gestapo. The *Funkspiel* operations in Holland were not only bringing agents, but numerous supply drops picked up by the Gestapo. Each new *Funkspiel* developed broadened the experiences of the Germans involved and made for better handling of information given to the enemy in Moscow or London, and also made the plans of the enemy better understood—not only for Holland. What information the enemy required revealed a weak spot. One SOE plan for Holland that these captured agents had been meant to establish—an underground army to be trained and ready for action when orders came—was easily made a paper tiger by SS-*Hauptsturmführer Kriminalrat* (from November 1943, SS-*Sturmbannführer Kriminaldirektor*) Josef Schreieder working in conjunction with Abwehr Major Hermann Giskes. The success of the *Funkspiel* operations in Holland were due in no small measure to one of Schreieder's counter-intelligence officers, SS-*Untersturmführer Kriminalobersekretär* Ernst May, who played a major part in deceiving SOE Dutch Section with the numerous *Funkspiel* messages. May worked out the security and 'bluff' checks after examining the back radio traffic of the first radio operators captured. In London, before being dropped into Holland, one agent who survived stated he had been told to answer any questions should he be captured as they would pick up the false messages within three weeks. With the knowledge May had picked up from past radio messages and the gullibility of the captured agents and SOE Dutch Section when every message they received came from the Germans, it reveals what disinformation can do when supplied by professional counter intelligence officers of the Abwehr and Gestapo.

With fifteen different *Funkspiel* operations working back to London, finally SOE Dutch Section realised in May 1943 that something was wrong in Holland and stopped dropping agents and supplies. The last three agents were dropped in the night 21–22 May 1943 and captured on landing. Radio communications between Holland and Britain continued through the summer and autumn of 1943, though without the earlier intensity. Giskes mentioned: 'In the first ten days of December [1943] London's signals became so dull and colourless compared with their usual quality that it did not need all our knowledge to enable us to guess that the enemy was trying to deceive us in his turn'.[49] Why did SOE Dutch Section take almost eighteen months to realise that their radio traffic from Holland was under German control, when SIS realised almost immediately when their agents in Holland had been compromised. Was it bungling in London by amateurs that lead to the loss of life among SOE Dutch Section agents, errors of judgement by many of those involved? Blame was allocated in London. In Holland and Germany, Schreieder and Kopkow believed the whole operation a success for them.

Across the frontier in Belgium, SOE suffered similar disasters mainly at the hands of the Abwehr. The German Army, under its Commander-in-Chief General Alexander von Falkenhausen, held power in Belgium and this meant the Abwehr controlled counter-espionage affairs. SS-*Sturmbannführer Regierungsrat* Dr Constantin Canaris, a nephew of Admiral Canaris, the Chief of the Abwehr, had made his career in the ranks of the Gestapo. Between June and September 1940, he had command of a small Security Police unit (*Sipo-Einsatzkommando*) in Holland, mopping up any last remnants of civilian resistance and seizing police station and Dutch intelligence service locations. His last few weeks in The Hague were spent as deputy of the newly created BdS Holland, SS-*Standartenführer* Dr Wilhelm Harster. Before the end of December 1940 came his posting to Brussels, although not as BdS; he was Plenipotentiary of the Chief of the Security Police and SD (*Beauftragter der Chef der Sicherheitspolizei und des SD*) attached to the Military Commander for Belgium and Northern France. When Canaris managed to establish himself and his Gestapo and SD structures in Belgium and Northern France, the army denied him a counter-espionage section as the Abwehr officers in Belgium carried out this function to the extent of discussions between Admiral Canaris and Heydrich in Berlin on this point.[50] In 1942, when the *Sonderkommando* Rote Kapelle run by RSHA Berlin arrived in Brussels under the command of SS-*Untersturmführer Kriminalkommissar* Karl Giering, which operated against this Soviet network, it did so independently of Gestapo Brussels.

It would not be until 1944 that a Gestapo counter-espionage section would form in Brussels and begin tracking down enemy agents. This meant that the Abwehr captured enemy parachute agents or others infiltrated into Belgium between 1940 and 1944. At least eight *Funkspiel* operations using the ciphers of SOE Belgian Section were run by the Abwehr. With few exceptions, most captured SOE agents in Belgium were tried before German military courts and sent to prisons in Germany; those associated with more serious damage to the German war effort were sentenced to death and beheaded or shot. Two SOE radio operators, André Flotte and Charles Fonck, were turned over to Gestapo Brussels; in 1944, they were sent to Gross Strelitz prison and, later, to Gross Rosen concentration camp. Only Fonck survived the war.[51]

The Abwehr began operations in 1940 to defend the interests of Germany in France from SIS and SOE agents and early French resistance organisations (Interallié and Overcloud). The Abwehr were using their ciphers in *Funkspiel* operations with SIS London from 1941, though initially deceived by the Interallié *Funkspiel,* SIS knew of the Overcloud *Funkspiel* when it began in February 1942 and still allowed it to run in 1943. BdS Paris was allowed to begin its own counter measures against SOE following the intervention of Heydrich in 1942. SS-*Hauptsturmführer Kriminalrat* Hans Kieffer had begun Gestapo counter-intelligence operations in summer 1940 from Paris and co-ordinated these operations through the regional KdS offices through France. These were primarily actions against French communists and communist resistance. Similarly, as in Brussels, when *Sonderkommando* Rote Kapelle under Giering moved to Paris in summer 1942, it again operated independently of Kieffer's activities. This move into active counter intelligence against British and French intelligence agencies operating in France meant Kieffer needed to bring in more personnel. To some extent, this was met by the absorption of the army's Secret Field Police (*Geheime Feldpolizei*, GFP) by the Security Police (*Sicherheitspolizei*) during the autumn of 1942 and by postings arranged through RSHA I personnel section.

The two most important men who came from the GFP were Dr Josef Götz and Josef Placke; they would play significant roles in the Gestapo *Funkspiel* operations from Paris. No sooner had they joined the section than it moved during January 1943 from the French Sûreté headquarters building on Rue des Saussaies to 84 Avenue Foch, where they spread themselves over six floors. The move to Avenue Foch also coincided with a reorganisation of Kieffer's section, which became IV A1 and IV A2. Interrogations of captured agents took place on the second floor, cells for the prisoners were on the top floor (the fifth floor). The *Funkspiel* operations, including ciphering and deciphering messages and radio transmissions, were on the second and third floors. In overall charge of the radio counter-intelligence operation, Kieffer appointed SS-*Untersturmführer Kriminalsekretär* Erich Otto from Dresden; he had been posted to Paris in 1940 and would remain with Kieffer until the end of the war. Once the results of *Funkspiel* operations with SOE French Section brought air drops of supplies and weapons, Otto took the teams of Gestapo men to the drop zone to pick up the containers dropped by parachute. On several occasions, when agents were being dropped under arrangements made by *Funkspiel* messages, both Otto and Kieffer went out to the drop zone for the arrests.

Otto remained very much in the background—most surviving agents only remembered Dr Götz. In civilian life, Dr Josef Götz had been a school teacher before being called up by the army and assigned to the *Geheime Feldpolizei* (GFP). In November 1942, when stationed in France along with hundreds of other GFP personnel, he was transferred into the *Sicherheitspolizei* and, with his fluent English language skills, sent to BdS France where he was assigned to Kieffer's section as a SS-*Untersturmführer* (Lieutenant). Dr Götz was not a member of the SS and simply classified as a 'uniform-wearer' (*Uniformtraeger*); his GFP colleague Josef Placke had to make do with the acting rank of SS-*Hauptscharführer* (senior sergeant). These two men formed the backbone of the *Funkspiel* operations. Dr Götz readily admitted that when assigned to this job, '[he] had neither practice nor knowledge in the matter' and needed to be instructed by Captain Schneider of the German police direction finding station in Paris; SS-*Obersturmführer Kriminalkommissar* Karl-Heinrich Büchert, RSHA IV A2, a sabotage and weapons expert; and a French interpreter called Offen. These instructive talks came about when KdS Toulouse in southern France arrested the first SOE radio operator to fall into Gestapo hands. SOE organiser Maurice Pertschuk and his radio operator, Marcus Bloom, had been arrested in April 1943 and taken to Toulouse military prison. Bloom's radio set and ciphers had also been seized. When the news came to Paris and passed to Kopkow in Berlin, Kieffer soon received orders from Kopkow to undertake a *Funkspiel* with London, having Dr Götz use Bloom's ciphers and radio set. Dr Götz arrived in Toulouse on 19 April 1943 and talked with Pertschuk and Bloom. Neither man gave him any help. Dr Götz stated:

> Every incoming message had to be sent to Berlin and every outgoing message had to be submitted to and agreed upon by Berlin. The greatest possible importance was attached to this scheme, both by Berlin and Paris, but it was obvious to me that we had not succeeded in deceiving London and, in fact, the transmission ceased towards the end of May.[51]

Pertschuk and Bloom were sent up to Paris and held at Fresnes prison should more interrogations be needed. Both men were sent to German concentration camps in 1944.[52]

Dr Götz returned to Paris from Toulouse at the end of May 1943 and soon afterwards went on leave to Hamburg where his wife was in the last stages of pregnancy. On 20 June 1943, another prize fell into Gestapo hands. After the unsuccessful first attempt of a *Funkspiel* with SOE French Section in London, Dr Götz's second attempt rivalled that of the radio games being played from Holland. Two Canadians, Frank Pickersgill and John Macalister, trained by SOE had the task of forming a new circuit called ARCHDEACON to be based at Sedan in the French Ardennes region. They were dropped at Villeny (near Blois) during the night of 15–16 June 1943 to a SOE reception. After a night or two spent with SOE agents in place (Pierre Culioli and Yvonne Rudellat), all four went by car driven by Culioli to a railway station for Pickersgill and Macalister to pick up a train for Paris. *En route* to Dhuizon, they found a police checkpoint, and the two Canadians unfortunately found their papers not quite good enough—Culioli and Rudellat roared off in the car. The chase did not last long, and, shot up by Germans in pursuit, the car ran off the road into a ditch. Ruddelat had a head wound and Culioli had a bullet hole in his calf. In an injudicious move by SOE French Section, reminiscent of Moscow's radio message to their radio operator in Brussels that revealed addresses in Berlin that led to the downfall of their Rote Kapelle network, the 'Canadians had brought with them several work messages for other agents, which the [London] staff had been trusting enough to send in English, and in clear, addressed to each agent by his field name; particularly some new crystals and detailed instructions for Gilbert Norman'.[53] After the arrests in Dhuison, Pickersgill, Macalister, and Culioli were taken to the Gestapo at nearby Blois. Yvonne Ruddelat was taken to a hospital for treatment. All three men were soon on their way to Paris and handed over to Kieffer with all their belongings. Their arrival and examination of the documents found on them proved disastrous for SOE agents in Paris and Kieffer's men took full advantage. It lead to the downfall of the PROSPER network and creation of the phantom ARCHDEACON network and a very successful *Funkspiel*.

Gilbert Norman, known as ARCHAMBAUD, had parachuted into France on 31 October 1942 as main radio operator for Francis Suttill (PROSPER), organiser of the PHYSICIAN/PROSPER network in Paris. Gilbert Norman had been under Gestapo surveillance for about two weeks according to Kieffer before the arrests of Pickersgill and Macalister, and the arrests apparently were decisive for he was arrested in Paris on 24 June 1943.[54] The courier Andrée Borrel was also arrested with Norman. The following day, Suttill returned to his Paris lodgings and was promptly arrested by Gestapo men who beat him up and broke his arm. All these arrests over a matter of days meant the cells in Avenue Foch were filling up fast. Kieffer now had the possibility of having two *Funkspiel* operations begin, using the ciphers of Norman and Macalister. Meanwhile, Dr Götz had gone on leave and had to be recalled.

Kieffer conducted the interrogations of Suttill, Norman, and Borrel using his interpreter Ernst Vogt. Through another agent, codenamed GILBERT (Henri Dericourt), Boemelburg (Kieffer's boss) acquired copies of various documents being sent back to SOE French Section from agents in the field via returning Lysander aircraft. Dericourt had the role of SOE Air Liaison Officer and arranged parachute drops of agents and supplies, and Lysander aircraft landings bringing agents from Britain and taking others back. Boemelburg had suborned Dericourt as a double agent in early 1943, the point when he began allowing the photography of documents entrusted to him for despatch to London. The use of these copied documents were used by Kieffer in his interrogation of Norman and Suttill to demoralise them into thinking SOE French Section had a traitor in London. Suttill remained silent, but Norman 'had not the integrity of PROSPER [Suttill], made a very full statement. Through Norman and through the documentary material available [they] received [their] first insight into the French Section, and also through DENISE [Borrel]'.[55]

Kieffer's comments also provide an insight into how the Gestapo worked. In Holland, the Gestapo had asked the SOE Dutch Section agents similar questions. They had done the same in Norway and Belgium. The Gestapo, by such innocent questioning of the agents, attempted to acquire information about their training, the locations where they trained, training personnel, other nationalities of agents being trained, and personal anecdotes about the instructors and their fellow agents.[56] By such careless talk, future captured agents were put at risk. Skilful Gestapo interrogators could place that seed of doubt in the agent's mind of a traitor in place at headquarters. By such means, agents were inveigled into telling their story, their tasks, who they worked with, addresses, and, of prime importance to Kieffer, who was the radio operator and where were the radio sets. The organisers, couriers, saboteurs, weapons, and explosive instructors were all arrested, but radio operators left at large could advise London of arrests—the last thing the Gestapo wanted. Kieffer did not have to be told twice:

> [RSHA] Berlin attached extraordinary importance to the French Section. K.R. [*Kriminalrat*] Kopkow and his department worked on the French Section cases, and all instructions concerning British officers came from Kopkow, or in particular matters from *Obergruppenführer* Müller himself.

> All other matters were pushed into the background, and Berlin showed interest again and again only for French Section matters and we were always obliged to neglect other matters because Berlin considered the French Section particularly dangerous.[57]

By Kieffer mentioning RSHA IV Chief Müller, it can be seen that when Kopkow sent instructions to Kieffer, it had the full backing of Müller. This interest in SOE French Section must have come about from experience gained in the *Funkspiel* operations of Holland, where SOE Dutch Section had been completely emasculated. If sabotage and insurrection could be completely eradicated through Gestapo control of SOE agents, the German armed forces could go about their business without worrying about their safety and security. Among military and political circles surrounding Hitler and his management of the war, the idea of a second front, a possible invasion by Allied armies in Western Europe naturally became a subject of discussion. *Reichsführer*-SS Heinrich Himmler was a close confidante of Hitler and held numerous discussions with him over the years, and attended the daily military briefings at Führer Headquarters when not going about his business elsewhere. The idea of a second front in Western Europe would mean an invasion of France. Therefore, resistance in France needed to be kept in check. By 1944, the invasion scare stories began and Kopkow demanded advance knowledge of when the Allies were coming.

The arrests in Paris in June 1943 broke up the PROSPER/PHYSICIAN network there and its activities beyond the city. The information found on Macalister led to further German penetration and arrests in other SOE networks. Dr Götz returned from his home leave to find Gilbert Norman (ARCHAMBAUD) and Francis Suttill (PROSPER) the subject of a pact agreed with Kopkow in Berlin. This was a pact not worth the paper it was written on, as later events would show. Kieffer informed Norman and Suttill that no harm would come to anyone they mentioned as long as he could confiscate all the arms and explosives dropped to them. Norman would not transmit himself, but he helped draft messages for coding and transmission by a substitute radio operator.[58] This *Funkspiel* did not last very long as London had been informed of the arrests of Norman and Suttill from other agents still at large. Another act of demoralisation for Gilbert Norman came from London, probably from his first message under Gestapo control. London responded: 'You forgot your double security-check be more careful'. Dr Götz spoke to Jean Overton Fuller, the biographer of SOE agents Noor Inayat Khan and John Starr, about this episode in the 1950s, adding that Norman 'was quite overthrown by shock and dismay'. As Fuller rightly remarked: 'What was the mentality of the people in London who made the blundering reply that gave the game away?'[59] Norman was soon assisting Kieffer in confiscating arms dumps at numerous places, and the arrests of the French helpers soon followed. In July 1943, Suttill found himself on a train to Berlin, where he was very probably held in the cells of Gestapo headquarters on Prinz Albrechtstrasse where Kopkow worked. After several weeks here, possibly being questioned by Kopkow, Suttill entered Sachsenhausen concentration camp, just north of Berlin, on 3 September 1943.[60] Norman remained in Paris, going out with Kieffer to seize the arms dump until one day, when being transferred to the small Gestapo prison at 'Place des Etats-Unis from the Avenue Foch … he made a bolt but was shot and wounded by von Kapri. He was sometime in hospital'.[61] This happened in 1944 before he was deported to Rawitsch prison (now in Poland), arriving with eighteen other agents on 18 April 1944.

After the *Funkspiel* with Gilbert Norman's cipher failed, it was probably July 1943 before Dr Götz turned his attention to the ciphers of John Macalister. He too refused to transmit or provide any information. It was a gamble, but Dr Götz and Kieffer, with the co-operation of Kopkow, proved able in concocting the new and false ARCHDEACON network. *Funkspiel* WALZEL began using Macalister's ciphers and would continue for over a year. It would be a disaster for SOE French Section, who dropped agents, weapons, and supplies to this fictitious network, bringing more radio operators and their ciphers to further expand *Funkspiel* operations in France. Dr Götz soon had *Funkspiel* WALZEL working well as SOE 'F' Section began parachute drops of supplies to designated drop zones arranged through false radio messages. Yet again, a home station sent information that led to the arrest of another agent. A safe house address in Paris, provided by 'F' Section over the *Funkspiel* WALZEL link, led to the Gestapo arrest on 23 September 1943 of Frank Michel, a newly arrived sabotage instructor destined to extend sabotage operations in the ARCHDEACON area.

German DF'ing units picked up transmissions from Pontoise, a small town 18 miles north-west of Paris. It seems likely that they were directed here by information given by Gilbert Norman to Dr Götz.[62] A raid on the house took place on 12 August 1943. In control was probably SS-*Untersturmführer* Otto, accompanied by the two interpreters August Scherer and Ernst Vogt and a few other Gestapo men. These three Germans burst into the house without taking care, and someone in the house started firing a pistol, fatally wounding Scherer; Vogt had a handful of bullet wounds himself, although none proved fatal. One person in the house was shot dead, while a second man made a run for the street, travelling only 100 yards before his own bullet wounds caused him to collapse. This was SOE radio operator Robert Dowlen, codename ACHILLE. Dr Götz attempted a *Funkspiel* with Dowlen's ciphers, and after two messages on 31 August and 1 October 1943, SOE 'F' Section broke off radio contact as acting 'probably under duress'.[63]

Dr Götz had better success with the cipher of Marcel Rousset (codename LEOPOLD), arrested in Paris on 7 September 1943 together with two other SOE agents (Fox and Garel/ Bouguennec). Rousset did attempt to warn London that he had been captured when he had errors put in his *Funkspiel* messages by Dr Götz. Despite errors given by Rousset about his security checks and the language used in the messages, London accepted them and only asked why he had changed languages. Another example of home headquarters not realising when agents were working under German control. For Dr Götz, the use of Rousset's cipher became *Funkspiel* ZEUS.[64]

In October 1943, after leading something akin to a charmed life since her deployment from a Lysander on 16 June 1943, SOE radio operator Noor Inayat Khan was arrested by the Gestapo in Paris and taken to Avenue Foch. Codenamed MADELEINE, her set had been DF'd several times, but a denunciation finally brought about her arrest on 13 October. After the arrest of Gilbert and Suttill in June 1943, her radio set became the most important in the Paris for passing information back to London. Inayat Khan made determined efforts to stay on air longer and from different locations to avoid capture. When arrested, her radio set, ciphers, and a number of documents were seized and handed over to Dr Götz at Avenue Foch. By a most unfortunate understanding, Inayat Khan had retained copies of her past radio traffic in plain and coded messages, which made Dr Götz's job a lot easier as he could see the security and bluff checks, in addition to the language being used. Therefore, he did not need much additional information for the successful playback using her cipher as *Funkspiel* DIANA. Inayat Khan did not take kindly to be held at Avenue Foch, in the cells on the fifth floor, and she made two attempts to escape. Although her captivity at Avenue Foch only lasted about four weeks, her demeanour made an impact: 'She was magnificent and everyone at Avenue Foch admired her'.[65] The escape attempts had repercussions: '[They] angered Kieffer very much and in any case she had not helped us in any way, Kieffer arranged with Berlin to have her sent to Germany'.[66] Kopkow arranged with the Ministry of Justice to have Inayat Khan imprisoned at Pforzheim prison, and after arrival in November 1943, the provisions laid down by Kopkow stated she should be shackled day and night.

Between June and October 1943, Dr Götz had finally made successful and continuous contact with SOE 'F' Section in London and had three *Funkspiel* operations accepted. Using the ciphers of Macalister, Rousset, and Inayat Khan (operations WALZEL, ZEUS, and DIANA), Dr Götz set about deceiving London. Kopkow was insistent that 'Berlin had the absolute and exclusive view of events, supervision and authority' at all times and that he controlled 'execution of radio deception plans all questions connected with it'.[67] Dr Götz had the most regular contact with Kopkow once the *Funkspiel* operations began:

> The decision as to whether or not a transmission was to be embarked upon rested ultimately with the [RSHA] Berlin office. This office also had to approve any transmission which was to be sent out. This, it is true was possible only at first when there were still not many decoy-transmission. Lately [*sic.*—Later] there was simply not enough time to obtain permission on each occasion and from then on reports were made from time to time only.[68]

After the war, Kopkow in his British interrogations resolutely denied his involvement with the *Funkspiel* operations in France and Holland. This obvious untruthfulness was designed to limit his involvement in what happened to the SOE agents after their capture, especially those arrested on landing following arrangements made by *Funkspiel* messages. Careful management of these messages through to the end of 1943 enabled Kieffer to seize supplies drop by parachute and in 1944 agents began arriving.

Two more SOE radio operators were arrested in November 1943. Marcel Clech was DF'd and caught by the Abwehr while transmitting from Neuilly on 19 November 1943. After being handed over to Kieffer, Dr Götz began a *Funkspiel* using Clech's ciphers, but London would not respond. Gestapo Rennes caught Georges Clement when transmitting on 28 November 1943.[69] His ciphers were used in messages sent in December 1943 and January 1944 before London noted the absence of his security checks and broke off contact.

When did SOE French Section in London realise before the end of 1943 that something was seriously wrong with the communications from their agents in France? In October 1943, agent Henri Frager had returned from France to London for discussions, during which he voiced his opinion of what was happening and charged the SOE air liaison officer Henri Dericourt as a traitor. Did SOE know, he told them, 'that a number of our [radio] transmitters were in the hands of the Gestapo, and were working for them … that the chief source of the Gestapo's information was the agent in charge of receptions (GILBERT)?'[70] GILBERT was the SOE cover name for Dericourt. Bringing this to the attention of London station chiefs appears to have done little as Gestapo penetration and playback of their ciphers did not diminish, it increased. Dericourt did not return to London until February 1944 (with his wife) and remained there until the end of the war.

In January 1944, another successful set of arrests in St Quentin brought in Yolande Beekman, who had been caught transmitting. After her radio set and ciphers were brought to Avenue Foch, Dr Götz made successful radio contact with London and this became *Funkspiel* JUNO. Additional staff were assigned to Dr Götz in January 1944 to take up some of the radio playbacks that were divided, and he retained under his supervision *Funkspiel* operations DIANA (Inayat Khan) and ZEUSS (previously named as ZEUS, Rousset); SS-*Hauptscharführer* Placke ran *Funkspiel* JUNO (Beekman). A new staff member, SS-*Untersturmführer* Alfred von Kapri, ran *Funkspiel* BLANC, and this may have been a BCRA cipher. Dr Götz later stated he worked only on English and American *Funkspiel* operations; the French *Funkspiel* operations were not his responsibility.[71]

False messages sent by Dr Götz and his team were successfully accepted by London in 1943 and 1944 and their first arrangements for new parachute agents to be dropped took place. The first radio messages using Inayat Khan's cipher, *Funkspiel* DIANA, had been treated with suspicion in London as they did not seem right, and only in December, after some questions about her early life, did London finally trust the messages. Plans were made to make two parachute drops during February 1944 with messages to her now captive radio set to arrange the reception committees. During the night of 8–9 February, four SOE agents (Alexandre, Byerly, Deniset, and Ledoux) were dropped near Poitiers to a Gestapo reception committee and arrested on landing. They were taken to Paris where the radio set, cipher, and schedule documents of Robert Byerly were handed over to Dr Götz, who soon sent a message to London announcing their safe arrival. London soon broke off contact.[72]

Two parachute drops took place during the night of 29 February to 1 March. One had been organised through *Funkspiel* DIANA (Inayat Khan) and another through *Funkspiel* ZEUS, and they involved three and two agents respectively. The three agents dropped east of Chartres included France Antelme, who famously became enraged that he had been arrested on landing, Madeleine Damerment and Lionel Lee, who was a radio operator, were his companions. MI6 Chief 'C' informed SOE on 2 March 1944 that the three had been arrested, and on 6 June 1944, radio messages received in London were noted 'W/T message on controlled circuit from Geheime Staatspolizei'.[73] The second drop that night took place at Daon, on the fringe of Brittany, where Julian Detal and Philippe Duclos dropped to a Gestapo committee and arrested.

In March 1944, three separate groups of SOE agents dropped. Two at different locations on the night of 2–3 March, when six 'F' Section agents were captured on landing by Kieffer's men. One of these two groups consisted of three men, including two American OSS agents (Lepage and Lesout), who were destined to create a new network in the Valenciennes area. The SOE agent in this group, radio operator David Finlayson, greatly interested Dr Götz for he quickly began a *Funkspiel* operation with his cipher, which 'F' Section noted: 'Telegrams continued to arrive on his plan until the end of May [1944], all of which must have been under German control'.[74] The second group of three agents (McBain, Sabourin, and Rabinovitch) landed a little way from the reception committee and had already shrugged off the parachute harnesses when they heard German voices nearby. They began shooting at the Germans, killing two before being overpowered and arrested. The Gestapo importance placed on messages sent, and presumably answers received, using McBain's cipher can be seen in what later happened when he had to be recalled to Paris from Rawitsch prison a month after arriving. The third parachute drop at Daon during the night of 7–8 March 1944, which had been used in February, this time led to the arrest on landing of two more agents, Defence and Octave Simon.[75]

Within four weeks, between 8 February and 7 March 1944, four Gestapo *Funkspiel* operations operating back to SOE 'F' Section in London had brought in seventeen trained agents, which included seven radio operators. These were the only agents dropped to a Gestapo reception committee before 'F' Section began to realise something was seriously amiss and stopped sending agents via arrangements with these radio links. With D-Day and the Allied invasion of France (although unknown to the Gestapo) only three months away, SOE needed to have agents in place to organise resistance, so they instead began dropping agents in blind to make their own way from the drop zone to their allotted area of work.

SOE historian M. R. D. Foot states 'F' Section had realised long before that a number of their radio operators were acting under duress, under German control, and this was the major reason for dropping new agents blind. However, with seventeen agents dropped to Gestapo reception committees between February and March 1944, quite apart from the numerous stores dropped by parachute also arranged through Gestapo *Funkspiel* messaging, such recognition can only have happened after 7 March 1944. Furthermore, Foot explains that 'F' Section had two objectives when facing the fact that their agents were in German hands: the first was to 'lull the Gestapo into a false sense of security' and the second was where it organised its reception committees. There may be some truth in the first reason, but the second reveals a complete misunderstanding of how the Gestapo operated, especially Kieffer's section. Regardless of distance from Paris, Kieffer always sent his own men to organise the reception committees.[76] Foot also believes that Dr Götz was 'slow in realising that the British had seen through their played-back wireless traffic as the British had been in realising that some of these sets were being played back at all'.[77]

In a series of radio messages, reminiscent of the radio messages sent over the German-controlled radio sets of SOE Dutch Section on 1 April 1944, a similar series were sent by Kieffer with Kopkow's agreement over nine German-controlled sets of SOE 'F' Section on D-Day, 6 June 1944:

> Many thanks large deliveries arms and munitions.... Have greatly appreciated good tips regarding your intentions and plans. Buckmaster replied the same evening: Sorry your patience is exhausted and your nerves not so good as ours.... Give us ground near Berlin for reception organiser and WT operators but be sure you do not clash with our Russian friends.[78]

The decision to end the *Funkspiel* operations with Britain came from Hitler himself. According to Oberg, HSSPF France, about 11 a.m. on 6 June 1944, Knochen received a telegram from RSHA IV Chief Müller ordering a stop to transmissions. Knochen then telephoned Müller in Berlin and was given confirmation of the order, saying 'it was by order of the Führer through the army high command [OKW]'.[79]

The German direction-finding unit in Paris sent a radio message on 14 June 1944 to its headquarters in Berlin; this was intercepted and decrypted by Bletchley Park. The message not only revealed nine *Funkspiel* operations and that RSHA sent the message cancelling them, but also that Kieffer had disputed why this message should have been sent:

> Concerts DIANA, MINOS, HERAKLES, APOLLO, JUNO, ATLAS, VULKAN, ZEUS, SATURN suspended as from 10.6.44 at source. Reason, a signal arrived during operational time on 6.6.44 from the RSHA, head of the Security Police, that the lines mentioned above have been covered for some considerable time by the Security Police. The local chief of Security Police [BdS] did his utmost to prevent this incomprehensible order, but was eventually obliged to obey. A more detailed report is following.[80]

After the war, Colonel Maurice Buckmaster faced several calls to explain and justify why some of his agents had been sent to their certain death when parachuted to Gestapo reception committees. He responded in an appendix to E. H. Cookridge, *Inside SOE*, published in 1966: 'Perhaps the most appalling accusation against us is that we deliberately sent out agents into the hands of the Gestapo.... I flatly deny these monstrous and intolerable accusations...'.[81]

As Foot had previously noted in his own SOE study in 1966 (revised edition), SOE 'F' Section apparently did know that some of their agents were transmitting under German control. At least they assumed it was their agents tapping on their Morse key, when, of course, it was usually trained German radio operators imitating the personal style of the SOE agent. Noor Inayat Khan had not touched a radio set after her arrest in October 1943—a German radio operator transmitted 'her' messages until June 1944. Buckmaster felt it necessary to defend himself and 'F' Section and said nothing about huge quantities of stores (money, weapons, explosives, clothing, and food) dropped into German hands, involving the loss of RAF aircraft and crews. In his SOE study, Foot again produced a chart of money dropped to nine resistance circuits 'under German control' between June 1943 and June 1944.[82] The total amount quoted, 8,572,000 French francs, became the equivalent of £43,000 in 1966 and probably over £500,000 in 2016. An enormous sum of free money in 1944 that contributed to the German war effort.

In civilian life before the war in Paris, John Starr had been a commercial artist. He was captured working as a SOE agent and brought to Kieffer's section at Avenue Foch in 1943 for interrogation. He began drawing the Gestapo men to fill the time and eventually, Kieffer had him use his artistic talents, inserting new information on the office maps of the various resistance networks. Questioned after the war by British interrogators, Starr described the roles of Kieffer, Dr Götz, and Ernest Vogt and the main reasons why so many agents had been captured. As with the Rote Kapelle radio operators, Starr stated the SOE radio operators transmitted too often from the same place, for too long and too frequently, so they became easy targets for DF'ing. The British were too trusting of their resistance networks to continue unchecked, otherwise they would have discovered the Gestapo running them as phantoms, one for almost a year.[83]

The influence of Horst Kopkow in the *Funkspiel* operations of Knochen and Kieffer in Paris with SOE French Section, by Schreieder and May in The Hague with SOE Dutch Section, was denied or pointedly not mentioned in any of Kopkow's post-war interrogations. The reasons for this can be laid at the doors of BAOR Intelligence Division (basically SIS in Germany) and Vera Atkins. BAOR Int. Div. concentrated their interrogation efforts on Kopkow's Rote Kapelle knowledge and any Soviet agents not picked up by the Gestapo during their wartime interrogations, about Kopkow's knowledge of other wartime German resistance organisations who might now be a threat to Allied security, and, lastly, his encyclopaedic knowledge of other Gestapo officers and their roles. They put their head in the sand about the fate of agents from another British intelligence organisation in which Kopkow played a significant role. This was left to Vera Atkins.

Kopkow had been hidden from view by BAOR Int. Div. in Germany, keeping him from the prying eyes of war crimes investigators while he was intensively interrogated. In October 1946, Vera Atkins raised a 'Haystack Wanted Report' for Kopkow, circulated among British authorities holding Germans in various camps and prisons. BAOR Int. Div. responded on 18 October 1946 advising that Kopkow was now available for interrogation at No. 7 CIC (Civilian Internment Camp) at Minden.[84] On 21 January 1947, Vera Atkins turned up at 'Tomato Minden' to interrogate Kopkow about the missing SOE agents from France and came away with a miserable two-page statement. Kopkow spoke about the *Funkspiel* operations in France in which he had played a significant role, but he very much reduced his role in favour of his subordinate Thomas Ampletzer. As regards the missing agents, Ampletzer also arranged things and Kopkow stood back. Nowhere does Atkins press Kopkow for a fuller explanation of his role in France and Holland as though mesmerised by his persona. The statement signed under oath by Kopkow on 21 January 1947 (German original) and 5 February 1947 (English translation) is a masterpiece from a professional policeman and counter intelligence officer agreeing to limited knowledge but putting the blame elsewhere—on the missing and presumed dead Thomas Ampletzer.[85] As a consequence of the small circle of RSHA IV A2 officers who went missing after the end of the war, such knowledge can hardly have been unknown to Kopkow because no statements from them had been put to him for explanation or denial. Kopkow was saving himself and BAOR Int. Div. provided the lifeline.

8

The Tide Turns: What to do with the Captured Agents—Decisions, Murders

What happened in 1944 that led to the systematic murder of Allied agents in German concentration camps did not happen by chance. By January 1944, over 100 men and women—captured British, Dutch, French, and Soviet agents from various intelligence agencies—were in Gestapo hands. Their numbers increased over succeeding months. They were held in a variety of national prisons, such as Fresnes in Paris, and in various smaller Gestapo prisons. Noor Inayat Khan became the first British agent to be transferred from Paris to Germany when sent to Pforzheim High Court Prison (*Gerichtsgefängnis*), arriving on 27 November 1943. This transfer can be seen as a forerunner to the mass deportation of agents that began six months later.

The transfer of Inayat Khan was not a simple arrangement. Kieffer originally requested Kopkow at RSHA Berlin to have her transferred to a prison at Karlsruhe in Germany. The decision to take her to nearby Pforzheim prison instead was made by the Ministry of Justice, who controlled the German prison service—its officials were the prison directors. They were not responsible to the Gestapo or RSHA. Kopkow therefore needed to ask the Ministry of Justice for a place. The same request had to be made a few months later when the first mass deportation arranged between Kopkow and, on this occasion, BdS Holland resulted in fifty-one SOE Dutch agents being deported from Assen prison to Rawitsch prison in what was then eastern Germany and is now Poland. According to Kopkow, he delegated these administrative arrangements to his deputy for *Funkspiel* operations and parachute agents, SS-*Hauptsturmführer* Thomas Ampletzer.

Between November 1943, when Inayat Khan transferred from Paris to Pforzheim, and April 1944, when fifty-one Dutch agents were transferred to another German prison (Rawitsch), more deportations followed on a regular basis—an indication that something had changed in those five months. Kieffer, when questioned after the war, spoke of RSHA Berlin's suggestion of having the captured agents put on trial, having heard this from Kopkow. Such a trial, a show trial, came from the news that the first war crimes trial involving Germans had taken place in Kharkov, in the Soviet Union, during December 1943. Three German officers, including a SS-*Untersturmführer*, and a Russian collaborator were tried for murders and mass murder carried out in Kharkov. The public trial (15–18 December 1943) in the newly liberated Soviet city of Kharkov was followed by a public hanging of the four men, and it made the news across the world.[1] Minister of Propaganda Joseph Goebbels and Hitler wanted show trials carried out in Germany. Allied secret agents captured wearing civilians clothes could be tried for sabotage and murders of German soldiers in the German-occupied territories, in addition to acts of terrorism. Cooler heads may have prevailed when weighed against the mass murders actually carried out by Himmler's *Einsatzgruppen* and police forces in the Soviet Union. The trials were dropped, but the idea of 'Anti-Kharkov Actions' did not, as will be detailed later.

The decision to transfer the captured Allied agents to concentration camps came about in the wake of the Kharkov trial. Kieffer had the romantic notion that the agents would be held captive until liberated or released. This was a notion not held in RSHA IV Berlin, which had already organised mass murder on an industrial scale through Eichmann's department. Such thoughts of release or liberation were not on their agenda as these agents had undermined and attacked the Reich and its organisations. Kopkow's department had prepared judicial indictments for trials of many men and women before the People's Court (*Volksgerichtshof*). Many Germans and others working in the Rote Kapelle network in Berlin, Brussels, and Paris had sentences of death and imprisonment handed down by the People's Courts. No such trials were necessary for countless other enemies of the state, who were sent to concentration camps under the Protective Custody (*Schutzhaft*) emergency decree dating back to 28 February 1933. Protective Custody began in the first days of the new Gestapa Berlin, organised by Hermann Göring, and it became one of the main stepping stones of the new Nazi Government, which allowed the police to arrest persons for political reasons. In 1933, these police powers were directed at various communist officials. Later, it would be used by the *Sicherheitspolizei* as legislation enabling them to place anyone who politically opposed the Nazi regime in a concentration camp without having to go through legal prodecures.[2] After the communists came the social democrats, trades unionists, and Jews. In these early days, transfers to the first camps were *ad hoc* arrangements, while during the war, a whole department, RSHA IV C2 (from March 1944, redesignated as IV A6), employed several hundred women clerks to complete and file index cards for every prisoner sent to a concentration camp or prison under the Protective Custody system. This department, under SS-*Obersturmbannführer* Dr Emil Berndorff, communicated with the Political Department of the concentration camp about the prisoners and what needed to be done: either moved to another camp or executed. The head of the Political Department (*Politische Abteilung*) came from the Gestapo or Criminal Police and was responsible to RSHA, not the camp commandant, and each office had its own records for Protective Custody prisoners. The records held were extensive, and prisoner clerks were used to complete and maintain them.

The histories written about the concentration camps speak of the barbarism and sadism of the guards towards the prisoners who were sometimes shot out of hand. This was undoubtedly true in the pre-war years, and during wartime in the camps established in Poland, but regulations did exist for running the camps. Take for example the post-war interrogation of Martin Weiss, who had served in Neuengamme, commandant of Dachau (1 September 1942 to 1 November 1943), commandant of Majdanek, Poland (1 November 1943 to 25 April 1944), then with WVHA until the end of the war. The WVHA was part of Himmler's SS empire, and administered all the concentration and forced labour camps, assigning and posting personnel. Execution of prisoners had regulations to be followed:

> The orders for execution (shootings and hangings) came from the *Reichsführer* (Himmler) through the *Reichssicherheitshauptamt*, signed *Gruppenführer* Müller and previously Heydrich. Toward the last these orders were occasionally signed by Kaltenbrunner. These orders came by wire (teleprinter). By order of the *Reichsführer* the Camp Commandant was not permitted to take part in any execution.[3]

At Natzweiler camp, Polish prisoner Conrad Schultz worked as a clerk and interpreter in the Political Department, and he examined many official documents that came into the office:

> When orders for the execution of prisoners came from the RSHA Berlin, they arrived by means of teleprinter. A carbon copy was made in the machine, and the original came to the *Politische Abteilung*, while the carbon copy went to the *Kommandantur*.[4]

Rudolf Höss, the former commandant of Auschwitz, was questioned at Nuremberg on the stand at the International Military Tribunal prosecuting the major German war criminals. On 15 April 1946, he said:

> ...Order for the executions carried out in the camps came from the RSHA... [by teleprinter] ... in urgent cases, the RSHA sent the orders directly to the camps concerned.... Only very few teletypes which I ever seen [*sic.*] came from the *Reichsführer* and still fewer from the Defendant Kaltenbrunner. Most of them, I could say practically all, were signed 'Signed Müller'.

US prosecutor Colonel Amen cross examined Höss on the point of the signatures. Höss agreed that rather than just 'Signed Müller', the teleprinter messages said 'i.V. Müller', meaning acting as Deputy for Kaltenbrunner, as overall RSHA Chief.

The administration side for RSHA departments, Gestapo, and Criminal Police offices across Germany sending Protective Custody prisoners to concentration camps did so through Berndorff's department. On the other side of the coin, once a decision was made about the fate of prisoners, the office responsible for the prisoner informed Berndorff's office, which then informed the Political Department of the concentration camp. Some prisoners were released from camps in Germany throughout the war. Whereas Ampletzer contacted the Ministry of Justice for prison spaces for prisoners from France and Holland, their later transfer to concentration camps to be murdered would have been arranged through Kopkow and Berndorff directly. The groundwork for this arrangement between the two SS officers had begun in 1942, first with Soviet-trained German communist parachute agents Erwin Panndorf (shot at Sachsenhausen on 10 or 12 December 1942) and Willi Börner (shot at Dachau between the same dates), then the Soviet mole and Gestapo officer Willi Lehmann (shot at Sachsenhausen on 13 December 1942). There was no let up in 1943, when two more communist parachute agents were shot at Sachsenhausen (Georg Tietze and Albert Hössler) and one at Mauthausen (Hermann Köhler). All were shot without a trial.

Many more individual communist parachute agents were shot in concentration camps in 1944, and this year also saw the mass deportation of Allied intelligence agents from France and Holland to German prisons and camps prior to their execution. After the war, Kopkow told his British captors that he little to do with the agents of SOE captured in France or Holland or in other parts of Western Europe, stating that he had concentrated on fighting the Soviet menace. Unfortunately, his British captors took him at his word and did not challenge him on this serious point. Senior Gestapo officers from France and Holland, Knochen and Schreieder, were in British war crimes custody at the same time as Kopkow and did not vary a jot in naming the key officer they dealt with at RSHA Berlin, the department chief responsible for all parachute agents, SS-*Sturmbannführer* Horst Kopkow. There are also statements from Dr Josef Götz who ran the *Funkspiel* operations from Paris and confirmed Kopkow and RSHA Berlin took an enormous amount of interest in SOE French Section activities. Dr Götz also mentions that Kopkow came to Paris in April 1944 to discuss the *Funkspiel* operations, a visit not mentioned by Kopkow. It can therefore be rightly said that Kopkow told blatant lies to his British captors about his involvement in the fate of the agents captured in France and Holland in order to avoid incriminating himself.

Kopkow blamed his superiors for the transfer of the agents to concentration camps. He dated the decision to transport the 'F' Section agents from France to a conference between Himmler and Oberg, HSSPF France, in spring 1944. Himmler did visit France at the time and is known to have visited *Waffen*-SS divisions in Thouars and Montauban on 10 and 11 April 1944.[6] Oberg took the opportunity to discuss with Himmler his growing poor opinion of Knochen as a BdS. The SOE agents are not mentioned by Oberg and had only a few words to say about the end of the *Funkspiel* operations, which was ordered by the Führer on 6 June 1944. Kopkow came to Paris in April 1944 to discuss continuity of the *Funkspiel*, but the order from Hitler on 6 June 1944 stopped it and sealed the fate of the 'F' Section agents. Much the same can be said of the Dutch Section agents and the end of the *Funkspiel* in Holland on 1 April 1944. The decision to stop the *Funkspiel* operations first in Holland then in France became the key factor for the deportation of the agents to the concentration camps, where they could be killed in secret. They were no longer needed and their lives were now expendable.

Kopkow said that, in spring 1944, he 'was verbally informed' by RSHA IV Chief Müller about the 'transportation of the agents from France'—a decision arranged between Himmler and Oberg, which is only partially true. Kopkow, in his attempt to save himself, played mischief by only mentioning the SOE French agents. He does not mention the fifty-one SIS and SOE Dutch Section agents, all captured in Holland, who were the first to be deported in a large group, arriving at Rawitsch penitentiary on 15 April 1944. A week later, on 22 April 1944, they were joined by twenty-four agents of SOE French Section (British and French nationalities). SOE 'F' Section agent Marcel Rousset who was among those arriving on 22 April, later said the agents were 'all in solitary confinement and were handcuffed at night. They wore convict clothes and worked at rope-making during the day. The food was extremely poor' and they had only thirty minutes' exercise a day.[7] That they were handcuffed at night is remarkably like the prison conditions endured by Noor Inayat Khan who was shackled—one of the conditions laid down by Kopkow at RSHA. No other officer was going to make these conditions. Six more agents arrived at Rawitsch on 18 May 1944 from France. Of these three deportations, Kopkow later said this was dealt with by SS-*Hauptsturmführer Kriminalrat* Ampletzer, who 'arranged the accommodation of the male agents of the "French Section" in the Rawitch Prison, Posen, in agreement with the *Reichsjustizministerium*'.[8] Kopkow had earlier mentioned that Ampletzer had made similar arrangements for Inayat Khan's transfer to a German prison through the Ministry of Justice. Obviously, with the prisons under control of the Reich Ministry of Justice, permissions and prison space had to be sought, and the procedure became much simpler when the next agents were deported to concentration camps for they were under the control of the SS.

Before 24 June 1944, a decision must have been made at RSHA Berlin for killing the agents. The invasion of France on D-Day, 6 June 1944, probably influenced the decision to begin systematically killing the agents. Prior to 6 June 1944, any SOE agents killed had been due to other factors. After the war, Kopkow came up with an explanation for the decision making process, which was never challenged. According to Kopkow's explanation for the execution, the order came when *Reichsführer*-SS Himmler, via the Chief of the RSHA, SS-General Kaltenbrunner, requested the files of the captured SOE French Section officers. Since 1943, Himmler had supposedly been kept 'continually informed about the "French Section" … [and now wanted] the entire records about each agent, as he intended to decide on their fate'. If Kopkow is to be believed, the files came via Ampletzer to Kopkow, then to RSHA IV Chief Müller to Kaltenbrunner, and finally to Himmler at his field headquarters (*Feldkommandostelle*).[9] Himmler's whereabouts are known: on

6 June 1944 he was at Klessheim, just outside Salzburg in Austria; on 21 June 1944, he gave a talk at a meeting of army generals being held in Sonthofen in southern Bavaria; and on 22 June, he was in the French Alsace meeting with *Gauleiters*. Government ministers such as Himmler would not have the time to personally examine over 100 individual files of captured French Section agents, though Kopkow says Himmler annotated each file with his instructions in green pencil. Kopkow only mentions the French Section agents in this connection, he never mentions the fifty-one SIS and SOE Dutch Section agents deported from Holland to Rawitsch who would all share the same fate. As a civil servant, Kopkow would have produced a brief, a summation, with a foregone conclusion that sought approval. Himmler had already signed off the murder of millions of Jews and the dozen or more communist parachute agents who had already been murdered without trial in concentration camps. Why would the procedure change for 200 parachute agents from the west? All had been deemed enemies of the German state and its institutions and Himmler's simple signature on his briefing note would be adequate.

Continuing with Kopkow's first version of events, when Himmler had seen all the individual records, they came back with his order for the French Section agents at Rawitsch to be shot. '*Amtschef* IV, SS-*Gruppenführer* Müller himself gave and personally dictated the order for the shooting' as decided by Himmler. Kopkow then unwittingly revealed prior knowledge of events by stating that Müller's execution instructions 'that came back to Referat IV A2b', which was under Ampletzer, 'and [which were] addressed to the head of Staatspolizeistelle Breslau… SS-*Obersturmbannführer* Scharpwinkel' ordered the transfer of agents from Rawitsch to Gross Rosen. Kopkow goes on to say that these execution orders include the place of execution, which, if remembered correctly, 'concerned the Gross Rosen Concentration camp'. In another order attached to his instructions, Müller included 'a detailed special order' for the commandant of Gross Rosen to shoot the agents.

Kopkow concluded:

> Having been asked I state, that no proper trial took place in the case of the agents of the 'French Section', but that the instructions for this execution had been issued by *Reichsführer*-SS Himmler. For this purpose he was in possession of an authority given by the Führer, which lasted for the duration of the war. The order for the shooting of the agents was exclusively issued by the *Reichsführer*-SS.[10]

What is more likely is that Kopkow prepared the documentation and RSHA IV Chief Müller signed it off, informing Himmler and Kaltenbrunner of his actions. This is more in keeping with the *modus operandi* of their working patterns. Gestapo men were trained policemen who followed administrative guidelines of having their superiors sign-off orders above their remit. It is noticeable that among surviving captured records of RSHA IV A2, few letters and orders are signed by Kopkow himself—invariably, they are signed by RSHA IV Chief Müller using the RSHA IV A2 heading and reference.

One question seemingly never raised during Kopkow's long post-war interrogation period was why the captured intelligence agents were not put on trial. The Hague regulations on the rules of war, Article 30, states: 'A spy taken in the act shall not be punished without previous trial'.[11] Under Nazi regulations, such as the cover all 'protective custody laws', anyone considered a threat to the regime could be sent to a concentration camp, but those laws do not permit execution. At a time of heightened tension, following the Dieppe Raid—when over 6,000 mainly Canadian troops landed on 19 August 1942 in the hope of showing British capability turned into fiasco, with half the landing force either killed or taken prisoner—and pinprick raids by British raiding parties elsewhere, Hitler issued his 'Commando Order' on 18 October 1942.

This *Führerbefehl* was distributed across the entire German armed forces and it called for all Allied commandos captured in Europe and Africa—in uniform or not—to be killed immediately and without trial. Whether the enemy landed by ship, aircraft, or parachute would make no difference. Captured saboteurs and agents, whether or not in uniform, were to be immediately handed over to the SD. This order from Hitler was confirmed to be still in operation at various times until the end of the war.[12]

Its first application took place less than a week later. British commandos making a raid in Norway resulted in the capture of seven of them in late September 1942. After interrogation by the German Army in Norway, the seven were transferred to Germany and held at Colditz Castle as prisoners of war. On the day the Commando Order was issued (18 October 1942), the seven men were brought from Colditz to RSHA Berlin headquarters on Prinz Albrechtstrasse at the command of RSHA IV Chief Müller. Being involved in sabotage, they came under Kopkow's remit. The seven remained at RSHA until 22 October, when they were taken to Sachsenhausen concentration camps and executed the following day. They were the first victims of murder without trial under this new ruling from Hitler. More British commandos were captured and executed in Norway and France before the end of 1942 with more following over the next three years.

The Commando Order, this *Führerbefehl* by Hitler, provided the legality in Kopkow's eyes for the murder without trial of the captured Allied intelligence agents. It still resonated in Kopkow's mind forty-four years later. The first paragraph of the Commando Order contains the sentence 'Especially brutal and treacherous is the behaviour of the so-called Commandos, who, as is established, are partially recruited even from freed criminals in enemy countries'. In 1986, during a talk with Robert Marshall, Kopkow claimed: 'It was well known the British just emptied all their prisons of murderers and criminal types, and offered them clemency if they would parachute into France. We only did what the British would have done to them'.[13] That is not what the British did; German parachute agents captured in Britain were given an option: if they did not work with the British, they would be tried before a court, sentenced to death as a spy, and executed. If they chose to work with the British, their lives were spared, and at the end of the war, they were returned to Germany as undesirable aliens. Extremely different to what Kopkow ordered the concentration camps to do.

None of the orders about the SOE agents sent to KL Gross Rosen or the instructions sent to Staatspolizeistelle Breslau have survived. Recently, Dutch historians researching in Poland found the Rawitsch penitentiary logbook of arrivals and departures during 1944.[14] This logbook records that ten prisoners—they may have been SOE Dutch or French Section agents—were taken from the prison on 24 June 1944 by men of Gestapo Breslau; post-war British war crimes investigations reveal they were taken to Gross Rosen concentration camp, where they marched off towards the crematorium and were shot. Their bodies were cremated. This was the first mass shooting of SOE agents brought to a concentration camp, and the date of 24 June 1944 must mean that the shooting decision had been made just days before. There would have been no delay in carrying out the order. This recent Dutch research also reveals the remaining SOE agents (British, Dutch, and French) remained in Rawitsch until September 1944. The most diligent research does not always answer the problems and this has happened with the Rawitsch prison records. More prisoners were deported than are recorded. This could indicate that one or more groups of SOE prisoners deported from Paris went directly to Gross Rosen and would therefore not be recorded at Rawitsch. At the British war crimes trial of Gross Rosen personnel in 1948, the question of multiple transfers of SOE agents from Rawitsch to Gross Rosen was not raised.[15] Current research among SOE papers does show many more agents were deported from Paris to Rawitsch and Gross Rosen than the war crimes prosecution identified and shown on the present-day commemorative plaque at the former camp site.

Eight SOE women agents captured in France had been deported on 13 May 1944 to Karlsruhe prison. According to the post-war British investigation into the fate of these women: 'As time went on the prison staff got worried about the presence of the British officers as it was unusual and against regulations to detain prisoners for more than a fortnight in the police prison. It was very overcrowded and air raids made conditions difficult'.[16] Representations were made to Gestapo Karlsruhe, whose chief, SS-*Obersturmbannführer* Josef Gmeiner, twice reminded RSHA Berlin about the SOE women. Due to the nature of urgency owing a top secret teleprinter message arriving for Gmeiner from RSHA IV Chief Müller, probably on 5 July 1944, four of the named women were to be immediately sent to a concentration camp. Gmeiner put the matter in the hands of his counter espionage chief, SS-*Sturmbannführer* Hermann Rössner.[17] The instructions from Berlin requested the four women be escorted to Natzweiler concentration camp 'for execution'. This camp lay about 90 miles south, the other side of Strasbourg. On 6 July 1944, the Gestapo escort detail under Max Wassmer arrived at Karlsruhe prison and took away Andrée Borrel, Vera Leigh, Diana Rowden, and Sonia Olschanezky. They travelled by ordinary railway train via Strasbourg to Rothau, the railway station for Natzweiler. A truck collected them from the station to take them up the steep hill to the camp where Wassmer reported to the camp administration and obtained a receipt for the four women. At the camp, barrack blocks were built on descending terraces, down to the cell block and crematorium, all surrounded by barbed-wire fencing and watchtowers. Natzweiler was a camp for male prisoners, so the four women stood out. They were observed by two particular prisoners, SOE French Section agent Brian Stonehouse and Albert Guérisse (Pat O'Leary), who had run an escape line through France to Spain for shot-down Allied aircrew. The four women descended the terraced walkway, down to the crematorium. Late that afternoon, SS camp Doctor Werner Rohde gave them lethal injections, in the guise of an anti-typhus injection, and the bodies were then cremated. A few days later, Gestapo Karlsruhe received official confirmation of the death of the four women from Natzweiler, which was sent on to RSHA.[18]

The day after the executions in Natzweiler, another Soviet-trained German communist Erna Eifler was shot at Ravensbrück concentration camp for women, north of Berlin. Eifler had been in Gestapo custody since October 1942 and, working with Ampletzer, carried out a *Funkspiel* operation with Moscow using her ciphers. Her usefulness had now run its course and Eifler was shot on 7 July 1944 and her body was cremated.[19]

August 1944 in Paris meant Kieffer's men clearing out the prisons and deporting the agents before the Allied armies arrived. A handful of SOE French Section agents had gone to Buchenwald as early as January 1944, and fifteen others went to Flossenbürg concentration camp in April 1944; one of these, Frank Michel, had been shot in June 1944. Forty SOE agents, including three women (Denise Bloch, Lilian Rolfe, and Violette Szabo), left Paris by train on 8 August 1944. The men went to Buchenwald and arrived during the night of 16–17 August, the women to Ravensbrück where they arrived almost two weeks later.[20] By the end of August 1944, at least 136 captured SOE agents were scattered among German concentration camps and prisons:

Pforzheim & Karlsruhe prisons	Four female agents
Rawitsch penitentiary	Sixty-one agents
Buchenwald camp	Forty agents
Flossenbürg camp	Fourteen agents
Ravensbrück camp	Eleven agents
Sachsenhausen camp	Six agents

September 1944 would be the month when most of these agents were murdered. It began on 3 September 1944, when forty-seven agents (American,

British, and Dutch) left Rawitsch prison and were transported by rail via Breslau and Prague to Mauthausen concentration camp in Austria, a few miles from Linz. The remaining fourteen agents (eleven Dutch and three French and/or British) were picked up on 4 September 1944 by a bus organised by Gestapo Breslau and taken to Gross Rosen camp where they were shot and cremated. The forty-seven agents arrived at Mauthausen and were all shot over 6 and 7 September 1944.[21] Most of the victims were SOE and SIS agents captured in Holland; among the four British agents was Gilbert Norman, who had signed up to Kopkow's pact in Paris in June 1943 that had the proviso that everyone would be spared if they gave up the arms and weapons parachuted to their network. What differentiated these men from one another and why some executed in one place and others at different camps is unknown.

At Flossenbürg, the Canadian SOE French Section agent Gustave Bieler, still suffering from a back injury that occurred at his parachute landing in France during November 1942, was singled out. Bieler was apparently shot by an SS honour guard on 5 September 1944, leaving thirteen other SOE agents in solitary confinement in the Cell Block.[22]

The executions at Buchenwald began on 11 September, when sixteen agents (British, Canadian, and French) were called out by name to report at the camp gate. They were hanged during the night of 11–12 September in the cellar of the crematorium and their bodies cremated. Their surviving comrades remained in a state of anxiety about their own lives, at least until October when they too were taken.[23]

On 10 September 1944, Gestapo Karlsruhe received another teleprinter message from RSHA Berlin ordering the execution of the remaining four women SOE agents. The arrangements were made and, the following day, Noor Inayat Khan was brought under Gestapo escort from Pforzheim prison to join her three fellow agents at Karlsruhe prison. At 2 a.m. on 12 September 1944, the four women (Yolande Unternahrer/Beekmann, Madeleine Damerment, Eliane Plewman, and Inayat Khan) left the prison escorted by three men from Gestapo Karlsruhe, catching a train from nearby Bruchsal to Stuttgart for the fast train to Munich, which arrived in the late afternoon; the danger of Allied aircraft strafing and bombing of trains no doubt caused the delay, for the journey today is less than two hours. In Munich, they waited for a local train for the journey north to Dachau. From Dachau railway station, they walked the mile or so to the camp, arriving about 10 p.m. The four women were handed over in exchange for a receipt, and the three Gestapo men billeted above the guard house for the night. Early the following morning, the women were shot and their bodies immediately cremated. Before they left Dachau concentration camp on 13 September 1944, the Gestapo men were given a report that the execution had been carried out (*Vollzugszettel*).[24]

Käthe (Katya) Niederkirchner had been held in the basement cells of Gestapo headquarters on Prinz Albrecht Strasse, Berlin, since October–November

1943. Kopkow's men must have dragged every last piece of knowledge out of her before sending her to Ravensbrück in May 1944. On 18 September 1944, Niederkirchner was brought to the cell block (*Zellenbau*). During the night of 27–28 September, together with a Polish woman, they were brought a few yards to the end of the 'shooting alley', adjacent to the crematorium, and shot by SS guard Artur Conrad. Their bodies were then cremated.[25]

The situation at Buchenwald for the SOE agents worsened in October. In four separate shooting actions between 5 and 9 October 1944, sixteen SOE agents were killed and cremated.[26] After these killing actions (ten female agents, 104 men), there was another execution in 1944 at Dachau. Enzo Sereni (codename Captain Shmuel Barda), an Italian Jewish professor of philosophy, had been dropped with a companion near Florence, Italy, during the night of 15–16 May 1944. By misfortune, Sereni was arrested shortly after landing and was handed over to the Gestapo. On 9 October 1944, Sereni became prisoner No. 113160 at Dachau concentration camp and was sent to work at Mühldorf sub-camp, where, in huge underground caverns, component parts for the Messerschmitt Me 262 jet fighter aircraft were manufactured. On 17 November 1944, Sereni was escorted back to Dachau and three days later was shot.[27]

During January 1945, the killings began again. A Soviet-trained German communist, one of the Pickaxe agents who had been dropped by the RAF in southern Germany, Elsa Noffke (codename Kersti Poska), told her fellow prisoner Odette Sansom/Churchill that she was being released on 10 January 1945. Kopkow was not renowned for releasing agents, and as Noffke was never heard of again, it appears that Noffke was shot that day. Four French female agents, radio operators working for the French intelligence agency BCRA, had been caught in summer 1944 and sent to Ravensbrück. Their execution order arrived and the four were shot on 18 January 1945.[28]

Towards the end of December 1944, German military forces taking back control of Slovakia after three months of insurrection came across members of an American and British military mission working to get shot-down Allied aircrew back to Allied territory. They flew pick-up aircraft from an airstrip in Slovakia. Operation Windproof under its mission commander, John Sehmer, had several tasks including intelligence gathering from Hungary, assisting OSS mission Dawes under its commander, US Navy Lt James Holt Green. The Slovak Rising in September 1944 meant German forces began sweeping the country for insurgents, moving ever more into the mountainous areas around Banska Bystrica. At Christmas time 1944, their position was precarious, but despite the snow, German forces captured eighteen members of the two groups: Sehmer had four men and a woman under his command when captured, and Holt Green had thirteen men. After almost two weeks, eighteen members of these missions were sent to Mauthausen concentration camp in Austria. When knowledge of this arrangement found its way to RSHA Berlin, RSHA IV (Kopkow) and RSHA VI (SD Foreign Intelligence) sent interrogators to Mauthausen. Hans Thost worked for RSHA VI as an English translator and interpreter, and he stated that it was 8 January 1945 when he arrived at Mauthausen to help the Gestapo in their interrogation of these English and American agents captured in Slovakia. Thost helped *Kriminalkommissar* Walter Habecker, one of Kopkow's men from RSHA IV A2, who had been ordered down from Berlin to interrogate the captives. They started with the radio operator Jack Wilsen, and Habecker decided Wilsen was not being cooperative so he tortured him according to Thost. Wilsen admitted he was August Warndorfer, an Austrian Jew. He had been dropped by SOE in October 1944 to work in Vienna, but his aircraft overshot the drop zone and he landed 40 miles further north-east in Slovakia where partisans took him to the military mission. The following day, Sehmer was interrogated by Habecker, the Mauthausen Protective Custody Camp Commander (*Schutzhaftlagerführer*) Johann Altfuldisch and the Mauthausen camp commandant Franz Ziereis with Thost interpreting. Sehmer wore his uniform with rank badges and answered most of the questions in a quiet and courteous way. After a while, Habecker got impatient and subjected Sehmer to his 'Tibetan wheel' torture device that painfully crushed his fingers. Two British-trained Palestinian parachute agents, Abba Berdichev and Zvi Ben Yaakov, were also questioned. A Gestapo interpreter from RSHA IV B1, Werner Müller, questioned the American contingent. Müller's post-war statement mentions the RSHA party, which included SS-*Untersturmführer* Arndt, Habecker, and Thost, arrived at Mauthausen during the evening of 6 January 1945 (two days earlier than Thost said); in charge of the whole interrogation commission was SS-*Sturmbannführer* Dr Manfred Schöneseiffen, the Gestapo chief in Chemnitz. Between 7 and 11 January, Müller interviewed the Americans, although Habecker beat Holt Green who had a broken arm in a plaster cast. Habecker also beat one of the Palestinians, who was known as 'Willis', because he was a Jew; Müller attempted to interpose: 'Habecker threatened me if I wouldn't get out of the way, saying he would otherwise beat me instead'. Müller returned to Mauthausen on 23 January for more interrogations of the Americans. The following day (24 January 1945), all eighteen members of the Anglo-American missions were killed at Mauthausen.[29]

Three days later at Ravensbrück, three SOE agents were shot. Denise Bloch, Lilian Rolfe, and Violette Szabo had been deported from Paris on 8 August 1944 and arrived at Ravensbrück towards the end of the month. Together they had done forced labour at Torgau and then at Königsberg an der Neumarkt, east of Berlin (now Chojna, Poland), where an airstrip was being lengthened and the women were digging out tree stumps in the snow and icy conditions. They were recalled by name from this work and brought back to Ravensbrück. All three were shot at the end of the 'shooting alley' in the early hours of 27 January 1945.[30] The fourth SOE agent, Cecily Lefort, who came with them from Paris, was very ill on arrival back from Königsberg/Neumarkt, and was taken into the hospital block. On 15 February 1945, Cecily Lefort was selected for gassing and taken to the makeshift gas chamber at Uckermark camp, just half a mile from Ravensbrück, where she was gassed to death.[31] Three

SOE agents were still being held at Ravensbrück—Odette Sansom/Churchill, Eileen Nearne and Yvonne Ruddelat. Only Churchill and Nearne survived. On 1 March 1945, Ruddelat (using her cover name Jacqueline Gauthier) was sent on transport from Ravensbrück to Bergen-Belsen camp. Still suffering from the effects of the head wound when captured in July 1943, Ruddelat's health continued to fail and she died from typhus and dysentery on 23 April 1945 at Belsen.[32] One of many other thousands whose unidentified bodies were given a mass burial by the liberating British forces.

During February 1945, probably at Sachsenhausen camp, SOE-trained German POW turned agent Kurt Koenig (codename Krotzky) was executed. He had two successful parachute missions behind him when he was arrested after his third parachute jump on 8 January 1944 near Baden in the Black Forest region. Koenig was brought to Gestapo Karlsruhe offices where he was interrogated by Walter Herberg. Koenig stated this was his third mission into Germany for the British and that he was given the job of sabotaging a railway viaduct in the Black Forest region. On his return through the advancing Allied front lines, he was to bring back 'some German papers, in particular food tickets used by Wehrmacht personnel'. Herberg informed RSHA Berlin and Koenig was escorted there and handed over to *Kriminalrat* Kopkow. After the war, Kopkow could remember Koenig, but not his subsequent fate.[33]

By March 1945, the German military situation had deteriorated to such an extent that defeat stared every German in the face. Kopkow, however, was still clearing the decks of the few captured agents still alive. Those surviving on poor food and worsening in health were being held at Sachsenhausen and Flossenbürg camps. If the teleprinter links were down, radio messages were sent. On 23 March 1945, at Sachsenhausen camp, the six remaining agents (Charles Grover-Williams and Francis Suttill, both captured in France; Lieutenant Commander Cumberledge and three of his NCOs, captured in Greece and brought to Sachsenhausen) were shot.[34] A few days later, Flossenbürg camp received instructions from RSHA Berlin about the remaining thirteen SOE and OSS agents. After almost a year in solitary confinement in the cell block, these men were taken out individually on 29 March 1945 and hanged.[35] On 6 April 1945, Bletchley Park intercepted a radio message between RSHA and the Senior SS and Police Commander (HSSPF) in Nuremberg.[36] The message probably refers to the transfer of Abwehr officers Admiral Wilhelm Canaris and Hans Oster and others to Flossenbürg 'on the order of the Rf.SS [Himmler]. For this purpose use the cells which became vacant as a result of the "Anti-Kharkov" operations, as arranged with Roman 4 (= Amt IV). If supervision is really difficult, your proposal will also be accepted. Good treatment—no "special treatment"'. The coy wording shows that the SOE agents had been killed as part of the Anti-Kharkov operation, mentioned before, and Amt IV is RSHA IV. No 'special treatment' (*Sonderbehandlung*) was a German euphemism for killing and used widely in Gestapo documentation. Unfortunately for Canaris, further instructions for his execution came within days as he was hanged on 9 April 1945 together with Hans Oster and Pastor Dietrich Bonhoeffer.

These killings of agents in 1944 and 1945 did not happen by chance. They were systematic and took place in several concentration camps within weeks of each other. The personnel in these camps did not kill the agents until they received instructions from RSHA Berlin. Whether the instructions were signed by Himmler, Kaltenbrunner, or Müller, these very senior officers—the 'top brass'—who ran the Gestapo and Security Police did not take a personal interest in each individual agent—that was left to their department chiefs. Who was responsible on a national basis across Germany and the entire German-occupied territories for parachute agents and *Funkspiel* operations? SS-*Sturmbannführer Kriminaldirektor* Horst Kopkow was the person responsible for issuing the killing orders regardless of the signature at the bottom of each teleprinter message from RSHA IV Berlin to the camps.

With so many agents losing their lives, it could be expected that Allied post-war justice would pursue and prosecute the perpetrators. This is a myth because very few paid the price. The first trial before a British military court in Wuppertal, May–June 1946, charged nine men from Natzweiler concentration camp involved in the murder by lethal injection of four SOE female agents on 6 July 1944. One of the defendants, SS Doctor Werner Rohde, was convicted of administering the lethal injections and sentenced to death; he was hanged on 11 October 1946. The others received prison terms including the former camp commandant, Fritz Hartjenstein, now at his second British trial. He was then handed over to the French authorities for another trial in Metz. In France, he received his second death sentence. Hartjenstein languished in a French prison until he died of natural cases in 1954.

A second British trial in Hamburg, December 1946 to February 1947, charged nineteen defendants with war crimes at Ravensbrück concentration camp for women. SOE men and women agents had been murdered here in 1944 and 1945, but a specific charge relating to their murder did not appear on the charge sheet. An examination of events that led to their execution in the camp was covered in the only charge against the former camp staff—that they committed a war crime 'in violation of the laws and usages of war, were concerned in the ill-treatment and killing of Allied Nationals' at the camp between 1939 and 1945. The SS officer in charge of the execution of the three women, Johann Schwarzhuber, admitted being present when they were shot on orders from RSHA, and he was sentenced to death and hanged.[37]

The British trials of concentration camp staff from Gross Rosen and Natzweiler, and indirectly those from Ravensbrück, were the only SS men ever held responsible for a small number of the murders of well over 200 captured intelligence agents from many different Allied intelligence agencies, who were all murdered without trial. The US judicial authorities did prosecute the camp staffs of Dachau, Flossenbürg, and Mauthausen without directly mentioning the murders of US or SOE intelligence agents. The Russian authorities carried out trials of camps staff from Buchenwald and Sachsenhausen and again those prosecuted were not directly charged with the murder of intelligence agents.

Not a single Gestapo or SD official has been prosecuted for involvement in the murder of over 200 captured intelligence agents.

Soviet Agents Executed Without Trial in German Concentration Camps and Prisons

Anna Ouspenskaya*	Paris	summer 1942
Erwin Panndorf	KL Sachenhausen	10–12 Dec 1942
Willi Börner	KL Dachau	10–12 Dec 1942
Willi Lehmann	KL Sachsenhausen	13 Dec 1942
Walter Gersmann	Hamburg	beginning of 1943
Willi Fellendorf	Hamburg	beginning of 1943
Georg Tietze*	probably KL Sachsenhausen	spring 1943
Otto Ulnoti*	probably KL Sachsenhausen	spring 1943
John Wilhelm Kruyt (snr)*	Berlin	1943
Albert Hössler	KL Sachsenhausen	1943
Elsa Noffke*	FKL Ravensbrück	6–7 Nov 1943
Georg Kennerknecht	KL Mauthausen	1944
--- Brandt	KL Sachsenhausen	1944
Theo Winter	KL Sachsenhausen	1944
Siegfried Schmidt*	probably KL Sachsenhausen	1944
Otto Bach*	probably KL Sachsenhausen	1944
Josef Weingart	FKL Ravensbrück	1944
Elvira Eisenschneider	FKL Ravensbrück	7 July 1944
Käthe Niederkirchner	FKL Ravensbrück	28 September 1944
--- Augustin	probably KL Sachsenhausen	end of 1944
Elsa Noffke*	FKL Ravensbrück	10–11 Jan 1945
Emil Kammler	KL Mauthausen	April 1945
Olga Gulikowa	Graz	2 April 1945
Soja Bogomnjan	Graz	2 April 1945
Johann Tominitsch	Graz	2 April 1945
Wladimir Iwanow	Graz	2 April 1945
Anton Dominitrenko	Graz	2 April 1945
Anton Blinko	Graz	2 April 1945
Johann Modovan	Graz	2 April 1945
Hermann Köhler*	KL Mauthausen	17 April 1945

* Pickaxe agents, dropped by the RAF on behalf of the NKVD.

SOE, SIS, OSS, BCRA, IIe Bureau Agents, Captured in France, Greece, and Holland, and Executed Without Trial in German Concentration Camps and Prisons

11 May 1942	KL Sachsenhausen	Hans Zomer
12 May 1944	Verona (Italy)	John de Lucia
9 June 1944	KL Flossenbürg	Francois Michel
10 June 1944	KL Vught (Holland)	Aart van Giessen
10 June 1944	KL Vught (Holland)	Jan van Rietschoten
24 June 1944	KL Gross Rosen	Ten unnamed SOE French agents taken from Rawitsch prison to KL Gross Rosen for execution and possibly these: Roland Alexandre, Robert Byerly, Francois Deniset, Roland Dowlen, Jean-Roger Dubois, David Finlayson, Henri Gaillot, John Hamilton, Charles Hayes, Maurice Lepage
6 July 1944	KL Natzweiler	Andrée Borrel, Vera Leigh, Sonia Olschanesky, Diana Rowden
20 August 1944	Fort Côte-Lorette (near Lyons)	Alcide Beauregard
4 September 1944	KL Gross Rosen	Remaining SOE agents held at Rawitsch taken to Gross Rosen for execution, possibly these: Edmond Lesout, Claude Malraux, Adolphe Rabinovitch, Francois Vallée, France Antelme, Lionel Lee, Paul Pardi, Octave Simon, Jacques Ledoux, Andre Maugenet, Marcel Defence, Philippe Duclos, Jakob Bakker, Ernst de Jonge, Jan Kist, Humphrey Macare, Andriaan Mooy, Felix Ortt, Herman Overes, Hermanus Parlevliet, Charles Pouwels, Frederik Rouwerd, Antonius van Steen
5 September 1944	KL Flossenbürg	Gustave Bieler
5 September 1944	KL Vught (Holland)	Nikolaas Celosse

6–7 September 1944	KL Mauthausen	Forty-seven French, Dutch & SIS agents brought from Rawitsch and shot: Georges Clement, Leonardus Andringa, Pieter Ardense, Arnoldus Baatsen, Thoe Beukema, Pieter Boogaart, Klaus van der Bor, Cornelius Braggaar, Oscar de Brey, Johannes Buizer, Josef Bukkens, Jan Dane, Kees Drooglever, Jan de Haas, Gerard van Hemert, Jan Hofstede, Cornelius van Hulstyn, Georg Jambroes, Roelof Jongelie, Pieter Kamphorst, Barend Klooss, Meinert Koolstra, Arie de Krujff, Anton Mink, Gerard van Os, Michels Pals, Laurentius Punt, Gozewijn Ras, George Ruseler, Hendrik Sebes, Horst Steeksma, Thijs Taconis, Ivo van Uytvanck, Pieter van der Wilden, Willem van der Wilden, Antonius Wegner, Aart Alblas, Jan Emmer, Willem Niermayer, Evert Radema, Johannes ter Laak, Marcus Bloom, Sidney Jones, Isidore Newman, Gilbert Norman, Edward Wilkinson, John Young
8 September 1944	Haidari Camp, Athens	Lela Karayanni
11 September 1944	KL Buchenwald	SOE agents executed: Eliseé Allard, Robert Benoist, Angehand Defendini, Julien Detal, Francois Garel, Emile Garry, Pierre Geelen, Desmond Hubble, Gerald Keun, Marcel Leccia, Yves Loison, John Macalister, John Mackenzie, James Mayer, Frank Pickersgill, Charles Rechenmann, Romeo Sabourin, Arthur Steele
13 September 1944	KL Dachau	Yolande Beekman/Unternahrer, Madeleine Damerment, Noor Inayat Khan, Eliane Plewman
September–October 1944	FKL Ravensbrück	Frank Chamier
5 October 1944	KL Buchenwald	Henri Heusch
6–7 October 1944	KL Buchenwald	Denis Barrett, Jacques Chaigneau, Marcel Corbusier, Jean de Leguier, Henri Frager, René Gerard, Pierre Mulsant, Christian Raimbaud, Paul Vellaud, Alfred Wilkinson, Charles Skepper (possible)
7 October 1944	KL Buchenwald	Jean Avallard, Jean Evesque

20 November 1944	KL Dachau	Enzo Sereni
20 November 1944	Shot after capture, Slovakia	Havivah Reik, Rafael Reisz
21 November 1944	KL Dachau	Charles Gonest
November–December 1944	KL Sachsenhausen	'Josef Bauer'
1–2 December 1944	Apeldoorn, Holland	Seerp Postma
18 January 1945	FKL Ravensbrück	Suzanne Boitte/Mertzisem, Marie Louise Cloarec, Jeannie Djendi, Pierrette Louin
26 January 1945	KL Mauthausen	All members of American and British military missions.
		American: Edward Baranski, Robert Brown, James Gaul, James Holt Green, Charles Heller, Joseph Horvath, Tibor Keszthelyi, Jaroslav Mican, Lane Miller, Joe Morton, Nelson Paris, Daniel Pavletich, Francis Perry
		British: Margita Kockova, John Sehmer, Zvi Ben-Yaakov, Abi Berdichev, August Warndorfer
27 January 1945	FKL Ravensbrück	Denise Bloch, Lilian Rolfe, Violette Szabo
15 February 1945	FKL Ravensbrück	Cecily Lefort
23 March 1945	KL Sachsenhausen	William Grover-Williams, Francis Suttill, C. M. B. Cumberledge, Thomas Handley, Jean Kotrba (Davies), James C. Steele
29 March 1945	KL Buchenwald	Maurice Pertschuk
29 March 1945	KL Flossenbürg	Jack Agazarian, Philip Amphlett, James Amps, George Demand, Roland Dowlen, Marcel Fox, Harry Graham, Eugen Levene, James Menesson, Brian Rafferty, David Sibree, Victor Soskice, Jean Worms
3 April 1945	Graz, Austria	Friedrich Berliner

Agents Missing Believed Killed in Concentration Camps

1944	SOE 'F' Section	Louis Berteau, Edward Coppin (possibly at Ravensbrück), Jules LeBon, George McBain, Jack Sinclair
1944	BCRA (France)	Jean Kammerer
1945	SOE Austrian Section	Georg Dereatti, Josef Hemetsberger, Hubert Mayr, Rudolf Moser
1945	SOE German Section	Peter Weisz

9

The Walls Come Tumbling Down (1944–1945)

The year 1944 began on a high note for Kopkow as he finally managed to have his offices moved out of Berlin due to the chaos of regular Allied air raids. Having moved office to Kurfürstendamm 140 in Berlin-Halensee, he now moved to the Security Police Officer Training School (*Sipo-Führerschule*) at Drögen, near Fürstenberg. This had the additional bonus of nearby Ravensbrück concentration camp for women, which was just 4 miles (6 km) away and had a large prison block where prisoners (male and female) could be held in solitary confinement for further interrogation. He left behind in Berlin a Liaison Office staffed by *Kriminalkommissars* Richard Haupt and Walter Habecker, who liaised with RSHA IV Chief Müller and RSHA Chief Dr Kaltenbrunner, and provided a courier service between RSHA Berlin and Fürstenberg.

On 19 January 1944, Kopkow gave a paper on 'Parachute Agents' at a meeting of all BdS and IdS commanders from across Germany and German-occupied territories that took place at Königsberg on the Baltic coast (now the Russian enclave of Kaliningrad). *Reichsführer*-SS Himmler also attended the meeting and made mention of Kopkow's forty-five-minute talk during his round-up of the various threats now facing Germany, reinforcing the measures to be taken against all Allied parachute agents and outlining the possibilities of *Funkspiel* operations.[1] In April 1944, Kopkow and Ampletzer conducted a short course about countering enemy radio operators at Fürstenberg to ten Security Police officers who were being posted to Italy to organise counter-intelligence operations against British and American agents infiltrating northern Italy and how to use captured ciphers. One of these officers was Richard Schnur, who found himself then posted to Paris to help Dr Götz rather than receiving a posting to Italy.[2]

The attempted assassination of Hitler took place on 20 July 1944 at his 'Wolfsschanze' headquarters near Rastenburg, in East Prussia. This sensational act by an army colonel, Claus von Stauffenberg, had deadly repercussions across Germany and the occupied territories when the surviving

Hitler took his revenge. RSHA was quick to act, and under Kaltenbrunner's direction, Kopkow was ordered to the 'Wolfsschanze' to take charge of the investigation. Kopkow arrived at the 'crime scene' on 21 July 1944 with his team of sabotage experts and they began their work; he reported: 'I had the task of establishing the facts of the matter at Führer Headquarters and worked there for several weeks before returning to Berlin'.[3] Kopkow's experts quickly established that explosives had been used and had pinpointed where they had originated from. Captain Georg Gerhard of the Kürfurst Regiment, which reported to the Abwehr, admitted when interrogated by Kopkow that 'he had furnished the explosive for the Putsch', but he had no knowledge of why it was needed. Gerhard happily confirmed that on 15 August 1944 he had been 'cleared by Kopkow of the charge of complicity' in the plot.[4] Gerhard was lucky to save his life; many hundreds would lose theirs as the RSHA investigation spread to identify anyone who acted positively in the plot or had supported it. RSHA created its *Sonderkommission 20.Juli* with twelve separate groups investigating different sections of the German armed forces and political societies. Kopkow's role in the 20 July investigation was chief of the first group, investigating the crime scene, which ran its course over a matter of weeks. The investigation did not end for some of his officers who had been seconded to other groups and based in Potsdam, and were interrogating lesser offenders connected to the plot until March 1945.[5] Only the advance of the Soviet armies threatening Berlin caused them to stop their activities and retreat.

In spite of air raids, RSHA hosted a conference of Gestapo Chiefs and representatives of BdS and KdS offices across Germany and the rapidly diminishing occupied territories. It took place at RSHA headquarters on Prinz Albrechtstrasse, Berlin, with RSHA IV Chief Müller as chairman. Over three days (30 September to 2 October 1944), they heard from RSHA IV desk officers about the current situation and fighting the enemy within and without. Kopkow gave his talk on parachute agents and *Funkspiel* operations; other desk officers spoke about resistance, communism, and Jews. One of those attending, SS-*Sturmbannführer* Dr Fritz Kranebitter, Gestapo Chief for Italy at BdS Italy in Verona, recalled meeting Kopkow at this conference and that 'Müller mentioned that Soviet agent groups in Great Britain, USA and Turkey had been penetrated by the Germans, and were being used for their own purposes in the reports they sent to Moscow.... Müller also said that the Rote Kapelle had been fairly successful in Holland, Poland and Spain'.[6] Although half-remembered by Kranebitter in a post-war interrogation report a year after the conference, Müller mentioning Rote Kapelle at this late stage of the war highlights that investigations were still on-going.

In spring 1944, RSHA wanted all its offices centralised because of delays in communication between the centre on Prinz Albrecht Strasse and locations found by the different departments across Berlin and its suburbs. Two new centres had been prepared from large numbers of barrack blocks at special camps east of Berlin. They were known as 'Dachs I' and 'Dachs II', and Kopkow's section moved from Fürstenberg probably in October 1944 to Dachs II near Trebnitz railway station on the Berlin–Küstrin rail line; this was only 10 miles (16 km) east of Küstrin, which sat on the Oder River border crossing. This was poor planning on behalf of RSHA as these locations were in the centre of Soviet military plans for the forthcoming attack on the Reich capital, Berlin, and within a few months, it would become a battle zone. Kopkow was evacuated from Dachs II by 3 February 1945, taking his office and staff back to Berlin. Conditions for working in Berlin had improved since the transfer to Dachs I and II, and on the return, two groups were quickly established—a 'management group' (*Führungsstab*) and a 'working group' (*Arbeitsstab*). The former consisted of senior RSHA IV department chiefs such as Kopkow, who remained in Berlin, whereas the latter consisted of large numbers of office staff and departmental officers transferred to Hof in northern Bavaria. They eventually became known as the Northern Group (in Berlin) and the Southern Group (in Hof).

Soviet military successes in 1944 included recovering vast regions of the Soviet Union from German occupation, which resulted in huge numbers of German prisoners. During 1941 and 1942, the German Army conscripted hundreds of thousands of men regardless of their political views to fill the ranks. This meant many communists and social democrats joined the army and served on the Eastern Front. When possibilities arose on the front lines, some communists serving in German units deserted to the Soviet side. These men could then be retrained and used by Soviet military intelligence and either parachuted or infiltrated across German lines of defence. Throughout 1944, Kopkow noted 'a new era of Soviet parachute agent activity' when large numbers of newly trained German communists and other non-Nazis began being dropped into East and West Prussia, the Warthegau, and Silesia for military reconnaissance missions. When captured, the ciphers of these agents could be used in *Funkspiel* operations to provide disinformation about the strength of German forces on the Eastern Front (claiming them much stronger), and if the Soviets accepted this disinformation, it might lead to a lessening demand for German reinforcements moving from the Western Front in France after the invasion on 6 June 1944.

The year 1945 began badly militarily for Germany and defeat looked ominously inevitable. Soviet armies were massing in eastern Poland for their advance westward, and Allied armies were massing on the western border of Germany, having repulsed attempted German military operations through the Ardennes forests in hope of recovering Belgian territory. In the Reich itself, supplies of food, the necessities of everyday life, communications, and travel by road or rail were all being seriously hampered or destroyed by Allied air raids. Berlin and many other German cities had been left with their hearts torn out, leaving skeletal buildings and forcing the population to live among the ruins. RSHA headquarters on Prinz Albrechtstrasse had suffered serious air-raid damage, and its officials were now forced again to work in temporary office accommodation inside and outside Berlin. The Allied air raids continued to wreak havoc in Berlin, and an especially devastating raid by 1,000 Flying Fortresses of the USAAF on 3 February 1945 practically carpet-bombed the government quarter of Berlin, causing even more damage to RSHA headquarters on Prinz Albrechtstrasse.[7] In spite of all these difficulties for the civilian population, German propaganda continued prophesising new 'wonder weapons' (*Wunderwaffen*) that would tilt the war in Germany's favour.

In Poland, Soviet armies had stopped on the eastern bank of the river Vistula, across from Warsaw, for several months—probably for political reasons as they arrived during the period of the Warsaw Rising (1 August–2 October 1944)—and they did not interfere with its suppression and destruction of central Warsaw by German forces. Soviet armies rested and resupplied until 12 January 1945, when they stormed across the Vistula on a front well over 100 miles long, travelling south towards the border with Czechoslovakia. Warsaw fell into Soviet hands on 17 January, and the Auschwitz concentration camp complex fell on 27 January, followed by Gross Rosen where the SOE agents had been murdered. The following week, Soviet armies faced Germany across the River Oder at Küstrin with Berlin just 35 miles (56 km) to the west. Kopkow now faced increasingly large numbers of agents being dropped north, south, and west of Berlin, reporting to Soviet military headquarters about rail transports, military crossing points, German troop concentrations, and their movements. Orders were also given to the agents to kidnap German officers in the rear areas and smuggle them back across the lines for interrogation. Ampletzer's section, RSHA IV A2b, sent out a circular to all Gestapo offices across Germany reminding them about increasing numbers of German POWs now being dropped as agents by the Soviets and what they needed to do with their ciphers and communications equipment to effect a *Funkspiel*.[8]

At this stage of the war, Soviet intelligence agencies picked through the ranks of their German POWs for the most suitable candidates to be trained as agents. In a post-war interrogation by the British, Sergeant Lesmeister of the Secret Field Police (*Geheime Feldpolizei*—GFP) stated:

> Later more German prisoners were sent over by the Russians with sabotage, espionage and propaganda missions. The majority sent on missions were passed through the German (front) lines; some were dropped by parachute in groups of 8 to 10 further in the rear.
>
> The number of German prisoners infiltrated by the Russians grew ever greater until as many as 30 to 40 a week were arriving in the Northern sector alone.... [At this time (beginning of 1945), Lesmeister was stationed in the Danzig area and stated] that only about 5% ever completed their mission; about 75% surrendered voluntarily to the

> German authorities … estimates that between Jun 43 and Jan 45 [some] 700 German prisoners sent back by the Russians on the Northern sector passed through the hands of [GFP] Gruppe 713.

These prisoners were taken to an interrogation centre at Lissa (now Leszno, Poland), not far from Posen (Poznan), established jointly by the army and Gestapo. After interrogation, these prisoners were either shot, continued to be detained, or were sent to military units fighting in the west. Towards the end of January 1945, when Soviet armies were threatening Danzig, Lesmeister's GFP unit still had 300–400 agents in custody and could not send them to Lissa for interrogation due to the worsening military situation. He provides no information on what then happened to these agents in GFP custody.[9]

Since arriving back in Berlin from Dachs II in January 1945, Kopkow had taken offices at Wrangelstrasse 6/7, Berlin-Steglitz. Some of his officials were based in Potsdam investigating the lesser offenders involved in 20 July 1944 bomb plot against Hitler, while Kopkow continued the prosecution of those involved in the much earlier Rote Kapelle network.[10] Under Kaltenbrunner's signature, RSHA IV A2a (Sabotage) wrote on 23 February 1945 to OKW confirming that Allied commandos captured in uniform were the responsibility of the army; the SD (i.e. the Gestapo) would take responsibility for any captured in civilian clothing.[11] With the destruction in and around Berlin, Kopkow could only stand back and take in the radio messages from the various Gestapo offices across Germany announcing the dropping or capture of agents. If Allied air raids did not destroy the Gestapo offices and its files by fire, the official messages that had already gone out to Gestapo offices to burn all documentation certainly did. After the war, there was little Gestapo documentation to salvage, meaning intercepted and decrypted German radio messages by Bletchley Park are possibly the sole means of identifying when agents were captured during the last months of war. Between 19 February and 23 March 1945, the German radio traffic reveals twenty-three agents were dropped at fourteen locations and nineteen of these agents were captured. As late as 23 March, the Gestapo office in Magdeburg requested help from Kopkow in beginning a *Funkspiel* with the Soviets using the ciphers of their latest captive. Most of the twenty-three agents that were dropped by the Soviets in Germany had intelligence gathering duties, including a party of five Soviet agents at Kwittkau (Bohemia). As British and American military forces advanced across Germany, they began to overrun their own agents. At least twelve agents captured in West German locations were a mix of OSS and SOE agents. Those captured in Central Germany (Halle, Chemnitz, and Magdeburg) were former German POWs trained by the Soviets.[12]

Kopkow decided in his post-war interrogations to recall only those agents arrested that would be interesting to the British and Americans, especially as some of them, according to Kopkow, would continue sending information after the German surrender about British and American forces. A group of Soviet-trained German agents were dropped at the end of January to beginning February 1945 near Torgau, about 50 miles (80 km) south of Berlin. The leader of the group posed as an army captain and wore Germany's highest military decoration, the *Ritterkreuz*. Their tasks chiefly concerned transmitting military information before moving westwards and being overrun by British forces. After the surrender, they were to establish themselves 'legally', and after a few months, they were to begin transmitting information about the British forces to Moscow. According to Kopkow, this group had the following objectives in the British Zone:

1. Administrative measures initiated in the British Zone.
2. Behaviour of the English civilian administration towards the German population.
3. To what administrative level are Germans employed in civilian posts (e.g. in local councils).
4. What armaments factories have been brought back into production and which have not?
5. What are the production figures for these armaments factories and where is the produced material sent?[13]

Another group of similar agents that were dropped at Strausberg, on the outskirts of eastern Berlin, at the end of February 1945 were also told to go west and be overrun by Allied armies before recommencing radio communications with Moscow. Having captured these groups of agents that provided these details, Kopkow does not mention what then happened to them. Although Kopkow remained circumspect in what he told his British interrogators about their SOE agents, he could have been more open about Soviet infiltration of agents into Germany. They were far more numerous than alluded to by Kopkow. Most of these agents trained by Soviet intelligence continued to be from the ranks of German POWs, but in 1945, they began to include Polish communists and the occasional Russian army officer. Heinz Gosling, a Luftwaffe bomber pilot shot down over the Soviet Union in 1943, returned to Germany as a parachute agent in late March 1945 with three other former German POWs—one of whom had been trained as a radio operator and had a radio transmitter and ciphers. Gosling managed to avoid his comrades at the drop zone and sought refuge at his parents' home in Jessnitz; four weeks later, this was overrun by American forces. After surrendering himself, he told his interrogators that 'he has information on Russian plans to use indoctrinated Military Government officials in Germany'.[14]

Other groups did get to work, carrying out intelligence gathering operations. One group of four Polish agents under Lieutenant Bogdan Locki dropped in February 1945 at Neustrelitz, not too far from Ravensbrück concentration camp. Among their tasks was making contact with Polish and

Soviet forced labourers for information on likely targets, and they identified a munitions depot where they worked. Locki reported this back by radio transmission, and it was subsequently destroyed by Soviet air attack. This group continued its work, and in April, they were found and attacked by a German patrol. Locki and his radio operator were the only survivors when they were overrun by Soviet forces in May.[15]

German Army Colonel Karl Friedrich Heuer had been captured at Stalingrad in January 1943, and after interrogation, he was found to be a suitable agent. After training, he was dropped near Berlin in February 1945 with a mission to surrender himself to the Abwehr and allow a *Funkspiel* to take place. At this stage of the war, the Abwehr had been absorbed by RSHA Berlin, and Heuer found himself handed over to Ampletzer who began a *Funkspiel* with his radio set and ciphers. Heuer claims that 'only he and Ampletzer knew about the true nature of the transmissions, while Kopko [*sic.*] and possibly a few others thought a '*Funkspiel*' was being run'. In March 1945, Heuer transmitted from a location in Berlin-Spandau, and together with Ampletzer, he travelled to the front at Frankfurt-Oder and north to Stettin, collecting military information, troop movements, and military headquarters. Heuer sent thirty to thirty-five radio messages and received three during his time with Ampletzer. When Kopkow began dividing his officials into a Northern and Southern Group, Heuer was evacuated with the Southern Group at the end of March 1945 and was eventually overrun by the Americans in Bavaria. Moscow had intended that Heuer be overrun by Allied forces in Germany and begin transmitting information about their troops. Instead, Heuer was arrested by US forces in Bavaria in May 1945, interned and interrogated, before eventually giving up his 'secret' radio codes.[16]

Two more former German POWs were dropped during the evening of 20 February 1945 near Bitterfeld, north of Leipzig. One of the men, Captain Krämer, had been captured at Stalingrad in January 1943, and in June 1943, after volunteering for espionage missions in Germany, he began training in various Soviet intelligence schools together with other German POWs who had similarly volunteered. Their 'mission was to report on the defences of the [River] Elbe in the area of Wittenberg and Bitterfeld'; they had two radio sets and were 'expected to maintain daily [radio] contact with [their] home station'. They were both arrested the following day and handed over to the Gestapo office in Halle. The Gestapo chief in Halle, Bauer, questioned Krämer and allowed him to send a radio message stating that they had arrived safely and were beginning their work. On 26 February, Krämer and his fellow agent were taken from Halle to Hof in northern Bavaria, where Kopkow's Southern Group had established a base. At the end of February 1945, after being interrogated several times by Kopkow's men—*Kriminalkommissars* Johann Strübing and Hans Müller—Krämer was returned to Halle with Gestapo official *Kriminalinspektor* Berg. A *Funkspiel* with Moscow began from Halle, in which Krämer included accurate military information and some false information supplied by the Gestapo. Krämer says that, in total, he transmitted to Moscow six times. After the last *Funkspiel* message to Moscow on 2 April 1945, Krämer began pressing the Gestapo to release him to his home in Giessen as the Allied armies were advancing towards Halle and the *Funkspiel* was no longer necessary. Krämer's release came on 9 April and he left the following day. He was captured by US troops in Erfurt on 12 April 1945, and two months later, he was interrogated by the British.[17]

Krämer was not the only captured Soviet agent being played back to Moscow from Halle by the Gestapo at this time. Captain Friedrich Demmer had also been captured at Stalingrad in January 1943 and volunteered for espionage work. Demmer had been overrun by US troops on 26 April 1945 and sent to a US interrogation centre where he was not entirely forthcoming about his 'espionage work' in the preceding months; he omitted to tell his interrogators that he had been arrested by the Gestapo and that there had been a *Funkspiel* operation with Moscow using his ciphers. Krämer had told his British interrogators that, in the Gestapo office in Halle, he had seen a file marked 'Demmer Interrogation'. What Demmer told the Americans about his mission had a sting in its tail, which was probably his failure to mention that he had been captured by the Gestapo:

> … with mission to go to Leipzig and Dresden locating any NS [National Socialist, i.e. Nazi] resistance groups. If overrun by Americans was to report only after there was no danger of blowing himself to any remaining Nazis. Was also to report on [River] Elbe fortifications, also try prevent sabotage.… Has sent and received three times. Set and codes intact.… In case of trouble with Americans was to get in touch with Russian Attache [*sic.*]. Has political aspirations.[18]

Demmer's 'political aspirations' would be very well forfeit in the Soviet Zone should he have given in to Gestapo pressure and helped a *Funkspiel* operation with Moscow. Soviet intelligence viewed assisting the enemy in this way as treason—other captured agents who survived found this out after the war.

The Gestapo office in Halle became a centre for interrogating parachute agents captured south of Berlin. After Krämer's arrival around 25 March 1945, followed by Demmer, a party of three agents (a Pole, a Yugoslav, and an Austrian) were dropped by the Soviet air force near Cottbus. The Pole betrayed the group to a local patrol and they were all taken to Gestapo Halle with their two radio sets and ciphers. A day or two later, a party of seven (two Red Army officers, two Poles, and three Germans) were accidentally dropped too close to a German airfield outside Halle. At least one of the Germans arrived at Gestapo Halle for interrogation.[19]

Some of the agents infiltrated were long-standing German communists who had migrated to the Soviet Union in the 1920s and 1930s, surviving numerous purges that carried off comrades; they now returned to Germany to rekindle communism while Hitler's thousand-year Reich died among the ruins of bombed-out buildings. A prime example is Georg Thiele, who had been on a Gestapo watch list from 1935. In 1938, he had been with the International Brigades in the Spanish Civil War along with thousands of other communists from all European nations and many Soviet intelligence officers. In 1939, Thiele was interned by the French authorities in Algeria, and in 1943, he managed to travel to Moscow. The central committee of the German communist party based in Moscow, since fleeing there in the 1930s, decided Thiele could be trained as an agent and returned to Germany. In November 1944, with Thiele in charge of a group of agents, they dropped to a Polish communist partisan group, and with their help, the group infiltrated into Germany during January 1945: 'The group should make contact with German resistance fighters and with Soviet prisoners of war and "inform the Party leadership" [in Moscow] about the situation in Berlin'. It is unlikely that Thiele found many 'German resistance fighters' due to Gestapo infiltration of remaining communist circles, and therefore, he kept his head down until the surrender. After the war, Thiele became a member of the ruling East German government central committee and died in 1978 as a colonel in the East German Army.[20]

SOE 'X' Section (the German Section) had been created on 18 November 1940 with office space at 64 Baker Street, London.[21] At this early stage of the war, its aims were 'to establish channels of communication into Germany and Austria for subversive activities and to build up inside those countries a network of agents suitable for such activities', and for such lofty ideas, 'it was clear from the start that 'X' Section was faced with a stupendous task. There had been no attempt on the part of the Secret Services during peacetime to maintain contacts inside Germany who might be useful for subversive activities in War'. Taking the battle to the enemy, the much-daunted British secret service gave this new organisation no 'assistance whatever' and, as such, 'there was no point in starting'. SOE German Section therefore started with a clean slate and made their first attempts at creating lines of communication through neutral countries (Sweden, Switzerland, and Turkey). It would be three years before they were able to begin parachute drops of agents. Until that time, they arranged for the RAF to drop forged ration cards and clothing coupons to create administrative havoc for the German authorities when the population used them. The agent infiltrated into Austria in April 1942 came from Switzerland and involved a SOE radio operator (Operation Aquavit).[22] The year 1942 also saw a series of sabotage actions in Germany and Austria, instigated by SOE German Section. One agent was dropped into Germany by the section happened during the night of 16–17 February 1943.[23]

Those agents dropped by Soviet intelligence were all targeting areas where Soviet armies would be advancing towards. In 1945, British and

American agencies increased their parachute operations and agents were dropped in areas that would constitute the Soviet Zone (Chemnitz, Leipzig, and Magdeburg in the sector south of Berlin) and in the neighbourhood of Berlin itself. OSS also dropped twelve teams during March–May 1945 along the line of the advance of General Patton's Third US Army, with teams dropping between Ulm through Munich and eastwards to Regensburg and Passau.[24] Some of these teams transmitted coded radio messages back to London, whereas others had the 'Joan-Eleanor' system—a very early version of mobile telephones that operated only between an agent on the ground talking to an agent in an aircraft circling several thousand feet above him. The British intelligence agencies SOE and SIS and the American OSS agency continued infiltrating agents from southern Italy into northern Italy and into southern Austria during 1944 and 1945. The British called their Austrian operations 'Clowder missions' and they consisted mainly of Austrian POWs recruited for their anti-Nazism and that their relatives in Austria were also anti-Nazi and could be called upon to provide food and shelter.[25] Intelligence operations into Germany itself had been seen by SIS/MI6 as unnecessary because they were able to intercept and decipher thousands of radio messages from a wide range of German government agencies and this 'Sigint' (signals intelligence) provided the information needed without risking lives. SIS had sent in a team in 1944 but without success. During the night of 10–11 April 1944, the RAF dropped Frank Chamier and a recruited German POW, Hermann Reschke, near Gündringen about 30 miles south-west of Stuttgart in southern Germany. On 12 April, they made for the nearby railway station at Nagold with the intention of travelling to Pforzheim. Reschke denounced Chamier to the railway staff and he was soon arrested by the local gendarmerie and handed over to the Gestapo in Stuttgart. Having been caught with their radio set and ciphers, Stuttgart informed Kopkow in Berlin, and Chamier, with his belongings, was escorted to Berlin. Kopkow related that a *Funkspiel* using Chamier's ciphers was attempted with 'Daventry', but after 'a few weeks', they no longer replied.[26] In summer 1944, Chamier was being held at Sachsenhausen concentration camp and made contact with RAF Wing Commander 'Wings' Day, calling himself 'Frank of UPWAY 282'—his British telephone exchange and number. A little while later, Kopkow had Chamier brought up to Ravensbrück concentration camp, just a few miles from his headquarters at Fürstenberg. Chamier's mission was old history, and what Kopkow possibly wanted of Chamier now was a detailed explanation of SIS and its organisation. The Gestapo had established SIS's pre-war organisation from detailed interrogations of Richard Stevens and Sigismund Payne-Best, following their kidnapping by Walter Schellenberg in November 1939 at Venlo, Holland. In 1944, with the Abwehr now absorbed by various departments of RSHA Berlin, department chiefs like Kopkow needed to keep producing intelligence material and a detailed explanation of the wartime SIS organisation would be very useful. Whatever knowledge Chamier had he possibly kept to himself. Kopkow moved his headquarters from Fürstenberg to the new barracks camp Dachs II near Trebnitz in October 1944, at which point, Chamier's life became expendable. After the war, Kopkow claimed Chamier died in Berlin when held at police headquarters on Alexanderplatz, which was seriously damaged during an air raid. There being no good reason for Chamier to be held in Berlin, being Kopkow's responsibility, and with Kopkow based in Fürstenberg at the time, it is most probable that Frank Chamier was shot at Ravensbrück camp in October 1944 just before Kopkow left for new headquarters at Dachs II.

There were other attempts by SIS at infiltrating agents into Germany. A report dated 31 October 1943 by the Gestapo office at Marburg–Lahn (between Frankfurt–Main and Kassel in western Germany) has details of three 'British agents' dropped by the RAF on behalf of SIS.[27] The men had been dropped near Düsseldorf on 2 October 1943, and they were discovered on 30 October in Duisburg hiding in the cellar of a bombed-out house, where they were arrested. The leader of the group had the cover-name 'Louis Dupuis'; he was about thirty-two years old and spoke fluent German, French, Spanish, Dutch, Polish, and English. His real name, according to the Gestapo report, was 'Snets', and he had a signet ring engraved with the initials 'L.S.'. The radio operator, described as 'Ali Mohamed', an Arab, was about twenty-eight years old and spoke fluent French. The third man is not described. Although dropped in western Germany, the report states their intelligence operations were to be conducted in Rybnik, Upper Silesia, several hundred miles to the east. Rybnik, now in Poland, is less than 30 miles (50 km) from Auschwitz, and whether reconnaissance of the area was planned can no longer be ascertained as there is no further trace of the three men. They disappeared, probably into a concentration camp, and as parachute agents, they were Kopkow's responsibility. A single agent of Czech Sudeten origin was dropped into the Sudetenland during May 1944—SIS never heard from him. Two Germans were dropped in the wrong place in southern Austria on 5–6 September 1944 and ended up in the hands of Yugoslav partisans. Two agents who were to go to Vienna were dropped in the wrong place and ended up in Slovakia—one was picked up by Slovak partisans and the second man was never heard of again.[28] Official historian Keith Jeffery offers rather disparate views of SIS's objectives in sending out these agents who, at best, he says, could only radio back what he calls 'humdrum observation reports' on German troop movements. Had German military operations in the Ardennes in December 1944 been successful, the military scenario may have been different and any information sent by these agents could have proved valuable. However, these German military operations in the Ardennes were not successful and SIS basically sent out several agents on meaningless and dangerous missions.[29]

At a meeting of the German Committee that included senior SOE top brass and SOE German Section officers on 25 October 1944, the question of using communists as agents led to prolonged discussion. The minutes record that the SOE Assistant Director and Administration 'stressed the danger of using communists as agents ... [as they] should be providing the Russians with a readymade communist organisation in the American and British sectors ... without any comparable pro-Anglo-American element in the Russian sphere'. This comment led to whether the very small number of communists involved would have any effect in the greater scheme of power once the German collapse had taken place. SOE German Section remarked that its communist agents being trained would be dropped by parachute into Germany. Its infiltration agents from Sweden and Switzerland into Germany and Austria would continue to be German former Social Democrats.[30] Although SIS stated that they had no agents in Germany and that they felt no need to risk the lives of agents, Chamier, with his German POW partner and the three unknown agents, dropped near Düsseldorf indicating otherwise—SIS continued sending more agents into Germany. On the other hand, SOE German Section had sent in agents, their first agent with a radio set infiltrated into Austria during April 1942 from Switzerland as 'Operation Aquavit'.[31] Their first parachute agent, Kurt Koenig (alias 'Krotzky'), was dropped during the night of 16–17 February 1943. The operation on the ground failed and Koenig made his way to Spain, crossing the border near Biarritz, and with the help of British Embassy in Madrid, he returned to Britain. In July 1943, an internal SOE report, using his experiences, summarised the problem its German Section faced following agent reports from the field in Germany and Austria over 'the non-existence of organised oppositional elements inside and the difficulty of obtaining suitable [local] agents'.[32] From Switzerland, SOE had several infiltration agents passing into Germany and returning. A report from a woman agent dated 7 June 1944 noted her three-week journey as far north as Hamburg, travelling via Göttingen and Hannover, renewing old Social Democrat contacts.[33] Some had been conscripted by the army and were killed in action, some died, and one was sent to a camp after sheltering Jews. The report also stated: '[A] small minority of Germans still believe in victory; many think compromise peace possible if invasion repulsed; and many are convinced of defeat'. The report also makes it clear that 'organised resistance on [a] national plane' is unlikely, mainly because the opposition had no footing in national life as the Nazis had crushed most signs of dissent. Resistance cells eventually brought about through SOE's efforts in the Reich were by necessity small and localised, and proved capable over time of extending their subversive activities through increased acts of sabotage in the industrial sector. These infiltration tactics proved a very valuable source of information and there are only two reports of these agents being detected. In December 1944, one agent was detected at Innsbruck, where he was arrested and held in the local Gestapo prison until released on

2 May 1945. The second, a woman, was shot to death by a German border guard as she attempted the clandestine crossing into Switzerland from the Austrian Vorarlberg in April 1945.[34]

Growing numbers of SOE and OSS agents were dropped into Germany in 1945 by blind parachute drop into Germany. As with their counterparts in Soviet intelligence, they now used communists who had sought refuge from Germany before the war or recruited anti-Nazis from the ranks of Austrian and German POWs. Under the umbrella of SHAEF (Supreme Headquarters Allied Expeditionary Forces, under General Dwight D. Eisenhower), an agreement was reached for SOE and OSS to conduct missions in Germany independently of each other, while they still had to maintain a close liaison on mission planning and information exchange. SHAEF's directive, dated 29 January 1945, also set the objectives for their missions:

1. Hastening the surrender or disintegration of all German Armed Forces.
2. Crippling the German war effort as a whole.[35]

The SHAEF directive also laid down how these objectives were to be obtained by agents on the ground: subversion, sabotage, organising foreign workers, deception, and intelligence gathering. Nowhere in the document does SHAEF promote political activities, and the activities of any SOE and OSS agents were directed at assisting the military war, unlike the Soviet-trained agents—some of whom had distinct political objectives. During 1944 in Moscow, Soviets, backing the Central Committee of the German Communist Party, established the 'National Committee Free Germany' (*Nationalkomitee Freies Deutschland*, NKFD). Suitable German POWs were trained in anti-fascist schools (*Antifa-Schulen*) in the Soviet Union and were to be parachuted into Germany for political and espionage purposes. Adherents leading this new political development based in Germany were Bernhard Bästlein and Anton Saefkow, long-standing communists.[36]

Bästlein had spent most of the 1930s in Nazi concentration camps and prisons for his political beliefs. After being released in 1940, he returned to his Hamburg home and began working again in the docks where he also instigated acts of sabotage. He maintained his freedom from arrest until 1942, when the two parachute agents Erna Eifler and Wilhelm Fellendorf made contact seeking shelter. Their arrest by the Gestapo in Hamburg preceded his own, and again, they were held in prisons and Sachsenhausen concentration camp awaiting trial and bearing witness at the trials of others. Bästlein was being detained at the notorious Plötzensee Prison in Berlin when it suffered air-raid damage, which enabled him to escape along with other prisoners. Apparently, by good fortune, Bästlein ran into an old comrade, Anton Saefkow, travelling on the Berlin S-Bahn (metro), and together with another old comrade, Franz Jacob, they created the 'Free German Movement' based on ideas gleaned from NKFD radio broadcasts from Moscow. Using their links to other communists, they began disseminating truthful news about the war taken from foreign radio broadcasts. This information spread across the military, factories, the resistance movement, encouraging sabotage, and passive resistance. Extending their contacts into other civilian areas of resistance is what probably led to the downfall of the group. The Gestapo swooped in and arrested Bästlein in Berlin on 30 May 1944. Many more followed in June and July when the entire leadership was arrested.[37] In his post-war interrogation, Kopkow strangely mentioned that another RSHA department, IV A1a, responsible for Communist and Marxist Opponents, had taken the lead in the Gestapo drive against this 'new development of the NKFD and its recruitment of German prisoners of war for political and espionage purposes'. Why Kopkow should share the success with another department is unknown because on 4 August 1944, an unsigned report addressed to *Reichsführer*-SS at his Field Headquarters and using the letterhead of RSHA IV A2, quoting Kopkow as departmental chief, recorded '82 persons, including the entire leadership, and its activists' had been arrested by '*Sonderkommission*' IV A2.[38] More reports were issued by Kopkow's department as the investigations continued, and the reports included notifications of additional arrests from Gestapo offices across the Reich. In a long report, dated 2 August 1944, two days before the report to *Reichsführer*-SS Himmler, Gestapo Leipzig stated that thirty people arrested in connection with NKFD activities had been charged and, as instructed by 'RSHA—*Sonderkommission* IV A2', their cases were referred to the People's Court in Berlin, with further arrests expected.[39] The *Sonderkommissions* IV A2 continued its investigation into 1945 when it was based at the Gestapo office in Potsdam, having been bombed-out of Berlin when a last report mentioned arrests as far afield as Leipzig and Lübeck. A post-war report on the Saefkow group alone lists eighty-six executions mainly at Brandenburg-Gorden prison between September 1944 and 20 April 1945, in addition to several suicides.[40] Little wonder Kopkow did not want to explain these executions and shifted the blame onto another RSHA department.

A new development by RSHA IV as the Soviet invasion of Germany itself grew ever more imminent was Operation Nibelungen. If the Soviets could plant agents behind the lines to provide intelligence on enemy forces and troop movements, then so could the Gestapo assist in fighting back against the Allied armies whether from the east or the west. The original demands for this action according to Kopkow came from *Reichsführer*-SS Himmler in autumn 1944, when Himmler held a field command in south-west Germany. Kopkow was incorrect in his timing since Himmler did not take up command of Army Group Upper Rhine (*Heeresgruppe Oberrhein*) until 26 November 1944. Himmler held this position until 21 January 1945, so it can only have been during these eight weeks that Himmler demanded action. After taking up this command on the Upper Rhine, Himmler discovered a serious lack of crucial information about the Allied armies he faced across the River Rhine in France. Kaltenbrunner, as RSHA Chief, ordered his *Amtschef* III (SD-Inland, under Otto Ohlendorf), *Amtschef* IV (Gestapo, Müller), and *Amtschef* VI (SD Foreign Intelligence, under Walter Schellenberg) to organise intelligence gathering in France 'in the German territories now occupied by the enemy', as Kopkow put it.[41] When Kopkow received his orders from Müller, he set about making plans with Ampletzer and the staff of IV A2b, who carried out the *Funkspiel* operations. With agents having to transmit information by radio, using the experiences of Kopkow and Ampletzer deemed necessary since Kopkow recalled that SD Foreign Intelligence under Schellenberg could offer virtually nothing. The biggest problems at this stage of war (probably December 1944) were a lack of schools, instructors, equipment of every description, and radio transmitters. In April 1945, he burned all the paperwork.[42]

Very little is known about the 'Nibelungen' operations carried out in 1944 and 1945 as Soviet armies drove the Germans from Poland, back towards the border of Germany on the River Oder. In September 1944, the Abwehr in Breslau (now Wrocław, Poland) received orders to prepare stay-behind agents to be overrun by Soviet armies and then 'to report on matters of operational and counter-intelligence interest, to spread confusion and even engage in sabotage'. The Abwehr found it difficult to recruits any agents with these abilities, and in the end, they were unable to create a network before the Soviets arrived.[43] A radio message, dated 20 February 1945, intercepted and deciphered by Bletchley Park, from Ampletzer in Berlin to SS-*Hauptsturmführer* Paul Fuchs at KdS Radom (Poland) asked for a status report on the various Nibelungen operations in Fuchs' area. With the Russian advance, KdS Radom had abandoned Radom and fallen back northwards to Waldenburg, leaving stay-behind agents with radio sets.[44] These agent teams were called 'Aries' and 'Orion' and comprised agents numbered one to six and one to two respectively. This radio message showed things were not going well and new attempts would need to be made as the position and difficulties resulting from the shortage of Polish-speaking instructors did not help. Kopkow recalled that in January to April 1945 they had twenty-five agents in training, but only ten to fifteen completed the course.[45] They had been hard pressed to find suitable candidates with a knowledge of radio transmitting, and those who finished the course were German, Belgian Flemish, Russian, Poles, and two Frenchmen. They were deployed in the west at Saarbrücken, Koblenz, Bad Godesberg (a Frenchman named Lemoine was sent here), and near Heidelberg; in the east, Kopkow could only recall one in the area of Frankfurt–Oder and another further eastwards at Litzmannstadt (Lodz). From his cursory narrative, it can be concluded that he was scornful of the entire plan devised by his superiors and thought it unlikely to have any measure of success. Neither Kopkow nor anyone else mentions who would be picking up the transmissions of these stay-behind agents, evaluating and disseminating their information, and giving new targets. The speed of the Allied armies advancing through Germany from the east and west with no stable German defence shows it to have been another waste of time and effort caused by thoughtless RSHA top management.[46]

Operation Nibelungen took up lengthy periods of time, taking Kopkow and Ampletzer away from the ever growing menace of Allied parachute agents. This meant leaving the poorly prepared local Gestapo offices attempting *Funkspiel* operations and having little success. After Berlin, Hamburg continued to be a hotbed of communist and general resistance activities. During 1943 and 1944, SOE infiltrated agents from Sweden through Denmark into northern Germany to establish resistance networks and carry out sabotage in the shipyards of Hamburg and Bremen.[47] Among the first SOE German Section agents dropped into Germany following the loss of Kurt Koenig in January 1944 were two teams dropped during the night of 26 November 1944, a two-man team (Alois Buchtik and Heinz Döring) and a single agent (Paul Penczok)—all former German POWs.[48] Neither team succeeded in their tasks; it did not help that one of the two-man team, Döring, denounced the other to the German authorities after landing. In fact, these and other recent parachute drops had not escaped the Germans. Bletchley Park had intercepted and decrypted three German radio messages as their report of 30 November 1944 makes clear:

1. A warning issued that parachute agents had landed in the Stühlingen and Donaueschingen area in S.S. uniform and carrying explosives. (Buchtik).
2. Another warning was issued about other agents being dropped in the Ingolstadt area, but not all these agents had been captured.[49]

Buchtik and Döring comprised Operation Frilford and had been dropped with explosives 'to blow up any one of the three tunnels on the single-track railway running between Zollhaus/Futzen and Waldshut. This line was used for military transports'. The two had not met up in the drop zone and Buchtik was determined to carry out the operation alone. He set off alone southwards on the road from Stuhlingen to Waldshut, south of Stuttgart in southern Germany, when, at 5 a.m., he fell in with a military patrol looking for him and was arrested; he was then taken to the small Gestapo office in Stuhlingen. The following day (28 November 1944), he was transferred to the large Gestapo office in Waldshut where he met Döring, smoking and drinking schnapps with the Gestapo Chief. At the beginning of December, Buchtik was escorted to Berlin and placed in the cells below Gestapo headquarters on Prinz Albrechtstrasse. Buchtik was beaten and interrogated for several weeks, on one occasion he was questioned by someone like Kopkow. This Gestapo officer asked Buchtik 'to describe his training; location of the schools; what life was like in London; what were the effects of V1 (remote missiles, the "doodlebugs")'. On 19 January 1945, the Gestapo handed Buchtik over to the army as a deserter, and he was imprisoned in Torgau military prison, 60 miles south of Berlin. Buchtik remained here until about 14 April 1945. During this time at Torgau, he found Penczok imprisoned, and he reported the executions of Kurt Koenig and two other SOE German Section agents, Zwick and Schmid. Buchtik managed to avoid this fate and survived the end of the war.[50]

Meanwhile, Kopkow fell back on the Soviet-trained German communist parachute agent Robert Barth, who had been captured by Kopkow's men on 9 October 1942 in Berlin. Barth was lucky to be alive as all his fellow agents had been executed when Barth assisted Ampletzer in a *Funkspiel* operation with Moscow using his ciphers. Between October 1942 and February 1944, this had taken place from a Gestapo office and radio station in Berlin-Spandau. In March 1944, contact was broken off by Moscow and Barth then languished in solitary confinement in the prison bunker at Ravensbrück concentration camp until November 1944, when Kopkow decided he could be made use of as a stay-behind agent for the Gestapo. There was some training in new codes and a radio set, and on 7 November 1944, he was taken to Saarbrücken in western Germany, which most likely would be overrun by American forces. His mission to transmit military information would begin once the Allied armies had overrun Saarbrücken, which they did on 20 March 1945, and Barth surrendered at the very earliest opportunity without transmitting any information, telling American interrogators of his pleasure at being able to double-cross the Gestapo. In May 1945, as a Soviet agent, Barth was turned over to the Soviet Mission in Paris who sent him to Moscow. Following his arrival in Moscow, Barth was charged with assisting the enemy in a *Funkspiel* operation and condemned to death for treasonable activities. Robert Barth was executed in November 1945 in Moscow.[51]

With several teams of agents dropped into Germany being caught and handed over to the Gestapo, on 1 March 1945, Kopkow had to send out a report to the remaining Gestapo offices in Germany and Austria reminding them of 'Employment of British Parachute Agents'.[52] Kopkow emphasised that most of these agents were captured German soldiers and being dropped in western and south-western Germany. This report provides a wealth of detail, showing how SOE German Section went to great lengths to maintain the mythical character agent legends they had adopted. The forged identity documents supplied by SOE 'could only be detected by special examinations'. A recently caught agent wearing civilian clothes carried not only well-forged identity documents, but also 'identity discs of the Secret State Police and the State Criminal Police'. Kopkow's report ends with the warning that the Allies have taken huge numbers of German soldiers as POWs and the Gestapo should now expect an increasing number of them returning as agents. They should expect an increase in 'full-moon periods', when single aircraft detach from bomber formations. This report by Kopkow was among enemy documents found after examining Gestapo offices that fell when overrun by advancing British armies. A SOE report, dated just ten weeks later

(12 May 1945), by SOE Assistant Director German Operations read the Kopkow report 'with the greatest interest. A remarkable tribute to [his] Planning and Operations'.[53]

Between 21 February and 18 April 1945, SOE German Section dropped or infiltrated at least another twenty-three agents (in thirteen teams) into Germany. Most were given specific targets such as the derailment of trains to block particular railway tracks at certain locations, and they continued sabotage and subversion work in the dockyards of Hamburg and Bremen. Others were sent to organise resistance and carry out acts of sabotage and subversion as far afield at Berlin, Halle, and Koblenz. Of the twenty-three agents sent in, two were missing (believed captured), two had surrendered themselves voluntarily to the German authorities, and the rest had been overrun by Allied armies and returned to Britain. One of those captured, Marcel Goethals had been arrested by Gestapo Würzburg, and he survived and was returned to Britain in May 1945.[54]

Agent operations into Germany of SIS still remain mostly clouded in secrecy. In his history of SIS, Keith Jeffery contends that the organisation also used former German POWs among other recruits. They also dropped radio operators into Germany between 'late 1944 and early 1945, but produced little or no information' and they were then overrun by Allied armies. After the war, some of these agents 'were retasked as agents in Germany'.[55] Jeffery does describe one particular SIS mission that involved 'an anti-Nazi Yugoslav … recruited in Uruguay' and brought to Britain in 1944 for training. During the night of 2–3 October 1944, this anti-Nazi Yugoslav, now renamed Josef Bauer, and his 'German-Jewish radio operator' were dropped near Heilbronn, north of Stuttgart, with instructions to travel 300 miles (500 km) north to Magdeburg and make it their base. They were to report on army and Luftwaffe bases, production figures in the armaments industries, air raid damage, and civilian morale. On 11 October, they were in Berlin and had made contact with another SIS agent. At this point, things went drastically wrong: they were denounced by an informer and the Gestapo went into action. Josef Bauer was captured, tortured, and revealed the address of his radio operator, which the Gestapo stormed. Jeffery concludes this episode by quoting an official of the German security police who confirmed that the two were dead.[56] This official could only have been Kopkow, who told the story in his interrogation dated 19 October 1945.[57] His version is slightly different from that quoted by Jeffery; was Jeffery trying to protect Kopkow? In Kopkow's version, a woman denounced Josef Bauer, who was arrested by Gestapo Berlin. Under interrogation, Bauer gave away the name and Berlin address of his radio operator. According to Kopkow, a squad of Gestapo men with a number of German policemen then raided the address and, during a gunfight, one German policeman was killed and the radio operator himself was 'killed while trying to escape'. On an unknown date, according to Kopkow, Bauer 'was executed by order of the RFSS' Himmler.[58] The execution, like those of the earlier Soviet parachute agents caught in Berlin, probably took place at Sachsenhausen concentration camp in November or December 1944.

The American OSS (Office of Strategic Services) wanted to become active in 1943 by sending agents into Germany. SIS and the Dutch intelligence service turned them down, and it was not until September 1944 that they were able to send in their first agent. During the night of 2 September 1944, the German social democrat Jupp Kappius dropped from a RAF Lancaster bomber over the industrial Ruhr area of western Germany.[59] Kappius made his way to the Bochum safe house, whose address he had been given by OSS, and began fulfilling his tasks. These were based on similar lines to the tasks of SOE agents dropped into France: establish a clandestine resistance that would act against Nazi government institutions, begin acts of sabotage and subversion, and encourage dissent among the German military and political organisations. Kappius proved successful in this role and survived the war. OSS dropped a three-man team during the night of 13 October 1944 from a RAF aircraft having left from Bari, Italy, with the target area of the Neusiedler See, south of Vienna. Three Austrian former POWs and US Navy Captain Jack Taylor comprised the DUPONT Mission, which did not get off to the good start it needed. Their radio set and supply containers dropped with them landed in the lake and were lost. They survived for over a month at safe houses while Taylor tried to contact make contact by courier with the DAWES Mission in Slovakia and the DILLON Mission south of them in Carinthia. Neither attempt at communication worked, and in late November, their luck ran out. The Gestapo raided their safe house (a farmhouse at Schützen), not too far from their drop zone the previous month. On 1 April 1945, Taylor arrived at Mauthausen concentration camp and managed to survive; he was liberated by USA forces in May. The three Austrians from his mission also survived.[60]

More Germans and other European nationals trained by OSS were dropped into Germany and Austria, with the last being dropped in April 1945. According to Joseph Persico, during this period, OSS dropped or infiltrated almost 200 agents into the region; of these, thirty-six were lost (killed, captured, or missing).[61] Of these thirty-six, fourteen were shot at Mauthausen concentration camp in January 1945.[62] One team of OSS agents caught in Munich were brought to the attention of Kopkow, who tried a *Funkspiel* with their ciphers; this was known as *Funkspiel* CHICAGO. By the end of February 1945, any continuing *Funkspiel* operations by Kopkow and the Gestapo offices with the Allies could hardly be worth the time and trouble. The Allied military onslaught quite simply was unstoppable and any false information provided by *Funkspiel* messages in the last two months of warfare were not even pin-pricks; they were simply a means to possibly keep the captured agents alive. Most OSS and SOE agents sent in at this time were given sabotage objectives, mainly on railroads to stop troop and supply movements near the front. These agents were overrun and returned to their base.

It cannot have been a peaceful life for Kopkow in Berlin: first the Allied air raid and then the approach of Soviet armies, who began encircling the city. However, there was still time to send out the execution teleprinter messages in March 1945 to Buchenwald, Sachsenhausen, and Flossenbürg. The last SOE agents in these camps managed to survive in very poor conditions, which only got worse in 1945 as the war drew ever nearer. Russian archives quoted by Francis Suttill in the biography of his father have a note that, on 23 March 1945, he was sent for execution at the crematorium. Seven days later, the last remaining agents held at Flossenbürg were sent for execution. This was an execution the camp would not have decided upon themselves; such orders had to come from the agency that sent the prisoners to the camp—RSHA IV A2 (Kopkow). RSHA IV Chief Müller decided he would stay in Berlin, giving orders for the rest of RSHA to evacuate. Kopkow was among the last to leave the city during the night of 22–23 April 1945 with thirty others, including his secretary, Berta Rose, a few other secretaries, and remaining RSHA officers. At dusk, two cars and two trucks made their way to Müller's home south of the city centre in Berlin-Lankwitz, Corneliusstrasse 22, and after a short discussion with him, the convoy made its way west before the Soviet armies completed their encirclement of Berlin. The night passed without mishap, and early the next morning, they arrived in Schwerin safely. Kopkow and some of the men and secretaries obtained quarters in a local temporary school. Two days later, they were on the move northwards through Lübeck to another school building at Breiholz. With British armies pushing north, Kopkow and other RSHA officials moved further northwards on 28 April to Ostenfeld, just a few miles from Husum, and they were given accommodation in a civilian work camp (*Arbeitsdienstlager*). Large numbers of RSHA and security police officials were here, just waiting for decisions to be made.

Reichsführer-SS Himmler had also made his way north to Flensburg, north of where Kopkow had his accommodation in Ostenfeld. Himmler had been disappointed by the last message he had received from Hitler, who, having heard of Himmler's peace contacts with the western Allies, passed on the post of Chancellor of Germany after his death to Admiral Dönitz. Himmler had to pledge his service to Dönitz, there being little else he could have done, but eventually Dönitz too severed Himmler from the last government of the German Reich. Himmler held a last meeting with his senior SS generals in Flensburg on 4 May 1945 and disappeared the following day. Kopkow heard of the meeting from another RSHA department chief, SS-*Sturmbannführer* Hermann Quetting.[63] The news of Himmler's disappearance spread among the sheltering RSHA officials who decided it was time for them to also disappear. Kopkow and his men changed into civilian clothes and, with their false identity papers, decided to take their cars southwards. They left on 6 May 1945, travelling through Winnert and Schleswig, dodging Allied aircraft strafing motor vehicles, making their way to Kiel then partly along the Baltic coast road towards Dahme, where they arrived two days later. Kopkow does not say why they ended up at Dahme, a small seaside village where Berliners took their summer holidays before the war. Kopkow's men took up residence in the Strandhotel on the day of Germany's surrender and waited for someone, the British, to find them. They waited for three weeks, then one of Kopkow's men decided to take matters into his own hands. On a trip into Lübeck, he surrendered himself to the British authorities and denounced Kopkow and the rest of the men. That same day (29 May 1945), a party of British military policemen arrived at the Strandhotel in Dahme at 4 p.m. and arrested Kopkow with his remaining three men, taking them back to Lübeck.

Horst Kopkow began his post-war life in Lübeck-Marstall prison and it would be another two and a half years before his freedom arrived.

10

Salvation

Horst Kopkow stayed one night in Lübeck-Marstall prison, a medieval tower over the gateway into Lübeck old town. On 30 May 1945, he was transferred to the newly renovated Lübeck court prison, another temporary detention centre, before being taken to the long-standing civilian prison at Lübeck-Lauerhof—which is still a prison today. Before his transfer to the Civilian Internment Camp (CIC) No. 1 at Neumünster, Kopkow was held at the British Military Arrest Station in Lübeck's Grosse Burgstrasse, where he had his photograph taken which was placed on his Detention Report.[1]

Kopkow's standard Detention Report is a double-sided document showing his date and place of birth, weight (80 kg (176 lb) (12 st. 8 lb)), height (1.83 meters tall (6 feet)), hair colour (dark brown), eye colour (grey), skin type (fair complexion), and also that he has gold-filled teeth. There is a listing of his positions held since 1939 and his rank. Being a SS-*Sturmbannführer*, he fell into the 'automatic arrest category'; this meant that he would be sent to an internment camp, which he duly was. Under escort, Kopkow was taken from Lübeck to CIC 1 at Neumünster, where British counter-intelligence officers realised they had a prize prisoner who could tell them what they wanted to know about Gestapo activities and, just as importantly at this time, Gestapo personnel and their likely whereabouts. British and American intelligence officers were very keen to track down all Gestapo and SD personnel (regardless of rank), who would be capable of carrying on underground Nazi activities in their respective zones of occupation in Germany. In the early months after the German surrender, many interrogation reports of Gestapo and SD officials have long appendices describing their colleagues and officials they knew, identifying them down to a short description. Kopkow soon became the man to go to because he seem to know everyone.

SS-*Sturmbannführer* Dr Georg Kiessel found himself recalled to RSHA by Kaltenbrunner in June 1944 after several years with the military administration in France and Serbia, which was followed by several months with the *Waffen*-SS. Until a suitable post became available, Kiessel was ordered to reacquaint himself with current working practices of RSHA IV A departments and the different sets of enemies the Gestapo now faced. He spent a month with Kopkow and he was allowed to examine the department's files and see for himself their work against Soviet-inspired communist subversion and 'plots against Germany'. After the war, when questioned by British interrogators, Kiessel gave a detailed sketch of Kopkow: despite his six years in Berlin, Kopkow still retained a 'heavy East Prussian accent' and continued to be a strong believer 'in Hitler and [was] a great critic on [*sic.*] Himmler'; he also possessed a '[v]ery sharp insight especially against all deviations in the [Nazi] party and its organisations'. Kiessel ended his pen picture of Kopkow by confirming he was a '[s]trong opponent of Bolshevism and a strong anglophile'.[2]

Following Kopkow's arrest in the afternoon of 29 May 1945, his arrival at CIC 1 Neumünster is not noted. From his movements in Lübeck and travel to Neumünster (35 miles (55 km)) his most likely arrival at Neumünster would have been 2 June 1945. The date is important because his first interrogation report (on 7 June 1945) of over forty-five pages in German shows a clear, methodical approach to his work ethic. A complete copy in German of this interrogation report can be found in archives of the German Resistance Memorial Centre (*Gedenkstätte Deutscher Widerstand*) in Berlin, but not in the national archives of Germany, Britain, or the USA. The English translation of seventy-one pages can be found in US National Archives (College Park), but not in UK National Archives (Kew). The US copy was held in the 'CIA Special Collections' and was declassified in 2000 due to activities of the Inter Agency Working Group established by US Congress to examine holocaust-era records held by US intelligence agencies. In Britain, two MI5 'name files' of Horst Kopkow were declassified in 2004 and released to UK National Archives. They contain a partial copy of Kopkow's first interrogation report that he dictated and most, but not all of his subsequent interrogation reports spanning the next two years.[3]

The preamble to Kopkow's interrogation report of 7 June 1945 notes that his former secretary and stenographer Berta Rose had also been arrested and was held at Neumünster. A typewriter was provided and Kopkow dictated for Mrs Rose, a war widow, who typed his words 'directly into the typewriter'. The preamble also mentions there are two reports. The first report (030/8/64/1) concerned Kopkow and his career; the highly complex second report (030/8/64/2) describes RSHA and how its power was exercised, the various activities of his particular department in counter-intelligence and counter-espionage against the Soviets, Rote Kapelle network and its roll-up, Soviet-trained German communist parachute agents, and details of the *Funkspiel* operations. Kopkow barely mentions his role in the fight against SIS, SOE, and OSS agents in France, Holland, or Germany. Possibly at the direction of his interrogator, in an appendix, he covers the case of SIS agent Frank Chamier in 200 words, including his apparent death in a Berlin prison during an air raid; he also covers the case of SOE agent Kurt Koenig in 100 words or less, though mentions nothing about his fate. He makes no mention of what happened to over 100 captured SOE agents.

How was he able to do this? Again, the preamble gives one likely answer. The British interrogation officer stated:

> [Kopkow] has a very methodical brain, the structure of these statements was left to him, and is his responsibility apart from the end of Part 1 (the report on Kopkow and his career), where some things were added, which had been over looked. He was allowed more or less complete freedom, and was seldom interrupted. Only if a point seemed to need explanation, he was asked to go further into the matter; he then dictated the supplement directly into the type-writer. But several times he had to be checked as he was getting too lengthy.[4]

By allowing Kopkow 'complete freedom', he proved more than a match for the British interrogator, having been trained as such himself. He was able to manipulate the information he provided to show his comprehensive knowledge of the RSHA and the Gestapo across Europe, that he had a wealth of experience fighting Soviet agent infiltration measures, and that he was not a war criminal. The British interrogator who began the first interrogation of Kopkow and allowed him free rein to state what he wished also had words of warning for him:

> [Kopkow] was warned from the start, that he would not be treated as any small agent, but if one wanted to know something from him he would be asked point blank. That had the advantage for him that he always knew, where he stood, but on the other hand if he slipped up and tried to conceal something important—and he was bound to be found out sooner or later—then he had damaged his prospects for good and all.[5]

This interrogator also noted Kopkow's anti-Soviet attitude:

> [It] runs like a red thread.... He is not only through his East Prussian upbringing biased against them, but also through his whole career he was to 90% engaged on work against Communists. His knowledge of the West is far inferior often second hand with few exceptions, like the 'Funkspiel' in France, Belgium, Holland in respect to sabotage were dealt directly by the Asts [*Aussenstellen*—offices] Paris, Brussels, The Hague etc.

Yet Kopkow had deceived the British already by denying knowledge or responsibility for the *Funkspiel* operations in these very cities.

The British interrogator states that Kopkow's start on the Gestapo ladder in Allenstein was undoubtedly due to his Nazi Party activities as 'a convinced

National-Socialist', but thereafter he rose through the ranks 'due to his capabilities and intelligence. He [had] an extremely matter of fact and methodical brain, very suitable for police work'. His subordinates captured with him in Dahme had mixed views of their boss, but 'all considered him a good and efficient superior. On the whole he [seemed] to have bothered more about his staff in the end, than other members of the '*Führungsstabe*' [leadership] who only thought of themselves'. The interrogator ended his report on the interrogation of Kopkow saying that, after cross checking some of the major points of the report with other sources, he found Kopkow had not concealed any 'vital information, and his statements seem reliable'.[6]

It took a few weeks before Kopkow's first interrogation report had been seen by (British) 21 Army Group/Intelligence Division (the forerunner of the SIS organisation in the British Zone of Occupation) and the Counter Intelligence War Room in London, at which point, a decision was made to subject Kopkow to more extensive questioning. CI War Room had access to the German radio messages decoded by Bletchley Park in which many Abwehr officers were identified and were of prime interest to all Allied intelligence agencies. The role of the Gestapo in counter intelligence was little known or understood, apart from the growing number of decoded messages that related to Otto Skorzeny and his possible activities in stay-behind networks. Kopkow is named in less than half a dozen decoded messages, all of which relate to Soviet parachute agents, and only one mentions a possible French agent. It is clear that by the end of the war, very little had brought Kopkow to the attention of the Allied intelligence agencies as a target for arrest. A file note, dated 3 July 1945, stated: 'Arrangements have been made for the transfer of Kopkow to Dept. CSDIC for detailed interrogation'. On the same day, SS-General Rauter, Kopkow, Berta Rose, and one of Kopkow's former subordinates, Helmut Steinert, arrived at the British Military Arrest Station in Lübeck, accompanied by various sums of Reichsmarks; Kopkow had 3,108.00 RM and Berta Rose had 979.80 RM.[7] From Lübeck, Kopkow was taken to the new British interrogation centre at Bad Nenndorf, CSDIC/WEA (Combined Services Detailed Interrogation Centre/West European Area), to the west of Hannover. Rauter, Rose, and Steinert did not go with him. The move had been initiated as CI War Room did not have sufficient information about the RSHA reorganisation of December 1944.

Counter Intelligence War Room in London had been established in November 1944 by SHAEF G-2 (Intelligence) as a centre for British and American interrogation reports of German intelligence officers. It had several tasks: it would collate and disseminate intelligence reports to the various British and American intelligence agencies based on information received and it would issue search and find directives for missing German intelligence officials to further Allied knowledge of German intelligence agencies. One primary task after evaluating incoming interrogation reports was any evidence that the Germans intended to put in place a stay-behind agent network to work against Allied operations. Intercepted and decrypted German radio traffic by Bletchley Park showed indications that such plans in 1945 had been formulated, but evidence from interrogation reports showed the enemy had had serious problems finding potential stay-behind agents and equipment for them. Unlike the aftermath of the First World War, when a beaten Germany was not occupied by the Allies to any great extent (for example, the French occupied the Saarland in western Germany), there would be total occupation of Germany at the end of the Second World War. In the last weeks of the war, March–April 1945, evidence from the field showed German units disintegrating and disbanding with no thought of installing a stay-behind network. As a result, German intelligence agencies ceased to have any central control or meaningful direction and many individual officials simply returned to their homes and waited for the end.[8] One of the motives behind the requested move of Kopkow to Bad Nenndorf was to fill in the gaps about RSHA IV as Counter Intelligence War Room regarded him as 'the best source available to us'.[9] In spite of this request for more information about RSHA, it would be October—over three months after the move from Neumünster to Bad Nenndorf—before these questions were put to him. Between times, counter intelligence officers had more pressing matters to discuss with Kopkow—the Rote Kapelle case. There are two interrogation reports of Kopkow from Bad Nenndorf (one taken on 11 September and another on 9 October 1945) that are still classified. It can be ascertained that these two interrogation reports are about Rote Kapelle because small extracts appear in a separate file.[10] The 11 September report concerns Rote Kapelle networks in France and Belgium, and Kopkow reveals what he knew about Henry Robinson and how the network was financed. The second report from 9 October has a detailed explanation of Rote Kapelle operations in Paris and various communist agents on the side lines who were involved; MI5 made an extract from this report on 15 September 1960 indicating that, fifteen years later, there were still loose ends.[11] The background to the latter report can be seen in a telegram dated 22 September 1945 from Major S. H. Noakes of 21 Army Group Intelligence Division in Germany to the CI War Room in London confirming 'detailed interrogation of Kopkow commencing shortly at CSDIC [Bad Nenndorf]. Full questionnaire urgently required. Briefs on Russian matters being obtained independently through WOLG [War Office Liaison Group]', which meant the SIS organisation now stationed in Germany.[12] British and American counter intelligence officers were keen to hear of German wartime successes and failures in their fight against communist agents from post-war interrogation reports—reports shared between the two nations. Before the war was over, these two allies had already identified that, come the German surrender, agents of the Soviet Union would seek to resurrect their former networks or at least the remnants of them after being driven further underground by the Gestapo. Although Kopkow's complete interrogation report, dated 9 October 1945, is still classified, a small extract available explains further his *Funkspiel* operations with Moscow from Berlin using the ciphers of captured parachute agents (Erna Eifler, Robert Barth, Albert Hössler, and others) sent by Moscow to help Rote Kapelle in Berlin with their radio communication problems. The small extract also mentions the elusive Henry Robinson, a Soviet agent active in a Paris-based communist espionage network long before Trepper arrived, having fled Brussels in 1940. British and American agencies looked everywhere in post-war Europe for Henry Robinson, not quite believing Kopkow when he told them Robinson had been executed in Berlin during 1943.

An interrogation of Kopkow took place in October 1945, following questionnaires from Counter Intelligence Branch, Counter Intelligence War Room, and US Intelligence (disguised as USFET (US Forces European Theatre). This was Interim Report 19, dated 19 October 1945, and it is available in UK national archives. The British were interested in further explanations of RSHA IV organisation, its various departments, and its personnel, and he mentions the case of the SIS agents tracked down in Berlin during autumn 1944, resulting in one being captured (named as Josef Bauer alias Fritz Betzinger) and one killed during an exchange of gunfire during the Gestapo raid on his safe house. US Intelligence wanted to know about *Funkspiel* operations from what was now the American Zone. Kopkow mentioned that Kiefer and Dr Götz having retreated from Paris in the last weeks of the war, conducted *Funkspiel* CHICAGO through the Gestapo offices at Konstanz. Kopkow knew that '*Funkspiel* CHICAGO had previously been operating from France, where contact had been established with the American Intelligence Service in Italy'. Of interest to the British and Americans was Kopkow's comments about '*Siegrune Kommandos*', whose creation had been demanded by RSHA Chief Dr Kaltenbrunner in February–March 1945. Kaltenbrunner had sent out the '*Siegrune*' decree to all Gestapo offices in the Reich who were likely to be overrun Allied forces. They were to use their existing informers, the '*V-Leute*', normally under the control of desk officer IV N at every Gestapo office, 'to collect military information on Allied troops and troop movements'. All information was to be passed through the lines to the nearest army unit fighting the enemy. Like all similar schemes decreed from above in the latter stages of the war, they collapsed due to the German surrender and Allied military occupation.[13]

The British Army occupying Germany after the war, known as BAOR (British Army of the Rhine), was created in August 1945 from 21 Army Group under its commander Field Marshal Bernard Montgomery. BAOR soon began producing its own reports, and in the Periodical Counter Intelligence Report, No. 25 for period ending 30 September 1945, it gave a short account of the career of Horst Kopkow: '[It] is interesting to note that on only one occasion was it found possible to turn an English W/T agent and their success with him was only short lived'. By 30 September 1945, Kopkow had been more than able to fool his British interrogators into believing that he had nothing to do with English parachute agents. This same report concludes by confirming that Kopkow's very first interrogation, which he dictated himself: '[It] is considered to be the most important C.I. document since Schellenberg's interrogation, and it is intended to hold him at CSDIC/WEA as his knowledge of the GIS [German Intelligence Service] is encyclopaedic'.[14] This point is confirmed by later interrogation reports where Kopkow is questioned together with former SS-*Sturmbannführer* Harro Thomsen (Gestapo service, then three years with RSHA IV D2, Polish Affairs) and SS-*Obersturmbannführer* Gustav Adolf Nosske (long service with Gestapo office, killing squads in the East, and six months in 1942 with RSHA IV D3, supervision of foreign migrants to Germany). This report, Combined Interim Report No. 47, issued on 14 November 1945, is a long explanation of the early Gestapa in Berlin and its reorganisation as RSHA in 1939. The interrogators were keen to have a better understanding of what the different departments did and how the organisation changed as circumstances and enemies changed. Kopkow, who had a background in anti-communism in his Gestapo service, confirmed that the German communist party had been at its peak from 1933 to 1935 then gradually diminished as Nazi terror took hold and sent many of its leaders and activists to concentration camps. In its place began the rise of industrial security and fighting sabotage. Kopkow said that the growing changes did not create undue problems or confusion in the regional or local Gestapo offices as they were the ones instigating changes in many cases. This report ends with Kopkow stating the last RSHA organisational changes in late 1944 did create problems and was not really necessary, but 'claims it was ascertained on several occasions that the reorganisation had so confused both the British and the American Intelligence Services that, in spite of their admitted efficiency, they were unable to ascertain the system of organisation of the RSHA until their troops had reoccupied France'. Oddly, Kopkow believed the enemy intelligence services in 1944 knew more about RSHA than they actually did. Anyone reading this report would realise the majority of the information had been given by Kopkow, Nosske's contribution is not mentioned.[15] The result of these interrogation reports of Kopkow—when coupled with those of RSHA Chief SS-General Dr Ernst Kaltenbrunner and SS-*Hauptsturmführer* Leonhard Halmanseger of RSHA IV N (who was also responsible for regularly advising the individual Gestapo offices on the informer network across Germany)—appeared on 7 December 1945 when the Counter Intelligence War Room issued its Situation Report No. 4 entitled 'Amt IV of the RSHA'.[16] This report was widely distributed to British and American intelligence agencies to help them identify other RSHA members. In 1944, SIS had appointed Kim Philby 'as head of anti-communist counter-espionage', and once the Allies militarily defeated Germany, he no doubt passed onto the Soviets anything that concerned them. The interrogations of Kopkow that passed across Philby's desk would be welcome to Soviet Intelligence as they would know what happened to their networks under the Third Reich and what steps were now being taken by western intelligence agencies, including SIS and MI5, to find every last agent.[17] In late 1946, Philby was promoted to SIS resident in Turkey, and afterwards, probably had no further information about Kopkow to pass on to the Soviets.

In December 1945, Kopkow, Thomsen, and Nosske were questioned again in a joint session, resulting with the Second Combined Interim Report IR No. 51, issued on 7 December 1945. This time they discussed the 'comparative strength of Kripo, Stapo & SD in regional *Kommandos*' in the Reich and in occupied territories; the word '*Kommandos*' seems to be a translation of '*Dienststellen*' meaning 'offices', which would make more sense in the context in which it is used. Again, Kopkow supplied most of the information. The copy of this interrogation report declassified by MI5 to UK National Archives has some interesting observations. Sections dealing with individual countries occupied by Germany were marked by hand for extract to MI 5 'Subject Files', the MI5 foreign country desks. This report had been produced following questions set by BAOR Intelligence Division and the Counter Intelligence Branch, who also set a number of additional questions that resulted with the Third Combined Interim Report IR 52, issued on 28 December 1945. This last interrogation report of 1945 represented a need by SIS for more information on individual Gestapo and SD personnel. Within the report, 187 individuals are named along with their positions over nineteen pages, and in an appendix, they are separated out by countries in which they served.

The year 1946 saw a change in the interrogation themes for Kopkow; gone went knowledge of RSHA and the Gestapo, in its stead came a much closer focus on his work against Soviet agents, infiltration, and communication methods. In London, the counter espionage department of MI5, Britain's domestic security service, had been examining a number of interrogation reports by various former Gestapo and Abwehr connected to the Rote Kapelle network. MI5 officer John Gwyer carried out a study of this network, which had a number of connections to Britain. On 29 January 1946, he sent a letter to Mrs Spring at BAOR Germany counter espionage branch asking whether she would 'be in a position to make one or two enquiries' in regard to Kopkow's first interrogation report of 7 June 1945; this report related to Rote Kapelle radio links with Moscow from Belgium and France. On the same day, Gwyer also wrote to SIS London and referred to Kopkow's 7 June 1945 interrogation report. This enquiry sought information about the elusive Soviet agent Henry Robinson, the cut-out between Trepper in Paris, and the Soviet Rote Drei espionage network operating out of Switzerland until they were arrested by the Swiss police in 1943. Gwyer had the thought that because Henry Robinson, according to Kopkow, was his actual name, 'it seems reasonable to deduce that he may have been a British subject'.[18] This was far off the mark. Henry Robinson had been born in Brussels on 8 May 1897, and after spending his youth with young communist organisations, he was recruited by Comintern, becoming an agent by 1930. When Trepper fled to Paris in 1940 and made contact with Robinson, he was then running his own Soviet network. Kopkow had confirmed his arrest and execution, but MI5 had a number of loose ends that lead to Britain—these needed examination. Gwyer wrote to the Deputy Commander, Special Branch (London), on 22 March 1946, asking whether Scotland Yard had any information from Germany during the 1920s or 1930s about Henry Robinson. The file does not have a reply.[19] MI5 had no powers of arrest, and when it needed to have persons arrested or when it needed a check of Britain's national police force indices, such requests were made through its liaison office with the Special Branch—a section of the London Metropolitan Police.

BAOR Intelligence Branch (SIS) had Kopkow again interrogated at Bad Nenndorf, leading to the Second Interim Report IR 56, dated 14 March 1946. This time their questionnaire was specifically connected to Rote Kapelle, especially how Schulze-Boysen was connected to Trepper in Brussels and how the radio link with Moscow worked, as well as more information about Rote Drei in Switzerland. The last item covered similar ground about Henry Robinson, who seems to have been a bogeyman for British intelligence agencies trying to find traces of him; yet again, Kopkow confirmed he had been 'tried and condemned to death by the same Luftwaffe Court Martial which tried … Schutze-Boysen [*sic.*]'[20] SIS were not standing back, sending two officers (Nicholas Elliott and Klop Ustinov) to Switzerland in 1946 to investigate any remaining Rote Kapelle members who might still be working for the Soviets.[21]

In May 1946, John Gwyer travelled to Germany as MI5 decided to make their own interrogation of Kopkow. Obviously, the information they had asked for and had been supplied with did not satisfy them. Between 3 and 10 May 1946, Gwyer stayed in Bad Oeynhausen, beginning a number of meetings with SIS (Major Shapiro and Mrs Spring, BAOR Int. Div.) about Rote Kapelle 'and the progress of their enquiries'. On 6 May 1946, Gwyer interviewed Kopkow at Bad Nenndorf about some additional aspects of the Rote Kapelle case and the characters involved. In the case of Trepper, who had run Rote Kapelle, Kopkow certainly made remarks about some of their ideas about who Trepper was and how he went about his business of deceiving the Germans. As Kopkow did not know what happened to Trepper after he escaped from the Germans in Paris in 1943, and MI5 had not picked up any trace of him, Gwyer took a rather false view: 'Trepper is keeping out of the way of the Russians, and might therefore be open to an offer from us, were we able to identify his whereabouts'.[22] Trepper had already fled the coop following the Allied liberation of France. He reported to the Soviet military mission in Paris, and using a false name, he was flown to Moscow where he ended up for several years in Lubyanka Prison. However, Gwyer, in his report of the visit to Germany, noted that Kopkow had answered his questions satisfactorily, but expressed dissatisfaction with the quality of some interpreters at CSDIC Bad Nenndorf who had assisted in his questioning of Kopkow. He added: 'I mention this point only because of its bearing on our future treatment of Kopkow and any similar cases which may find their way to CSDIC'. Did MI5 have future plans for Kopkow once out of the hands of SIS? Both organisations were following up the leads provided by Kopkow. That SIS was also involved in the Rote Kapelle post-war investigation meant it was also liaising with the intelligence agencies of France, Belgium, and probably Holland, where Rote Kapelle agents had been active. Two months later, in July 1946, SIS sent MI5 an extract of a report (in French) on Rote Kapelle by 'Int.Bureau Detachment (Belgium)' about RSHA IV A2b, the *Funkspiel* section of Kopkow's department. After leaving Bad Nenndorf, Gwyer travelled south with the deputy SIS chief in the British Zone (Mr Long) to the US Zone, where they had a meeting on 10 May 1946 with SSU (the Special Services Unit of OSS) and CIC (Counter Intelligence Corps). They discussed Rote Kapelle and the enquiries made of them in the past, and the British officers were 'disappointed to find that so far no progress of any kind [had] been made' in the US Zone. Gwyer and Long returned to Bad Oeynhausen, and after a few more briefings, Gwyer left by air for London. Gwyer wrote to SIS London on 13 June 1946, advising them of his visit to Germany and the interview with Kopkow. He passed on information that they could follow up regarding French and Czechoslovakian links of Rote Kapelle.[23]

Gwyer had interviewed Kopkow on 6 May 1946, and over the next three days, two more interrogation reports from Kopkow were issued by CSDIC/WEA Bad Nenndorf. The first was another joint report by Kopkow, Thomsen, and Nosske (Sixth Combined Interim Report IR 62, dated 8 May 1946) on the subject of German Security Police Schools, their location, and types of candidates; the report also dealt with security of the armaments industries, first by the '*Abwehrbeauftragten*', who were Abwehr officials until they were replaced by the '*Werkschutz*' in 1943. Another joint interrogation of Kopkow, Thomsen, and Nosske (Seventh Combined Interim Report IR 63, dated 9 May 1946) is entitled 'General Study of the Relative Efficiency of the Russian and British IS [Intelligence Service]' and it includes a short discourse entitled 'General Account of DF and Cryptographic Resources of the GIS [German Intelligence Service]'. Kopkow gave practically all the information, with Nosske making no contribution and Thomsen agreeing with Kopkow's views. Gwyer probably took a copy back to London with him to read on the plane.

Kopkow persists in the line of avoiding incrimination by claiming an inability to provide details of British radio agents because their activities were chiefly in the occupied countries and any responsibility for dealing with them rested with the local BdS office. Russian radio agents were chiefly directed against Germany itself and they were dealt with through RSHA (i.e. through Kopkow) and the regional Gestapo offices across Germany. At a stroke, Kopkow distances himself from any responsibility for the fate of captured agents, which is never mentioned. Neither SIS nor MI5 wanted to make anything of this as they were more intent on Kopkow's information about Russian espionage activities. Gwyer returned to London on 13 May

1946, and CSDIC/WEA Bad Nenndorf issued his interrogation of Kopkow as Third Interim Report IR 68, dated 28 May 1946. At his eloquent best, brought out by Gwyer, this Kopkow report shows the information MI5 wanted about Rote Kapelle links and personnel and the Rote Drei. The Robinson link with London, dating to the pre-war years, could only be half-remembered, whereas he could remember the twenty-five people connected to Rote Kapelle network in Berlin and what happened to them. Kopkow stated that the Rote Kapelle network in Germany had been destroyed and would not be able to be resurrected by the renewed post-war Soviet intelligence efforts. Kopkow also stated—possibly now with an eye to his future—that he did 'not mean that the activities of the Russian IS in Germany had been liquidated', only the Rote Kapelle network had been thoroughly eradicated. Another Kopkow interrogation report, Fourth Interim Report IR 70, issued on 10 July 1946, dealt with 'activities against Russian IS' in Germany. This came about following two questionnaires from the Counter Intelligence Bureau, dated November 1945—the delay for this is unknown. This is a wide-ranging report, covering a multitude of subjects in which SIS had an interest. MI5 were also interested and extracted many paragraphs for their separate Subject Files. Kopkow explained about Soviet intelligence recruitment of agents, espionage activities in the field, the armaments industries as special targets, agent contacts with communist relatives or communist organisations, and communist activities in Italy at length; this information was seemingly well-received by MI5.[24] OSS/SSU London sent a copy of this latest Kopkow interrogation, IR 70, to Washington on 4 October 1946; Washington officials marked paragraphs in their copy much the same way as MI5 had done.[25]

October 1946 arrived and Kopkow awoke from the safety of Soviet espionage and intelligence activities to the danger of the fate of captured SOE agents and what happened to them. SOE London had been closing down its various country desks since the German surrender, but the problem of what happened to its agents who had not returned still rankled. Vera Atkins, a squadron officer and conducting officer of SOE French Section, took matters in hand and travelled to Germany to find out where they were or what had happened to them. Over 100 men and women SOE agents were missing. Before Atkins received permission to visit Germany, British War Crimes Group/North West Europe (WCG/NWE), based in Bad Oeynhausen, established that a great number of the missing agents had been executed at Natzweiler, Gross Rosen, Flossenbürg, and Dachau concentration camps. The War Office finally gave Atkins permission to go for four days in December 1945 and her first objective on her first day in Berlin was to find a grave of SOE agent Marc Jumeau at Buch hospital complex, north of Berlin. Accompanied by a British war crimes investigator, Atkins professed satisfaction at Buch and then, having heard that two former concentration camp commandants (Anton Kaindl of Sachsenhausen and Fritz

Suhren of Ravensbrück) were being held in the British Zone, demanded she be taken there. Atkins received approval of WCG/NWE to see both commandants. Kaindl was interviewed at Staumühle camp near Paderborn and said nothing of interest. They travelled down to a camp at Recklinghausen to see Suhren, who denied any English women had been held at his camp, apart from Odette Churchill (Odette Sansom). Atkins returned to London having achieved something, but she was aware that she needed to go back. After pulling strings, Atkins returned to Germany in January 1946 attached to the war crimes unit at Bad Oeynhausen, with open-ended permission to find out what had happened to the missing agents. Between times, Atkins assisted in the normal war crimes investigation work and she was present when Rudolf Höss, the commandant of Auschwitz, having been tracked down and arrested in the British Zone, was brought in for his first interrogation. Over the next nine months, Atkins discovered a great deal, and in September 1946, she was able to issue a 'Haystack' Wanted Report for Horst Kopkow. Working on the principle of needles in haystacks, WCG/NWE issued so-called Haystack reports to the commanders of the Civilian Internment Camps and prisons across the British Zone of Occupation where German POWs were being held. These Haystack reports provided the names and details of charges of persons the war crimes investigators were keen to find. Internment camps and prisons made a return with positive or negative answers.

This Haystack report for 'Kopkov or Kopkow' stated:

> Wanted in connection with murder of various British agents in various Concentration Camps, particularly women in Natzweiler and Dachau. All reports and documents of captured agents were sent to Kopkov and he ordered their removal to Concentration Camps and ligquidation [*sic.*].[26]

A positive reply, dated 18 October 1946, came to the Judge Advocate General office at BAOR: 'Held in custody by Int. Div. CCG [Intelligence Division, Control Commission Germany] at an Interrogation Centre; location not known'. The chief of the Intelligence Division (SIS) wrote on 30 October 1946 to War Crimes Investigation Unit (Research Branch), at HQ BAOR, confirming that Kopkow was now being held at 7 CIC, the Civilian Internment Camp No. 7 at Eselheide, near Paderborn, having been moved from the Bad Nenndorf Interrogation Centre where he had been for the past year. Int. Div. remarked that although Kopkow '[had] given a great deal of important information whilst under interrogation, he [would] not be released without reference of this Headquarters'.[27]

It was December 1946 before Captain Alexander Philipson, Investigating Officer from the War Crimes Investigation Unit, was able to interrogate Kopkow at 7 CIC. On 18 December, the two had a general discussion and

Kopkow 'gave the impression through-out the interrogation of being a very unreliable witness'. Kopkow so far had an easy life because he gave SIS a wealth of counter-espionage materials they could use, but now he faced questioning that might incriminate him in events he had so far been able to dodge. His first interrogation report of 7 June 1945, in which he had volunteered information about captured SIS agent Frank Chamier, came back to haunt him. Philipson asked:

> What he [Kopkow] knew about the Chamier case and what part he played in it, his face registered fear, he turned quite pale, closed his eyes, bit his lips and began to sway. Pressed to answer the question, he said in a low voice: *Ich weiss nichts davon* and staggered to the wall, propping himself against it. He then asked for a glass of water, and after drinking some, he partly recovered his self-control. He later explained his behaviour by ill-health and under-nourishment.[28]

When Philipson later described this incident to camp management, he was told that, as a special prisoner held in separate compound of the camp, Kopkow received better food and more tolerable conditions than in other compounds. His fainting trick was used 'whenever one puts him awkward questions, which he would prefer not to answer'. This is the only reported information on his fainting to be found because his interrogations about Soviet counter-espionage must have been a diet on which he happily feasted and could regard as non-self-incriminatory. What interrogations led to his fainting trickery are unknown.

Philipson continued his own report on meeting with Kopkow and persisted in his line of questioning about Chamier. Kopkow 'tried to avoid answering in every possible way' and eventually stated:

> [From the beginning] Chamier had refused to cooperate, but that he probably was in the end persuaded to do so by word of mouth, having been promised that his life would be spared and that later he would be released. He described Chamier as being a weak character, but how he knew this, having never spoken to him or having no knowledge of the way he was interviewed, he could not explain.

In conclusion, both Philipson and his interpreter, Sergeant Ullmann, agreed Kopkow 'was lying when he denied any knowledge of how Chamier was persuaded to cooperate and of the details of the interrogation in general':

> Undoubtedly he was trying to hide facts with which he was probably directly or indirectly concerned. He also could not give a satisfactory explanation of the reason why Chamier was held in the Berlin prison with very important Communist personalities.

The reasons were clear, Chamier had been held in a Berlin prison before being sent up to Ravensbrück concentration camp in 1944, to be near Kopkow's headquarters in Drogen, should he be wanted for further questioning. In the end, Chamier's life became expendable, and like so many other deaths, he was murdered on orders from Kopkow.

Kopkow gave a deposition, sworn on oath, for Philipson at 7 CIC on 18 December 1946, in which he gives the bare bones that he could admit to about Chamier.

In the new year (18 January 1947), Kopkow was moved from 7 CIC (Eselheide) to No. 1 War Criminals Holding Centre (WCHC) at Minden, known as 'Tomato Minden'. Vera Atkins finally met with her adversary Horst Kopkow in January 1947. Having been unprepared for the interrogation and deposition at Eselheide the month before, Kopkow was much more prepared for the meeting with Atkins at Minden. There is no background report to their conversation, simply a deposition on oath by Kopkow (dated 21 January 1947).[29] He was much more cunning this time and was quite able to tell lies to save himself when it came to avoiding incriminating himself. This deposition is about his involvement, kept to a minimum, with the SOE 'F' Section agents in France and his interaction with the senior Gestapo men in Paris. According to Kopkow, the *Funkspiel* operations carried out in France were the responsibility of Kieffer in Paris and Kopkow's subordinate, Ampletzer. These two are said by Kopkow to have had 'close contact', whereas Kieffer and Dr Götz both mention having contact only with Kopkow. The section in the deposition that *Reichsführer*-SS Himmler had a healthy interest in the 'F' Section is undoubtedly correct and Himmler did discuss the regular reports from his man in Paris, SS-General Oberg, with Hitler. Kopkow is correct (as confirmed by Kieffer and Dr Götz) that the invasion of Europe via France was expected in the summer of 1944, and all the way down from Himmler to Kopkow, with their respective contacts at HSSPF and BdS France, a demand was created that the BdS, through the interrogation of captured 'F' Section agents and the *Funkspiel* operations with SOE in London, should establish the precise date of the invasion. Before the invasion took place, the first 'F' Section agents were deported from France to Rawitsch penitentiary and Kopkow asserts this decision came from Himmler-Oberg discussions; RSHA IV Chief Müller ordered Ampletzer to arrange this. Naturally, Ampletzer was not around to dispute this, so could easily be blamed. Except, of course, such orders went through the department chief, i.e. Kopkow, who then arranged a subordinate to make the arrangement. The Reich Justice Ministry were responsible for German prisons and Ampletzer made the arrangement for accommodation at Rawitsch. Kopkow carefully does not mention the fifty-one SOE Dutch Section agents who arrived at Rawitsch on 15 April 1944, followed seven days later (on 22 April) by twenty-four SOE 'F' Section agents. Kopkow then tells a tale about how the decision for the shooting of the 'F' Section agents at Rawitsch came about. Kopkow never deviates from mentioning only the 'F' Section agents. According to Kopkow, the decision rested on the Soviet military threat towards Rawitsch, and *Reichsführer*-SS Himmler, through RSHA Chief Dr Kaltenbrunner, requested the files of the individual 'F' Section agents. At this time, BdS France had evacuated Paris and it took some time for Kopkow to get the files for Himmler.

It is surprising that Vera Atkins allowed Kopkow to get away with conflating these timings. Firstly, Rawitsch would not be under Soviet military threat until January 1945 (along with Gross Rosen concentration camp); secondly, BdS Paris evacuated around 18 August 1944, at which time, ten agents sent to Rawitsch had already been transferred to Gross Rosen and shot (June 1944). Allowing two weeks for BdS Paris to recover its files and have the hard copies sent to Berlin would mean them arriving around 2 September 1944, a date that does not fit well with what happened. On 3 September 1944, forty-seven SOE Dutch and 'F' Section agents were transferred from Rawitsch to Mauthausen concentration camp, arriving on 5 September; all were shot between then and 7 September. The remaining fourteen SOE agents left at Rawitsch were transferred to Gross Rosen camp on 4 September 1944 and shot.

Kopkow explains that once he had all the files, they were passed to Himmler. When they came back—a date Kopkow does not remember—they were accompanied by an order from Himmler's field headquarters for the shooting of the agents. The *Reichsführer*-SS himself had made handwritten notes in green pencil on each file: 'The order for the shooting on the basis of the returned files and instructions of the *Reichsführer*-SS given to [RSHA] *Amtschef* IV, SS-*Gruppenführer* Müller, were personally dictated'. Müller then contacted Ampletzer, who informed the regional Gestapo office in Breslau of the orders, directing Gestapo Breslau to pick up the prisoners from Rawitsch and take them to Gross Rosen where they would be executed.

The problem with Kopkow's explanation and the orders from Himmler for shooting the agents simply do not hang together. Kopkow continually and solely mentions SOE 'F' Section agents, and by the time Kieffer's men had evacuated Paris along with other BdS officials in August 1944, almost 100 SIS and SOE 'F' (and RF) Section agents had been deported from Paris to German concentration camps. An additional fifty-one SIS and SOE Dutch Section agents had been deported from Holland to Rawitsch. Did Himmler really have the time to examine each individual file (151 at least) of these agents and personally annotate each in green pencil? No, he did not. Such actions were daily fodder for RSHA IV Chief Müller, and Kopkow had been no slouch when it came to giving orders for the execution without trial of Soviet agents. With no personal comeback in 1944, he needed a concoction in 1947 to avoid being charged with war crimes. Unfortunately, Vera Atkins swallowed the lies and half-truths in this sworn deposition and Kopkow got away with murder.

His luck continued in February 1947 when Captain A. W. H. Nicolson of BAOR Legal Staff arrived at Tomato Minden to depose Kopkow. This deposition practically duplicated the one Kopkow had signed for Vera Atkins. There was a slightly different addition to the ending:

> Having been asked I state, that no proper trial took place in the case of the agents of the 'French Section', but that the instructions for this execution had been issued by *Reichsführer*-SS Himmler. For this purpose he was in possession of an authority given by the Führer, which listed for the duration of the war. The order for the shooting of the agents was exclusively issued by the *Reichsführer*-SS.[30]

The ink was barely dry on this deposition of 5 February 1947 when problems came from a different direction. The US Army came calling on 22 February 1947 through their War Crimes Investigating Dept. No. 6/7708, who were 'searching for Stubaf Horst Kopkow, wanted in connection with the murder by shooting of 2 American aviators in or near Drogin [*sic.*] (Mecklenburg, Russian Zone), in May or June 1944'. This was followed on 14 March 1947 by a US extradition request for Kopkow. Whether this was a ruse to get Kopkow into US hands might never be known as WCG/NWE wrote to the US War Crimes Liaison Detachment 'by hand' on 9 April 1947: 'It is regretted that the extradition of Kopkow is not possible at this time. US Authorities will be informed of the outcome of his trial by Great Britain'.

There may have been something behind WCG/NWE comment that Kopkow may be facing a trial. BAOR HQ Int. Div. wrote to BAOR Judge Advocate General (War Crimes) on 19 February 1947 in reply to their letter of 23 January 1947. JAG (War Crimes) must have asked Int. Div. what their interrogations of Kopkow comprised. Their reply reported: 'An immense amount of material here arising out of subject's many interrogations, therefore it is impossible for us to know precisely what evidence is required, and as we have no spare reports available, it is suggested that we send you his personal files'. Seemingly, it did not take long for WCG/NWE to peruse two files sent over from Int. Div. for they returned them on 26 February commenting that 'it [was] regretted that the interrogations carried out at CSDIC [Bad Nenndorf] did not touch on the subject matters' they had sought; as JAG and WCG/NWE were investigating the murder of SOE agents, it can be assumed that CSDIC at the behest of SIS (Int. Div.) and MI5 had not bothered asking Kopkow about such matters. The question of German orders for killing captured agents and British commandos came up at an important trial in Wuppertal, beginning 7 March 1947, of members of BdS Paris.

In July 1944, as the result of a *Funkspiel* operation by Kieffer's section, they were expecting a parachute drop of supplies in containers. At the drop zone near Noailles, west of Paris, a group of Gestapo men were surprised to find that, instead of containers, there were a dozen British SAS commandos coming down—a firefight ensued. Three SAS men were wounded and handed over to the army, five were captured and kept by Kieffer's men, and the rest fled. Kieffer reported the event to Kopkow in Berlin, who, when faced with a similar capture reported in Yugoslavia, referred Kieffer to the army. Military men captured in uniform were not the business of Kopkow, who no doubt referred Kieffer to Hitler's decree of 18 October 1942 that specifically mentioned that, in cases like the capture of the SAS men, they should be handed over to the army. Unfortunately, the BdS himself, Knochen, received instructions from RSHA Berlin to execute the SAS men, and passed an order to Kieffer to shoot the five SAS men. The execution of four of them (one fled from the execution site) resulted in a prosecution brought by a British Military Court in Wuppertal, 7–12 March 1947. Knochen, Kieffer, Schnur, and Ilgenfritz were all condemned to death and two others were given prison sentences. Kopkow appeared as a prosecution witness on 10 March, and said the executions had been carried out pursuant to Hitler's decree of 18 October 1942. Under questioning of the lawyer defending Schnur, the handwritten proceedings report Kopkow saying 'the S.D. complained to the Wehrmacht that they were not to hand over the commandos to the S.D. The S.D. could refuse to receive such commandos'. Under cross-examination, Kopkow stated: 'I know of no case when refusal to carry out the "*Führerbefehl*" resulted in a death sentence being carried out on those who refused to obey it'.[31] If Kopkow was trying to help Kieffer's case, it was in vain. Having been condemned to death on 10 March 1947, his subsequent appeals for clemency denied, Kieffer went to the gallows at Werl prison on 26 June 1947 along with Schnur and Haug; Knochen was handed over to the French for a different trial and eventually returned to the British authorities who did give clemency.

Kopkow's appearance before a Wuppertal court was the only one he would ever appear before for the rest of his life. In 1948, his deposition of 5 February 1947 from Tomato Minden was used in evidence in the case against Gross Rosen concentration camp personnel, including its former commandant Johannes Hassebroek. On this occasion, a British Military Court sitting in Hamburg tried three men charged with the murder of ten SOE agents at Gross Rosen between 1 July and 31 August 1944. Research fifty years later by Dutch historians showed the basic prosecution charges that agents had been murdered without trial was correct, but the dates of the murders and the numbers involved were flawed. The three defendants were condemned to death; Hassebroek's sentence was reduced to life imprisonment, then fifteen years, and, finally, he was released on 18 November 1958 from Werl prison. The two sentences on his subordinates were not confirmed and they were released in 1948.

The year 1947 began badly for Kopkow—with the pointed interrogations at Tomato Minden—although it picked up following his appearance at a witness in Wuppertal and WCG/NWE seeing off an unlikely extradition to the Americans. WCG/NWE also agreed to let Kopkow be questioned by the Norwegians. Kopkow had made a visit to BdS Oslo in October–November 1943 to discuss the work of RSHA IV A2 and the possibilities of *Funkspiel* operations. This letter is the first mention of Kopkow visiting Norway and is not mentioned again, nor is any interrogation by the Norwegians. The last months of 1947 about Kopkow are clouded by the destruction of official British documents, noted in the MI5 'name file' of Kopkow.[32] Six separate pieces of correspondence between 20 October and 18 November 1947 are noted 'Destroyed 9/1/62'. According to the Enclosure List in the file, MI5 corresponded with SIS Germany (BAOR Int. Div.) about Kopkow and this included MI5 acknowledging the receipt of a 'Top Secret document from BAOR'. Until SIS open their Kopkow files, we will never know the subject of this correspondence.

The year 1948 dawned and Kopkow was almost home and dry, salvation at hand. Just one more deposition then he really would have put incarceration and the threat of criminal proceedings behind him. His long-time subordinate *Kriminalinspektor* Walter Habecker, a bald-headed thug of the old school, had been arrested on 8 March 1946 in Hannover. Brought to CSDIC/WEA Bad Nenndorf, he met again with Kopkow and together they produced a very short (three pages) interrogation report, mainly about Rote Kapelle.[33] Habecker went on to languish in various internment camps in the British Zone while BAOR Int. Div. wondered whether to allow his extradition to the US Zone. The Americans wanted him for torturing members of the American and British military missions at Mauthausen concentration camp in January 1945, a few days before their execution. Why Habecker was not handed over to the Americans is unknown; his MI5 file contains only two short interrogation reports as though no one from MI5 or SIS wanted to talk to him more about Rote Kapelle (to ensure Kopkow told the truth) or about the missing agents. Habecker was undergoing denazification in Wuppertal when Kopkow provided a deposition (11 April 1948) in his favour. It did not do much good as Walter Habecker hanged himself in his cell on 25 January 1949 at Paderborn Prison.

The nub of the question about Kopkow's recruitment by SIS is did they regard the loss of wartime comrades in execrable circumstances count as nothing in the post-war grander scale of events when facing the new enemy from the east? The answer can be found in a letter dated 19 March 1948 from WCG/NWE (signed Major A. E. E. Reade) to JAG at BAOR HQ, which stated the case against Kopkow had been shelved due to lack of evidence. This letter goes on that WCG/NWE had 'provisionally released him for special employment under an 'I' agency here [SIS Germany] who, however, have specially requested that the case against him should not be dropped'.[34] There is another inference to be drawn from Kopkow's recruitment by SIS: protection from judicial proceedings. Kopkow had been a longstanding SS member and senior Gestapo officer, and both organisations had been declared 'criminal organisations' by the International Military Tribunal at Nuremberg, and Kopkow should have appeared before a denazification tribunal charged with membership of them. Typically, he may well have been sentenced to time served by internment. In his case, SIS did not want Kopkow subjected to public scrutiny in a denazification trial so protected him from this process. In his statement for the West German police years later (9 May 1961), Kopkow stated that, in autumn 1947, he was released to Unna/Westphalia where he had a room organised by the British Intelligence Service who employed him for the following months. In the same statement, he states that, in 1948, he worked as a coal miner at Unna/Königsborn for eight months, which was a cover-up to conceal from the West German police that he worked for the British secret service in Germany throughout this period. At the Knochen/Kieffer trial in Wuppertal in March 1947, he gave his address not as CSDIC/WEA Bad Nenndorf, but as Sachsenstrasse 6, Detmold, quite some distance away.[35] This may indicate that Kopkow had indeed been released, but there is no information available to confirm this. What the files do reveal is that Kopkow was brought to London at the time of the first major Cold War crisis, when the Soviets severed all land links between Berlin and western Germany and when the Berlin airlift of supplies was about to begin using Allied aircraft. A report dated 25 May 1948 shows Kopkow being accommodated at the London District Cage, 6–7 Kensington Palace Gardens, London. This address, today part of 'Embassy Row', looks similar to a large country house, but bugged throughout for secretly monitoring POWs held there thinking they would not be overheard when talking to their fellow prisoners. There are no reports of Kopkow volunteering or receiving information from his SIS handlers, but what happened next confirms they wanted people to believe that Horst Kopkow had died in London. Lt-Col. R. Paterson of London District Cage wrote to WCG/NWE back in Germany, in his letter dated 15 June 1948:

> Re Horst KOPKOW.
>
> The above as you know was sent to England about ten days ago for special interrogation and when he arrived here he was found to be running a temperature and after two days was sent to hospital, where we regret to say he died of Bronchopneumonia before any information was obtained from him. We enclose a certificate of death issued by the Hospital Authorities and would request that you duly advise his relations of his decease. He has been buried in that portion of the local Military Cemetery allocated to Prisoners of War who have died.[36]

SIS invented this fictional death in order to disguise their plans for Kopkow and his past did not figure in his future. The new name found for him was Peter Cordes, and when he felt safe in later years became Horst

Cordes-Kopkow. Apart from this story being available in archival records (at UK National Archives), it was also repeated in the history of SIS by Keith Jeffery, who then remains silent about how Kopkow was employed by SIS.[37] In a nod to Kopkow's recruitment, Jeffery described him as one of the 'pretty unattractive former (and not so former) Nazis' employed by SIS, wanted because of their knowledge of 'the growing Soviet threat ... German counter-intelligence expertise on communist networks and techniques was much in demand' by the British and the American agencies as well as the nascent Gehlen Org in the US Zone—and what a bunch of mass murderers these organisations recruited. Jeffery did not think to name these men employed by SIS, but others have. Real Nazi mass murderers have turned up on the books of SIS, revealing SIS to be no different than the American, the French, the Soviet, and the Gehlen organisations when it came to recruiting people of a dubious counter-intelligence past.[38]

It is easy to see why Kopkow appealed to SIS; his wartime experience alone in counter-espionage against the Soviets was much broader than anything SIS and MI5 had had to cope with, but was this the real reason why they wanted him? Like any professional intelligence agency, SIS Germany would soon have got to grips with counter measures against Soviet intelligence and espionage activities in the British Zone in this new Cold War era. Although the land border between the Soviet and British Zones was several hundred miles long, the British Army regularly patrolled it—no less often after the Soviets erected a barbed-wire fence with watch towers. Everything Kopkow told them about Soviet infiltration measures and Gestapo counter measures had been learned and acted upon. Countering Soviet methods cannot have been why they recruited Kopkow and used him throughout the 1950s. SIS reasons lay elsewhere.

SIS recruited Kopkow not as an agent, but as a consultant for the continuing examination of Rote Kapelle in Western Europe. SIS and MI5, in common with the intelligence agencies of other Western European countries, were keen to ensure that wartime Soviet espionage networks as represented by Rote Kapelle were no longer in operation. To ensure SIS and MI5 had all the same information, John Gwyer of MI5 had steadily accumulated a vast quantity of reports from Abwehr and Gestapo prisoners like Kopkow who had any knowledge of Rote Kapelle. In October 1949 (the file cover has a handwritten date of 17 October 1949), MI5 issued its comprehensive report, 'The Case of the Rote Kapelle', which ran to 344 pages and was divided into three parts: (I) examines each of the seven networks identified under the Rote Kapelle umbrella; (II) a chronological review of how these groups developed and operated; and (III) is the longest section and lists alphabetically every identified member of Rote Kapelle, agents, and informants. Kopkow's various interrogation reports at Bad Nenndorf provided the backbone to this report. He did not name everyone at the time, and those listed in this MI5 report show a much deeper look into anyone associated with Rote Kapelle. As Kopkow was in London during the summer 1948, is it too obvious to suggest that he provided more information, names, and personal background at this time?

There is little information available to show when Kopkow returned to Germany. His wife, Gerda, when interviewed by the British journalist Sarah Helm in 2004, said the family had lived in Berlin before they were evacuated to the west, probably in late 1944. Gerda did not see her husband again for over two years after the war and the first confirmation of where he was came from his former secretary, Berta Rose, who visited her after being released from her own internment. It is worth noting that most of the SS women held in detention in the British Zone, typically former concentration camp wardresses, were held at CIC Staumühle outside Paderborn. It is more than likely that Rose was held here before her release. The address Kopkow gave at Detmold in March 1947 is not too far from Staumühle, and it is the most likely place for the Kopkow family to be living. Sarah Helm, from her interview with Mrs Kopkow, stated: 'Gerda Kopkow remembers that he was promised immunity and within months of his arrest. Gerda and Horst were even allowed to meet during his captivity, in a special house provided by the British. They were very kind to us'. Indeed they were, providing Kopkow with a mantle of protection from war crimes prosecution and denazification. Berta Rose afterwards returned to West Berlin and began working as a stenographer with the criminal police.

After his bogus death, Kopkow returned to Germany to live again with his family. Mrs Kopkow said to Sarah Helm that it was 1950, but in his CV prepared for the Bundesarchiv (Federal German National Archives) at Freiburg im Breisgau in 1986, Kopkow states that in 1949, he joined the textile company Bekleidungs-Union Harald Feilgenhauer GmbH at Gelsenkirchen, in, it is said, a position provided by the British. Gelsenkirchen is where the Kopkow family lived under the name 'Cordes'. At this textile company, which manufactured and sold clothing, Kopkow began in the legal and personnel affairs department, and four years later, in 1953, he was entrusted as director of the company when the owner went off to South America; Kopkow was left responsible for most departments of the company. In 1960, he was appointed CEO (*Geschäftsführer*) and was responsible for the entire company in Gelsenkirchen until he retired in the 1970s. The factory site was torn down in the 1980s and replaced by apartment blocks. In common with CVs, Kopkow skated over several cracks in his career, omitting all connections with the British. Many times during the 1950s, SIS called Kopkow back to London, so often that he became 'comfortable with BEA' (British European Airway), flying into Heathrow airport at a time when air travel was expensive. These London meetings undoubtedly involved more discussions about Rote Kapelle as SIS found more leads to other possible agents. In June 1957, Kopkow met with Reinhard Gehlen, then President of the West German Foreign Intelligence Service (Bundesnachrichtendienst), in Munich to discuss Rote Kapelle. A file note in a MI5 file, dated 15 September 1960, shows one of their desk officers taking an extract from Kopkow's interrogation of 9 October 1945 regarding Soviet intelligence networks in Western Europe.[39]

Fifteen years after the end of the war, MI5 were still chasing down possible Rote Kapelle leads.

By the mid-1950s, Kopkow decided it was safe to write to West German newspapers as Horst Kopkow-Cordes. Heinz Höhne, in the introduction to his own book on Rote Kapelle mentions this. As Kopkow-Cordes, he wrote to *Neues Deutschland* (13 December 1955) and *Münchener Abendzeitung* (12 August 1959, this letter was about the suicide of Fritz Panzinger in Munich three days before). The West German journal *Der Spiegel* dated 24 August 1959 (Nr. 35/1959) carried an obituary from the *Süddeutschen Zeitung* that no doubt carried the flavour of what Kopkow wrote about Panzinger: 'Dear Panz, We mourn for you with all the fervour the heart is capable of. Your dear friends'. Old comrades did not forget old friends.

In 1960, the state prosecutor in West Berlin began an investigation into the activities of RSHA IV Chief Heinrich Müller. Since the end of the war, there had been any number of reports that Müller had survived the war and escaped war crimes charges by hiding out somewhere, possibly South America, possibly Eastern Europe, helping another intelligence agency. At the request of the West Berlin prosecutors, Horst Kopkow-Cordes was invited to attend the criminal police headquarters in Gelsenkirchen for a discussion. This discussion, held on 9 May 1961, resulted in Kopkow's very first interrogation since 1947. The questions followed what Kopkow knew about Müller in the last weeks of April 1945. Kopkow described their last meeting in Berlin, alone, at Müller's private residence on Corneliusstrasse, where Müller said he had been ordered to remain in Berlin. Müller advised Kopkow that he would have nothing to fear about leaving Berlin, the end was near, and he should take advantage of any offer from Western intelligence agencies as they would be very interested in him and want to use his experience in the counter-espionage sector. Müller said his career was over, played out, and he would stay in Berlin. Kopkow was adamant that Müller died during the battle for Berlin in May 1945. The only people who had made contact with him since the war were Heinz Pannwitz, who had visited him in Gelsenkirchen, and Fritz Panzinger, Müller's deputy and group leader of all the Department 'A' sections at RSHA Berlin. Both of these men contacted Kopkow in 1955 within weeks of their release from Soviet captivity. At the end of this interrogation report, Kopkow states that he 'dictated himself directly into the typewriter', reminiscent of his very first interrogation on 7 June 1945. Sixteen years later, he still had the keenest of minds.

Kopkow was invited to criminal police headquarters in Gelsenkirchen again on 23 April 1970. On this occasion, he was questioned about the activities of the Gestapo office in Allenstein where his Gestapo career had begun. A single-page statement resulted.

The West German judicial authorities did not bother Kopkow again, but historians now beat a path to his door. BBC television programmers had a story for their *Timewatch* history series about SOE 'F' Section agents and how the Gestapo in Paris were able to capture so many. The programme took the view that Henri Dericourt had played a major role in betraying agents to the Gestapo, more especially to Kieffer's boss in Paris, SS-*Sturmbannführer* Karl Boemelburg. Programme maker Robert Marshall went to Germany in 1983 and was surprisingly able to talk with former Gestapo officers about the disaster that befell SOE in Paris. Kopkow agreed to talk with Marshall and the two met at his Gelsenkirchen home on 10 June 1983. The report on their talks discusses the *Funkspiel* operations and how the Gestapo marvelled at the riches that came by parachute. 'Whole trainloads of parachuted arms and explosives were shipped off to Berlin' said Kopkow, who gave a good pen picture of Kieffer and Boemelburg and confirmation of the 6 June 1944 invasion date by judicious use of *Funkspiel* messages with London. The Gestapo had the date but not the place: 'We passed it on to von Rundstedt and Goering only to find out after the war they did nothing with it.'

Marshall also went to talk with Helmut Knochen in Frankfurt-Main, but he said little. Josef Schreieder lived in Munich when Marshall and his colleague Larry Collins went to see him. Schreieder mentioned Kopkow's name in connection with Rote Kapelle, but little else, as though Kopkow had no connection with the SOE Dutch Section agents he had taken off Schreieder's hands—also not mentioned by Kopkow and murdered. Schreieder was purposefully vague about Kopkow's post-war career, but as a Gehlen organisation operative for many years after the war, Schreieder knew all about Kopkow. Dr Josef Götz was also interviewed and recalled once Kopkow had come to Paris—a visit never mentioned by Kopkow: '[He] was in charge of all these [radio] games, at all the frontiers.... [Kopkow] was a man of the [Nazi] party.... I think he lived for these things'. These words of Dr Götz are reminiscent of what Kopkow told Marshall at their meeting and which Marshall called Kopkow's leitmotiv: 'I love treason. I hate traitors'. This is how Kopkow looked at the Soviet-trained German communist parachute agents who appeared in front of his desk, before they were sent off to a concentration camp and executed without trial as German traitors.

In a surprising outburst, what Kopkow said to Robert Marshall at a second meeting on 27 February 1986 reveals a still held contemptuous view of the SOE 'F' Section agents: 'It was well known the British just emptied all their prisons of murderers and criminal types, and offered them clemency if they would parachute into France. We only did what the British would have done to them'.

Did SIS completely misjudge Horst Kopkow in 1945 or were these words of a grumpy old man already on the way to dementia at the age of seventy-six? Had Kopkow really provided a glimpse of what he really thought about trained agents who did not come from prisons, was he finally voicing an opinion kept hidden since the war? It appeared to be a final kick at SIS and MI5, who had taken care of him in many ways; they picked an employer for him where, on merit alone, he could rise to the top and provide a good life for himself and his family. His usefulness to SIS undoubtedly closed in the early 1960s, when every possible Rote Kapelle lead had been run down. The Cold War had moved on to a more technology driven level, and Kopkow's expertise and knowledge had run their course—his was yesterday's war, not today's.

Kopkow lived another ten years, dying on 13 October 1996 in a Gelsenkirchen hospital. In May 2004, two Horst Kopkow name files from MI5 were declassified to UK National Archives. By no means do they contain all of Kopkow's interrogations and they come to a halt in 1948; however, while they unlocked the door, full disclosure from SIS is still needed to push the door open.

Endnotes

UK National Archives, Kew—TNA
US National Archives, College Park—US NARA
BStU Berlin—BStU
Bundesarchiv Berlin-Lichterfelde—BArchB
Bundesarchiv Dahlwitz-Hoppegarten—BADH
Bundesarchiv Koblenz—BAK
Bundesarchiv Ludwigsburg—BAL

Chapter 1

1. TNA, WO 309/1771, Detention Report.
2. Helm, S., 'A Nazi in Her Majesty's Secret Service', *Sunday Times* Magazine (London), 7 August 2005.
3. The most complete copy of this interrogation report is held in the Gedenkstätte Deutscher Widerstand, Berlin; less complete copies at TNA Kew, KV 2/1500, and US NARA, RG 263, CIA name file Horst Kopkow.
4. TNA, KV 2/964 and 965, MI5 name files Carl Marcus.
5. TNA, KV 2/1500, MI5 name file Horst Kopkow.
6. TNA, KV 2/269 to 272, MI5 name files Ernst Kaltenbrunner.
7. TNA, WO 208/4176, PW Paper 133, Otto Ohlendorf (Oct. 1945).
8. TNA, KV 2/96, MI 5 name file Walter Schellenberg.
9. TNA, WO 309/1022.
10. Tuchel, J., 'Zwischen kriminalistischer Recherche und brutaler Folter', in Gerhard Paul/Klaus-Michael Mallmann, eds, *Die Gestapo—Mythos und Realität*, (Darmstadt: WBG, 1995) pp. 373-387; BStU, MfS-HA IX/11, FV 98/66, Vol. 570, pp. 16-20.
11. TNA, WO 309/1295; BAL, B162/16669.

Chapter 2

1. TNA, KV 2/1500.
2. Beckmanns Welt-Lexikon und Welt-Atlas A-Z, (Leipzig: Verlag Otto Beckmann, 1931), p. 94.

3. BArchB, SS-Officer file, Horst Kopkow.
4. Orlow, D., *The History of the Nazi Party*, Vol. I, 1919-1933 (Newton Abbot: David & Charles, 1971), p. 215.
5. *Ibid.*, p. 269.
6. *Sunday Times* Magazine, 7 August 2005.
7. TNA, KV 2/1501, 4th Interim Report by Kopkow, pp. 8-9.
8. BArchB, SS-Officer files, Kopkow and Felix Rühl.
9. US NARA, RG 498 Box 80, interrogation report CIR 4/2 dated 24 May 1945, Kurt Bethke, pp. 12-13.
10. Krausnick, H., Buchheim, H., Broszat, M., and Jacobsen, H.-A., (eds.), *Anatomy of the SS-State*, (London: Collins, 1968), p. 146.
11. *Ibid.*, pp. 157-160.
12. *Ibid.*, p. 162.
13. BAL, B162/465, pp 71-73, statement of Josefine Pautz dated 26 August 1959.
14. Buber-Neumann, M., *Unter Two Dictators. Prisoner of Stalin and Hitler*, (London: Pimlico Press, 2009), pp. 143-146, 155-160.
15. TNA, KV 2/1500, Kopkow interrogation 7 June 1945.
16. BArchB, R58/245.
17. USHMM, RG-15.032M reel 3, has numerous examples.
18. TNA, FO 371/24380, report by Yugoslav Minister in Berlin, 2 March 1940.
19. Gedenkstätte Deutscher Widerstand, Berlin, their copy of Kopkow interrogation dated 7 June 1945 only.
20. Höhne, H., *The Order of the Death's Head*, (London: Secker & Warburg, 1969), pp. 287-289.
21. Grundmann, S., *Der Geheimapparat der KPD im Visier der Gestapo – das BB-Ressort*, (Berlin: Karl Dietz Verlag, 2008), pp. 117-118.
22. *Ibid.*, p. 109.

Chapter 3

1. BArchB, R58/245, organisation chart.
2. Cookridge, E. H., *Gehlen. Spy of the Century*, (London: Hodder, 1971), p. 275.
3. McKay, C. G., *From Information to Intrigue. Studies in Secret Service based on the Swedish Experience, 1939-1945* (London: Frank Cass, 1993), p. 204.
4. TNA, KV 2/1500, Kopkow interrogation dated 7 June 1945.
5. Werner Röder, *Sonderfahndungsliste UdSSR*, (Erlangen: Verlag D+C, 1976).
6. Nuremberg document NO-2939.
7. TNA, KV 3/190, translation of captured document.
8. TNA, KV 2/1500, Kopkow interrogation dated 7 June 1945.
9. TNA, KV 3/190, translation of captured document.
10. Cookridge, E. H., *Inside SOE*, (London: Arthur Barket), p. 38; the evidence for 'set Europe ablaze' appears anecdotal.
11. Foot, M.R.D., *SOE in France*, (London: HMSO, 1966), pp. 7-11.
12. TNA, HS 7/108, history of SOE Czechoslovakia.
13. Witte, P., and others (eds.), *Der Dienstkalender Heinrich Himmlers 1941/42*, (Hamburg: Hans Christians Verlag, 1999), p. 438.
14. BArchB, R58/331, notes of Gestapo officer attending the meeting.

15. Macdonald, C., *The Killing of Obergruppenführer Reinhard Heydrich, 27th May 1942*, (London: Papermac, 1990), is one of several on the subject.
16. BArchB, R58/331, R58/2314, Heydrich order of 15 May 1942.
17. *Ibid.*, Müller order of 6 June 1942.
18. USHMM, RG-15.032M reel 3.
19. TNA, KV 2/1501, Thomsen interrogation FR 18, 3 Jan 1946.
20. Höhne, H., *Codeword: Direktor. The Story of the Red Orchestra*, (London: Secker & Warburg, 1971), pp. 79-81.
21. *Ibid.*, pp. 93-94.

Chapter 4

1. US NARA, RG 65, Entry 179, Box 751. Interrogation of Hauptmann Krämer.
2. TNA, KV 2/2752, MI 5 name file Walter Habecker; TNA, WO 311/607, interrogation of Dr Hans Thost, 26 Nov. 1946.
3. TNA, KV 2/1500, Kopkow interrogation, 7 June 1945.
4. BArchB, SS-Officer file Horst Kopkow.
5. BArchB, SS-Officer file Friedrich Panzinger.
6. BArchB, SS-Officer file Heinrich Müller.
7. Griebel, R., Coburger, M., and Scheel, H., (eds.), *Erfasst? Das Gestapo-Album zur Roten Kapelle*, (Rendsburg: Drückhaus Heinrich Möller Söhne, 1992), pp. 341-342.
8. BArchB, R58/1131, Kopkow report dated 22 Nov.1942.
9. SS-Officer file, Panzinger.
10. TNA, WO 208/5220, interrogation of Dr Georg Kiessel, 31 May 1945.
11. TNA, WO 309/184, interrogation of Dr Joseph Schreieder, 5 Sept. 1946.
12. Information from Robert Marshall on his interview of Kopkow.
13. *Ibid.*

Chapter 5

1. Witte, P., and others (eds.), *Der Dienstkalender Heinrich Himmlers 1941-42*, (Hamburg: Hans Christians Verlag, 1999), p. 438.
2. *Ibid.*, p. 451.
3. Nollau, G., and Zindel, L., *Gestapo ruft Moskau*, (Munich: Heyne, 1980), pp. 12-17.
4. Höhne, H., *Codeword: Direktor. The Story of the Red Orchestra*, (London: Secker & Warburg, 1971), pp. 79-81.
5. Trepper, L., *The Great Game*, (London: Michael Joseph, 1977), p. 156.
6. BArchB, R58/2314, Gestapo-Abwehr negotiations.
7. Trepper, *op. cit.*, p. 415.
8. Niedersachsisches Archiv, Hannover, Nds 721 Lüneburg, Acc 69/76, Box 3 Vol. 10, statement of Johannes Strübing, 18 Jan. 1950, pp. 192-204.
9. Höhne, *op. cit.*, pp. 150-152.
10. BStU, MfS HA IX/11, FV 98/66, Bd. 86, pp. 3-5, RSHA IV A2 order, 22 May 1942.
11. US NARA, RG 263, CIA name file Johann Sanitzer.

12. *Ibid.*
13. *Ibid.*
14. BArchB, RY I/1/2/3/142.
15. BStU, MfS HA IX/11, FV 98/66, Bd. 185, p.138.
16. Höhne, *op. cit.*, pp. 94-95.
17. Tarrant, V. E., *The Red Orchestra*, (London: Arms & Armour, 1995), p. 58.
18. Witte, *op. cit.*, p. 524.
19. TNA, KV 2/1501, Kopkow interrogation FR 68, 28 May 1946.
20. Befehlsblatt des Chef der Sicherheitspolizei und des SD, Nr 4/43, January 1943.
21. BAL, B162/129834, pp. 9-15, Pannwitz interrogation, 27 Oct. 1965.
22. Höhne, *op. cit.*, pp. 171-172.
23. Witte, *op. cit.*, p. 577.
24. *Ibid.*, p. 593.
25. BArchB, R58/1131, Kopkow report dated 22 Nov. 1942.
26. Witte, *op. cit.*, p. 645.
27. Höhne, *op. cit.*, p. 192.
28. *Ibid.*, pp. 163-164, 203.
29. Griebel, R., Coburger, M., and Scheel, H., (eds.), *Erfasst? Das Gestapo-Album zur Roten Kapelle*, (Rendsburg: Drückhaus Heinrich Möller Söhne, 1992), pp. 342-348.
30. BStU, MfS HA IX/11, FV 98/66, Bd 570, pp. 15-20.
31. Landarchiv Berlin, Oberfinanzpräsident report 26 March 1943.
32. BArchB, R58/1131, Kopkow report dated 22 Nov.1942.
33. TNA, HS 4/327, has full text of the agreement.
34. TNA, HS 4/358.
35. TNA, HS 4/340, KV 2/2827.
36. TNA, HS 4/342, KV 2/2827.
37. TNA, HS 4/342.
38. TNA, KV 2/991.
39. USHMM, RG-15.032M reel 3.
40. BArchB, R58/331, R58/2314, RSHA IV A2 order, 4 April 1942.
41. BArchB, R58/331, details of the instruction course.
42. *Ibid.*
43. Nollau, Zindel, *op. cit.*, pp. 17-25, 70-72.
44. Trepper, *op. cit.*, p. 417.
45. *Gedenkbuch für die Opfer des Konzentrationslagers Ravensbrück 1939-1945*, (Berlin: Metropol, 2005), p. 186.
46. *The Rote Kapelle. The CIA's History of Soviet Intelligence and Espionage Networks in Western Europe, 1936-1945*, (Washington DC: University Publications of America, Inc., 1979), p. 292.
47. TNA, KV 2/2238, MI5 name file Robert Barth.
48. *Ibid.*
49. TNA, KV 2/2752, MI5 name file Walter Habecker.
50. *The Rote Kapelle. The CIA's History*, pp 383-384.
51. TNA, KV 3/349, MI5 investigation into Rote Kapelle.
52. Trepper, *op. cit.*, p. 423.
53. TNA, KV 2/3785, MI5 name file Daniel Gouloose (alias Gouwlooze).

54. Höhne, *op. cit.*, pp. 212-213; Perrault, *op. cit.*, p. 213.
55. Höhne, *op. cit.*, p. 215; Trepper, *op. cit.*, p. 165.
56. Trepper, *op. cit.*, pp. 171-172.
57. Höhne, *op. cit.* p. 223; Trepper, *op. cit.*, p. 422.
58. BArchB, NS 19/2040, Kopkow report dated 24 Dec. 1942.
59. Witte, *op. cit.*, p. 638.
60. US NARA, RG 242-Entry23B-Box 6, instruction dated 23 Sept. 1942.
61. BArchB, R58/331, order dated 5 June 1943.
62. Sudoplatov, P., and Sudoplatov, A., *Special Tasks*, (New York: Litt, Brown, 1994), p. 143.
63. Simon, M. J., *Gone to Ground*, (London: Profile Books, 2014) p. 193
64. US NARA, RG 263, CIA name file Johann Sanitzer.
65. BArchB, R58/331.
66. Trepper, *op. cit.*, p .328
67. TNA, KV 3/190, interrogation of Eduard Stobbe.
68. TNA, KV 2/2238, MI5 name file Robert Barth.
69. Nollau, Zindel, *op. cit.*, p. 163.
70. *Ibid.*, pp. 159-160.
71. TNA, HS 4/344.
72. TNA, KV 2/2827, interrogation report Gerd Haneberg, 24 Aug. 1944.
73. TNA, HS9/59/2, interrogation report Walter Herberg, 2 Aug. 1946.
74. TNA, HS 7/187; *Gedenkbuch Ravensbrück*, *op. cit.*, p. 448.
75. Nollau, Zindel, *op. cit.*, p. 75.
76. US NARA, RG 263, CIA name file Johann Sanitzer.
77. *Ibid.*
78. TNA, KV 2/2827.
79. *Ibid.*
80. *Ibid.*
81. TNA, HW 17/48, decrypted messages.
82. *Gedenkbuch Ravensbrück*, *op. cit.*, p. 446.
83. TNA, KV 2/2827.
84. *Ibid.*; US NARA, RG 263, CIA name file Johann Sanitzer.
85. TNA, HS 4/346, HS 7/187.
86. *Justiz und NS-Verbrechen*, (Amsterdam: University Press, 1969), Vol. II, pp. 519-535.
87. TNA, KV 2/2827.
88. *Ibid.*
89. BAK, Nachlass Heinrich Himmler.
90. Höhne, H., *The Order of the Death's Head*, (London: Secker & Warburg, 1969), p. 537.
91. TNA, KV 2/1500, Kopkow interrogation 7 June 1945.
92. *'Spiegelbild einer Verschwörung', Die Opposition gegen Hitler und das Staatsstreich vom 20.Juli 1944 in der SD-Berichterstattung*, (Stuttgart: Seewald, 1961), pp. 18-22.
93. TNA, KV 2/1500, Kopkow interrogation 7 June 1945.
94. US NARA, RG 65, Entry 179, Box 751. Interrogation of Hauptmann Krämer.

Chapter 6

1. TNA, WO 309/282.
2. TNA, HS 9/59/2.
3. TNA, WO 208/5543 interrogation report SIR 1674, 24 May 1945.
4. West, N., *MI6: British Secret Intelligence Service Operations 1909-1945*, (London: Weidenfeld, 1983), p. 143.
5. TNA, KV 3/418.
6. TNA, HS 9/195/4.
7. West, *op. cit.*, p. 145.
8. Ibid., p. 152.
9. Ibid., pp. 154-155.
10. Mackenzie, W. J. M., *The Secret History of SOE: The Special Operations Executive 1940-1945*, (London: St Ermin's Press, 2000), p. 240.
11. Reile, O., *Der Geheimdienst im II.Weltkrieg. Westfront*, (Munich: Weltbild Verlag, 1989), pp. 185-186.
12. *Ibid.*, pp. 186-187.
13. Fuller, J. O., *Dericourt*, (Salisburg: Michael Russell, 1989), pp. 285-301.
14. TNA, WO 235/560, statement of Helmut Knochen, 21 Feb. 1947.
15. TNA, KV 2/962.
16. TNA, KV 328, interrogation of Friedrich Dohse, 19 Aug. 1945.
17. Reile, *op. cit.*, p. 190.
18. *Ibid.*, pp. 202-209.
19. *Ibid.*, p. 208.
20. TNA, HS 9/836/5, interrogation report LDC 11, Dr Josef Götz, 21 Nov. 1946.
21. TNA, KV 6/29, interrogation report Ernest Vogt, 19 June 1948.
22. Foot, M. R. D., *SOE in France*, (London: HMSO, 1966), p. 174.
23. *Ibid.*, p. 194.
24. TNA, KV 3/238, interrogation report Arthur Katzemich, 30 April 1946.
25. IWM, London, AL 1681.
26. *Ibid.*
27. TNA, HS 9/836/5, interrogation report LDC 11, Dr Josef Götz, 21 Nov. 1946.
28. Foot, *op. cit.*, p. 212.
29. TNA, WO 311/733.
30. TNA, HS 9/836/5, interrogation report LDC 11, Dr Josef Götz, 21 Nov. 1946.
31. Fuller, *op. cit.*, p. 307.
32. King, S., *Jacqueline*, (London: Arm & Armour, 1989), pp. 310ff.
33. BArchB, SS-Officer file, Karl Boemelburg.
34. Fuller, *op. cit.*, p. 226.
35. TNA, KV 2/1131-1132, MI5 name files Henri Dericourt.
36. Foot, *op. cit.*, pp. 302-304.
37. Fuller, *op. cit.*, pp. 309-312.
38. Foot, *op. cit.*, pp. 313-314.
39. *Ibid.*
40. TNA. HS 6/426, Kieffer interrogation.
41. Foot, *op. cit.*, p. 315.
42. TNA, HS 6/426, Kieffer interrogation.
43. Suttill, F. J., *Shadows in the Fog*, (Stroud: History Press, 2014), p. 218.

44. *Ibid.*, p. 225.
45. Verity, H., *We Landed by Moonlight*, (London: Ian Allan, 1978), p. 99.
46. TNA, HS 9/836/5, SOE PF file Noor Inayat Khan.
47. Saward, J., *The Grand Prix Saboteurs*, (Milton Keynes: Morienval Press, 2006), p. 311.
48. *Ibid.*, p. 317, Suttill, *op. cit.*, p. 227.
49. TNA, HS 9/836/5, Kieffer interrogation.
50. TNA, HS 9/836/5, interrogation report LDC 11, Dr Josef Götz, 21 Nov. 1946.
51. TNA, HS 9/451/6, SOE PF file André Dubois.
52. Foot, *op. cit.*, p. 295.
53. *Ibid.*, pp. 238-241.
54. TNA, WO 208/4679, interrogation report LDC 1213, Emil Rühl, 29 June 1946. Interrogation report LDC 1268, Josef Stork, 26 July 1946.
55. TNA, HS 9/1225/2, SOE PF file Brian Rafferty.
56. TNA, WO 311/103, statement by Christopher Burney, June 1945.
57. Marshall, B., *The White Rabbit*, (London,: Pan Books, 1954), p. 136.
58. TNA, HS 9/648/4, SOE PF file Odette Sansom/Churchill; also FO 950/2253.
59. TNA, HS 9/1395/3, SOE PF file Maurice Southgate.
60. TNA, KV 6/29, interrogation of Ernest Vogt, 19 June 1948.
61. TNA, HS 9/980/7, SOE PF file Claude Malraux.
62. TNA, HS 9/114/2, SOE PF file Yvonne Beekman/Unternahrer; HS 9/166/7, SOE PF file Marcus Bloom.
63. TNA, HS 9/1395/3, SOE PF file Maurice Southgate.
64. TNA, HS 9/1435, SOE PF file Violette Szabo.
65. TNA, HS 9/890/1, SOE PF file Maurice Larcher.
66. TNA, HS 9/111/1, SOE PF file Alcide Beauregard.
67. Foot, *op. cit.*, pp. 409-410.
68. TNA, HS 9/836/5, Kieffer interrogation.
69. www.bddm.org/liv/details.php?id=I.173.
70. Churchill, P., *The Spirit in the Cage*, (London: Hodder, 1954), pp. 117-125.
71. TNA, HS 9/836/5, Kieffer interrogation.
72. *Ibid.*
73. TNA, HS 1409/8, SOE PF file John Starr.
74. TNA, WO 309/418.
75. TNA, WO 235/560, Statement by Helmut Knochen, 21 Feb. 1947.
76. *Ibid.*
77. TNA, WO 208/4679, interrogation LDC 1213, Dr Josef Götz, 26 June 1946.
78. Foot, *op. cit.*, p. 473.
79. *Ibid.*, pp. 473, 505-517.
80. TNA, HS 7/159.
81. West, *op. cit.*, pp. 97-98, Jeffery, *op. cit.*, p. 387.
82. Kelso, *Errors*, p.52.
83. TNA, KV 2/1170, MI5 name file Mattis Adolf (George) Ridderhof.
84. TNA, HS 9/1438, SOE PF file Thijs Taconis.
85. TNA, HS 9/894/3, SOE PF file Hubertus Lauwers.
86. TNA, KV 2/961, MI5 name file Hermann Giskes.
87. TNA, KV 2/1332, MI5 name file Josef Schreieder.
88. *Ibid.*

89. TNA, KV 2/961, MI 5 file Hermann Giskes.
90. Schreieder, J., *Das war das Englandspiel*, (Munich: W. Stutz Verlag, 1950), p. 257.
91. BArchB, NS 19/2560.
92. *Ibid.*
93. TNA, KV 2/961, MI5 name file Hermann Giskes.
94. Dourlein, P., *Inside North Pole*, (LondonL Wm Kimber, 1953), pp. 110-117.
95. Kelso, *op. cit.*, p. 151; West, *op. cit.*, pp. 98-99.
96. Kelso, *op. cit.*, p. 152.
97. TNA, HS 9/1569, MI5 name file Antonius Wegener.
98. US NARA, RG 498 Box 16, interrogation of Josef Schreieder, 28 Dec 1945.
99. www.englandspiel.eu/index.php?taal=en last aacessed 24 March 2017.
100. US NARA, RG 498 Box 16, interrogation of Josef Schreieder, 28 Dec 1945.
101. TNA, KV 2/1332, MI5 name file Joseph Schreieder.
102. Birn, R. B., *Die Höheren SS-und Polizeiführer* (Düsseldorf: Droste Verlag, 1986), p. 216.
103. Kelso, *op. cit.*, pp. 191-201.

Chapter 7

1. Höhne, H., *Codeword*, p. 75.
2. Höhne, *Der Krieg im Dunkeln* (Munich: C.Bertelsmann, 1985), p. 374.
3. Reile, O., *Der Deutsche Geheimdienst im II.Weltkrieg. Ostfront* (Munich: Weltbild Verlag, 1989), p. 410.
4. Sudoplatov, P., and Sudoplatov, A., *Special Tasks*, (New York: Little, Brown, 1994), pp. 107, 160.
5. Nuremberg document NO-2939.
6. Nuremberg document NO-4428.
7. BArchB, R58/1131, Kopkow report dated 22 Nov.1942.
8. US NARA, RG 263, CIA name file Johann Sanitzer.
9. Höhne, *op. cit.*, p. 150.
10. US NARA, RG 263, CIA name file Johann Sanitzer.
11. Höhne, *op. cit.*, p. 151.
12. US NARA, RG 263, CIA name file Johann Sanitzer.
13. BArchB, RY/1/1 2.3.142, Stapoleitstelle Hamburg, report dated 24 October 1942.
14. TNA, KV 2/1501, Kopkow interrogation IR 63, 9 May 1946.
15. US NARA, RG 263, CIA name files of Heinz Pannwitz and Johann Sanitzer.
16. Wiener Library, London, microfilm 2/46.
17. Witte, P., and others (eds.), *Der Dienstkalender Heinrich Himmlers 1941-42*, (Hamburg: Hans Christians Verlag, 1999), pp. 635-639.
18. Copy from Institut für Zeitgeschichte, Munich (courtesy Dieter Pohl).
19. BArchB, RY I/1/2/3/142, interrogations of Erna Eifler and Wilhelm Gersmann.
20. TNA, KV 2/1501, Kopkow interrogation IR 68, 28 May 1946.
21. *The Rote Kapelle. The CIA's History*, p. 302.
22. Griebel, R., Coburger, M., and Scheel, H., (eds.), *Erfasst? Das Gestapo-Album zur Roten Kapelle*, (Rendsburg: Drückhaus Heinrich Möller Söhne, 1992), pp. 341, 351.

23. TNA, KV 2/1501, Kopkow interrogation IR 68, 28 May 1946; BBL 4/43; www.spiegel.de/einestages/spionage-im-zweiten-weltkrieg-a-948520.html
24. TNA, KV 2/2238, MI5 name file Robert Barth.
25. *Ibid.*
26. TNA, HS 6/289, report on SOE Belgian agents.
27. BStU, FV 98/66, Bd 310, pp. 380-386, interrogation of Wenzel, 26 Dec 1945.
28. Höhne, *op. cit.*, p. 94.
29. TNA, KV 2/411, MI5 name file Rudolf Rathke.
30. BStU, FV 98/66, Bd 310, pp. 38-48.
31. BStU, FV 98/66, Bd 352, pp. 31-76.
32. Trepper, L., *The Great Game*, (London: Michael Joseph, 1977), p. 115.
33. *Ibid*, p. 165.
34. TNA, KV 3/349, MI5 report on Rote Kapelle, 1949.
35. TNA, KV 3/190, interrogation of Eduard Stobbe.
36. BADH, ZR 773 A.2, T1-170.
37. TNA, HS 4/344.
38. BStU, FV 98/66, Bd 310, pp. 92-118, Panzinger interrogation by Russians, 29 July 1951.
39. TNA, HS 4/344.
40. TNA, KV 2/1501, Kopkow interrogation IR 68, 28 May 1946.
41. Philipp, G., *Kalendarium der Ereignisse im FKL-Ravensbrück 1939-1945*, (Berlin: Metropol, 1999), p. 136 fn 22.
42. US NARA, RG 263, CIA name file Johann Sanitzer.
43. *Ibid.*
44. *Ibid.*
45. *Ibid.*
46. *Ibid.*
47. *Ibid.*
48. *Ibid.*
49. Giskes, H. J., *London Calling North Pole*, (London: Wm Kimber, 1953) p. 129.
50. TNA, WO 204/12806, Constantin Canaris interrogation, SD 45.
51. TNA, WO 208/4679, interrogation report LDC 1213, Dr Josef Götz.
52. TNA, HS 9/166/7, SOE PF file Marcus Bloom, and HS 9/1172/7, SOE PF file Maurice Pertschuk.
53. Foot, M. R. D., *SOE in France*, (London: HMSO, 1966), p. 315.
54. TNA, HS 6/426, Kieffer interrogation.
55. *Ibid.*
56. US NARA, RG 242-Entry 23B-Box 6, RSHA IV A2 instructions (19 Jan. 1943) on interrogating parachute agents.
57. TNA, WO 235/560, Kieffer interrogation.
58. TNA, WO 208/4679, interrogation report LDC 1213, Dr Josef Götz.
59. Fuller, J. O., *The German Penetration of SOE*, (London: Wm Kimber, 1975), p. 79.
60. Suttill, F. J., *Shadows in the Fog*, (Stroud: History Press, 2014), p. 224.
61. TNA, KV 6/29, reports by John Starr.
62. TNA, HS 9/836/5, interrogation report LDC 11441,Dr Josef Götz.
63. TNA, HS 9/447/2, SOE PF file Roland Dowlen.
64. TNA, HS 9/1283/3, SOE PF file Marcel Rousset.

65. TNA, KV 6/29, reports by John Starr.
66. TNA, WO 208/4679, interrogation report LDC 1141, Dr Josef Götz.
67. TNA, WO 235/560, Kieffer post-trial plea for clemency.
68. TNA, WO 208/4679, interrogation report LDC 1213, Dr Josef Götz.
69. Foot, *op. cit.*, p. 262.
70. *Ibid.*, pp. 299-300, 311.
71. TNA, WO 208/4679, interrogation report LDC 1141, Dr Josef Götz.
72. Foot, *op. cit.*, p. 342.
73. TNA, HS 9/905/4, SOE PF file Lionel Lee.
74. TNA, HS 9/513/8, SOE PF file David Finlayson.
75. TNA, HS 9/412/1, SOE PF file Marcel Defence.
76. Foot, *op. cit.*, p. 344.
77. *Ibid.*, p. 347.
78. Fuller, *op. cit.*, pp. 144-147.
79. TNA, KV 2/1668, MI5 name file Karl Oberg.
80. TNA, HW 16/12.
81. Cookridge, E. H., *Inside SOE*, (London: Arthur Barket), p. 603.
82. Foot, *op. cit.*, p. 345.
83. TNA, KV 6/29, reports of John Starr.
84. TNA, WO 309/1022.
85. TNA, HS 9/59/2, interrogation report, Horst Kopkow, 21 Jan. 1947.

Chapter 8

1. Bazyler, M. J., and Tuerkheime, F. M., *Forgotten Trials of the Holocaust*, (New York: NYU Press, 2014)—the most recent account of the trial.
2. Krausnich, *SS-State*, pp. 401-403; Wachsmann, N., *Hitler's Prisons. Legal Terror in Nazi Germany*, (New Haven and London: Yale UP, 2004), pp. 166-167.
3. IMT Nuremberg, Kaltenbrunner Prosecution document by Manfred Weiss.
4. TNA, WO 311/76, Conrad Schultz statement, 26 April 1946.
5. IMT Nuremberg, Rudolf Höss witness testimony, 15 April 1946.
6. TNA, KV 2/1668, MI 5 name file Karl Oberg; BArchB, NS 19/4012.
7. TNA, HS 9/1286/5, SOE PF file Marcel Rousset.
8. TNA, WO 309/350, interrogation report, Horst Kopkow, 5 Feb. 1947.
9. *Ibid.*
10. *Ibid.*
11. IMT Nuremberg, quoted in testimony, 27 July 1946.
12. Nuremberg document PS-498.
13. Marshall, R., *All The King's Men: The Truth behind SOE's Greatest Wartime Disaster*, (London: Collins, 1988), p. 247.
14. www.englandspiel.eu/index.php?taal=en last accessed 24 March 2017.
15. TNA, WO 235/552, British war crimes trial proceedings against the personnel of KL Gross Rosen.
16. TNA, WO 309/282.
17. TNA, WO 309/1022.
18. *Ibid.*

19. *Gedenkbuch Ravensbrück*, p. 186.
20. Philipp, G., *Kalendarium der Ereignisse im Frauen-Konzentrationslager Ravensbrück 1939-1945*, (Berlin: Metrolpol, 1999), p. 161.
21. TNA, WO 311/607, has list of those executed from Mauthausen archive.
22. TNA, HS 9/147/5, SOE PF file; Gustave Bieler.
23. TNA, WO 309/1366, Buchenwald executions.
24. TNA, WO 309/282, Dachau shootings; HS 9/836/5, SOE PF file Noor Inayat Khan.
25. Philipp, *Kalendarium*, p. 169.
26. TNA, WO 309/1366.
27. Bondy, R., *The Emissary. A Life of Enzo Sereni*, (London: Robson, 1977), p. 241.
28. TNA, HS 4/344.
29. TNA, HS 4/246, WO 311/607.
30. Philipp, *Kalendarium*, p. 191; TNA, HS 9/1435, SOE PF file Violette Szabo.
31. *Gedenkbuch Ravensbrück*, p. 376.
32. *Ibid*. p. 525.
33. TNA, HS 7/145.
34. Suttill, F. J., *Shadows in the Fog*, (Stroud: History Press, 2014), p. 233.
35. TNA, HS 8/880; TNA, WO 328/21, statement of Hans Lunding.
36. TNA, HW 16/49, GPDR 56 transmitted 6 April 1945.
37. TNA, WO 235/309, statement by Johann Schwarzhuber, 15 Aug. 1946.

Chapter 9

1. BArchB, SS-Officer file Hans Thielecke, has copy of the agenda.
2. TNA, WO 235/560, statement by Richard Schnur.
3. BAL, B162/3233, pp 110-118, statement by Kopkow, 9 May 1961.
4. US NARA, RG 65-Entry A1-136P-Box 186, statement by Georg Gerhard.
5. US NARA, RG 242-Entry 23B-Box 28, has SK 20 Juli investigations March 1945 at Potsdam.
6. TNA, WO 310/123, interrogation report SD 49, Dr Fritz Kranebitter.
7. *Daily Telegraph* (London), 5 February 1945.
8. BArchB, R58/331.
9. TNA, WO 208/3616, interrogation report SIR 1675, 24 May 1945.
10. BStU, FV 98/66, Bd 244, case against Hannelore Thiel.
11. Nuremberg document 535-PS.
12. TNA, HW 16/43, GPDs 4021, 4023, 4027, 4034, 4039, 4040, 4044.
13. TNA, KV 2/1500, Kopkow interrogation report 7 June 1945.
14. TNA, KV 6/57.
15. Nollau, G., and Zindel, L., *Gestapo ruft Moskau*, (Munich: Heyne, 1980), p. 194.
16. US NARA, RG 65-Entry A1-136P-Box 186, statement by Karl Heuer.
17. US NARA, RG 65, Entry 179, Box 751, interrogation of Hauptmann Krämer.
18. *Ibid*.; TNA, 6/57.
19. US NARA, RG 65, Entry 179, Box 751, interrogation of Hauptmann Krämer.
20. Nollau, Zindel, *op. cit.*, p. 164.

21. TNA, HS 7/145, SOE X Section.
22. *Ibid.*, Operation Aquavit out of Switzerland into Austria, 1942.
23. TNA, HS 9/855, SOE PF file Kurt Koenig.
24. Persico, J. E., *Piercing the Reich*, (New Yok: Ballantine, 1979), pp. 424-426.
25. TNA, HS 7/146, Clowder missions.
26. TNA, WO 309/248, WO 309/1078.
27. US NARA, RG 242-Entry E23B-Box 6, report by Gestapo Marburg/Lahn, 31 Oct. 1943.
28. Jeffery, K., *MI6: The History of the Secret Intelligence Service (1909-1949)*, (London: Bloomsbury, 2010), pp. 546-547.
29. *Ibid.*, p. 547.
30. TNA, HS 6/621.
31. TNA, HS 7/145.
32. *Ibid.*
33. Persico, J. E., *Piercing the Reich. The Penetration of Nazi Germany by American Secret Agents during World War II*, (Viking Press, 1979), p. 113.
34. *Ibid.*, p. 338.
35. TNA, WO 219/5307.
36. BArchB, RY 1/I/2/3/142.
37. BArchB, RY 1/I/2/3/139 and 140; FBS 110/1974.
38. BArchB, FBS 110/1974.
39. BStU, SV 1/74, Bd 1, pp 300-343.
40. BArchB, RY 1/1/2/3/139.
41. TNA, KV 2/1500, Kopkow interrogation, 7 June 1945.
42. *Ibid.*
43. TNA, WO 204/12925, CI War Room, Situation Report No. 215, Abwehr Breslau.
44. TNA, HW 16/42, message GPD 4020.
45. TNA, KV 2/1500, Kopkow interrogation, 7 June 1945.
46. *Ibid.*
47. TNA, HS 6/652, Operation Calvados.
48. TNA, HS 6/652, WO 311/20.
49. TNA, HW 5/705.
50. TNA, HS 6/664, statement by SOE agent Alois Buchtik.
51. TNA, KV 2/2238, MI5 name file Robert Barth; execution in Moscow, BStU, FV 98/66, Bd 353, Teil 2/2.
52. TNA, HS 8/852, Kopkow order 1 March 1945.
53. *Ibid.*
54. TNA, HS 9/594/3, SOE PF file Marcel Goethals.
55. Jeffery, *op. cit.*, p. 549.
56. *Ibid.*, p. 550.
57. TNA, KV 2/1501, interrogation report IR 19, Horst Kopkow.
58. *Ibid.*
59. Persico, *op. cit.*, pp. 2-3.
60. *Ibid.*, pp. 158-174.
61. *Ibid.*, p. 419.
62. *Ibid.*, p. 278.
63. TNA, KV 2/1500, Kopkow interrogation, 7 June 1945.

Chapter 10

1. TNA, WO 309/1771, Kopkow Detention Report.
2. TNA, KV 2/1500, interrogation report, Georg Kiessel.
3. TNA, KV 2/1500, Kopkow's first report. 7 June 1945.
4. *Ibid.*
5. *Ibid.*
6. *Ibid.*
7. TNA, WO 208/5209.
8. Hinsley, and Simkins, C. A. G., *British Intelligence in the Second World War: Volume 4, Security and Counter-Intelligence*, (London: HMSO, 1990), p. 268; Breitman, R., and others, *US Intelligence & the Nazis*, (Washington DC: US NARA, 2004), pp. 148-149.
9. TNA, KV 2/1500.
10. TNA, KV 3/137.
11. *Ibid.*
12. Jeffery, K., *MI6: The History of the Secret Intelligence Service (1909-1949)*, (London: Bloomsbury, 2010), p. 551.
13. TNA, KV 2/1501.
14. TNA, KV 2/1500.
15. TNA, KV 2/1501.
16. TNA, WO 204/12924
17. Roper, H. T., *The Secret World*, (London: I.B. Tauris, 2014), pp. 105-106.
18. TNA, KV 2/1501.
19. TNA, KV 3/137.
20. TNA, KV 2/1501.
21. Macintyre, B., *A Spy Among Friends*, (London: Bloomsbury Press, 2014), p. 106.
22. TNA, KV 2/1501.
23. *Ibid.*
24. *Ibid.*
25. US NARA, RG 263, CIA name file 'Horst Kopkow'.
26. TNA, WO 309/1022.
27. *Ibid.*
28. TNA, WO 309/248, WO 309/1078.
29. TNA, HS 9/59/2.
30. TNA, WO 309/350.
31. TNA, WO 235/560.
32. TNA, KV 2/1501.
33. TNA, KV 2/2752.
34. TNA, WO 309/248.
35. TNA, WO 235/560.
36. TNA, WO 309/248.
37. Jeffery, *op. cit.*, p. 654.
38. Tyas, S., 'Ghosts from the Past. Nazi War Criminals recruited by Great Britain's Secret Intelligence Service', *Journal for Intelligence, Propaganda and Security Studies*, Vol. 6 No. 1/2012, pp. 62-79.
39. TNA, KV 3/137.

APPENDIX I

German Successes from *Funkspiel* Operations in Holland, 1942–1944

During the period 1942–1944, 190 parachute drops of agents and supplies had been agreed with SOE Dutch Section in London using false radio messages, and ninety-five parachute drops of supplies were actually made to designated locations, consisting of 570 containers and about 150 packages.

Agents captured:
Sixty, of whom fifty-one were executed
Stores captured:

Explosives	15,200 kg
Sten guns	3,000
Pistols	5,000
Silenced pistols	Six
Bren guns	300 (machine guns)
Hand grenades	2,000
Radio transmitters	Seventy-five
Radio telephones	Three
Special torches	100
Aircraft trackers	Three
Infrared lamps	Two
Bullets	500,000
Bicycle tyres	200
Raincoats	Ten
Pairs of boots	Ten
Pairs of shoes	Ten
Dutch Guilders (cash)	450,000
Other currencies also supplied	

APPENDIX II

German Successes from *Funkspiel* Operations in France, 1941–1944

The capture of radio operators in France happened on a regular basis and all of them could be used for *Funkspiel* operations. Many succeeded for only a little time before being ignored by SOE London. In 1943 and 1944, Gestapo Paris had at least six successful *Funkspiel* operations that created serious damage both in the capture of new agents, but also the capture of stores, ammunition, and money:

30 July 1943: Using the ciphers of Gilbert Norman (PROSPER circuit), agent Jack Agazarian was lured to a rendezvous at a Paris apartment and arrested by waiting Gestapo men.

8–9 February 1944: Using the ciphers of Noor Inayat Khan (PHONO circuit), four agents were captured on landing (Alexandre, Byerly, Deniset, and Ledoux).

29 February–1 March 1944: Using the ciphers of Marcel Rousset (BUTLER circuit), two agents were captured on landing (Detal and Duclos).

29 February–1 March 1944: Using the ciphers of Noor Inayat Khan (PHONO circuit), three agents were captured on landing (Antelme, Damerment, and Lee).

2–3 March 1944: Using the ciphers of John Macalister (ARCHDEACON circuit), three agents were captured on landing (McBain, Rabinovitch, and Sabourin); the false ARCHDEACON radio traffic had also previously enabled capture of agents at safe houses and a rendezvous nominated by the circuit: Francois Michel (Paris, 23 September 1943), Robert Gieules, and Maurice Duthilleul (Paris, 29 September 1943), and Angehard Defendini (Paris, 21 March 1944).

2–3 March 1944: Using the ciphers of Yolande Beekman (MUSICIAN circuit), three agents were captured on landing (Finlayson, Lepage, and Lesout).

7–8 March 1944: Using the ciphers of Marcel Rousset (BUTLER circuit), two agents were captured on landing (Defence and Simon).

20–21 June 1944: Using the ciphers of Denise Bloch (CLERGYMAN circuit), the agent L. A. Blondet managed to avoid the Gestapo reception party and escape.

Dropping of supplies, requested via *Funkspiel* radio messages:

ARCHDEACON circuit:

Parachute drops	Forty-six
Agents captured	Three
Containers	328
Packages	Fifty-six
Money	2,267,000 French Francs
Aircraft lost	Three

MUSICIAN circuit:

Parachute drops	Thirty-two
Agents captured	Three
Containers	182
Packages	Twenty-four

PHONO circuit:

Parachute drops	Seventy-nine
Agents captured	Seven
Containers	491
Packages	126

BUTLER circuit:

Parachute drops	Seventy-six
Agents captured	Four
Containers	523
Packages	Ninety-three
Money	1,150,000 French Francs

DELEGATE circuit:

Parachute drops	Twenty-three
Containers	182
Packages	Thirty-five
Money	580,000 French Francs

PRIEST circuit:

Parachute drops	Fifteen

Containers	162
Packages	Thirty-six
Money	655,000 French Francs

SATIRIST circuit:

Parachute drops	Four
Containers	Thirty
Packages	Two

LIONTAMER circuit:

Parachute drops	Two
Containers	Twelve
Packages	Seven
Money	700,000 French Francs

The author gratefully appreciates the assistance given by Francis Suttill in preparing this appendix.

APPENDIX III

Funkspiel Operations Carried Out

France

The INTERALLIE circuit (SIS) operated in Paris from 1941 until 1942, when it was penetrated by the Abwehr and a *Funkspiel* took place. On 1 December 1942, MI5 noted: 'Recent [radio] traffic shows that the Germans do not realise that we know the set is controlled by them'.

Radio operator Comte de Kergolay for the OVERCLOUD circuit (SOE RF Section) was arrested February 1942 by the Abwehr. He transmitted until 1943, with London knowing he was under German control.

The POLENBLUT circuit (Polish Intelligence) was noted as an Abwehr *Funkspiel* with London from Marseille in December 1942.

The JULITTE circuit (French BCRA) was an Abwehr *Funkspiel* operation with Algiers from Marseille, January–March 1943.

The MITHRIDATE circuit (French BCRA) was penetrated by the Gestapo in 1943 and at least one set of ciphers was used in a *Funkspiel* operation.

SOE radio operator Marcus Bloom was arrested on 19 April 1943 near Toulouse. First Gestapo attempt at *Funkspiel*, stopped in May 1943 when SOE London was not deceived.

SOE radio operator John Macalister was arrested on 21 June 1943 at Dhuizon. *Funkspiel* operation began at the end of June 1943 and continued until March 1944.

SOE radio operator Gilbert Norman was arrested on 24 June 1943, Paris. *Funkspiel* operation took place until 18 August 1943 when stopped.

SOE radio operator Marcus Rousset was arrested June 1943, Paris. His ciphers became *Funkspiel* ZEUSS and this continued until March 1944.

SOE radio operator Robert Dowlen was arrested on 2 August 1943, Pontoise, outside Paris: '... messages from him 31.8.43 and 1.10.43 probably under duress'.

SOE radio operator Noor Inayat Khan was arrested on 8 October 1943, Paris. Her ciphers became *Funkspiel* DIANA and were in use until March 1944 when SOE suspected her messages 'were controlled by the Germans'.

SOE radio operator John Young was arrested on 18 November 1943, near Lons-le-Saunier (Jura). His ciphers were used in a *Funkspiel* operation with SOE London during 1944.

SOE radio operator Marcel Clech was arrested on 19 November 1943, Tours. In December 1943, he 'came up under duress'.

SOE radio operator Georges Clement was arrested when transmitting in December 1943 near Rennes. His first message after arrest came up on 4 January 1944 and London decided he was controlled due to a lack of security checks.

SOE radio operator Yolande Beekman was arrested when transmitting on 13 January 1944, St Quentin. Her ciphers were used for at least two months.

SOE radio operator Robert Byerly was arrested on landing on 8 February 1944. His first message was sent on 25 March 1944, and in April 1944, London decided his set was German controlled, but 'went on transmitting messages to and receiving ... in the hope of receiving possible clues or information'.

SOE radio operator Lionel Lee was arrested on landing on 8 February 1944. 'C' reported his arrest on 2 March 1944; SOE noted on 6 June 1944 that his 'W/T message on controlled circuit from Geheime Staatspolizei'.

SOE radio operator Madeleine Damerment was arrested on landing on 29 February 1944. On 6 June 1944, London realised her set was German controlled.

SOE radio operator David Finlayson was arrested on landing on 2–3 March 1944: 'Telegrams continued to arrive on his plan until the end of May [1944], all of which must have been under German control'.

SOE radio operator Arthur Steele was arrested late March 1944, near Marseille. A *Funkspiel* with his ciphers lasted through April–June 1944. On 30 June 1944, SOE London noted: 'We presumed his [radio] traffic controlled'.

SOE radio operator Christophe Janik was arrested on 17 April 1944, Cannes. When he came up on air (27 April 1944) without his Bluff and True checks, it was not continued.

SOE radio operator Denise Bloch was arrested on 20 June 1944, near Evreux. Her ciphers were used until August 1944.

SOE radio operator Alcide Beauregard was arrested on 16 July 1944, near Lyon. According to his SOE PF file, he sent fifty-six radio messages and received sixty-five, 'some of the later ones sent by him must have been controlled' by the Gestapo.

SIS radio operator Réne Beck (Réne Caumont) was arrested on 4 August 1944. Played back (no details available).

More radio operators from SOE and other Allied intelligence agencies operating in France had been captured. A German radio message dated 14 June 1944 intercepted and decoded by Bletchley Park lists nine *Funkspiel* operations:

DIANA (Noor Inayat Khan)
MINOS
HERAKLES (Andre Dubois)
APOLLO
JUNO (Yolande Beekman)
ATLAS
VULCAN
ZEUS (Marcel Rousset)
SATURN

In another intercepted and decoded German radio message, dated 16 June 1944, four more *Funkspiel* operations are listed:

FAUST
LISZT
RAVEL
LULLI

As the names of Greek gods and goddesses were used for SOE radio operators, it is likely that the four musical terms refer to BCRA radio operators in contact with their Algiers base.

SIS and OSS both had radio operators captured by Kieffer's section and *Funkspiel* operations made using their ciphers. In March 1944, OSS radio ciphers were being played back from Marseille to their base in Algiers.

In November 1944, following the withdrawal from France into southern Germany, Dr Götz reported that he had two new *Funkspiel* operations in use—one British and one American—and involved they four captured agents, who were later released.

Austria

Funkspiel operations against Soviet intelligence agencies began in July 1942, and by 1945, seventeen operations were in use (against the Comintern, GRU and NKVD).

In 1944, two *Funkspiel* operations were in use against French intelligence agencies.

Also in 1944, at least two *Funkspiel* operations (called Mississippi and Potsdam) were in use against OSS.

At least three *Funkspiel* operations in 1944–1945 were being used against British agencies (*Funkspiel* operations Enzian, Goldenes Horn, and Themse). SOE Austrian Section were aware of a *Funkspiel* being played with them in April 1945.

Funkspiel Operations Carried Out

Belgium

The Abwehr and Gestapo had four *Funkspiel* operations with Moscow using the Rote Kapelle ciphers from 1942–1944.

The Abwehr also had at least eight *Funkspiel* operations in use against SOE Belgian Section from 1942 and as late as 1944.

Bulgaria

From November 1942, the Abwehr began *Funkspiel* operations against Soviet intelligence agencies and eventually had seventeen operations in use with ciphers from captured agents.

In 1944, one captured SOE agent had his ciphers unsuccessfully used with the British in Cairo.

Czechoslovakia

From 1942, Gestapo Prague had at least two *Funkspiel* operations against Soviet intelligence agencies.

In April 1944, at least one set of SOE ciphers was in operation against London.

France

The Gestapo *'Sonderkommission Rote Kapelle' Funkspiel* operations against Moscow eventually had six Rote Kapelle and French Communist Party radio sets in use, 1942–1944.

Funkspiel operations against SOE French Section, BCRA, OSS, and SIS are listed above.

Germany

Major Frank Chamier, SIS, was arrested in Germany on 12 April 1944. Transmissions using his ciphers in a *Funkspiel* operation with London were broken off after messages indicated that he could not sent them 'of his own free will'.

Holland

The Abwehr and Gestapo, between 1942 and 1943, had fifteen SOE ciphers being used against London and two attempted using SIS ciphers.

Between 1943 and 1945, after the end of Operation North Pole (the *Englandspiel*), a further five new Dutch radio operators were arrested and their ciphers used in *Funkspiel* operations by the Gestapo.

In 1945, at least two sets of OSS ciphers were being used by the Gestapo.

Italy

In January 1943, the Gestapo attempted a *Funkspiel* operation with SOE following the arrest of their agent Gabrielle Adler on Sardinia: 'Heard on the air, but considered to be under duress'.

At least six SOE ciphers and four OSS ciphers were being used by the Gestapo in *Funkspiel* operations, 1944–1945. One *Funkspiel* operation played back to OSS was named Heckenrose and another Chrysantheme.

Norway

An unsuccessful *Funkspiel* operation using SOE Norway Section ciphers happened in 1942; in 1944, they were more successful and four SOE ciphers were being played back against London.

At least one Soviet agent was being played back to Moscow from Norway in 1944.

Bibliography

Binney, M., *The Women Who Lived for Danger: The Women Agents of SOE in the Second World War*, (London: Hodder & Staughton, 2002)

Birstein, V. J., *SMERSH. Stalin's Secret Weapon Soviet Military Counterintelligence in WWII*, (London: Biteback Publishing, 2011)

Blank, A. S., and Mader, J., *Rote Kapelle gegen Hitler*, (Berlin: Verlad der Nation, 1979)

Breitman, R., Goda, N. J. W., Naftali, T., and Wolfe, R., (eds.), *U.S. Intelligence and the Nazis*, (Washington DC: National Archives Trust Fund Board for the Nazi War Crimes and Japanese Government Records, Interagency Working Group, 2004)

Buckmaster, M., *They Fought Alone. The Story of British Agents in France*, (Watford: Odhams, 1958)

Churchill, P., *The Spirit in the Cage*, (London: Hodder & Staughton, 1954)

Cookridge, E. H., *Inside SOE*, (London: Arthur Barker, 1966)

Deutsche Widerstandskämpfer 1933-1945, Vols. 1 and 2, (Berlin: Dietz Verlag, 1970)

Dourlein, P., *Inside North Pole. A Secret Agent's Story*, (London: Wm.Kimber, 1953)

Erickson, J., *The Road to Berlin*, (London: Weidenfeld and Nicolson, 1983)

Felfe, H., *Im Dienste des Gegners. Autobiographie*, (Berlin: Verlag der Nation, 1988)

Flicke, W. F., *Spionagegruppe Rote Kapelle*, (Fackelverlag, Olten, 1967)

Foot, M. R. D., *SOE in France: An Account of the Work of the British Special Operations Executive in France 1940-1944*, (London: HMSO, 1968)

Fuller, J. O., *The Starr Affair*, (London: Gollancz, 1954); *Born for Sacrifice (Madeleine): The Story of Noor Inayat Khan*, (London: Pan Books, 1957); *Double Webs*, (London: Putnam, 1958); also published as *Double Agent? Light on the Secret Agents' War in France*, (London: Pan Books, 1961); *The German Penetration of SOE. France 1941-1944*, (London: Wm. Kimber, 1975)

Giskes, H. J., *London calling North Pole*, (London: Wm Kimber, 1953); *London ruft Nordpol*, (Bergisch-Gladbach; Bastei-Lübbe Taschenbuch, 1982)

Gourevitch, A., *Un certain monsieur Kent*, (Paris: Bernard Grasset, 1995)

Grehan, J., and Mace, M., *Unearthing Churchill's Secret Army: The Official List of SOE Casualties and Their Stories*, (Barnsley: Pen & Sword, 2012)

Grundmann, S., *Der Geheimapparat der KPD im Visier der Gestapo—Das BB-Ressort. Funktionäre, Beamte, Spitzel und Spione*, (Berlin: Karl Dietz Verlag, 2008)

Helm, S., *A Life in Secrets: The Story of Vera Atkins and the Lost Agents of SOE*, (London: Little Brown, 2005)

Höhne, H., *Codeword: Direktor: The Story of the Red Orchestra*, (London: Secker & Warburg, 1971); *Der Krieg im Dunkeln. Macht und Einfluss der deutschen und russischen Geheimedienste*, (Munich: C.Bertelsmann Verlag, 1985)
Jeffery, K., *MI6: The History of the Secret Intelligence Service (1909-1949)*, (London: Bloomsbury, 2010)
Kelso, N., *Errors of Judgement: SOE's Disaster in the Netherlands, 1941-1944*, (London: Robert Hale, 1988)
King, S., *Jacqueline: Pioneer Heroine of the Resistance*, (London: Arms & Armour Press, 1989)
Koch, P.-F., *Enttarnt. Doppelagenten: Namen, Fakten, Beweise*, (Salzburg: Ecowin Verlag, 2011)
Kogon, E., *The Theory and Practice of Hell*, (London: Secker & Warburg, 1959)
Kramer, R., *Flames in the Field: The Story of Four SOE Agents in Occupied France*, (London: Michael Joseph, 1995)
Macintyre, B., *A Spy among Friends: Kim Philby and the Great Betrayal*, (London: Bloomsbury, 2014)
Maclaren, R., *Canadians Behind Enemy Lines, 1939-1945*, (Vancouver: University of British Columbia Press, 1981)
Marshall, B., *The White Rabbit*, (London: Evans, 1954)
Marshall, R., *All The King's Men: The Truth behind SOE's Greatest Wartime Disaster*, (London: Collins, 1988)
McKay, C. G., *From Information to Intrigue: Studies in Secret Service based on the Swedish Experience, 1939-1945*, (London: Frank Cass, 1993)
McLoughlin, B., 'Proletarian Cadres en route. Austrian Agents in Britain 1941-1943', in *Labour History Review*, Vol. 62 ed. 3, 1997
Nicholas, E., *Death be not Proud*, (London: Cresset Press, 1958)
Nollau, G., and Zindel, L., *Gestapo ruft Moskau. Sowjetischer Fallschirmagenten im 2.Weltkrieg*, (Munich: Wilhelm Heyne Verlag, 1980)
O'Connor, B., *Churchill's and Stalin's Secret Agents: Operation Pickaxe at RAF Tempsford*, (Stroud: Fonthill, 2012)
O'Donnell, P. K., *They Dared Return: The True Story of Jewish Spies Behind the Lines in Nazi Germany*, (London: Simon & Schuster, 2009)
O'Sullivan, D., *Dealing with the Devil: Anglo Soviet Intelligence during the Second World War*, (New York: Peter Lang, 2010)
Orlow, D., *The History of the Nazi Party*, (Newton Abbot: David & Charles, 1973)
Perrault, G., *The Red Orchestra*, (London: Arthur Barker, 1968)
Persico, J. E., *Piercing the Reich: The Penetration of Nazi Germany by American Secret Agents during World War II*, (Viking Press, 1979)
Philipp, G., *Kalendarium der Ereignisse im Frauen-Konzentrationslager Ravensbrück 1939-1945*, (Berlin: Metrolpol, 1999)
Reile, O., *Der Deutsche Geheimdienst im II.Weltkrieg. Westfront. Der Kampf der Abwehr im westlichen Operationsgebiet in England und Nordafrika*, (Munich: Weltbild Verlag, 1989)
Roewer, H., *Die Rote Kapelle und andere Geheimdienst-Mythen: Spionage zwischen Deutschland und Russland im Zweiten Weltkrieg 1941-1945*, (Graz: Ares Verlag, 2010)
Saward, J., *The Grand Prix Saboteurs: The Grand Prix Drivers who became British Secret Agents during World War II*, (London: Morienval Press, 2006)

Schafranek, H., and Tuchel, J., (eds.), *Krieg im Äther. Widerstand und Spionage im Zweiten Weltkrieg*, (Vienna: Picus Verlag, 2004)

Schreieder, J., *Das war das Englandspiel*, (Munich: Walter Stutz Verlag, 1950)

Simon, M. J., *Gone to Ground*, (London: Profile Books, 2014)

Smith, S., *'Wings' Day: The Man who Led the RAF's Epic Battle in German Captivity*, (London: Collins, 1968)

Stephan, R. W., *Stalin's Secret War: Soviet Counterintelligence against the Nazis 1941-1945*, (Lawrence, KA: University Press of Kansas, 2004)

Sudoplatov, P. and A., *Special Tasks: The Memoirs of an Unwanted Witness—a Soviet Spymaster*, (New York: Little Brown, 1994)

Suttill, F. J., *Shadows in the Fog*, (Stroud: The History Press, 2014)

Tarrant, V. E., *The Red Orchestra: The Soviet Spy Network inside Nazi Europe*, (London: Arms & Armour Press, 1995)

The Rote Kapelle: The CIA's History of Soviet Intelligence and Espionage Networks in Western Europe, 1936-1945, (Washington DC: University Publications of America, Inc., 1979)

Trepper, L., *The Great Game: The Story of the Red Orchestra*, (London: Michael Joseph, 1977)

Trevor-Roper, H., *The Secret World: Behind the Curtain of British Intelligence in World War II and the Cold War*, (edited by Edward Harrison), (London: I. B. Tauris, 2014)

Tyas, S., 'Im Dienste Seiner Majestät. Die Nachkriegskarriere des Horst Kopkow', in *Die Gestapo nach 1945. Karrieren, Konflikte, Konstruktionen*, Mallmann, K.-M., and Angrick, A., (eds.), (Darmstadt: WBG, 2009)

Verity, H., *We Landed by Moonlight: Secret RAF Landings in France, 1940-1944* (Manchester: Crécy Publishing, 2000)

Weber, H., and Herbst, A., *Deutsche Kommunisten: Supplement zum Biographischen Handbuch 1918 bis 1945*, (Berlin: Dietz Verlag, 2013)

West, N., *MI6: British Secret Intelligence Service Operations*, (London: Hodder & Staughton, 1983); *Secret War: The Story of SOE, Britain's Wartime Sabotage Organisation*, Hodder (London: & Staughton, 1992); (ed.), *The Guy Liddell Diaries. Vol. II: 1942-1945: MI5's Director of Counter- Espionage in World War II*, (London: Routledge, 2005)

Wildt, M., *Generation des Unbedingte: Das Führungskorps des Reichssicherheitshauptamtes*, (Hamburger Edition HIS, 2002)

Witte, P., and seven others (eds.), *Der Dienstkalender Heinrich Himmlers 194½2*, (Hamburg: Hans Christians Verlag, 1999)

Wolff, W., *An der Seite der Roten Armee: Zum Wirkes des Nationalkomitees 'Freies Deutschland' an der sowjetisch-deutschen Front 1943 bis 1945*, (Berlin: Militärverlag, 1982)

Index